Computer Fraud Casebook

Computer Fraud Casebook

THE BYTES THAT BITE

Edited by
Joseph T. Wells

WILEY

John Wiley & Sons, Inc.

Library of Congress Cataloging-in-Publication Data:

Computer fraud casebook: the bytes that bite/[edited by] Joseph T. Wells.
    p. cm.
    Includes index.
    ISBN 978-0-470-27814-7 (cloth)
    1. Computer crimes. 2. Computer crimes–Investigation. 3. Fraud. 4.
Fraud investigation. I. Wells, Joseph T.
    HV6773.C657 2009
    363.25'9680973–dc22

                                                                    2008032267

Printed in the United States of America

10 9 8 7 6 5 4 3 2 1

Contents

Foreword   ix

Preface   xi

Chapter   1   Just What the Doctor Ordered   1
                  George Kyrilis

Chapter   2   Of Botnets and Bagels: Vaccinating the Hospital
                  against Cybercrime   13
                  Frank Riccardi and Jennifer Campbell

Chapter   3   Pandora's Box   21
                  Dr. Vishnu Kanhere

Chapter   4   Mail-Order Fraud   35
                  Robin Conrad

Chapter   5   Lancelot Gone Missing   45
                  Carolyn Conn, Paul Price, and Karon Murff

Chapter   6   Double Trouble   57
                  Stephen P. Weber

Chapter   7   Unimaginable Wealth   67
                  Sandra Burris

Chapter   8   Hacked   75
                  Jon Lambiras

Chapter 9   Bad Education   85
                 Russ Allen

Chapter 10   If Only His Nose Could Grow   97
                 Barry Davidow

Chapter 11   Keeping Up with the Jamesons   105
                 Mike Andrews

Chapter 12   Imaginary Satellites   115
                 George Kyriakodis

Chapter 13   Never Pass Your Password   125
                 James Martin and Harry Cendrowski

Chapter 14   Why Computers and Meth Don't Mix   135
                 Stephen R. Menge

Chapter 15   Fishing in Dangerous Waters   143
                 Joe Dervaes

Chapter 16   The Man Who Told on Himself   155
                 Alan Greggo and Mike Jessee

Chapter 17   Triple Threat   163
                 Jean-François Legault

Chapter 18   Swiped   173
                 Peter Belloli

Chapter 19   Have Computer, Will Video   181
                 Dominic A. D'Orazio

Chapter 20   Server, We Have a Problem   191
                 Marty Musters

Chapter 21   Do It for the Kids   199
Michael Ammermon

Chapter 22   Moving Money   209
Neil Harrison

Chapter 23   Operation: Overnight Identity Theft   219
Bruno Pavlicek

Chapter 24   The Karma of Fraud   231
David Clements and Michael Cerny

Chapter 25   Secret Shopper   241
Jay Dawdy

Chapter 26   Would You Like a Receipt?   251
Shirley Quintana

Chapter 27   The Coupon Code Crooks   261
Danny Miller, Michael P. Rose, and Conor Donnelly

Chapter 28   He Fought the Law   269
Clifford Hunter

Chapter 29   Eyes on the Company Secrets   281
Tyson Johnson

Chapter 30   French Connections   289
Michael Nott

Chapter 31   Irreconcilable Differences   299
Jennifer Birtz

Chapter 32   Keeping It In the Family   309
Eric Sumners

Chapter 33   I Due   319
              Rebecca Busch

Chapter 34   What Lies Inside the Trojan Horse   329
              Johnathan Tal

Chapter 35   Lost in Transition   339
              Amy Cron

Chapter 36   Superhero Syndrome   351
              Hatitye Zhakata

Chapter 37   Stealing for the Sale   363
              William J. Pederson and Timothy M. Strickler

Chapter 38   Do as I Say, Not as I Do   371
              Richard Woodford

Chapter 39   Cinderella: One Glass Slipper Just Wasn't Enough   383
              Antonio Ivan S. Aguirre

Chapter 40   Bloggers: Separating the Wheat from the Chaff   389
              Steven Solieri, Joan Hodowanitz, and Andrew Felo

Chapter 41   The Campus Con   401
              Kevin Sisemore

Chapter 42   One for You, One for Me: A Tale of Crooked Insurance   413
              Steve Martin

Index   **421**

Foreword

It was almost a decade ago that a colleague introduced me to Joseph Wells. At the time he was chairman of the Association of Certified Fraud Examiners (ACFE), a membership group he had founded only 10 years earlier but which was already recognized as a major player in the fight against business fraud and corruption. At the meeting he proposed writing a monthly column for the *Journal of Accountancy;* I, being its editor-in-chief, reacted with a journalist's natural skepticism about working with a new writer and agreed to try it on the condition that *JofA* readers proved they valued his articles. We assigned Joe the task of targeting his articles to small-business fraud, and he chose the format of presenting real case studies to make his points. What a fortuitous meeting that was. Not only did the *Journal's* readers praise his work from day one, they went on to vote his articles as the best in the *JofA* for three years running and catapulted him into the *Journal of Accountancy's* Hall of Fame, a very rare honor that only four writers have attained. Our partnership lasted for eight fruitful years.

Based on that highly successful working relationship, I am very pleased to write this introduction to the ACFE's fourteenth book and the first one devoted entirely to computer fraud. As Joe's editor at the magazine all those years, I had gotten an eye-opening education on small-business fraud and a great respect for the ACFE's mission when I saw the pressing need in the marketplace for the information and education the ACFE delivered. From today's vantage point those crimes seem relatively simple: Each case consisted of three elements: a perpetrator (an employee), a victim (the small-business owner), and a fraud investigator who was continuously honing his or her skills as a Certified Fraud Examiner. The average small business lost $127,500 to fraud (ACFE 2002 Report to the Nation). In the vast majority of the stories, the opportunity to defraud presented itself in the form of an administrator who had not set internal controls in place, had placed trust in the wrong person, or who believed that a fail-safe system was not necessary. How easy it was for a thief to filch money from a cash drawer or forge a check or cook the books or doctor a bank reconciliation. We even managed to find humor in the ineptitude of some of the would-be crooks. How could you not chuckle over the bank robber who wrote the holdup note on the back of his utility bill? Or the Wal-Mart shopper who tried to pay for her $1,672 bill with a $1 million bill? Or the genius check writer who used disappearing ink to pawn off bad checks, but didn't notice they had his name and address in permanent ink?

But the fraud landscape has changed dramatically by adding one more element—the computer. Computer fraud is sophisticated, global, annihilating, and unimaginably expensive. High-tech criminals can obliterate records, bankrupt companies, steal money, cheat consumers, rob identities, and cause unprecedented havoc, sometimes with a single mouse click. In cyberspace, the fraudster has morphed from a hapless rip-off artist into a clever, diabolical techno-thief who deliberately sets out to steal, manipulate, deceive, or in some other way destroy on a grand scale—just count the current frauds that cost companies and consumers in the billions of dollars. Sounds alarming? You bet it does. It is not an exaggeration to say this book is appearing at the right moment. Technology experts and professional crime fighters alike predict that computer crime will explode in the coming years.

As you read this book, many of the case studies will astonish you, but at the same time you will gain an understanding of the scope and complexity of computer crime. You will be introduced to scam methods and techniques that were unheard of just a few years ago and to some as old as the pyramids. For example, you will read about a fraudster who began as a 15-year-old spammer making thousands of dollars a day while still in high school, who then moved on to peddling illegal drugs on the Net and laundering money through a computer network that spread far beyond the United States. His every action preyed on the unsuspecting. He amassed untold illicit millions by age 25, but ended up being sentenced to 30 years to life before he was 30.

Yet, in my opinion, the true value of this book lies not in knowing the criminals, as cunning as they are; rather it is in the telling of their downfall. For each and every schemer in this volume, there was a fraud investigator or team of them whose dedication, skill, and intelligence uncovered the fraudster and put an end to the corruption. As I read the case studies, I marveled at how smart the investigators were, their dogged determination, and the number of resources they used—and which you can use—to snare the criminal. The detailed plan of action outlined in each case should prove invaluable to fraud fighters everywhere. I heartily recommend this book to anyone who has an interest in fraud detection and prevention, or, for that matter, to anyone who uses a computer—for everyone is at risk. Fraud examiner, client, employer, manager, consumer, student—read and absorb, for you will never treat your computer casually again.

Colleen Katz, Editor-in-Chief, *Journal of Accountancy* (Ret.)

Preface

- Barings Bank, England's oldest, failed in 1995 due to the actions of one employee, Nick Leeson, who was in charge of arbitrage at Barings's Singapore branch. Through a computerized shell game, he was able to conceal $1.4 billion in trading losses from his superiors. When this computer fraud was uncovered, the bank collapsed.
- In 1996, Timothy Allen Lloyd, former disgruntled employee of Omega Engineering Co., hacked into their computer system to permanently delete all manufacturing software programs, causing losses of more than $10 million.
- In 2001, Geoffrey Osowski and Wilson Tang, former accountants for Cisco Systems, pled guilty to stealing about $8 million in company stock option refunds. They did so by computerizing certain aspects of their responsibilities to direct payments away from the rightful payees and into bank accounts the two had set up for their own benefit.
- Daniel Jeremy Baas pleaded guilty in 2003 to illegally accessing customer databases at Acxiom, a company that maintains information for various vendors. He was able to extract sensitive data on over 300 accounts maintained by Acxiom, which cost the company an estimated $5.8 million.

What all the case examples above have in common is that the means to carry them out did not exist 30 years ago. But that was then and this is now. We stand on the precipice of a whole new era that is forever changing our lives because of advancements in technology. Computer fraud is just one aspect of these changes, but a very important one.

In a worst-case scenario, hackers and cyber thieves could cripple the global economy. That hasn't happened—at least not yet. The U.S. Cyber Consequences Unit estimates such attacks could average $700 billion per incident. The Computer Security Institute believes annual losses by U.S. companies more than doubled from 2006 to 2007.

No one really knows the cost of computer fraud. Estimates range from well-researched opinions to wild guesses. There is no government agency or private sector organization that gathers comprehensive data on these crimes. Indeed, there is not even agreement on a definition of computer fraud.

Because there are so many variations, we decided to concentrate on cases committed in the workplace by employees to enrich themselves or their companies. So if you are looking for detailed information on malware, phishing, computer viruses, or hacking, this book might not be your best choice. One question that I am frequently asked is, "Why is there so much more computer fraud now and why does it seem to be growing?" The reason is that there are more and more computers. This trend, of course, is unlikely to reverse itself.

There are those of you reading this book who may share something in common with me: I know just as much about brain surgery as I do about computers. When I graduated with an accounting degree over four decades ago, classes on computers were not even offered. Now, in the first part of the twenty-first century, I can finally navigate e-mail and type a document in Microsoft Word. But that is about it.

In today's business environment, we are almost completely dependent on technology, which can be used for both good and evil. The bad part about computers is that they can enhance the ability of fraud perpetrators to carry out their nefarious schemes. But the good aspect is that the very computers used to commit these crimes can also help solve them; they can quickly hone in on statistical and other data that will lead fraud examiners and auditors to solid clues of fraud. In the following pages, you'll see multiple examples of both.

Computer Fraud Casebook: The Bytes That Bite is a collection of 42 real case studies written by the ACFE members who investigated them. There is no better perspective. You will see that in some situations, justice was served. But that is the exception, not the rule. You will also notice something that my experience has taught me: Once fraud occurs, recovering the victim's money is difficult if not impossible. That makes prevention the number one goal of the antifraud specialist.

As hard as it is for me to believe, this is my fourteenth book on fraud. That doesn't even count the 200 or so magazine articles I have published on the subject. The writing I have done has been a tremendous learning experience for me, and this work is no exception. That has been the reason I have continued, plus the fact that profits from all of my books are donated to the CFE General Scholarship Fund to assist worthy students in the antifraud field.

Some computer fraud takes real technical expertise; sometimes not. My first computer fraud case came from a Fortune 500 bank based in Dallas. A computer programmer named Nelson wished very much to return to Louisiana, his home state, so the company graciously arranged for him to transfer to New Orleans as head of the data processing department. They granted Nelson a $15,000 "bridge loan" to take care of miscellaneous moving expenses, with the understanding that the loan would be repaid in full after he sold his Texas home. That's where the trouble started.

He made a miniscule profit on the sale of his house, so he took the money from the bridge loan to pay some of his more pressing creditors—the squeaky wheel gets the grease. But Nelson eventually tallied his debts, which were in excess of a quarter of a million dollars. He was between a rock and a hard place. No one would loan him money because his credit had more holes than a block of Swiss cheese. And if he filed for bankruptcy, chances are he would have been given his walking papers by the bank.

So Nelson devised a scheme to get himself out of hock. First he opened a checking account under the name of an uncle. Why the bank allowed this serious breach of internal control is not known. Then Nelson wrote a program that would remove money from the ending balance field on a customer's account and transfer it to the uncle's, where Nelson would spend it. Had he moved the funds directly from the customer's account, the statement would have shown the transaction; hence, the ending balance method.

Because checking accounts cycled throughout the month, Nelson figured that he had exactly 29 days to reverse the transaction, which he would then move to another customer, so he wrote another program to remind him when to do that. All in all, it was a computerized lapping scheme. But Nelson's ''move the money around'' program didn't account for February, which has only 28 days except for leap year.

So, around the first week of April, customers started streaming in the bank, checking account statements in hand showing that the beginning balance for March was lower than the ending balance for February—a mathematical impossibility. The total losses to the bank were about $250,000 and Nelson spent three years as a guest of the Louisiana penal system.

You will learn some useful lessons from the *Computer Fraud Casebook*. The first is that most ''computer frauds'' are garden-variety embezzlements that are not technology dependent; the same crime could have been committed with pen and ink. Another lesson is that most computer frauds are committed by one fraudster acting alone. Were that not the fact, losses would be exponentially higher. The good news is the losses to date have been relatively small when compared to the risks. But will that continue? Only time will tell; the cases in this book deal with what *has* happened, not what *might*.

This book would not be in print without the efforts of two different groups. The first is the 42 contributing authors who wrote the original case studies. Writing well is difficult at best. And it's almost impossible to be done to perfection. Many of our members had never taken on such a project. But with diligence and hard work, they have produced something they can be proud of for a lifetime.

The second group is the ACFE's Research Department, led by John D. Gill, J.D., CFE. He and his staff, including Chris Kajander and Andi McNeal, worked tirelessly to edit the contributing authors' material into what we hope is a seamless style. Kassi Underwood, our research editor/writer, deserves special recognition. She was saddled with the details of conducting the next-to-last edits and handling dizzyingly diverse other assignments at the same time. She was principal liaison with our publisher, Wiley, ensuring that we got the book out on time. We did—Kassi never missed a single deadline. We also must recognize the contributions of Tim Burgard, my longtime colleague at Wiley, for his input. He was always there with his sage advice when we needed him.

Finally, it will be obvious to you—from reading *Computer Fraud Casebook: The Bytes That Bite*—that computer fraud is not going away. Our only real hope is to educate ourselves and potential victims on how to minimize the risks. This book is a start.

Joseph T. Wells, CFE, CPA
December 2008

Computer Fraud Casebook

CHAPTER 1

Just What the Doctor Ordered

GEORGE KYRILIS

By his mid-twenties, Cory Steele was already well-known on the Internet as one of the top ten spammers in the world. The golden-haired entrepreneur from Minnesota started writing software programs for distributing spam when he was just 15. He circulated his product throughout the globe in exchange for half the spammers' profits. This business venture earned him so much money that he dropped out of high school. When his father objected, Cory replied, "Dad, I made $69,000 online by 11 a.m. today."

The rebellious teenager spent his time sharpening his computer and online expertise. Once he paid five thousand dollars for a Russian computer programmer to fly to Minnesota and give him a one-day lesson. Cory began pedaling human growth hormones, penis enlargement pills, and other fake supplements online. He used the anonymity of the Internet to conceal his true identity and take advantage of gullible customers willing to buy his "pixie dust." Anyone was fair game as long as there was money to be made.

Shortly after his 24th birthday, Cory ventured into his most lucrative Internet scam—selling prescription drugs. With the help of Betsy Hartman, a computer programmer known as the "spam queen," he set up an illegal online pharmacy. The scheme made him a wealthy man. Before he turned 25, Cory was a multimillionaire. He bought a $1.1 million home in cash and added a Ferrari Spyder, Mercedes Benz C55AMG, and Lamborghini Murcielago to his collection of foreign cars.

Cory was obsessed with affluence, but his most prized possession was his artificially enhanced trophy wife, Amber. He often spied on her. Even though Cory frequented strip joints and had a dancer named Christie Kelly as a mistress, he expected Amber to remain faithful. He was insecure with their relationship and controlled her to the point of abuse. She was the one possession he couldn't stand to lose.

1

Fear and suspicion consumed Cory's life. Once when an officer came to serve court documents, he hid in a closet with his four-year old son, telling him that the police were bad and would hurt him. He protected his money and fleet of vehicles by constantly transferring safes full of cash and his luxury vehicles from one storage facility to another. Cory used disposable cell phones to avoid electronic eavesdropping. He had 24 cameras at the office watching his employees every hour of the day. They were required to walk through metal detectors where security guards, led by Cory's heavyset enforcer and confidant, Randy Mesher, confiscated their cell phones.

In spite of all his wealth, Cory failed to overcome his own weakness. He was addicted to Xanax, a prescription drug for anxiety. His addictive nature made him extremely erratic. He often had emotional outbursts. People were frightened by his unpredictable behavior, which was compounded by the fact that he brought a 9 mm pistol to work every day.

Cory originally established Advanced Express Systems as a billing company to facilitate online sales for his spammed products. But after realizing that it could be used as a marketing tool for his primary pharmacy operation, SwiftRX.com, he developed it into a call center employing more than 100 telemarketers working around the clock to sell prescription drugs. Next, he established another Web site, www.directdiscountdrugs.com, which served as the core for his online pharmacy operation by processing orders for customers of SwifteRX and connecting with a doctor to approve orders.

Pills and Abuse

I was a special agent with the FBI and assigned to the Minnesota Cyber Crimes Task Force in Minneapolis, a squad of highly trained agents from the FBI and U.S. Secret Service dedicated to investigating a multitude of computer-related crimes. After working white-collar crime investigations for most of my 28 years of duty, I decided that cybercrime would make a challenging finale to my career. This case, my last FBI investigation, proved to be my most fascinating and rewarding.

One frosty day in late November, I got a phone call from a colleague who had received a complaint regarding Cory. A tenant in the same building as Advanced Express Systems had grown suspicious of the operation. He had noticed several limousines in the parking lot that the employees used as break rooms. Many of Cory's workers were disorderly and disturbed others in the building. We later found out that quite a few had been recruited from a halfway house and were former felons. The curious tenant had seen the baby-faced entrepreneur arrive at work in a $300,000 Mercedes Maybach, driven by a chauffeur. Puzzled, he searched the Internet and discovered that Cory was named on several antispam Web sites as one of the world's most prolific spammers. He learned that several people who bought prescription drugs from his Web site, SwifteRX, complained about being overcharged and never receiving their orders.

I ran a Google search on Cory and discovered more information about his nefarious online activity. He had been linked with a group of individuals who hijacked IP (Internet protocol) net blocks to commit billing and credit card fraud, send spam, and launch attacks against spam opponents and Internet service providers (ISPs). A Whois (a domain search engine) check on www.swifterx.com revealed that it was registered with an ISP in Switzerland and had a United Kingdom business address—a dead end. Using a covert computer, which cannot be traced back to law enforcement, I visited the Web site. It offered a multitude of generic drugs available for sale without a prescription. SwifteRX claimed it had a network of doctors and pharmacies throughout the United States. The customer's patient history and an FDA-approved online questionnaire were said to be reviewed by these supposed physicians to approve prescriptions. SwifteRX would not accept any health insurance. Only major credit cards and COD payments were accepted and FedEx delivered the medication. I immediately opened an investigation on Cory's credit card fraud and spamming activity.

A few weeks into the case, Special Agent David Flynn of the IRS Criminal Investigation Division called regarding allegations that Cory was potentially involved with a money laundering scheme. We began working together. David was a meticulous investigator, one who accounted for every single dollar. He and I identified several former and current employees who were fed up with Cory's continual sexual harassment and appalling conduct at the office. They claimed he belittled them and would fire anyone without reason. He was even said to have used a taser gun on them to test their threshold for pain, laughing until they succumbed.

We learned from his employees that Cory was making millions of dollars through his online pharmacy business. The top sellers were pain-killers, usually hydrocodone-based drugs such as Vicodin and Norco. Customers were provided with an online questionnaire to describe medical symptoms, self-prescribe their own drugs, and place an order. For pain-killers, clientele rated their level of discomfort on a scale of 1 to 10. If their threshold did not link with their desired dosage, telemarketers coached customers to increase their pain level. It was confirmed that the call center used the Web site for Direct Discount Drugs to place orders. A Whois check on www.directdiscountdrugs.com revealed that it was registered in Seattle, Washington, to someone using the name RegisterFly. The registrant's real name was concealed by a security feature called Whois Privacy Protect, but after obtaining a subpoena, we reviewed the records, which proved that Cory used an alias and Visa business credit card to buy the domain name.

The former call center employees told us that all of their customer orders were electronically sent to one doctor, Paul Martel in New Jersey, for approval. Telemarketers were ordered not to call him for any reason. Dr. Martel had no face-to-face, telephone, or any other contact with the clients. And not one employee could recall the doctor ever rejecting a prescription.

Cory required his employees to work around the clock, demanding that they "Sell, sell, sell!" Those with the highest performance were placed on an elite team called the "Platinum Group." Staff contacted repeat customers, usually drug abusers, and pressured them into refilling their prescriptions. Advanced Express Systems was essentially an online drug dealer preying on addicts.

David and I interviewed more employees and learned that Cory had several other Web sites with servers located in different locations in the United States and the Bahamas. I looked at the SwifteRX Web site again and noticed a 1-800 number for placing orders and customer service. Google revealed several other online pharmacies with the same number. After performing a Whois search on each Web site, I discovered that the domain names were registered with different names and addresses, but some of them shared the same IP address. I then searched Netcraft, which provides Web server analysis, and found the locations of their servers, four ISPs in Texas, Ohio, and Minnesota. When David reviewed the bank records for Advanced Express Systems, he confirmed that Cory made payments to all four ISPs. David and I continued to build our case for credit card fraud and money laundering.

Shut Him Down

Our findings were reported to Assistant U.S. Attorney Sarah Rich. She immediately recognized that Cory's operations were illegal. Without a legitimate doctor consultation, each and every prescription was invalid under federal law. She noted that by using the Internet and FedEx, Cory also violated federal wire and mail fraud statutes. She invited Special Agent Rob Kinsey of the U.S. Food and Drug Administration to join our investigation and look at the illegal distribution of controlled substances. Rob was a tenacious investigator and quickly reviewed Cory's Web sites to gather evidence on the drug charges. He pointed out that the sites touted an FDA-approved online questionnaire, which was a lie. After Rob joined the team, there was never a dull moment. And his gift for gab meant there was no such thing as a short conversation.

Our team was almost set, anchored by Sarah, whom Rob accurately described as our "scary smart" prosecutor. There were no single federal statutes regulating the legality of prescribing pharmaceuticals over the

Internet. Sarah brilliantly deciphered the combination of federal regulations, state laws, pharmacy board rules, and medical association pronouncements applicable to our case. What initially appeared to be a grey area of the law became as clear as day. An online pharmacy selling pharmaceuticals without a valid prescription was illegal. She set the precedence for our investigative team, refocusing our efforts on drug charges. Rob was our resident drug expert and became our undercover agent to buy prescription drugs from Cory's online pharmacies.

Within a short period of time, we developed several confidential sources that provided critical information regarding the illegal operation. Unfortunately, one source gave Cory the heads-up about our investigation and kept him up-to-date on our progress. Despite his warnings and inside information, Cory continued to brazenly build his enterprise. Greed had swallowed him. After he opened the Minnesota call center in September, his prescription drug sales grew from $500,000 to $5 million per month. The marketing whiz kid deftly used the Internet, call centers, spamming, postcards, and facsimiles to produce more revenue. A few weeks after the winter holidays, David noticed a huge spike in deposits in the Advanced Express Systems' bank account. We later discovered that Cory had Betsy Hartman, the spam queen, hack into a competitor's online pharmacy operation and steal all of their customer information.

Cory had begun withdrawing huge amounts of cash each week. Coincidentally, we learned from a source that in February, a Brink's armored truck started making deliveries to Advanced Express Systems. It was unloading $125,000 in cash to their office two or three times each week. It didn't take long for Cory to accumulate more than $2.9 million in cash. David established that Cory's online pharmacy operation had generated more than $18 million in prescription drug sales. The number would soon round out at $28 million.

During this same time frame, between late February and April, we discovered that Cory and Sean Pitts, a manager at Advanced Express Systems, were traveling on a chartered jet to Montreal, Canada, each week. Cory enjoyed the private jet so much that he made a $385,000 deposit to buy a $1.16 Million British Aerospace Aircraft. He brought cash, luxury vehicles, and equipment to Montreal in preparation to set up a new call center. I ran a Google search on Sean and found that he had been charged with spamming online college diplomas—caught selling a master's degree to an investigator's cat. When I ran a Whois on Sean's diploma sales domain name, I recognized one of Cory's aliases as the registrant.

While we continued our interviews, Rob diligently arranged his undercover buys from several of Cory's Web sites and his call center. Each time he placed an order, he self-prescribed the quantity, dosage, and type of medication. All of his undercover buys were approved by Dr. Martel without any consultation and delivered by FedEx. He discovered that when he submitted false or incomplete information, even using a female name, his orders were filled. He also received up to five calls a day from tele-marketers asking the same question: "Are you ready for a refill?"

With the help of the Drug Enforcement Agency (DEA), we identified several U.S. pharmacies providing prescription drugs to Cory's customers. The DEA received grievances from doctors and pharmacists recruited to approve prescriptions and supply painkillers and controlled substances. Addicts complained that they had tried to stop abusing drugs but continued to succumb to the pressure of relentless telemarketers.

After Rob made a few undercover purchases, we learned that Cory was planning to move his Minnesota call center. A source informed us that he was transferring his luxury vehicles to different storage facilities. I rechecked his Web sites on Netcraft and found that he had also moved his servers to different ISPs. Cory was one step ahead of us, trying to hide his assets and destroy evidence. At the time, we had no idea what prompted his evasive measures.

Only five months into the investigation, Sarah decided that we had to shut down Cory's operation in the interest of public safety. A newspaper article linked a Minnesota man's suicide with his addiction to painkiller prescription drugs bought from several online pharmacies, including Cory's. Shortly thereafter, our FBI office received a phone call from one of the employees indicating that Cory knew we were planning a raid. Acting quickly, David obtained search and seizure warrants and I obtained a temporary restraining order to freeze Cory's assets and stop his online pharmacy operation. We gathered about 30 agents to help us execute the warrants.

This Is Not a Game

On May 10, we executed 13 search warrants on Cory's operations in five states. We found him at his million-dollar home sitting in the backseat of his limousine. He was wearing an empty holster with a 9mm pistol under the floor mat. As I approached Cory, he said, "This must be George Kyrilis." I was surprised he knew my name. I then served him with the temporary restraining order and explained that we were shutting him down and freezing all of his assets. Cory remained defiant and cocky. "Oh, I see. This is just a game," he replied.

"No, Cory, this isn't a game; your drugs are killing people."

The searches took all day and carried on until late into the evening. We seized boxes and boxes of documentary evidence, computers, and other items. We confiscated more than $4 million in assets, including $1.8 million in vehicles and $1.3 million in cash. On May 13, search warrants were executed at four pharmacies supplying the prescription drugs. The following week a federal judge froze the accused's assets by preliminary injunction and appointed a receiver to take control of and dissolve the pharmacy operation. Cory was ordered to stop his illegal online activity.

On May 24, Cory hopped on a plane and flew to the Dominican Republic. Randy Mesher flew down a few days later. Cory persuaded several people, including Amber, Sean, Christie, and Randy's wife, to smuggle cash out of the United States for him. Christie, his mistress, had stopped stripping at clubs when Cory offered to pay for her lost income. Cory needed the money to start a new online pharmacy offshore, out of the reach of U.S. law enforcement.

During the following month, several of Cory's employees came forward and provided information regarding his criminal enterprise. Betsy decided to cooperate after her house was searched. She proved to be our most valuable source of knowledge. The proficient programmer had been involved in Cory's operation from beginning to end. She designed and maintained his whole computer system. Betsy described nearly every detail of their drug business. With the assistance of an FBI computer forensic expert, she spent countless hours recreating their database and retrieving critical information. She confirmed that Dr. Martel was their one and only doctor and had approved 72,000 prescriptions. He received $7.00 for each prescription and often approved 25 orders at a time with just one click. The online pharmacy had $28 million in sales with a 90 percent profit margin. Nearly 85 percent of sales were of hydrocodone-based products. Using 17 Web sites and three call centers, Cory had quite the operation.

Death Threats

After the search warrants, Betsy recorded her instant message communications with Cory. He tried to retrieve his customer database for his new offshore online pharmacy. A former SwifteRX employee came forward and told us he sent two FedEx packages containing $70,000 in cash to New York and Florida. The U.S. Postal Inspection Service intercepted them. Cory sent one package to a shady online pharmacy operator. With the help of a merchant bank manager, we learned that his accountant, Ben Luserman, had opened a merchant account for Cory, which he needed to process credit card transactions for his offshore online pharmacy. The bald, skittish Ben opened the account with a fake name and helped set up a fake Web site to deceive MasterCard. The manager recorded the telephone calls and instant messages with Ben, who revealed Cory's domain names for two new offshore online pharmacies. I immediately located the servers through Netcraft and the ISPs were ordered to shut down the Web sites.

At this point, Assistant U.S. Attorney Liz Grayson, a prosecutor with a competitive attitude and experience in drug cases, joined the investigation. Typically, after executing search warrants, the investigative team will focus on reviewing the evidence. But Cory never slowed down—we stayed busy. He continued to rebuild his criminal empire, ignoring the preliminary injunction and defying the judge's orders. We filed a complaint charging criminal contempt of court and obtained an arrest warrant for Cory.

A week later, Sean decided to cooperate and informed us that Cory had smuggled more than $500,000 in cash to Montreal. He flew down to the Dominican Republic to meet Cory and go over a new business plan. Cory wanted his help to set up an offshore online pharmacy and hide in Honduras. The well-dressed former manager admitted that he helped Cory launder money through a bank account. Sean deposited the COD payments from Cory's customers in the account and then ordered Brink's to deliver cash to their office suite.

Soon after Cory realized that Sean had cooperated, he and Christie fled the Dominican Republic and went to the Turks and Caicos Islands. Cory discovered that Amber was having an affair, which sent him into a rage. He tried to slip back in the country on July 1st, arriving at the Minneapolis–St. Paul airport at midnight. When he exited the plane, I greeted him, "Cory, welcome back."

He withered when he realized his fate. We seized Cory's PDA and laptop and obtained search warrants for them. Cory had protected his laptop with PGP (pretty good protection) encryption and his PDA was password protected.

After a two-day hearing Cory was released with an electronic monitoring device and ordered to stay away from computers and from developing new Web sites. He ignored the order. On August 24, Cory and others were indicted on wire fraud, money laundering, and drug charges. We arrested Cory again and the judge placed him in a halfway house. Within a week he was found with a laptop and PDA. We placed the cuffs on Cory for the third time and took him to the county jail. This time breaking the rules landed Cory behind bars until his trial, 13 months later.

After three months in jail, Cory, now nicknamed "Crybaby," came to the U.S. attorney's office to cooperate on a possible plea deal. Cory was somewhat truthful during the eight-hour interview. When he returned to jail, the guards kept a close eye on him. But it wasn't enough; he found every loophole in the jail's telephone monitoring system to make unrecorded calls. When they deprived Cory of his Xanax, he had a defense attorney smuggle the drug into his cell.

In January, Cory came back to the U.S. attorney's office to explain the incident, but failed to give a full accounting of his unrecorded telephone calls. He admitted that, the day after the search, he took $1.1 million in cash from a safe hidden at a storage facility and put it in the trunk of Christie's car. A couple of weeks later, he said, he moved the money to his home, where he and Amber counted out bundles of $10,000, wrapped them in Saran Wrap, stuffed them into Apple Jacks cereal boxes, and hid the boxes in his parents' boathouse. His lack of credibility and compliance caused Sarah and Liz to end plea negotiations. Subsequent charges would be forthcoming, including operating a continuing criminal enterprise (CCE). Cory knew that the minimum prison sentence for CCE was 20 years and came up with a plan to derail the case.

In March, with the help of another inmate, Cory found the telephone number of a local defense attorney that was no longer in service but still recognized by the jail. Since the jail could not monitor calls to his supposed attorney, Cory had an associate in the Philippines set the number up through voice-over-Internet protocol (VOIP). The jail became suspicious and monitored the calls. They heard Cory make arrangements to kill Betsy and her children. He callously stated, "This is a kill or be killed world," and quoted Joseph Stalin, "No man, no problem."

Cory was immediately transferred to a supermax prison. Finally, he was under control and we could focus our attention on the trial. On March 8, a criminal complaint was filed against a Filipino associate who had helped Cory run an online casino in Costa Rica and, later, customer service for his online pharmacy; the charges were witness tampering and conspiracy to obstruct justice. On March 21, Cory was indicted on the same charges and with CCE on a superseding indictment on the main case.

In spite of all of Cory's distractions, we continued to build our case on the illegal online pharmacy. Sitting in a room with a view of a brick wall, we carefully reviewed and organized all the documentation and computer evidence obtained from the search warrants. We found key information in nearly every box and computer. It seemed that Cory spent more time trying to hide his assets than destroying evidence that might bury him. We interviewed more than 100 witnesses, including telemarketers, doctors, pharmacists, addicts, inmates, and defendants. Tirelessly, often working late into the evenings and on weekends, we located frightened and hostile witnesses. After serving more than 200 subpoenas and executing 45 search-and-seizure warrants, we stood atop a mountain of evidence.

Most valuable was the digital evidence, the information harvested from computers, e-mails, instant messages, and especially servers. Some of the computer documents revealed that Cory was fully aware that his online pharmacy was operating illegally. The flood of e-mails between Cory and his codefendants presented us with a detailed history of the entire operation. All his efforts to deceive and manipulate lawful doctors and pharmacies and his total indifference to the customers' health were evident. In spite of Cory's efforts to protect his data with encryption, passwords, and Skype instant messages, we persevered and defeated his blockade by finding his passwords.

Finally Behind Bars

Dr. Martel, Sean, and Betsy entered guilty pleas and agreed to testify at trial. Randy, the incorrigible security guard, pleaded guilty but remained loyal to Cory and refused to fully cooperate. After we had asked Randy for his laptop, he deleted everything and pawned it. The six-week trial started after Columbus Day and ended the day before Thanksgiving. An eerie silence filled the courtroom before the jury read its verdict. When his guilt was announced, the glimmer of hope in Cory's pale expression completely vanished. His face turned green as he trembled and began to vomit. Cory left the courtroom to the sounds of his sobbing sister.

Nearly nine months later, a sentence hearing was held for enhancements to Cory's 20-year sentence on the CCE conviction. Cory's flagrant defiance of judicial orders, his death threat against Betsy, and his reckless disregard of life were some of the issues argued. On August 1, the dismayed judge was left with no choice and elevated his sentencing range to between 30 years and life. The judge compared Cory to a drug kingpin. Cory was ordered to forfeit the fruits of his crime, nearly $5 million in assets.

Lessons Learned

Our team learned a thing or two about investigating a difficult Internet, money-laundering, and health-care fraud case. Foremost, we learned that teamwork was paramount to a successful outcome. Throughout the investigation we worked side by side, equally sharing responsibilities. We had the utmost confidence and trust in each other's judgment and ability.

We also learned that confinement in prison will not stop a criminal from breaking the law. Time and time again, Cory found ways to exploit and bypass the jail's security measures, ultimately leading to the death threat. Rob developed a superb liaison with the jail and monitored Cory's abuse of their telephone system.

Another lesson we learned was that confidential sources can be unpredictable and their trust should always be held in question. The source, the office landlord, betrayed us and compromised our investigation. I disregarded remarks that the source was a little too chummy with Cory; I should not have.

We also learned that digital evidence was crucial and should be quickly reviewed and analyzed. Our computer forensic examiners were overwhelmed by the number of computers seized on the investigation. Some examinations were delayed until just weeks before the trial, which interfered with our preparation.

Recommendations to Prevent Future Occurrences

Be Aware

The world of computer technology has created an overabundance of Web sites that sell prescription drugs over the Internet without requiring a prescription. People should be aware of the risks and the consequences associated with purchasing drugs online.

Develop Statutes

A single federal statute that clearly criminalizes the prescribing of pharmaceuticals over the Internet would make prosecutions easier. At least one face-to-face examination between doctor and patient should be required prior to prescription.

Publicity and Education

More publicity about prescription drug abuse and convictions of online pharmacy operators might curtail the growth of prescription drug abusers. Shutting down online pharmacies is effective to a point, but in reality it is merely attacking a symptom rather than the actual problem: drug abuse. People must be educated about the dangers of drugs. It is simple economics. The reason illicit online pharmacies exist is to meet a demand. If the demand is reduced, online pharmacies will be forced to close.

About the Author

George Kyrilis is director of Special Investigations for the Insurance Fraud Division of the Minnesota Department of Commerce. He served as a special agent of the Federal Bureau of Investigation for nearly 29 years. He was assigned to the Minnesota Cyber Crimes Task Force before his retirement in 2007.

Of Botnets and Bagels: Vaccinating the Hospital against Cybercrime

FRANK RICCARDI AND JENNIFER CAMPBELL

Anthony Baker fancied himself a brilliant advertising executive, but in reality he was a cybercriminal looking for an easy score. At 21 years old, he wore baggy shorts and a t-shirt, and stalked his victims in broad daylight. What was his weapon of choice? A scruffy laptop computer connected to the Internet, courtesy of a dilapidated coffeehouse that offered a free wireless "hot spot" to its patrons. Anthony, fully caffeinated and high on a scone-induced sugar buzz, scoured the Web in search of prey.

Anthony preferred to attack nonprofit organizations, particularly hospitals, because the workforce was customer-service oriented and not about to look for a wolf in sheep's clothing. The Internet, as usual, had returned the prey he was looking for. The headline read, "Stalwart Hospital Named Top 100 Cardiovascular Hospital."

In the early 1980s, anyone with a hard drive and a mouse was called a *hacker*. Today the term refers to highly skilled technology enthusiasts who deem themselves "White Hats" or "Black Hats." The reference to colored hats is derived from Hollywood's use of hats in old John Wayne movies to help an audience differentiate between good guys (white hats) and bad guys (black hats). In the world of hacking, those who use their knowledge of computer technology maliciously or criminally are Black Hats. Anthony didn't consider himself a Black Hat. He was just trying to make enough money to pay his rent and take a girl out once in a while.

Anthony's business model (he didn't think of it as a "scheme") was simple: He would hack into the networked information systems of un-suspecting companies and launch a malware virus that would allow him to remotely control any computer running on a Microsoft operating system. These hijacked "zombie" computers—or "botnets," as they are called by the hacking community—could be used to send thousands of SPAM e-mails or launch virtual vandalism known as denial-of-service attacks.

While vandalism was fun, it didn't pay the rent, so Anthony concocted a more profitable use for his botnets: advertising. Anthony struck a deal with a shady Internet marketing company that paid him 25 cents for each piece of advertising software, or "adware," he could install on a computer. Advertisements would pop up on the user's computer screen and hawk products and services ranging from bath soap to magazine subscriptions. Each piece contained a unique serial number that identified Anthony as the "installer" who was entitled to the commission. While a quarter doesn't seem like much, Anthony stood to make a fortune if the law of large numbers had anything to do with it.

To carry out his plan, Anthony designed a botnet that would highjack thousands of zombie computers and send spam e-mail in a deluge that would *exponentially* increase the amount of information being delivered. A "distributed" denial-of-service attack could slow down or "freeze" the end user's workstation. "No harm could come from that," Anthony mused, and he carried out his plan without a care in the world.

The law of large numbers didn't let Anthony down. Within four months, Anthony was able to infect over one million computers across the country. He used his zombie botnets to install adware on 425,000 machines at a commission of 25 cents each, bringing his total haul to $106,250. Anthony had found his calling: a mass marketing cybercriminal.

■ ■ ■

Stalwart Hospital was founded in 1909 as a medical facility for indigent patients with tuberculosis. In 1956, Stalwart became full-service, specializing in the treatment of cancer and heart disease. Today the hospital leads in its care for cardiac and vascular disorders, respiratory illnesses, various forms of cancer, as well as physical therapy and behavioral health. Stalwart has been named a "Top 100 Cardiovascular Hospital" for two consecutive years and performs 800 open-heart surgeries and over 9,000 cardiac catheterizations each year. Stalwart is nestled in the heart of a major cosmopolitan city, and serves a culturally diverse metropolitan community on the East Coast.

The Virus

It was silver and small—about the size of a pack of gum—and was easy to spot against the sea of tarmac that enveloped Stalwart Hospital. The shiny object, a USB flash drive, caught Sean McRae's eye as he arrived for his morning shift as a registered nurse in the hospital's intensive-care unit (ICU). A USB flash drive is a portable hard drive that can store prodigious amounts of information on a platform that's small enough to fit on a keychain. Sean popped the flash drive into his shirt pocket and went about his daily activities in the busy ICU. It wasn't until his lunch break that he remembered what he had in his pocket. Curious, he plugged the flash drive into the USB port of his clinical work station. The files he pulled up were innocuous enough—a few mundane spreadsheets, a couple of statistical reports, and so on. He yanked the flash drive out of the port and threw it in the garbage before heading home.

Forty-eight hours later the hospital was brought to its knees by a malware virus that infected the hospital's clinical information systems. For nearly a week, Stalwart was forced to route new patients to other area hospitals as its panicked and unprepared IT department struggled to cope with this vicious "cybercrime."

Anthony Baker smirked as he watched the news on CNN, thrilled that his scheme had made the national news. His ego swelled with the realization that his plan had worked without a hitch: He knew someone from Stalwart Hospital would find the virus-laden flash drive he nonchalantly scattered in the parking lot; and he knew that person would take the flash drive and plug it into a hospital computer. Curiosity always kills the cat, doesn't it? Anthony felt like a tiger.

Searching for a Cure

In my role as the hospital vice president, a position I held for two years, I was ill-equipped to handle a major criminal investigation. I had always been an "operations gal"—I supervised departments, launched business lines, and managed people. Never in my wildest nightmares did I contemplate being the lead investigator of a high-profile cybercrime.

On a Wednesday evening, starting as a trickle, the calls began to come in, continually increasing in volume. The ICU mission critical clinical systems were "bogging down," resulting in the inability of staff to perform their lifesaving jobs. Once the computer staff realized this was an attack on our network, my systems team and I immediately leapt into action.

My first order of business was to determine what exactly was happening. The second, to preserve evidence. We physically secured all ICU workstations and made copies of the hospital's security videos and computer backups.

Next, we contacted the CERT Coordination Center of Carnegie Mellon University.[1] Working with existing computer security incident-response teams

---

[1] CERT is not an acronym, but a registered trademark of Carnegie Mellon University. Its use derives from the term "computer security incident response team."

and establishing new teams, CERT specializes in analyzing vulnerabilities of organizations and countries, while also coordinating communication and emergency responses during major security events. They further examine artifact evidence for the purpose of cataloging and reverse-engineering malicious codes.

CERT was familiar with our situation, indicating it rose to the level of "federal interest computers," which is legally defined as the use of two or more computers across state lines for criminal purposes. They referred us to the Federal Bureau of Investigation's (FBI's) National Computer Crime Squad (NCCS), charged with investigation of cybercrime in relation to federal interest computers.

A botnet attack can last for two minutes, two years, or forever. When we contacted the NCCS, our attack had been going on for 10 days. Fortunately, the NCCS was able to launch an investigation while the botnet attack was still in process. NCCS immediately acted to further secure evidence in real time, interviewing Stalwart's rank-and-file workforce to hone in on the entry point of the attack.

They quickly performed a series of forensic studies on Sean McRae's clinical workstation. Unfortunately, since Sean McRae had thrown away the flash drive we were unable to recover it. By the time the attack had begun, it was long gone. As the whirlwind investigation unfolded, virus fragments were isolated and analyzed, and the NCCS conducted forensic examinations of the hospital's e-mail servers, Internet service provider (ISP) logs, hospital information system, ICU laptops, and peripheral devices. The NCCS was able to trace the IP address of the attack back to the coffeehouse. After reviewing all the information they were able to connect the attack to Anthony Baker.

On the Mend

In the end, the FBI got their man. Eleven months after the cyber attack, Anthony Baker pleaded guilty to conspiracy to intentionally cause damage to a protected computer and conspiracy to commit computer fraud. Anthony was sentenced by a U.S. district judge to three years in federal prison.

Incredibly, Anthony and his attorneys did their level best to portray Anthony as naïve about the potential consequences of his botnet attacks. Gone was his unkempt hair and goatee; he stood before the judge clean shaven, with a crew cut, and wearing a sport coat, khakis, and a silk powder-blue tie. "In my heart I'm a good person and I would never have intentionally hurt anyone," Anthony said to the judge. "I am only 21 years old and sometimes boys are immature and make stupid mistakes. I had no idea a computer could be a weapon of mass destruction."

The U.S. district judge didn't buy it. "Anyone with the ingenuity to launch a technologically complicated attack against hundreds of thousands of computers is not a misguided youth," the judge said, "but a grown man who knew that the consequences of his actions would result in hundreds of victims. As a result, a significant prison term is warranted not only as punishment for your actions, but as a serious deterrent to all other hackers who may consider following in your footsteps."

Lessons Learned

Although we often hear about cybercriminals who get caught, the sad truth is that most hackers are able to evade the law with relative ease. Hackers known as Black Hats have a multitude of objectives—they could be career criminals looking for an easy score, terrorists eager to make a political statement, or a motley crew of computer geeks looking for cheap thrills. They could be stalking their victims at the Starbucks on Main Street or they might penetrate your network halfway around the world in a smoky *Kasbah* or trendy European nightclub.

A hacker can stay one step ahead of law enforcement by literally becoming invisible to networks, a feat that is accomplished by switching between servers before conducting a cyber attack or by deleting the log files in servers that have been compromised. It is the virtual equivalent of a criminal wiping away his or her fingerprints at the scene of the crime.

Prior to this experience, our concerns relative to fraud were mainly focused on embezzlement and run-of-the-mill petty thefts. We never considered the scenario of unwitting employees accidentally exposing the hospital's vital information systems to high-tech predators. We have learned that hospital executives should be just as concerned about "virtual" computer-related threats as they are with "real world" physical threats.

Perhaps the greatest risk in the realm of health care is a unique vulnerability to a form of hacking known as "social engineering," as demonstrated by Anthony's attack on Stalwart Hospital. Social engineering requires little or no technical skills; instead, the attacker attempts to "trick" employees into giving away vital information that hackers can exploit to gain access to an organization's information systems. Hospitals are particularly vulnerable because social engineers prey upon the kindness and goodwill of a patient- and visitor-friendly workforce.

The *only* defense against social engineering is an educated workforce. If an organization's employees are not aware of the importance for system security, then there is a serious risk of a data breach, whether by determined hackers or well-intentioned users. An aware and educated workforce reduces many security risks and improves the organization's security posture.

Recommendations to Prevent Future Occurrences

System Backups

Once CERT and the NCCS identified the date our information systems were infected, we were able to pull copies of our backup tapes from offsite storage and conduct a full restoration. We lost little with the restoration, and discovered the importance of making sure that all our systems are backed up on a regular basis. We have since decided to conduct periodic "test" restorations throughout the year to monitor our state of security readiness. These mock drills will also keep our staff prepared, enabling them to move quickly in another emergency.

Employee Awareness

I have recommended that Stalwart Hospital implement a more visible and accessible employee security-awareness program to educate employees about good security practices. Our initial program consisted of annual Web-based security training and a 15-minute video shown during new-employee orientation. While we will continue the current training for new employees, we have improved our visibility by including articles in the monthly staff newsletter and have placed security "reminders" in high-traffic areas. We also conduct educational "Town Hall" meetings and promote an annual Privacy and Security Awareness Week to drive the message home. Finally, we now include a lesson on IT security in *all* computer-related trainings.

Strong Passwords

We are now mandating that all employees use "strong" passwords to access information systems. When employees use passwords that are simple and easily guessable (i.e., "weak"), it affords the opportunity for others to gain unauthorized access to the information system.

A weak password typically is alpha/numeric, no longer than six characters, and could take a hacker as little as 20 minutes to crack; even worse, an alpha-only weak password of six characters could be cracked in as little as five minutes. If the password is a word contained in a dictionary, then it can be cracked in less than five minutes. This is true no matter how many characters the word is, or whether it is a non-English dictionary, or typed backwards, or even a dictionary word with a number tacked on at the end. Weak passwords pose a serious risk to any organization concerned about computer security.

In contrast, a *strong* password that is up to eight characters long and uses an alpha/numeric and symbol format could take a hacker *years* to crack.

Strong passwords are tough to penetrate because of the exponentially increasing variations corresponding to the increase per character.

In an effort to educate our workforce about the use of strong passwords, we developed a flyer that provides easy examples of how to create them:

1. Take a familiar word and format it like an e-mail, such as "Goldsmith @2002.com" or "Rosa.G@2006.com"; this is easy to type, easy to remember, 15 characters long, upper and lower case, and uses 2 special characters.
2. Create "input rules" to help you remember the password. Example: For each password place a special character at the beginning, make the second character a capital, and place a number 1 character from the end (the user can also pick a word that is application specific, such as Cerner) = >cErne1r. This formula can be reused each time the user needs to change the password, making it easier to remember; additionally, the user can increase the number incrementally making the password easy to remember = >cErne2r.
3. Create a phrase, such as "I traveled to Key West in 2002," and then take the first letter from each word, change one character to a special symbol and use two digits from the year = I!tkwi02 OR Ittkwi02. OR !Ttkwi02; you can also move the numbers around = 0Ittkwi2; this allows the user to continue to use the same password repeatedly by just changing the sequence.

Encryption

Many organizations are diligent in encrypting data in transmission, such as e-mails containing sensitive information; however, the encryption of data at rest is often overlooked. Data at rest includes information stored on a laptop, external hard drive, "jump" or "flash" drives, CDs, backup tapes, and other movable storage systems. These devices are often lost or stolen, and laptops in particular are especially vulnerable to theft.

I have recommended that our hospital conduct a risk assessment to determine who within the organization should be allowed to store sensitive information on laptops and removable devices. Those that contain sensitive information should be encrypted and employees should be educated on good security practices.

All users whose laptops do not qualify for encryption will be educated on how to password-protect text documents, and they will be reminded to save documents containing sensitive content on their network drive rather than their workstation hard drive.

Ongoing Auditing and Monitoring

Our organization has developed internal security standards that will be audited on a quarterly basis to ensure that our policies and procedures regarding information security are being followed.

The audits will identify who is accountable for meeting the security standards and specify what corrective actions to take in the event of negative results. Further, the results of these audits will be reviewed by hospital leadership and used where appropriate to educate our staff of ongoing risks.

Computer Security Incident-Response Team

In working with CERT, we decided to create a Computer Security Incident Response Team (CSIRT) to be activated in the event of another incident. The CSIRT is, in essence, a rapid-response team that will take immediate steps to preserve evidence, conduct the investigation, and contact the appropriate state and federal authorities. The CSIRT will document the findings and recommendations of any investigations to further reduce vulnerability and mitigate risks.

About the Authors

Frank Riccardi, J.D., CFE, CPHRM, CHC, is the Executive Director of Organizational Integrity and Internal Audit (and Chief Privacy and Security Officer) for Adventist Healthcare, a faith-based nonprofit health-care system that includes three acute-care hospitals, a behavioral health hospital, a rehabilitation hospital, a home health agency, and five skilled nursing facilities.

Jennifer Campbell, B.S., RMA, CHC, is the compliance specialist for PHNS Inc., a technology company that provides information technology, health information management, and patient accounting services to over 400 hospitals across the country. Ms. Campbell has worked in the health care field for 12 years, the bulk of which has been devoted to information technology within the health care environment.

Pandora's Box

DR. VISHNU KANHERE

Paul Right was the brain and the face of Town Mark Ltd. From meeting distributors, dealers, shopkeepers, mall managers, and suppliers, to interacting with shareholders, he was at the forefront of all business interactions.

Always immaculately dressed, he loved ostentatious ties with equally flashy tie pins, often with a red ruby or a green emerald in its center. His wardrobe was impressive, with a different suit for every day of the week. Paul never looked ruffled—he dyed his hair and gelled it neatly into place. He worked hard for the company and loved to sacrifice his time, his earnings, and his future for its welfare. A day would not pass without him declaring this to an audience—whether to employees in a staff briefing, to visitors in a chance encounter, or to the directors in a board meeting. He seldom spoke of his family, but always had a good word to say about the business.

Town Mark Ltd is a well known and respected consumer-goods public company with 8 branches, 12 depots, and 5 main distributors. It grew from its early beginnings in a remote factory in the middle of nowhere by using outsourced production facilities spread across the major regions in India. The company has a network of dealers within and outside the country.

The key figure in Town Mark Ltd had always been Paul Right, the sincere and hardworking managing director of the company. He had been loyal to the promoters and owners, the house of Maharaja Ishwarchand. With a lineage dating back over 200 years, they had sprawling properties in the district of Chandnagar, India, where the factory was located. Everything was built on a massive scale—including the factory, the residential quarters, the staff colony, and the school for the employees' children. Many of these were built in the times when Maharaja himself ran the company. But successive generations had seen the business resting on past laurels. The sheer scale and size had kept it going. Dinesh Singh, the son of Maharaja, followed by Dinesh's wife, Mayawati, and now their son, Rahulji, fresh from business school, ran the affairs of the company.

Dinesh Singh was an easygoing person with a taste for the good things in life. During his tenure he had brought in Paul Right as an executive assistant in his office. Paul was then a young man who wanted to show his mettle. He quickly earned the trust of his boss and became a reliable retainer of the family. After the untimely death of Dinesh Singh, his widow took charge. But two or three years later she passed away too, felled by an attack of falciparum malaria contracted during one of her trips to the factory. The company's troubles now fell on the shoulders of Rahulji, the couple's son, a soft-spoken business school alumnus who became heavily dependent on Paul for guidance, support, and practically everything else. Rahulji never met anyone alone, be it lawyers, employees, branch managers, or company shareholders. At every board meeting or the annual general meeting, Paul Right was by his side. Paul boasted about how the company had seen glorious days in the times of "the Maharaja" and how he'd single-handedly struggled to keep the company alive since then.

The Initial Meeting

As a practicing accountant who handles system audits and investigates fraud, I was called in by Town Mark as a systems auditor. The company was going in for ISO (International Organization for Standardization) 9001:2000 certification, an international designation of the quality management system of an organization. Their consultant, Ravi Kumar, had suggested that the information systems be documented and streamlined by an expert. The cost auditor of the company, Nari Mehta, knew me well and recommended me for the position. That is how I found myself sitting face-to-face with Paul Right in April. He looked at me with his brown eyes framed in gold-rimmed reading glasses and in a firm voice said he wanted quick results.

"To tell you the truth, we're quite happy with our system. But our ISO consultant, Ravi Kumar, feels we need to improve and streamline our information system. That's why you're here. Please do what you can to satisfy Ravi. You can call me or meet me personally anytime you want, but on a regular basis you can meet our accountant, Goldie Jhaveri."

I learned a lot about Town Mark and its functioning on my first day and, thereafter, in my interactions with the staff. I met the accountant, his juniors, the system administrator, and a few other staff members, who briefed me on the company's past. Though it had potential, Town Mark had not shown good results for a while. It had experienced a perpetual resource crunch—a funds problem—and was plagued with bad debts. Control over debtors was weak.

Paul had been struggling to revive Town Mark. His remuneration was a fixed amount plus a commission on profits, which he had surprisingly voluntarily forgone for a few years because he felt the company had not made enough profits. It was a personal sacrifice he wanted to make. Paul was under pressure to perform. Rahulji also wanted to assert himself and use his own knowledge and experience more effectively. While the company appeared to have great potential, it was stagnating. The accounts were taking too long to finalize and management information system (MIS) reports were not readily forthcoming.

It was in this context that Paul brought in a new team, which reenergized Town Mark—sales rose and profits soared. Among the new team members were a chief operating officer and a chief financial officer, apart from the chief accountant. Paul also put new systems in place including a quality management team. The company now had regular reporting, MIS, and internal and external audit mechanisms. A system of budgets was introduced and the MIS information now comprised budgeted figures with actuals and variances presented with the cause of variations. Accounts were now being finalized within a week of the year-end. Shareholders and top management, including Rahulji, were pleased with the improvement. To top it all, for the first time in years the company was in a position to give higher dividends, as the profit had nearly doubled. Everyone was happy. It seemed a bit unusual for a managing director to be self-sacrificing forever, though, especially in light of a revival and growing profits, thanks to efforts by the new team. I started studying systems methodically, documenting each process—purchasing, stores, sales, marketing, delivery and dispatch, receipts and payments, accounting, etc. My work of documenting the systems was progressing well.

The Investigation

On a Monday in June, I arrived at Town Mark's administrative office. There had been a heavy downpour and the sky was overcast. I got out of the rush-hour traffic and looked up at the glass-fronted building that housed their offices. The reflection of the dark angry rain clouds in the large window panes looked ominous and depressing. I entered the office and asked for Paul Right.

"He's not in," said his secretary, Seema Gomes.

"When can I meet him?" I asked.

"He's been away for a week; I have no idea," she said, offering a smile.

"Can I meet Mr. Goldie Jhaveri then? I've finished documenting the information system, the network of computers in the company, and want some clarification," I added.

"I am afraid Goldie is not in either. He's on leave for a month in order to sit for an examination to become a certified accountant."

"What about Mr. Roy, the company secretary?"

"He just put in his papers yesterday," she said. "Why don't you have a cup of coffee? It's raining and cold. I'll fix you a cup," she said, going to the pantry.

I was feeling a bit lost and wondering what to do next when Nari, my cost auditor friend, walked in. I mentioned to him the absence of three top executives and expressed my concern, primarily because it would affect my project. Nari had his own share of difficulties. Last week he had discovered that the cost records did not match the financial accounts and balance sheet. There was an entry in the cost records of stock destroyed, valued at $500,000, which was not reflected in the financial accounts. As a reconciliation of cost and financial records was not a regular practice, he thought it would be a simple omission.

After the coffee break we both went in to meet the junior accountant, Sheila Gole. Sheila was having a tough time handling bank auditors who had dropped in to verify stock. It was normally Goldie who handled these matters. The auditors seemed to be agitated about the discrepancy in the stock of finished goods relating to the remote depots furnished to the bank. Sheila assured them that she would give them a proper explanation as soon as the accountant was back.

Satisfied with this answer, the bank auditors left, and we took seats opposite Sheila, whose long, black, shining hair hung well below her shoulders. She was remarkably impressive, carried herself well, and was considered close to Paul Right himself. It was reputed that she could get any papers approved or voucher signed with ease. I proceeded to tell her that I needed information to finish my project and any delay would affect my timelines. I wanted details on the procedures for reporting of financial information and accounts. Sheila was disturbed but promised to help.

"The MIS is drawn up in an Excel sheet where the information is extracted from the entries in the accounting package. However, the data is manually entered in the Excel sheet and not directly exported from the package due to formatting difficulty. The accounts package is a commercial off-the-shelf solution and the reports are not customizable. The company has its own formats and style of reporting due, which is why data entry was necessary." Sheila explained that these sheets were prepared by Goldie, with her help, and placed before the company executives and board of directors.

Nari then inquired about the sudden absence of Paul, especially as he had a meeting scheduled with him. Sheila confided that after the current year's balance sheet was finalized a week back, Paul had left the company for better prospects. There was some whispering among the staff that suggested he had developed differences of opinion with Rahulji on policy matters, she added. Rahulji had started questioning some of his decisions, which had annoyed Paul. This had surprised Sheila and quite a few other employees, as everyone in Town Mark felt that it was the managing director's initiative that had helped turn around the company's fortunes. At the same time, there was an overturn of both the accountant and company secretary position. The company secretary had left for better prospects and Goldie, the accountant, had gone on long leave to pursue further studies. The company was looking for a replacement for him.

The new accountant, Mrs. Rita Prabhu, was a graying middle-aged woman who had served as a secretary and then as a senior accountant in another large consumer product company. She was a complete contrast to Sheila, her junior accountant, who had an engaging personality and always got her way in the company. But Rita knew the business model, the MIS, and the accounting system quite well. When I met her, she asked me to come to her office to discuss the system audit and system overhaul after one week.

Opening Pandora's Box

After a week had passed, Rita appeared a bit harried. Her face looked tired sans her usual light makeup, and gray peaked from the roots of her dyed hair. But the office was buzzing with activity. Statements were being compiled, reconciliations done, accounts made up.

She glanced up from her cluttered desk and said, "There is a difference of over $2 million dollars in the books. There are debtors as per the final accounts that are not reflected in the books. I have gone over the books and extracted a trial balance. It means that figures of sales and debtors in the final accounts presented to the board and shareholders are inflated by 2 million. The inflation was made in the spreadsheet prepared from the trial balance extracted from the books. All subsequent processing is based on the inflated figures."

Over the weekend, Rita had checked and verified the balances of individual debtors and found the difference. The discovery was delayed due to inadequate circularization of debtors, some being disputed, others not yet reconciled, and some omitted from the list because they never responded in the past and mailing statements to them was considered a waste. It was also noticed that in the last four years, confirmation of balances was not obtained from the debtors, thereby weakening the control on receivables. Rita asked me if I could help. I agreed but requested that Nari join me, as he was the company's long-time cost auditor and knew most of the old hands in the accounts department, especially Sheila.

The next day Rita, Nari, and I sat down to sift through the papers, wondering where to start. Inflating sales and debtors for window dressing was "old hat." But what about invoices? Dispatch notes? How was the whole scheme tied up? A further prodding revealed that this was a completely MIS-based fraud. The original books, vouchers, and records were never tampered with. Monthly sales and debtor figures reported to the board and used for MIS were inflated. Figures in the final accounts were also upped by cleverly programming the spreadsheet template, used for preparing MIS and final accounts, to add a fixed sum to both sales and receivables. I remembered that Sheila helped Goldie compile the figures and the spreadsheets. Rita, the new accountant, immediately called Sheila and asked her point-blank: "Why did you fudge the spreadsheets? Or did you help Goldie do it?"

"We just followed Paul's instructions. I really don't know where the figures came from," she responded. We knew we wouldn't be able to extract much information from her. Sheila was rattled and left the company a week later. There was no formal investigation in process, so they couldn't hold her. There was no use catching the small fry, anyway, when the real brain in the scheme was someone much higher up in the hierarchy.

It was an amazingly simple, yet effective, scheme. But the question kept haunting us: Who was behind it and where did the money come from to keep the company running if the sales were inflated? Increased sales meant more profits, more bonuses, more commissions, and higher dividends. The sales could be inflated with higher receivables, but the bonuses, the commissions, and the dividends needed hard cash funds to be paid out.

We kept looking at the sources and the receipt side of the bank book and soon discovered a number of short-term loans and unsecured loans. They were all borrowed from associates of the top management, and at rates much higher than the market—from 18 percent to 36 percent per year. This was the method of bankrolling the operation. It effectively covered up the fact that sales were not genuine, as the company still had enough funds, received by way of these loans, to manage its activities.

We compiled this information and wrote the results on a piece of paper:

Inflated sales and debtors	$2 million
Missing inventory (written off as destroyed in cost and excise records—appearing in books)	$0.5 million

| Overcharged interest on borrowings— difference above the market rate over a period of two years | $0.6 million |
| Total | $3.1 million |

As we sat back looking at the total on the sheet of paper, Rita saw the staggering figure and remarked, "Are we not opening Pandora's Box?"

"We're still not sure who is involved and at what level. Let's look at the figures more carefully," I suggested.

Nari proposed we look at the commission and sales expenses. We found that there were substantial commission claims and charges of sales expenses by distributors and agents at a rate much higher than was accepted under the new management team. There was an avenue for personal profit. Someone was making excess cash at the cost of the company. Again, the difference was staggering—$4 million over the last two years.

Pandora's Modus Operandi

Rita, Nari, and I discussed the matter. We thought that the information and the findings were so significant and sensitive and the implications so far-reaching that it would be best to talk to Rahulji directly. The three of us met in his office and briefed him. He sat staring at us for a moment and then said softly, "I think my mother knew it but couldn't do anything. I had suspected that something was amiss, but before I could find out the details the whole team had left and was replaced."

We presented our information to him. The modus operandi was clear. We showed him a diagram that illustrated the chain of accounting and financial reporting and the cash flow in the company. See Exhibits 3.1 and 3.2.

Financial transactions were recorded in the books. Documents and records in respect to the same were preserved. The books of accounts were audited and the resulting assets and liabilities were duly verified. The trial balance was then extracted. The figures were used to generate final accounts, but the sales and debtors were inflated at this stage.

The accounting entries, along with supporting documentation and records, showed the true picture. Using this data, MIS reports were prepared for presentation to management and to the board for decision making. Once audited, the final accounts statements (profit and loss, balance sheet, and cash flow) were also presented to the shareholders, filed with the regulators, and given to relevant stakeholders.

Instead of using the actual figures from the books, figures of sales and debtors were inflated, resulting in apparently higher turnover and elevated

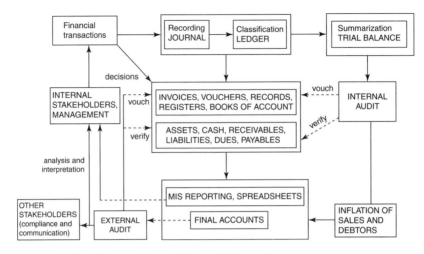

Exhibit 3.1   Chain of Accounting and Financial Reporting

profit. This was done by adding amounts to the corresponding total-debtors cell entry in the spreadsheets used for preparing the statements.

The cell matched the accounting records, but the resultant outputs were inflated by the fixed amount added in the formula. Thereafter, these figures were used for compiling and presenting financial statements for internal decisions as well as external reporting. The cash flow was maintained by taking short-term borrowings to cover the shortfall arising from the inflated debtors. These funds were used to pay increased commissions, margins, interest, and the dividends resulting from higher book profits. The cycle was thus complete.

Except for the inflated sales figures, the others—the higher-than-market rate of interest, the excessive sales expenses and commissions—were, at best, acts of financial impropriety or irregularity. They could have been a result of

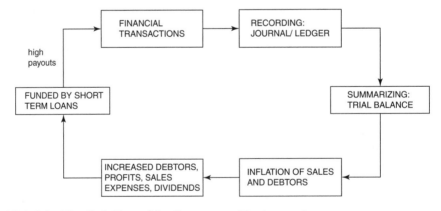

Exhibit 3.2   The Cash Flow of the Company and Its Accounting

lack of fiscal discipline but were not evidence of direct fraud. Like the proverbial Pandora's box, when the lid was lifted off the accounts, a whole lot of errors and issues tumbled out.

In hindsight, it appeared that Paul wanted to keep the company going at any cost, and that was how shoring up the results must have started. At this stage the only personal benefits appeared to be the accolades, the respect, the admiration of the employees and shareholders, and the trust shown by the owners. He was trying to maintain all that by showing improved results. But, down the line somewhere, he might have been deriving some benefit through overpriced sales margins and the higher-than-normal interest rates. The inflated values could also have been his last-ditch effort to keep the company afloat. Our dilemma was that since all the key personnel had changed, there was no way to find out the truth by direct interviewing and questioning.

Though a better showing helped the company, it could not have benefited any single group of executives directly. In the absence of a proven motive and direct evidence, the irregularities were looked on as mistakes, costly ones that taught the company valuable lessons. But there was always this lurking feeling about the whole episode. Paul appeared to be the mastermind. But was he? The way he portrayed himself as the ever-sacrificing saint seemed to be a dead giveaway.

It was not impossible to initiate legal action against the suspected perpetrators, but the likely impact on the image and reputation of the organization made it advisable not to pursue the matter. The correct remedy would be to strengthen and improve the systems.

Out With the Old, In With the New

Investigations and cases do not always lead to justice. Sheila Gole left the company in a week. She joined a competitor, but was relieved from her new job for suspected embezzlement. Paul Right joined a competitor and took his accountant, Goldie, along. Three years later, they were caught attempting to sell duplicate products with the Town Mark brand and are currently facing litigation.

Town Mark had a fresh look at its systems, cut down production and operating costs, put in place tighter controls over its operations, and re-negotiated sales margins, expenses, and commissions with its dealers, distributors, and sales force. This resulted in a remarkable turnaround. Today, Town Mark is a leading consumer-goods brand and is worth over $1 billion. Rahulji and Rita are both hoping that, with tighter and more efficient systems in place, the company will not face such problems in the future. The learning cost for the company was $7.1 million.

Lessons Learned

This fraud was not initially detected because spreadsheets of the management information system (MIS) reports were accepted without being checked by the managerial staff or the internal auditor. The statutory auditors failed to trace the final accounts in depth from balances in the books. MIS reports are intended for top management and offer quarterly, monthly, and annual results (profit and loss, balance sheet, and cash flow statements). During Town Mark's "Pandora" period, computer-generated MIS reports using spreadsheets, and final accounts generated from spreadsheet software using trial balance, were generally considered reliable, accurate, and acceptable, which led to figure fudging. This is precisely how management, in collusion with the senior accountant, could commit fraud. If the statements were extracted and prepared manually, they would not have been relied upon blindly. Similarly, if they were generated directly by the accounting software, the fraud would not have occurred so easily, as the statements directly generated from the accounting package would have been checked more carefully. It would have also been more difficult to interpolate and inflate the figures, as this would have required changing the accounting software program. Modifying the spreadsheet using macros was much easier and difficult to detect, as no one expected it.

Establishing management fraud beyond a doubt is always a difficult proposition, especially when it involves issues of propriety of decisions. What happened in this case could be fudging or window dressing (if it was deliberate), or an error or carelessness (if it was inadvertent). Since the key persons in the top management had changed, there was no way to find out the truth by direct questioning or confrontation. Before the heat could be turned on, they had fled the scene.

While it is easy to be wise after the event, vigilance, skill, and expertise are important in order to spot the telltale signs of wrongdoing, mischief, and system malfunction in time to prevent fraud. There were some weaknesses discovered in the company's internal controls, especially in the handling of debtors. A sound review mechanism to monitor the aging of debtors and review them for their realizable potential would have prevented or at least reduced the extent of the fraud.

In fact, the scheme was so simple and so ingenious that it not only yielded personal profits to the perpetrators by way of higher commissions, bonuses, and interest, but resulted in a higher profit and dividend payout, making the employees, shareholders, and owners happy. The shareholders and owners relished the dividend after a long break and the higher share prices pleased everyone. This created a situation where none of the key stakeholders—the owners, the board, the shareholders, the employees—were in a mood to look at things closely or ask searching, uncomfortable questions.

Top management should not have blind faith in their executives and there should be adequate checks and balances through proper systems of internal controls and regular internal audits. Disturbing facts like a liquidity crunch or a growing number of debtors should not be ignored, as they were in this case, merely because the company is making profits.

Recommendations to Prevent Future Occurrences

Proper Controls for Final Accounts and MIS

Proper control systems need to be put in place for tracing all MIS and final accounts spreadsheets to books and trial balance in the accounting package. The spreadsheet needs to be periodically verified against book figures and the formula validated for accuracy.

Executive Ownership of Financials

The final accounts are generally the ultimate responsibility of the board of directors and are eventually approved by the shareholders of the company at the general meeting. It is necessary to build among top executives a sense of ownership toward the financial statements of accounts to ensure their accuracy and fairness. One such healthy practice is to get the CEO, CFO, and the chief accountant to sign these statements every year, as is now required under the Sarbanes-Oxley Act of 2002. Even the MIS needs to be authenticated now to improve the quality of reporting.

Formal Internal Control Manual

Many of the processes would have been in place had a formal manual been written and adopted for internal control.

Greater Emphasis on Internal Audit

Internal audit is often viewed as a supplementary function to statutory audit when, in fact, it has a significant role to play in safeguarding assets and ensuring adherence to systems, policies, and practices. A robust internal audit could have revealed the problem involving debtors, the borrowings at high interest rates in excess of normal market rates, and the above-normal commissions and expense margins to distributors on sales.

Review the Appointment of Auditors

The work of auditors, both statutory and internal, is a significant input for the audit committee and board of directors. For effective governance, it is not only necessary to review and consider their findings, but also to communicate with them and identify and analyze the areas of importance and concern. This helps to focus the auditors' attention on issues that can help control deviations in the system.

Appoint a Fraud Officer/Establish a Fraud Hot line

All large corporations need a specialist to handle potential frauds. Fraud experts should set up controls and systems that can fix responsibility when frauds are discovered. It also helps to improve the success rate in bringing fraudsters to book, apart from preventing frauds and minimizing their impact through early detection.

Human Resources Policies

Human resources policies should address four key security needs:

1. Appropriate recruitment strategies to prevent the wrong kind of people from being recruited, including background checks
2. A whistle-blowing policy
3. Serious penalties as deterrents
4. A checklist to identify fraudsters and their lifestyles

System Audits

Computer systems need to be properly designed and continuously monitored and controlled. General internal and accounting controls are not adequate. Regular system audits are essential to ensure confidentiality, integrity, and availability of correct and timely information for decision making. Involvement of an auditor from the beginning might have helped prevent the event. An effective systems audit would have plugged the loophole that allowed inflation of figures at the spreadsheet stage, leading to erroneous MIS reports and final accounts.

About the Author

Dr. Vishnu Kanhere, CFE, CISA, CISM, is a practicing chartered accountant, cost accountant, and management consultant, and holds a doctorate in management. A renowned speaker and prolific writer, he addresses a range of specialized topics—valuation, taxation, information security, fraud examination, and environmental management—that reflect the wide canvas on which he operates.

Mail-Order Fraud

ROBIN CONRAD

Mail-order brides are certainly not new. For hundreds of years, Americans have imported wives from developing countries. According to the U.S. Citizenship and Immigration Services, from four thousand to six thousand marriages occur per year via mail order and the divorce rate in such relationships is only 20 percent, well below the average for most American couples.

As an online networking and dating site, my company, loveandcompanion-ship.com (LC.com), facilitates communication between individuals, but we prohibit mail-order bride listings due to the high probability of fraud that accompanies unverified foreign profiles.

Typically, networking/dating fraud is some variation of an advanced fee scam whereby perpetrators request funds for a fallacious reason and then abscond with the money. A potential love interest may ask for funds via Western Union for a plane ticket or to help with a family emergency. In the most extreme of circumstances, a mark—that is, the targeted victim—might be lured to a foreign country or drained financially for months. Usually, however, the scam takes the form of a one-time request for money.

Russia and former Eastern bloc countries represent a large portion of the bridal frauds and have the distinction of being more technologically advanced than African fraudsters. Additionally, when compared to the diversity of Nigerian 419 scams—named for the part of the Nigerian Criminal Code regarding cheating—which run the gamut from the "Spanish Prisoner" (a scam promising buried treasure) to fake lotteries to romance advanced-fee schemes, the Russian fraudsters are specialized when targeting their prey.

Most of the fraudulent Russian bridal scams that have been prosecuted were run by men, sometimes with organized crime connections. Online databases full of pictures available for download make the existence of a real woman unnecessary to the scheme.

Toying with Human Emotion

A few years ago, I came across an efficient Russian fraudster, Vlad, who was responsible for approximately 15,000 dating profile accounts in the span of a couple of months. The fraudulent e-mails sent included a brief introduction and a Yahoo e-mail address to direct his potential victims away from our supervision. Unfortunately, many of our users contacted the fraudster. In each case, the targets were sent at least five or six conversational e-mails. In the second e-mail, the female persona, Natasha, would confess to living in Russia but promise that she had plans to come to a city in America near the victim in the next month—and that she would love to meet him.

Each additional e-mail would include three pictures. As the conversation progressed, the pictures would become more suggestive but were never obscene. The fraudulent e-mails were carefully crafted to include questions about the mark's answers in the previous communications. Here's an example of an e-mail from Vlad:

Hello again,

How are you today? How is your day? I would like to see as many pictures of yours as possible, because its very interesting for me and I would like to get to know you better . . . Recently we celebrated my friend's birthday and I felt so sad because her boyfriend was with her. They were kissing and hugging each other. She got a great bouquet of flowers . . . I hope that my birthday will also celebrate with my beloved who can be my one and forever. Could it be you?

By the way I have something more to tell you about me. I didn't tell you that I like traveling. I have been in Moscow a few years ago with my friends. Also I have been in St. Petersburg. It was wonderful to go sightseeing and very interesting. But unfortunately I had no chance to visit any foreign country . . .

I have already told you that I work as a surgeon in a city hospital. I do different optional operations. But I earn not much in our country. About $200 in your money per month. I do think it is a small salary but all doctors have low salary in Russia . . .

So strange, time flies so fast . . . I will be 35 years old soon. My birthday is on 3rd of January. Can you believe it! But I should say that I don't want to spend it, because I always wanted to celebrate it with my life partner. That is my dream and I hope it will come true one day. You know, now I am very sad that you are so far away from me, cause we couldn't be together on my birthday. I have one more dream, a dream to have a family, to take care about my husband. It's all I want in my life, I just want to be happy as a woman. And it doesn't matter in what kind of country my future husband is living . . .

I guess that is enough for today and I would like to ask you a few questions:

What did you do during the week-end? Anything interesting? What did you do for fun? What do you feel about such relationships as we can possibly have? I will be waiting for your reply with great impatience. I have to run for my work right now . . .

The Natasha persona that Vlad created was subtly manipulative. She loves to travel but hasn't left the country. She has a great job, but it doesn't pay well. Her birthday is coming up and she'd love to spend it with the mark. In her first e-mail, she introduced herself and said she was visiting a friend that lived less than a hundred miles from the mark. In another, she claims her sister married an American and is very happy, supposedly spurring her excitement about a potential long-distance relationship. Vlad invested a lot of time in developing his marks' interest. Some of his text was standard, while some details were variable.

Each time, the week before the planned trip, ''Natasha'' claimed to have spent her travel money on a hospital visit for a family member and asked the mark to pay for her trip to the states. To add an air of legitimacy, Natasha then indicated that the mark should work directly with the travel agency.

Once the victim agreed, an e-mail from a phony travel agency would be sent to the victim. The total price for the flight was $945 and could be paid by Western Union. If the mark sent the money, the Russian bride completely disappeared. A couple of months later, the mark would often begin receiving e-mails from other potential foreign brides. To add insult to injury, after stealing the money, Vlad was selling his victims' e-mail addresses to other scammers.

Vlad differentiated himself from the average Russian fraudster by using personalized detail. The mark was made to feel as though he were truly engaged in a relationship. ''Natasha'' never responded immediately to the correspondence, there were no tell-tale professions of love in the first few e-mails, and instead of requesting wired money, she asked that he use a travel agency to purchase the plane ticket, adding a layer of false security. No genuine travel agency would insist on payment via Western Union, but not everyone is aware of that, and the fact that the phony company had a Web site made it appear legitimate.

Vlad's scheme stands in contrast to other e-mail scams that still work on occasion but are more obviously fraudulent. Following is a first e-mail in a Nigerian 419 scam:

> hello Walter
>
> i just look into your profile now its so lovely and i want to tell you that you are soo cuite, you are much like an angel to me with your cute smile on the screen here its soo lovely soo if you dont mind i want to know better than what you have on the site to tell you the fact you capture my heart no matter what i dont want you to say no the age is nothing to me okay i just want to love you for who you are thats all i want to do soo just for you to let me know you and I'm ready to settle down soon if you are ready to let me know cuz i want to be a responsible man for my life okay and if i may ask what is your lovely name angel?

This e-mail is clearly not personalized or well written. Notice that it is addressed to ''Walter'' but then asks for the mark's name. The majority of Internet users would be swiftly tipped off by this contradiction. Also, all of the Nigerian accounts and e-mails are created by hand, so the loss potential is much smaller.

Real Love

As a network and dating site, loveandcompanionship.com (LC.com) provides a safe environment for individuals to communicate. In addition to a searchable database of users, LC.com also provides a secure and anonymous e-mailing and messaging system. The company weathered the original dot.com bust and continues to be one of the best known of the dating and networking sites.

When I started at LC, there was no database of fraudulent accounts, no studies about fraudulent behavior, and no monitoring system. Overall, the company lacked a sense of urgency concerning fraud because nobody understood the extent of the impact on users. Fortunately, LC was not afraid of change. Now work never ends. I wear a pager that wakes me in the night whenever our monitor has detected large amounts of activity that could be fraudulent.

There were already some fraud protections in place, such as limits for e-mails sent to unique users per day per account. We also prohibit the same username or e-mail address from being used more than once, putting pressure on individuals who create multiple accounts because they usually operate with naming conventions that make finding patterns easier.

Going After Lover Boy

LC.com is in many ways my dream job. I sit quietly in a dark room surrounded by computers. I find systemic and repeat fraud perpetrators and recommend policy and system enhancements to help control them. My job is to detect user patterns. It might hinge on the use of one IP address for multiple account submissions, using the same password, e-mail provider, or profile. The accounts might seem distinct but send the same e-mail repeatedly. I use various computer programs, like MS Access, to monitor new accounts and look for similarities.

Upon first detecting Vlad's fraud, I wasn't impressed. All of his accounts shared a password, e-mail provider, and IP. They weren't difficult to find. I blocked that first group of accounts and set up detection based on the individual attributes, such as patterns in username, password, e-mail address, or IP used to establish the account, just in case he decided to use discretion. Once I began to study the accounts, I realized finding them wasn't the problem. Vlad was sending out the maximum number of e-mails in less than one minute of account registration, which meant the damage was done before the accounts were canceled.

Although I eliminated the dating profiles and warned our users about the dangers of sending money, we received quite a few complaints from customers who had already been tricked into sending funds. LC has no way of protecting our users once they begin using third party e-mail communication, but our filtering system would have captured the e-mails asking for money if they were sent using our communication system.

Since the fraudsters are aware of this and, in fact, most dating and networking sites employ some kind of filtering system, it's common practice to try to convince users to employ a third party e-mail system as quickly as possible.

We essentially act as a conduit for communication between singles, so our challenge was to stop Vlad and other fraudsters without interfering with legitimate communications. The first step was to block all Internet traffic coming from Russia and other countries with high instances of fraud.

Lovers' Protocol

Each computer on the Internet has a unique Internet protocol (IP) address. IPs are broken into four parts called octets. Each octet is a number from 0-255. Every computer on the Internet has an IP address based on location and service provider. All Internet service providers own blocks of IP addresses that are assigned to the individual computers. By looking at a complete IP address, location and provider can be determined.

Vlad was not fazed in the slightest by IP blocking. He began launching his scripts with botnets, or networks of zombie computers. A zombie computer is created when a computer is physically hacked or infected with a virus/trojan. Once infected, the computer joins a group called a botnet. This network is maintained by one person, typically referred to as a bot herder, but it can be

Enter the word as it is shown in the box below.

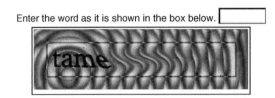

Exhibit 4.1   Example of a Capcha

"rented" for various nefarious purposes. One botnet might be responsible for thousands of fraudulent activities. Many of the zombie computers I've seen have been public machines, either at libraries or universities, but any computer with online access can be compromised.

Since botnets aren't necessarily geographically linked, it is difficult to effectively block them by IP. Additionally, a savvy user can spoof their IP address or use an anonymous proxy server service which allows them to create false credentials.

Our botnet defense was to introduce "capcha," or visual verification, to the signup process. A capcha is the box of text that a user is instructed to type into a provided field. Exhibit 4.1 gives an example.

The purpose is to disrupt bots while not impeding actual customers. The defense is used by many of the larger Web sites as a means of verifying that online services are being provided to humans and not to computer scripts. While the practice is fairly common online, it is the nature of network and dating sites to attract "newbies" (those new to the Internet) who might be confused by capcha.

Implementing capcha at LC brought an immediate 30 percent drop in fraud, but it did not deter Vlad or any of the other Russian bots. Unfortunately, it's common in Russia to employ individuals to monitor the script process and manually enter the capcha, so we only managed to add 15 seconds to their process.

Again I was failing, and by doing so, losing the confidence of upper management. While my job is to minimize the impact and prevalence of fraud, it is their job to ensure that the users have the best and quickest sales experience. Like many Web sites, our business revolves around a high number of transactions. While overall systemic fraud was down dramatically, Vlad and his Russian counterparts hadn't been impacted in the slightest.

Who Said Making Crime Pay was Cheap?

A cost/loss analysis for fraud in a high-transaction Web environment is difficult at best. Since I was finding and refunding the fake accounts created by Vlad within hours, there were no charge-backs associated with the accounts. And because the monetary losses happened off our site, I was not able to determine a loss total. While there were some customer complaints, the number was relatively low compared with the expense of my next pitch.

My idea was to benchmark legitimate customers. When they deviated from established behavior, one e-mail would go into a manual review process. The idea was to have these e-mails quickly sent through or blocked. The impact on legitimate users would be minimal, but the process would require a lot of development and administration. To justify the change and attached expenditure with almost no cost basis, I had to sell the idea based on the esoteric concept of user experience, which is not easily quantifiable.

A fraud task force was formed comprised of me and representatives from development, marketing, and customer service. It is always a challenge to explain the subtle nuances of fraud to professionals from different backgrounds. Perhaps the most common misconception is that fraudsters are dumb and do not employ creative problem-solving skills. Since the income potential for fraud is so high, it is in the fraudsters' interest to take the time to research their process; and since they live in developing countries, manpower can be cheaply obtained. Matching prevention methods to the evolution of fraud is an important aspect of a well-rounded detection and deterrence system, but determining the perpetrators' drive is just as critical.

I was able to sell the idea to management with the help of the task force. I told a story detailing the abuse new users would suffer if they fell for the scam, and what might happen if such stories were leaked to the public. There is no way to predict or control the impact or speed of Internet word of mouth. A horror story involving our company could potentially be sent and resent millions of times in a day—or not at all.

In the interest of research, I obtained copies of all of the communications between several victims and Vlad's operation. I created a packet that included my thoughts on how this group was different and far more dangerous to our users than the typical Russian or Nigerian scam. As shown in the example at the beginning, the difference is pretty dramatic.

The story, along with the number of fraudulent accounts and their obvious discrepancies in behavior when compared to legitimate clientele, was enough to convince upper management that a manual review process was necessary.

In addition to basic behaviors, a manual update process was added for any new patterns that I might discover as the fraudsters evolved. With every protection, their tactics changed. I had no expectation of actually exterminating the fraud; it was like a disease that mutates in response to new medicine.

It took Vlad about two weeks to successfully navigate through the tool. First, he began using unique passwords and different e-mail providers for each account. Since we were basing some rules on account age, he tried to create the profiles and wait a few days before sending the e-mails to counter our efforts. I was able to cancel those accounts before anyone incurred significant damage.

Eventually, the company began to use a statistical method that assigns a fraud probability to accounts. But the system requires regular updates to keep it relevant and to keep the majority of fraudulent e-mails from reaching our users.

I supplied our information to both the Secret Service and the FBI. They showed no interest in pursuing the case, both because the losses were relatively minor per complainant and because we had no way of finding all of the victims, given that the fraud had occurred offsite. Over the months, I was able to have Vlad dropped by several ISP services and to obtain the shutdown of all the supporting Web sites and the e-mail addresses his operation used.

Lessons Learned

Legal prosecution in international fraud matters is fairly rare in comparison with the amount of cases that actually occur. Often foreign countries directly or indirectly profit from fraud via payoffs or foreign money in the local economy. It is unreasonable to assume that prosecution of a few perpetrators will destroy this income stream. As long as there are developing countries where tech jobs are scarce and not necessarily lucrative, fraud will be rife.

Online antifraud professionals will continue to play cat and mouse games with people like Vlad, operators who are smarter and more adaptable than the average scammer. As detection and prevention grow, Vlad and his ilk will become the rule, and not the exception, for operating a fraudulent enterprise online. The drive and problem-solving skills of a good online fraudster should never be underestimated. Our side's ability to respond to new threats as they occur is the ultimate test of our intelligence and forethought.

In a way, I owe a huge debt to Vlad. He illustrated a scenario I had been warning the higher-ups against since taking my job at LC.com. While fighting his crimes, I was able to completely shut down others like him and impress on management the importance of fighting fraud.

The joy and challenge of fraud is that we, as antifraud professionals, operate within a framework of business rules, laws, and budgetary constraints. Our foes have no such limitations. It is far easier to rewrite a script than to change a functioning Web site. The sheer size of a business limits its ability to adapt quickly. By creating a system that operates with variables, fraud can be contained. It requires constant monitoring and updating, but it is worth the time and expense.

Network and dating sites provide a means and opportunity for fraud, although in many ways, they are safer than meeting strangers in person. According to fakechecks.org, "The best and worst thing about the Internet is anonymity." When personal information and money are exchanged online, the lack of physical interaction hides many of the clues that normally give away dishonesty. Using VOIP (voice-over IP) a fraudster can create the illusion of being anywhere in the world. There are so many methods that a fraudster can employ, it would be impossible to list them all.

It is hard to educate people without scaring them, which is not good for sales. As more stories of deception make it into the public arena, users will learn to be more leery of instant gratification in matters of the heart. But just as spam was once an effective means of fraud, dating and networking will eventually fade as a preferred medium.

Fraud is a living, breathing thing. I've since learned that when one person breaks through fraud protections, he or she often sells the techniques to other fraudsters, so the battle will not end anytime soon.

Recommendations to Prevent Future Occurrences

Study the Behavioral Patterns of Fraud

Continued studies on the behavior of fraudulent computer users versus legitimate ones are important to staying current with the evolution of fraud. As the fraudsters change tactics, it is essential to understand their behavior and how to distinguish it from regular customer habits.

Quality Assurance

Quality assurance is important to a company's specialized group that reviews potentially fraudulent e-mails. As the group at LC has grown, my interaction with the members individually has become much smaller. But through reviewing their work, I have had the chance to make recommendations and impart my applicable knowledge.

Allow Customers to Communicate Concerns

Enhance the methods available for customers to voice their concerns to companies. An instant message feature would facilitate the process. Their experience is critical to justifying company expenditures on fraud deterrence and detection.

Be Up-to-Date with Technology

Purchase new IP geolocation technology. NSA has patented a system of determining an IP address by sending messages back and forth a number of times to determine the physical location of a computer. This technology challenges IP address spoofing.

Continued Education

Continue antifraud education for executives. As companies change, it is essential that fraud remain a consideration. There is a tendency within management to consider fraud conquered, so regular reporting and communication are essential.

Fraud Classification System

A fraud classification system is important. By categorizing fraud by the level of innovation apparent, technical changes can be tracked and solutions can be offered by grouping.

About the Author

Robin Conrad, CFE, has been in the online fraud investigation industry for over 13 years and is currently the senior fraud analyst for a leading Internet social networking site. She has focused on the information-systems and IT aspects of fraud detection and deterrence. She is proficient in ACL, SQL, Access, and Excel.

Lancelot Gone Missing

CAROLYN CONN, PAUL PRICE, AND KARON MURFF

Back in his hometown of Pineland, Arizona, Richard Dawson had been dubbed "Lancelot" for his propensity to rescue women in distress. The nickname followed him from high school into college when he and his closest friends enrolled at Arizona Tech, located in nearby Jackson. So no one was surprised when Richard expressed his desire to save Patti Williams from a bad relationship.

Richard met Patti in an Internet chat room while he was home for the holidays between the fall and spring semesters of his junior year. He had been on the computer late one night checking his Organic Chemistry grade online, concerned that it might be his first B. A driven individual, Richard graduated as valedictorian of his high school class of more than 500 students. Dual-credit advanced placement courses that counted at both the high school and college level allowed him to enter Tech with the credits of a second-semester sophomore. At age 20, Richard was one year away from graduating with a bachelor's degree in information technology.

After seeing that his chemistry grade wasn't posted yet, Richard decided to distract himself by visiting his favorite chat room. That's where he met Patti, a senior prelaw student at Phoenix State University. Once Richard told her of his academic accomplishments and his fear of a B, she wrote:

> Chill out. Worrying about it now won't do any good. Tomorrow the grades will be posted and you'll make an "A."

Encouragement from Patti, a total stranger, made Richard feel better—plus, he had a new friend. In the following weeks, their relationship blossomed online. Patti seemed wiser than her years and seemed to understand him.

"I've never met a girl who can get inside my head like she does," he told his roommate, Bobby. "She really gets how guys feel about things."

Bobby kidded him about being in love. Richard denied it, but soon he was making plans to meet her in person. Patti said she would drive to Jackson for a basketball game with her brother, Clifton, a Tech sports fanatic.

They were supposed to meet at five o'clock on Friday, just in time to grab a bite and head to the game. About mid-afternoon, Richard received an e-mail from Patti:

> So sick. Threw up all day. Stomach bug. Can't make trip.

Richard was disappointed. Eager to meet this girl, he wanted to find out if she was as perfect in real life as she was online. Her message continued:

> Clifton's still coming ur way. Will u take him to the game?

"Sure. We'll miss you," he responded.

Lancelot to the Rescue

Tall and half-starved looking, Clifton Ray Williams was not what Richard expected. Evidently, he was sensitive to people's reaction to his frail and sickly appearance. Immediately after shaking hands, Clifton told Richard about his health problems. It started with jaundice when he was five. Ever since, he had been in and out of hospitals. He never had any close friends. As a child, his peers tormented him with name-calling and teasing.

Clifton said his father made things worse. He was a man's man, and so were Clifton's two older brothers. They hunted together and shot target practice in the off season. His dad drove an old, camouflage-painted pickup truck. He sounded like some kind of survivalist. "He divorced my mom about 20 years ago, when I was 14," Clifton explained. "He's been living in the mountains of northern Mexico—just him and a pack of guard dogs. Mom said he left the country so he wouldn't have to pay child support."

Richard inferred that the family had been verbally and physically abusive, which would explain why Patti stayed with her current boyfriend, who he suspected was behind all of her cancellations. He sounded like a real jerk. She described him as insanely jealous. In one conversation, she wrote:

> He'll never believe I've gone with my brother to a basketball game. He'll think I'm seeing someone and then he'll be all over me.

Patti said the guy belittled her, calling her dumb and ugly.

Nothing could have been further from the truth. As a prelaw major who had been on the dean's list with straight A's every semester, Patti obviously wasn't lacking in intelligence. And she wasn't ugly either. It took Richard quite a bit of coaxing—she had been hesitant, claiming she was new to the chat room culture and felt nervous about divulging so much information to a stranger—but finally Patti e-mailed him a photo. In response, Richard forwarded his own picture and referred her to a few articles about him on the Web. "This way you'll know I'm real and not some kind of pervert," he had written.

After reading an article about him winning the state math competition his senior year in high school, Patti relaxed and sent her photo. She wrote back:

> How could I possibly be afraid of a math geek?

Richard took the comment good-naturedly, knowing it wasn't accurate. He was not the kind of guy who spent endless hours in front of a computer screen. His technological savvy came naturally. He could figure out nearly anything software- or Internet-related. But he was social too, sported a perpetual tan from being outdoors as a member of Tech's track team, and lifted weights to maintain his physique for competitions. Girls described Richard as "buff," though he definitely was not the stereotypical jock.

When Patti finally did send her picture, it was of a petite girl with dark blonde hair, gray-blue eyes, and a timid smile. Richard was smitten. His heart ached at the thought of this girl being emotionally or physically abused.

Over the next two months, Richard and Patti made plans several times to meet in person. Once they were supposed to get together at a truck stop that was a halfway point between their colleges. At the last minute Patti canceled, claiming something had come up. Another time, they planned to see each other in Flagstaff, where both of their families would be visiting relatives over spring break. Richard went to the restaurant where they had agreed to meet, but she never showed. After waiting for nearly three hours, Richard turned on his laptop and found a message from Patti; her mom was apparently sick and their family had canceled the trip.

Then there was the time she couldn't meet because of dental surgery. Patti said her jaw was wired shut, which increased Richard's suspicions. She refused to answer his direct questions, but he was certain her boyfriend had become violent.

"If I can look her in the eye, I know I can convince her that she doesn't have to spend any more time with this guy," he told his roommate, Bobby.

"There you go again, Lancelot, always trying to take care of everybody."

Though Patti never made any of the promised meetings, her brother Clifton went to several sporting events at Tech with Richard. During one trip Bobby joined them at a bar near campus where they shot pool for several hours. Upon returning to their dorm room, Bobby said, "I don't understand how you can spend any time around Clifton. The guy's breath was so bad I couldn't stand to be near him. I had trouble even making my pool shots!"

Richard said he felt sorry for Clifton and the visits helped him know Patti a little more through her brother's eyes. Even though there was a significant age gap, Clifton said Patti was his only friend. She was the only one who showed real empathy toward him, understood his disappointments and recurring illnesses.

About 10 years earlier, Clifton was employed at a fast food restaurant where he had worked his way up to assistant manager. He planned to save money and enroll in the local community college, then later on transfer to Tech. Unfortunately, he became seriously ill and underwent surgery to remove part of his liver. He lost his job. For the past three years, Clifton said he had been unemployed and living with his mother and Patti in a suburb of Phoenix. Recently, his sister had tried to persuade him to pursue his college goal again.

His descriptions of his sister were consistent with the girl Richard knew online, but he still had trouble reconciling the broken promises to meet. She was always apologetic and the excuses seemed legitimate. But something wasn't right. He had to find out, particularly since Patti had recently been telling people in the chat room that she and Richard were getting engaged.

"Engaged? Where did she get that idea?!" Bobby was shocked. "You better get rid of this chick. She sounds like some kind of psycho," he said.

"No, she's not! She's just confused and feels powerless. I think she's telling people we're getting engaged because she really wants to be helped."

Richard had made up his mind. He would find where Patti lived and drop by her house unannounced. That way there would be no backing out, no rescheduling. Was this the girl of his dreams? His soulmate? He had to know and he had to save Patti from her abusive boyfriend.

With his computer skills, it took Richard less than 30 minutes of online research to find Patti's address in suburban Phoenix. She had said she lived at home with her mother and brother to save the cost of college room and board. Richard told Bobby he was flying out of Jackson early on Friday to surprise her for the weekend. "Don't worry. I'll be back Monday morning with time to spare for the exam in my three o'clock class."

Richard's parents became worried when they didn't hear from their son. He usually called home at 8 p.m. every Sunday, without fail. But they had repeatedly tried his cell phone and got no answer. When Richard hadn't spoken to them by Monday night, his parents decided to contact the university police. His mother was a nervous wreck. "Something is seriously wrong. Richard would never do this," she told an officer.

Gone Missing

As a patrol supervisor with the university police for 10 years, Sergeant Matthews had seen his share of "missing" college students. They usually reappeared after a partying binge or after they had cooled off from a fight with their parents. When Mrs. Dawson called on Tuesday morning, Matthews tried to calm her down. "Ma'am, I *do* hear what you're saying. But most of the time these kids are back on campus in three or four days. Maybe he had a fight with his roommate or something. Are you sure he didn't just need to get away for a while?"

Richard's mother insisted, "Absolutely not. I *know* my son and he would *never* miss an exam. And he's never missed calling home every Sunday night since he's been at Tech. I'm telling you—something's wrong. You've got to find my son!"

Mr. Dawson took the phone from his distraught wife and asked how to file a missing-persons report. He told the sergeant they would drive to Tech that afternoon.

After more than 25 years in law enforcement, Detective James Franklin of the university police had also seen his fair share of "missing" college students. He tried to be objective with the Dawsons. Their son sounded like a good kid, but parents cannot always predict their children's behavior. The Dawsons told Detective Franklin everything they knew about Richard's absence from campus. They had spoken with his roommate, Bobby, on the phone. He told them Richard had gone to Phoenix to see a new girlfriend. Perhaps he decided to stay with her for a while. Maybe he was in love. The more Franklin talked with the Dawsons, the more it seemed like there was some credence to this case. College kids who "go missing" usually surface after a few days and make some form of contact with friends or family via a phone call, e-mail, or text message. After running Richard's driver's license through the state and local law enforcement databases, Franklin found nothing. No parking tickets, no speeding tickets, no violations of any sort. This kid was squeaky clean.

He reassured Richard's parents, "Based on my experience, he'll be home soon. But first I'll talk to his roommate." Bobby, Richard's roommate, was defensive from start. "I'm telling you, he went to see some girl . . . someone he met on the Internet who sounds like she's got a screw loose. I don't know where he is!"

"Come on, Bobby," said Franklin, "This is your buddy, Richard. You were the last person to see him on Friday. Can't you think of anything else he said about his plans for the weekend?"

"I'm not talking to you anymore—not without an attorney!"

How Dead Men Talk

Franklin had seen roommates react with indifference to the absence of their friends, but Bobby's response was unusual. Was he hiding something? Franklin obtained permission to kick him out of the dorm room and call in crime scene investigators. In particular, he wanted a forensic examiner to go through Richard's computer. That seemed to be where the case began. And with Bobby refusing to cooperate, it was the only place to search for clues.

On Wednesday morning, Franklin was surprised by a phone call from Mr. Dawson. "My wife got an e-mail from Richard last night. He said not to worry and that he's just spending a few extra days with Patti." But Mr. Dawson said his wife was not convinced. The e-mail did not sound like her son. Franklin thought the message was pretty straightforward.

Over the next few days, there were more e-mails from Richard sent to his parents, Bobby, and other friends. The messages all claimed he was having a good time with Patti and urged everyone not to worry. Franklin found inconsistencies. After checking at the Jackson airport, he could not locate Richard's car. And the only airline with service to Phoenix had no record of Richard flying during the previous week.

Franklin contacted both city and state law enforcement agencies. He scheduled a meeting with their investigators for Friday morning. "We originally thought this was a simple case of a college kid going off for a long weekend, but things aren't making sense and we need your help," he told them.

He introduced the group to Gary Goodman, the forensics expert who had been examining Richard's computer files. Goodman distributed copies of online conversations between Richard and Patti and other participants in the chat room.

"We've been in touch with the chat room moderator," he began. "He's an older guy who's been running it for about two years. He had concerns even before we contacted him and mentioned the situation with Patti and Richard always seemed odd. Apparently she had set up dates with other college boys too but never showed."

Franklin asked the investigative team to review the copies of the online conversations for clues that might lead to the whereabouts of Richard Dawson. He reminded them, "All of you know that, if this is something more than a missing person, we're in trouble. If it's a homicide, the murderer has a big lead."

The first 24 to 72 hours are critical to any homicide investigation. The longer it takes to identify a murder suspect, the less likely the case will be solved. Goodman informed the group that Richard had been searching for an address in Phoenix and seemed to have found it from the county's online property tax records. He had also been searching newspaper, high school, and other databases for the names "Patti Williams" and "Clifton Williams."

"Patti Williams" was a name Goodman recognized. It was the girl Richard had met online. But there was not much information on Clifton yet. An online search of the state police database for "Clifton Williams" yielded a driver's license. The street address on the license matched the address in Phoenix contained in Richard's computer files. The investigators had not found any record of a driver's license for Patti. The results of an online search of Tech's academic records showed that Clifton had been admitted to the school several years earlier.

Because Detective Franklin had initially been working the case as a missing person, his efforts had been concentrated on the travel routes to Phoenix. After learning of Clifton's connection to Tech, he redirected his attention to the campus and surrounding area. He ran Richard's car and driver's license numbers through the campus traffic and parking database and found an odd result. Richard had been issued a parking ticket on-campus Monday when he was reportedly in Phoenix with Patti. Franklin immediately called parking services. "Have someone review all the videotapes of the parking garage where this ticket was issued," he instructed.

Several hours later, a parking officer reported that an individual who did not look like Richard Dawson was seen on the videotape driving Richard's car. Although the image on the videotape wasn't clear, it looked a lot like the photo on the driver's license of Clifton Williams.

With an attorney at his side, Richard's roommate, Bobby, came in the next day for questioning. He told Detective Franklin that the previous Monday his morning class let out early. He had returned to his dorm room and found Clifton sitting at Richard's computer. He recounted Clifton's explanation: "Richard said it would be OK for me to play some computer games. He knew I was coming to town and told me to make myself at home. He and Patti are spending the rest of the week together."

The forensic examination of Richard's computer revealed that a large number of files had been deleted after he left campus the previous Friday. The computer timestamps proved the deletions occurred on the same day Bobby said Clifton had been in their dorm room. Goodman recovered all the deleted files; their contents were the conversations between Richard and Patti. Even though his actions had been suspicious, investigators had been wrong about Bobby. Based on the content of the files recovered by the fraud examiner, Clifton Williams became the prime suspect.

Beware of the Chat Room Flirt

After his initial meeting with the Dawsons, Franklin sent a missing-persons report to other law enforcement agencies across Arizona. "Franklin, you ought to look at this," said the dispatcher. "It's a wire about a John Doe found by some hikers in the national forest northeast of Phoenix in Rockwood County."

Franklin's first thought was the body might be Richard Dawson. Five days later, DNA analysis and dental records proved his hunch was correct. The county coroner reported the cause of death as one rifle shot to the back of the head. The case was a homicide.

Officers from Phoenix and Rockwood County converged on the Williams' home in suburban Phoenix. Mrs. Williams confirmed the investigators' suspicions: she did not have a daughter. She also told them Clifton had been admitted to a nearby hospital the day before and urged the officers to be considerate of her ailing son. They seized multiple computers and a deer rifle, and they cut out a large chunk of the living room carpet that appeared blood stained. Clifton was arrested in his hospital room a short time later.

After he was in custody, Clifton admitted to masquerading online as Patti and confessed to the murder of Richard Dawson. He said he had never intended to harm anyone. He became desperate when Richard showed up unannounced demanding to see Patti. Clifton killed Richard to maintain his secret cyber life. He had utilized Richard's computer to gain access to his Tech e-mail, password, and chat room accounts. Using that information, he assumed Richard's identity online.

Police had planned to question Clifton the morning after his arrest about the use of his Patti persona. They wanted to know more regarding the online relationships reported by the chat room moderator between Patti and other male college students. Several law enforcement agencies across the state had received reports of similar cases and Clifton was the likely perpetrator. But they were not able to question him further. The next morning Clifton was found dead in his cell. He had committed suicide.

The evidence in the case did not indicate Clifton was a pedophile or that he had ever physically harmed any of the other victims. Some investigators hypothesized his motivation was the "thrill of the chase" and his ability to convincingly portray a female online. It was even likely he was on-site, but not visible, when the male dates went to the meeting locations Clifton's female alter ego had designated.

Lessons Learned

Solving Internet crimes requires new and innovative investigation techniques. Valuable information was gained from the moderator and participants in the chat room. This case would not have been solved quickly without their help. People who spend a lot of time on the Internet develop behavior norms, just like in the real world. Their insight into their cyber world can be an excellent source of intelligence. What they "see," as well as their technical skills, can prove invaluable.

Online witnesses may have crucial evidence in Internet crimes even if they live in another state or country. Investigators should not discount information from these sources.

Solving the digital component of many modern crimes requires the expertise of a trained forensic examiner who can properly collect and analyze computer-based evidence. Nearly every modern crime has a digital component. Computers, cell phones, PDAs, and other digital devices all store data that can be useful evidence in an investigation. First responders and investigators must be trained to recognize potential digital evidence and to know how to preserve it for review by a digital forensic examiner.

Solving Internet crimes requires cooperation among law enforcement officials from multiple jurisdictions. Such crimes usually cross jurisdictional boundaries. This can cause delays and miscommunication among investigators. Prior to the advent of the Internet, state, county, and city officials usually stayed within their own geographic borders and concentrated on crimes within their area.

Recommendations to Prevent Future Occurrences

Never Meet an Online Friend Alone

Richard Dawson might not have been murdered if he had taken some simple precautions with his new online friend. No one should go alone to meet someone in person from the Internet. Get together in a public place. Park a considerable distance from the meeting spot and assure that the other person cannot identify your vehicle or follow you home. To decrease the chances of being a victim of an Internet dating fraud, meet several times over a long period until you get to know the person. Ask to meet his or her friends and learn as much about the person as possible. Consider using a service that conducts background checks on Internet dates.

Don't Send Photographs Online

No one—male or female—should ever post or send photographs of themselves over the Internet. After a photo and other personal information are on the Web, there is little control over who can access it or what is done with it.

Know Your Resources

Computer forensic resources should be located and identified before investigators need them. Know their contact information and procedures for after-hours calls. Law enforcement agencies should receive training by a digital forensic examiner on the proper ways to seize electronic evidence to ensure it is preserved for use in their investigations.

Protocols and Communication

The state, city, county, and university law enforcement agencies working this case did have some challenges coordinating with one another. To prevent problems when investigating Internet crimes, protocols must be developed and followed for dealing with multiple jurisdictions. With the advent of the Web, law enforcement officials must recognize that the Internet has no boundaries. They cannot rely on other jurisdictions to solve Internet crimes and they cannot work Internet crimes alone. Cooperation is essential, regardless of the physical locations of the computers used by the victim and the perpetrator. The question of who's going to police the Internet is a tough one. The answer must be *everybody*.

About the Authors

Dr. Carolyn Conn, CFE, CPA, is an associate professor of accounting whose interests include fraud/forensic accounting and accounting ethics. She has extensive experience in both the academic and administrative areas of higher education. She also provides consulting services in the area of litigation support.

Paul Price is Director of Forensic Technologies at J.A. Compton & Co. Prior to entering the private sector as a consultant, Paul was a state law enforcement officer with 20 years of public service. His background includes specialized assignments in financial crimes investigation, crime scene investigation, computer forensics, and counterterrorism.

Dr. Karon Murff, CPA, CIA, is an associate professor in computer science and Director of the Center of Excellence in Digital Forensics at Sam Houston State University. Areas of interest include digital forensics, fraud examination, and computer fraud. She is experienced in fraud auditing, forensic investigations, and investigation of white-collar crime.

CHAPTER 6

Double Trouble

STEPHEN P. WEBER

Laura Romanoff fancied herself an upwardly mobile person, but circumstances always seemed to prevent her from moving to a big city to achieve the yuppie lifestyle of which she had always dreamed. Laura was born and raised in a small midwestern town where, after finishing high school, she graduated from the local junior college with an associate's degree in business management. But fashion was Laura's real passion. She loved the elegance of chic apparel and frequently treated herself to excursions to upscale department stores to get the scoop on the latest trends. The *Vogue*-style designs sparkled in her mind and stoked her desire to own and wear them.

After college graduation, Laura went to work for the county sheriff's department in the administration office. Of course, as the local fashion plate in a small midwestern town, she was noticed by many of the young men and attracted a number of suitors. Within 18 months of finishing school, Laura married a handsome young carpenter in the construction business named Nick Vanderhouse.

The midwestern work ethic permeated Nick's persona. He took his job responsibilities seriously and worked hard to support and improve the young couple's lifestyle. During the summer, Nick was busy building new homes. But in the winter, when construction season ended, he struggled to make ends meet. To compensate for his fluctuating income, Nick was a pragmatic financial steward of the family assets. He did not believe in having credit card debt and preferred paying cash. Nick's conservative fiscal strategies soon enabled the young couple to buy a new home, complete with furnishings. Not long thereafter, they began talk of having a child.

After four years on the job, Laura transferred to the county's land use department because of limited promotional opportunities within the sheriff's administration office. Starting off as a clerk receptionist, Laura worked hard for advancement—and it paid off. After two years, she was promoted to Customer Service Representative for building permits in the Land Use department's Building Division. Her supervisors were impressed with her attention to detail and her interpersonal skills. Laura was a natural at working with contractors and, after three more years, she was transferred to the division's contractor registration section. She quickly learned all sides of the job: the state and county regulating statutes; the computer software/database; hard-copy contractor backup files and daily posting procedures; annual contractor renewals; receipting; cash reconciliations; and daily deposit logs. To demonstrate her professional capabilities and dedication to the position, Laura flowcharted all the contractor registration processes. Impressed with her expertise, the building division manager, Joanne Puckett, promoted Laura to Contractor-Registration Section Manager. After six years with the land use department, she was finally on her way to the top. She had a staff of two clerical people and managed the entire process, including primary system administration responsibilities for the department's entire computer system/database. Things outside the office were equally as promising: Nick's new subcontracting business was benefiting from a local boom, and the couple had been blessed with a bouncing baby boy.

License to Build

The Williamson County Land Use Department is responsible for administrating and enforcing local ordinances relating to new and existing building development and contractor management throughout the county, with the purpose of guiding the county's overall growth. Its mission is "to protect and enhance the public health, safety, and welfare by effective land use planning, regulation, and enforcement." The department has five operation divisions: building, planning and zoning, subdivision engineering, historic preservation, and waste services. All Williamson County administrative departments report to the elected county executive. The land use department has over 65 employees. The total operating expense budget is over $3.2 million, the bulk of which is generated through permits, licensing (including contractor registration), and inspection fee revenues.

In the past 10 years, the county has experienced unprecedented population and development growth. The number of residents has increased by over 50% and the projected 10-year forecast indicates doubling. The county makes every effort to coordinate intradepartmental activities to best serve Williamson County residents. One of the services offered by the contractor registration section of the building division is the verification of contractor registration licenses in order to protect the public from unethical or fraudulent construction scams and contractors.

Needless to say, the building division counter is a busy place. At any one time, 5 to 10 employees in the land use department staff the building permit counter as residents and contractors line up to obtain permits that will let them remodel and embark on new construction projects, among other authorizations. Contractors can also register for a license to operate in the county.

The counter staff was indoctrinated to offer permit clients "one-stop" service—each client had one primary contact at the department throughout the entire transaction.

Local statutes mandate all contractors to have a current license with the county. Fees range from $75 to $250, depending on whether the individual or firm is categorized as a subcontractor, general contractor, or construction manager. To obtain a license, a contractor simply fills out a single-page application, including basic contact information and type of trade expertise, and provides proof that he or she meets the associated state requirements. A land use department employee then reviews the application for completeness and enters the data into the computer, collects the appropriate fee, and issues a computer receipt for the transaction, which the customer must keep since it bears his or her license registration number. Because the registration receipt number is manually assigned rather than automatically generated by a computer, the digits are not restricted to single use. The same receipt number could be used multiple times. After the receipt is printed, a copy is made and filed as a backup hard copy in a contractor's file folder. This file contains all documents pertaining to the specific contractor, including correspondence and customer complaints.

The contractor registration section typically generates $250,000 annual revenue for the county. For years prior to the fraud discovery, however, the land use department had reported income discrepancies to the county board. The calculated value of all permits and licenses were always more than the revenues. Some years the difference was six digits. Of course, there were plenty of "the dog ate my homework" excuses provided by the counter staff to justify these discrepancies.

During this period I had conducted several internal audits on land use department processes in an effort to rationalize these income variances. As a result, I had recommended over 16 procedural changes. The most significant recommendation was centralization of the cashier function, eliminating overlapping cash reconciliation duties. Of course, the labor union objected and numerous grievances were filed. Eventually, the problem grew so visible it became a real political fight between the board and the county executive.

Seeing Double

Early one Tuesday morning, Laura faked a cough over the phone as she whimpered, "I'm not coming in today. I'm not feeling well," to her boss, Joanne. The truth was Macy's was having a sale and she wanted to get there early.

That same Tuesday was not a good day for Norman Bentley. The drywall contractor had just been fired from a highly profitable job because the land use department had told his client that Norman's firm was not a registered contractor in good standing with Williamson County, which just wasn't so. But his customer refused to believe that the receipt that Norman showed him was valid.

"It's not authentic! You forged it!" his customer screamed at him.

Never had Norman been so insulted. He had worked hard to build his drywall contracting business, and after years of going it alone, he finally had a two-man crew and a backlog of jobs. Why would he forge a $75 contractor registration license and risk it all? He was proud of what he had accomplished and the mere thought of someone accusing him of a lack of integrity was infuriating.

"This has to be a mistake," Norman thought as he leaped into his truck and launched it toward the land use department. But by the time he screeched to a halt at his destination, all eight cylinders of his anger had shifted into overdrive.

Norman stormed up the stairs and shoved open the entry doors. The crowd waiting for service parted as he steamed to the permit counter, waving his contractor registration receipt. "I paid your registration fee!" he said, slamming down his proof. Startled by the outburst, everyone stopped and stared as Norman exploded into incoherent rage. "You guys are ruining my business with your bull****!" Norman shouted.

Gazing in shock from a distant office doorway, Joanne could not remember when she had ever witnessed such a meltdown. She scurried over to where Norman was fuming and attempted to defuse the eruption. "Mr. Bentley, I'm the building division manager, Joanne Puckett. I'm awfully sorry this happened to you. Let's see if we can clear up this mess." Stunned by the gesture, Norman slowly shook her hand. With the same conviction, she said, "Please come into my office; I'll fix this problem."

"Thank you," Norman replied, relieved.

After a 20-minute interview, Joanne walked to the permit counter computer and typed in the receipt number from Norman's contractor registration. "That's odd," she thought. "The receipt number belongs to Friedman Roofing." She checked Norman's number again with the same results. Pausing for a minute, Joanne searched the contractor backup files and pulled out Bentley Drywall's file, where she found a paid-in-full cash receipt identical to the one in her hand. Then she checked in the Friedman Roofing folder and discovered a receipt had the same number! Astonished, Joanne picked up the phone and called my auditing department, which performed daily audits of all vendor payments involving the land use department.

"Steve," she said to me, "Can you come over here right away? I think we have a problem."

The Investigation

Early the next morning, Joanne and I met in her office with her door shut.

"We had an incident at the counter yesterday that exposed some irregularities with contractor registration receipts," she said, before showing me the Bentley Drywall and Freidman Roofing files and documents. "See? The number on both receipts is the same. Only one was paid by check, and the other paid with cash."

"What does the computer system show?" I asked.

"That's the part I don't understand. Only Friedman Roofing is listed in the database with that receipt number. There is no record of Bentley Drywall in the system," Joanne said.

"Did you find any other duplicate receipts?" I inquired.

"Frankly, Steve, I was so drained after Norman Bentley left yesterday, I did not have time to look," Joanne declared.

She handed me the two files, and I asked her for all daily transaction-summary reports for the last few months. Something immediately caught my eye: On the two hard-copy receipts were the initials of Laura Romanoff as having received both payments. After reviewing the daily transaction summary for obvious red flags, I noted a couple of suspicious transactions that prompted me to call the land use department's computer-system administrator.

The Williamson County Land Use Department used a database called LIPP (Licensing Information and Permit Processing). The software was a locally developed, one-of-a-kind, proprietary computer program written years earlier by a land use department employee, Richard DeBois. In fact, department employees called it "Richard's Program." LIPP had a lot of shortcomings, including lack of connectivity to the county's main financial-information system, but when I called Richard that day, I was impressed with his programming expertise.

"Hi, Richard, this is Steve. I'm doing an audit for Contractor Registration and I need to find out what computer log-in systems reports LIPP can produce." He explained all the standard reports that were available.

"No, that's not what I am looking for," I said. "I need a report that shows who logged onto the system when specific transactions were initially entered and who may have later changed or voided that record." To my surprise, Richard responded: "I can do that! That's a custom report that only I have access to." I described the transactions I needed to analyze, and within 20 minutes that report was faxed to me.

Just glancing at the report from Richard, I had a pretty good idea of the nature of the problem and who was responsible. Laura's log-in information was on about 99% of the voided transactions listed. I pulled about a dozen contractor files that were identified as having voided receipts. In three of the hard-copy files, the contractor registration receipts were not voided, indicating that the contractor had paid in full for the license. According to the report, no deposit to the treasurer's office was ever made for these payments. Now there were two types of embezzlement: duplicate and voided receipts.

I immediately headed to Joanne's office.

"Joanne, have you noticed any changes in Laura's behavior over the last year or few months?" I asked.

"No," Joanne replied. "Laura's a good employee. She's my right-hand person."

"Do you know if she has been experiencing any family problems?" I asked.

Joanne answered, "Nothing out of the ordinary."

"Does she do anything different from the rest of your employees?"

"Now that you mentioned it, Steve, she does. All of her personal mail is delivered to the office," Joanne said.

"Anything in particular you've noticed about the mail?" I continued.

"Well, she does receive a lot of clothing catalogs, and on occasion I've seen credit card invoices too," she said.

Suspecting the worst, I had enough proof to contact the county sheriff to ask for his help with a formal investigation and interrogation.

A thirty-something, Marine-groomed detective in a tailored suit soon arrived at the permit counter and asked to speak with Joanne. One could sense the uneasiness developing among the department's personnel; it became clear that something beyond normal business activities was occurring.

"Good afternoon, ma'am. I'm Detective Norris for the county sheriff's office," he said as he flashed his badge. "The sheriff asked me to come down here and discuss the irregularities you identified to County Auditor Steve Weber this morning. We believe we have enough probable cause to have a conversation with Laura Romanoff, a person of interest in the case. May I speak with her here or would you prefer that I ask her to come to my office for questioning?''

"Here is fine," said Joanne. "I would rather not instigate any office rumors if Laura's not actually involved."

Knowing what had transpired the previous day, Laura meekly slunk into the office, where Detective Norris greeted her in his no-nonsense fashion. "Laura, I'd like to ask you a few questions about some discrepancies that were found with some of your contractor registration receipts."

He explained the problems I had discovered with voided and duplicate receipts. Laura immediately confessed.

"Detective, I know you've probably figured it out—I did it." Her face flushed as she continued to respond to his questions. "I'll pay back the money I owe. I just needed a loan to pay off some credit card balances. My husband doesn't know about these cards. I was always planning to pay. . . . ''

"How much do you think you owe, Laura?" Norris asked.

"About $5,000," she responded. After 10 minutes of additional questions and confessions, Laura was handcuffed and transported to the sheriff's station to videotape her confession for prosecution purposes. About an hour later, Detective Norris called me to discuss details of Laura's interview and her confession. Hanging up the phone, I thought to myself, "That was way too quick and easy. Something still is not right."

The Whole Truth

I called the state's attorney to inform him that I wanted to conduct a complete forensic audit. I suspected that Laura's confession might not have been the whole truth. He advised me that the statute of limitations was three years on fraud, but agreed it would be a good idea to find out the actual length of time and amount of money involved in Laura's scheme. I called my secretary and asked her to schedule a staff meeting the next morning.

After the meeting, three auditors attacked the land use department's contractor registration files with instructions to review all transactions. They scrutinized the electronic and hard-copy files, attempting to correlate each transaction to the treasurer's daily deposit slips, daily summary collection reports, and the daily receipts. They were instructed to continue this audit procedure until they found no receipt discrepancies.

Three weeks later the report was complete. Our investigation revealed 154 receipt discrepancy instances that totaled $17,761 in cash not deposited with the county treasurer over a seven-year period. Laura used three different methods to defraud the land use department: deleted or voided receipts, duplicate receipts, and cash received but not deposited. We also discovered that over the course of her scheme she had alternated her methodology between these techniques to avoid detection.

Upon examination of the contractor file folders, transactions that were marked as deleted or voided in the LIPP computer system were not marked as such in the hard-copy contractors' file folder. A valid receipt was found in each folder. However, the supporting transaction detail on the daily deposit summary sent to the county treasurer was marked "void" on the computer systems printout.

Laura was responsible for reconciliation and depositing the daily collections with the treasurer's office, in addition to receipting and receiving money for contractor registration. Numerous transactions were found where monies were received but not reported on the deposit slip sent to the treasurer. In some cases, cash was received and partial amounts were deposited. In other cases, complete transaction payments in both cash and check were not deposited.

Laura started to use the "duplicate receipts" technique two years prior to the discovery. She would issue the same receipt to two different contractors. For instance, receipt number 001 might be issued to Contractor A, indicating that the payment was cash. A copy of the receipt would be placed in Contractor A's folder. Then, because the LIPP computer systems allowed her to use the same receipt number for a different contractor, she would actually change the information on receipt number 001 and issue a duplicated receipt to Contractor B with this contractor's information for a payment by check. Contractor B's receipt number 001 was then filed and listed on the daily deposit slip.

The cause of this fraud was improper segregation of duties and inadequate controls with the accounting software. Within six months, the LIPP accounting software was updated. But it took about two years to convince the county executive to implement a centralized cashier because certain employees at the land use department did not like the idea.

What happened to Laura Romanoff? She took the state's attorney's plea deal by repaying $17,761. She pleaded guilty to a single count of theft, a class-two felony that allowed probation, which she received. And how did her husband react? Not in kind. After an explosive venting of his vexation about Laura's treachery, he canceled her credit cards and nixed her frequent shopping excursions. He mandated a complete metamorphosis—or else.

Lessons Learned

The primary lesson we learned from this case is to "sweat the small stuff," or pay close attention to the "soft" factors or observations that could possibly foster or identify fraud.

Feelings can be facts. My staff accountant, Lucy, who assisted with the land use department's monthly audits, was always suspicious of Laura. She mentioned to me that there was something "phony" about her. As the frequency of audits increased, Laura became more helpful—and even started treating my staff accountant like her best friend. In addition to this inconsistency, every time there was a problem with a voided receipt, Laura was involved or contributed to the issue. In both instances, I did not follow up on my accountant "gut feelings" and dismissed them as personality differences. We have instincts for a reason and they should be incorporated into our investigations.

After Laura confessed and the evidence was compiled, everyone involved in the discovery, audit, arrest, and prosecution had opinions regarding how to treat her crime and whether or not to expose the fraud to the public. Because some elected officials feared that publicity could damage the perception of the county's services, the consensus was to not aggressively prosecute or publish details of the case in the newspaper. The flip side of this decision is that one of the most effective deterrents is fear of public exposure. Hiding the fraud is what the perpetrator wants.

Furthermore, we learned that the real cost of fraud exceeds the actual amount stolen. Consider the time and resources funneled into this investigation and prosecution. These costs far exceeded the $17,761 Romanoff pilfered. As part of any fraud recovery, time spent investigating can be recovered by adding the fees to the total damages.

Recommendations to Prevent Future Occurrences

Communication and Education

Improving communication about fraud at the departmental level, either with one-on-one or in formal seminars, can be vital to preventing fraud. Laura's scheme could have been prevented—or the damage significantly reduced—if we had discussed identifying red flags with departmental managers.

Background Checks

A good way for a public agency or department to prevent fraud is to hire ethical employees by conducting criminal background checks. In most states, this is not illegal or a violation of privacy as long as the information on the report is not the sole reason a person is not hired. It is interesting to note that about a year after Laura's restitution was paid off and her probation had ended, I received a call from someone who runs the accounting department for the local school district. Laura had applied for a job in his division; her resume listed her work for Williamson County. He wanted to know if I knew her.

Computer-Risk Assessment Reviews

Computer-risk assessment reviews are vital to an organization's financial health. Williamson County had contracted with a local CPA firm to conduct a review of our major computer operating and financial information systems, and offer recommendations for updates. However, due to cost, this study was limited to the county's major operating structure and failed to examine the smaller subsystems, such as the land use department's LIPP accounting system. Now the county incorporates all of these subsystems into our formal assessments to identify internal control weaknesses and enhance security.

About the Author

Stephen Weber is a CPA with 22 years of governmental accounting experience. Elected as auditor of Will County, Illinois, Mr. Weber has investigated three major fraud cases, each time uncovering from $17,000 to over $130,000 in embezzlement. His pre-audits have saved taxpayers over $1.5 million. Weber has a bachelor's degree in accounting from Lewis University. Steve and his family reside in Mokena, Illinois.

C H A P T E R

7

Unimaginable Wealth

SANDRA BURRIS

Cyberspace is a fraudster's dream come true—a place where true identities are hidden and it is all too easy for a con artist to create a believable life history to facilitate nefarious goals. Usually, the aim is to steal hard-earned cash from as many unsuspecting victims as possible—and to get away scot-free.

It's difficult, if not impossible, to determine exactly how much of the online history Mike Gregory created for himself is real. Constructing an Internet persona as a cybersecurity guru, Mike claimed to own a company that had become an innovative leader in Web-based technology. His organization's success, he alleged, stemmed from a program he created that could restore even the dirtiest computer systems to like-new condition, protect against future viruses, and block spam, pop-ups, and spyware. To further his apparent credibility, Mike declared himself one of the top experts in the area of PC security and privacy, claiming that he had been a guest speaker on computer security at various seminars and conventions.

While these claims might seem quite bold, on their own they don't raise suspicions of fraud. However, the next step in Mike's history induced some serious doubts about the honest intentions of the self-professed Internet security expert. Mike created a Web site, www.UnimaginableWealthClub .com, and registered it through an anonymous server located in Saint Vincent and the Grenadines—an easy task that certainly doesn't require the skills of a cyberspace security leader. These anonymous service providers don't even ask their customers for any identifying information. Just pay the fee and you become the proud owner of a new Web site. Not surprisingly, Mike took full advantage of the anonymity in creating his online endeavor. Conveniently, nowhere on the site did he identify himself as an online security specialist or even as the mastermind behind the Unimaginable

Wealth Club (UWC) program. Omitting these personal details allowed him to swindle numerous investors out of hard-earned cash without leaving a trail of incriminating evidence.

On the UWC Web site, Mike promised participants that they would earn three, four, even five times their money back—with payouts made daily, sometimes starting the next day! All that was required of the victims was to send Mike money to purchase a position on the "2×9 company matrix," set up an online bank account so that all transactions could take place via the Internet, and wait for the money to roll in.

The Ponzi of Cyberspace

In the world of cyberspace, programs like UWC are commonly known as "doublers," "triplers," "bubbles," "cyclers," and "gifting." They are viewed by some as viable get-rich-quick schemes. In fact, there is a whole subculture of people who eagerly participate in these dubious online programs, using pretty sophisticated strategies like diversification to offset losses. They'll pick several variations of these "investments," hoping a few of them will pay off if they're early enough. Some risk-takers have made just enough money from one or more of these programs to entice them to try others. Most people don't realize that any money they're making is at the expense of others. Or perhaps they do realize it and they just don't care.

In the world of law enforcement these programs are known as Ponzi schemes. The term "Ponzi scheme" is derived from a scam perpetrated by Charles Ponzi, who duped thousands of New England residents into investing in a postage-stamp speculation scheme back in the 1920s. The fraudster told investors that he could provide a 40% return in just 90 days compared with 5% for bank savings accounts. To increase the appearance of legitimacy, Ponzi paid off a few early investors using the money provided by subsequent investors—a tactic that clearly would only work in the short term. Ultimately, the scheme crumbled, and the bulk of his investors were left empty-handed. As a result, Ponzi's name has become synonymous with any swindle where money paid in by later participants is used to pay off those who invested earlier.

The UWC Web site did its best to hide the organization's Ponzi-like operations, claiming that a participant's earnings did not depend on his or her ability to recruit new members. Instead, the Web site convolutedly explained that each member was given his own 2×9 matrix within the company. If the participant did not want to recruit new members to be added to his or her matrix, he or she would still receive "spillover" from the largess.

Further, in order to share the company's good fortune with as many people as possible, as well as to add a little more complication to the organizational structure, Mike decided that there would be three phases to his club. For $40 you could be a "Phase One" member. To be a "Phase Three" member, though, it would cost you $200. Each participant would receive a "commission" for members placed below him or her on the matrix. The Phase One member would earn $3 per person, and the Phase Three member would earn $9 for every participant added below him or her.

Adding even more complexity to the investment configuration, the 2×9 matrix did not, in fact, ensure that every member would receive commissions for nine generations, as many investors would assume. Instead, Mike decided that the average "do-nothing" members should only benefit from six levels of members below them. Participants had to earn the right to profit from levels seven, eight, and nine by "sponsoring" new members—in other words, they must pay additional fees to get new people "into the club."

According to Mike and his supporters, that was a great deal. Here's why: levels one through six, combined, only had 126 members; level seven added another 128 members; level eight, another 256 members; and level nine, 512 members. Investors only had to have 23 members under them at $9 per head to earn more than they put into the scheme. Further, by sponsoring six people at level nine status, UWC members could earn a whopping 220% on their money. Where are you going to find such profitable returns in the stock market?

Mike also boasted that participants could earn three, four, and five times their investment. By recruiting six other people, investors could earn the "Super-Duper Leadership Bonus." As a super-duper leader, members would earn commissions from an infinite number of levels underneath them, leading to the unimaginable wealth promised in the organization's name. This twist prompted many of the early participants to launch massive e-mail campaigns and even create their own Web sites to snare new UWC participants.

If It's Too Good to Be True . . .

Jack Porter, the naive investor who ultimately reported the scheme for investigation, provides a classic example of how Mike snared victims into the Unimaginable Wealth Club trap. Jack received an e-mail solicitation from a person he had never heard of, one who didn't even reside in the same state as he did but who was willing to sponsor Jack for a position on his matrix. One of the early e-mails received by Jack told about a "live conference call" held with the creator of the program and potential members in advance of the UWC program's official launch. The outlandish e-mail promised that "something financially BIG is waiting in the wings . . . good for those that just come in . . . but TREMENDOUS for those of you who bring some folks to the UWC Launch and establish yourself!" Of course, the sender of the e-mail claimed that his "sponsor will be receiving his signup link [for the conference call] directly from the company . . . then in turn will send his link to me to sign up . . . in other words . . . we're at the TOP Baby!"

Could Jack be any luckier? He had the opportunity to tap into this moneymaking program before it was even "launched"! And at the top, no less! Once UWC was open to the public, Jack believed, people would certainly be flocking to invest. After all, the cost to join was $200 at most, and the promise of earning "three, four, and five times your purchase fee" was practically unheard of.

Jack and the other "exclusive" invitees were instructed on the UWC Web site to set up an account with a particular e-bank so that all transactions could use online credit cards. He couldn't wait. Jack excitedly bought two positions and sponsored six people under each one for a total investment of $2,800. Then he thought he could just sit back and collect. Jack waited for the money to start pouring in. And waited. And waited. But he never received a penny.

Frustrated, Jack began submitting inquiries to UWC about the status of his investment proceeds. The reasons provided by the club for the delay in payment ran the gamut, from technical issues with the e-bank to lack of confirmation for payment transactions from new members to the altered explanation that the funds would be paid out based only on the "new" sales volume.

After about a month of paltry excuses from the UWC, Jack was fed up and suspicious. He filed a complaint with the state attorney general's office, which referred it to the enforcement section of the secretary of state's securities division.

Our securities division investigates many types of investment scams. Increasingly we are seeing scams offered over the Internet. When a complaint comes into the division, it is assigned to an investigator by the chief of enforcement. As a 10-year veteran with the division, I investigate a wide variety of fraudulent activities, among them Ponzi schemes, pyramids, pump-and-dump schemes, and failure to make full disclosure of material information as provided by state securities laws.

Faceless Fraud

Because the Internet provides fraudsters such easy access to potential targets worldwide, it is virtually impossible to determine the true number of victims and the extent of financial participation in an online Ponzi scheme like the Unimaginable Wealth Club. In one e-mail communication to its investors, UWC claimed that, in a span of just three days, 8,000 members joined the club and that 80% of them joined all three phases. If the e-mail was indeed accurate and 80% joined all three phases for a fee of $200 each, with the remaining 20% paying the lowest fee of $40 each, that would be a minimum of $1,344,000 generated in a three-day period. With that kind of money rolling in, if Mike paid commissions even to just those members that brought in the largest numbers of participants, enough buzz would have been generated to keep new members joining the club.

We began our investigation of the scheme with the basic searches of company information. Not surprisingly, we were unable to locate any legitimate entity named Unimaginable Wealth Club. And since the UWC Web site was set up through an anonymous server located offshore, it did not give any information about the identity of its creator or his whereabouts. However, a Google search of the program's name turned up quite a bit of "cyber chatter" about it, indicating that many people were soliciting members through their own Web pages. We landed a break in the case when we located one such Web site, created by an individual in Norway, which identified online security guru Mike Gregory as the creator of this program to convince potential members that it was legitimate. The owner of the Web site was given the information identifying Mike by an associate who participated in one of the early conference calls held by UWC.

A search of Mike's name, through Lexis-Nexis, revealed that a few years earlier, the UWC founder attempted to legally change his birth name to "Mike Gregory." By contacting the court clerk, I learned that "Mike" and two other family members all applied to have their last names changed to Gregory at the same time. Even though he still began using the name "Mike Gregory," the name change was never legalized because none of the three individuals gave the court a physical residential address. Unlike cyberspace, the court requires more verifiable information about people with whom it deals.

We also learned Mike's real name, Trevor Mussing. Again, using Lexis-Nexis, we were able to locate several addresses used by the UWC master-mind—three in Oregon and one in California. Now we were getting some-where. Unfortunately, our progress hit a minor snag as we discovered that all four locations were postal boxes rented from various mail-management services.

With the cooperation of the U.S. postal inspector and our sister agency in Oregon, we determined that Mike's two family members were also involved in Mike's scheme. The postal boxes were rented in their names, always paid in cash. The applications for the postal boxes listed either another postal box or a completely fictitious address as the applicant's residence. Additionally, we discovered that one family member routinely called the post offices and had the mail forwarded to a separate box located in Oregon.

All attempts to contact the individuals by mail failed. However, a search of DMV records in Oregon turned up drivers' licenses for Mike's two family members. Again, they listed two of the postal boxes as their residential addresses.

We also obtained information from the e-bank used by UWC to identify the owner of the account where Jack's money went. We found that it was located in Tennessee. The bank agreed to provide us information on the account. The owner was a Nevada corporation called ABC Inc.; but the only data required to open the account was an e-mail address, a telephone number, and a credit card number.

Transactions in the UWC e-account were logged by the participants' e-mail addresses. We were able to trace Jack's payments into the account by his e-mail address. Tracing disbursements, however, was virtually impossible, as they were identified only by generic-sounding e-mail addresses set up through anonymous servers. It was obvious, though, that the disbursements were not going back to the accounts associated with the victims.

The registered agent of record for ABC Inc. stated that he had no knowledge of the company, except that he had prepared the charter documents for it. Immediately after being contacted by our office, he filed a resignation with the State of Nevada. This was pretty much a brick wall.

Unfortunately, we were not able to determine how long the program lasted; how much money, if any, Mike paid to participants; or how much of the proceeds he personally harvested. When he felt the heat closing in on his scam, Mike just shut the Web site down and disappeared. In the end, it was by pure luck and dogged determination that we were able to identify the three individuals involved with this scheme.

Because the UWC program met the parameters of an investment contract, the commissioner of securities determined that it was a security as defined by state security laws. As such, the UWC had not met the applicable registration requirements and was found to have materially misrepresented and/or omitted facts that violated disclosure requirements. Consequently, the securities commissioner issued a pro se order to cease and desist and required the perpetrators to pay, jointly and severally, a limited fine of $10,000.

Lessons Learned

There is no way of knowing whether the con men behind the Unimaginable Wealth Club will change the name of the program and start afresh on another Web site. As these schemes evolve and become more sophisticated, detection of the individuals perpetrating the fraud will likely become more difficult.

But even with the ever-evolving nature of these frauds, certain factors can serve as warning signs to investors looking to cash in on a sure thing. Three bright red flags were present in this case: First, the business was operating through an anonymous server located in a foreign country. Second, the Web site did not prominently display the name of the entity and individuals who created it. Finally, anytime a return is offered on an investment without a feasible explanation of just how that money will be earned, investors should be especially wary. Money does not simply reproduce. If it is not being earned by some legitimate, verifiable means, the only other explanation is that it's being taken from other participants.

Recommendations to Prevent Future Occurrences

With computers in most households, and considering the ease with which anyone can anonymously communicate with a very large number of people worldwide, it is difficult to stop these scams.

Consumer education may be the only way to slow these programs down. Following our investigation of Mike Gregory and his accomplices, our office issued a press release reminding potential victims to be very skeptical of any Internet offer that sounds too good to be true, because it probably is!

About the Author

Sandy Burris, CFE, is a Securities Investigator, grade III, with the Missouri Secretary of State's Office. She has been investigating securities fraud for more than ten years. Prior to settling in Missouri, Sandy worked for the FDIC during the savings and loan crisis and assisted in the resolution of many failed savings and loan institutions.

Hacked

JON LAMBIRAS

According to nationwide news reports, hackers pointed a telescope-shaped antenna toward a retail store. A laptop computer helped decode data streaming through the air among handheld inventory management devices, cash registers, and store computers. From there the hackers found their way into the company's central database at its headquarters more than a thousand miles away. The hackers' entry point was an outdated wireless network connected to a computer system plagued with a host of data security shortfalls.

What followed was one of the biggest data-security breaches in history. At least 45 million credit card and debit card numbers were stolen, along with approximately 456,000 customers' driver's license, state, or military identification (personal ID) numbers with accompanying names and addresses. Many of the personal ID numbers were the same as the customers' Social Security numbers.

The hackers sold much of the stolen data on Web sites used to traffic stolen information. One cardholder's account experienced unauthorized transactions at a large discount store and at online vendors. Another account had $45,000 in fraudulent charges for gift cards. Fraudulent charges approaching $100 million surfaced throughout the United States and as far away as Mexico, Italy, Sweden, Thailand, China, Japan, and Australia.

At the heart of the data breach is RackCo, a major U.S. retailer. Parent company to a chain of several stores, it controls over 2,000 retail locations throughout the United States. The business boasts $17 billion in annual sales worldwide.

At first blush, RackCo appears to be a helpless victim of a highly specialized gang of data thieves. But a closer look shows that, because of numerous violations of core data-security standards, the company essentially invited the hackers in. As a result, the fraudsters methodically stole data from RackCo's computer system during a year-and-a-half–long period.

I am an attorney involved in litigation against RackCo. In light of my role in the litigation, this case study is limited, by necessity, to publicly available information. The data breach was a high-profile event and there is much publicly available information from which to draw, including exposes published in major national newspapers. I do not attest to the accuracy of the information from which this case study is drawn.

Reality Check

During the period when hackers were accessing RackCo's system, a routine audit at the company revealed that many security measures were not being adhered to. The auditor cited outmoded encryption and missing firewalls and software patches.

Three months later, another auditor noticed suspicious software on RackCo's network and anomalies in the company's credit card data. That prompted RackCo to conduct an internal investigation, hiring two large forensic consulting firms to assist. Within three days the investigation revealed that RackCo's computer system suffered a massive intrusion by the hackers, who continued to maintain access to the system—suggesting the thieves could be caught in the act.

RackCo notified the Justice Department, the Secret Service, the U.S. Attorney's Office, and later the FBI, and all played active roles in the investigation.

Shoddy Security

An investigation reportedly revealed that the hackers were able to gain illicit access because RackCo's wireless network used a flawed and out- dated encryption system called Wired Equivalent Privacy (WEP), a pro- gram that was highly susceptible to intruders and whose vulnerability was well known to RackCo.

The outdated technology reportedly provided less security for the company's wireless network than many people have on their home networks. After intercepting RackCo's wireless system and cracking the encryption code, the hackers stole usernames and passwords by digitally eavesdropping on employees who logged into RackCo's central database at its headquarters. The stolen information enabled the hackers to enter RackCo's system remotely from any computer on the Internet. By using Web addresses of private individuals and public places, such as coffee houses, the hackers were able to hide their whereabouts.

The hackers set up their own accounts in RackCo's system, saving credit and debit card data into about a hundred large files for their own access.

They stole roughly 83 gigabytes of cardholder data, which was transferred from RackCo's system to an Internet site in California. (One gigabyte of data equals roughly 65,000 pages of Microsoft Word text. Therefore, the equivalent of 5.4 million pages of text was stolen.)

The hackers left traces such as altered computer files, suspicious software, and mixed-up data involving time stamps in the wrong order. They also left encrypted messages to each other on RackCo's system to communicate which files had already been copied and to avoid duplicating work.

Some of the stolen data was encrypted by RackCo. However, the hackers had access to the decryption tool for the encryption software. They stole credit and debit card data that RackCo routinely stored on its system for lengthy periods of time, a procedure which violated credit-card industry rules.

The fraudsters also lifted credit and debit card information as customers waited in line for their transactions to be processed and approved by their card-issuing banks. To do this, they equipped RackCo's network with a traffic capture program called a "sniffer," which captured cardholder data as it was transmitted during the purchase process in an unencrypted format.

Investigators believe the hackers' style of operation had the hallmarks of Romanian hackers and Russian organized-crime groups. These gangs are known for scoping out the least secure target and being methodical in their intrusions, in contrast to other types of hackers who often enter and exit quickly and clumsily, leaving a telltale trail.

Card-Carrying Crooks

All told, at least 45 million credit and debit card numbers with accompanying expiration dates were stolen. The exact number of affected cards cannot be pinpointed because, before discovering the intrusion, RackCo deleted in the normal course of business much of the illicitly accessed information. The hackers also used deletion technology, making it virtually impossible to determine the contents of much of the data. Nearly 100 million credit and debit card transactions occurred during the at-risk period.

For many of the affected cards, the stolen information included full "Track 2" data obtained from the card's magnetic stripe. This includes sensitive information including a card's 16-digit account number, expiration date, and other discretionary information that banks may include, such as issuance date and country code. Fortunately, it does not contain a cardholder's name and address.

A number of the credit and debit card numbers were expired at the time of the theft, but that did not eliminate the risk—expired cards are often renewed with the same card number. Identity thieves use guesswork and the process of elimination to determine the new expiration dates.

Roughly 456,000 customers' driver's license, state, or military identification (personal ID) numbers with accompanying names and addresses were also stolen. In some cases the personal ID number was the same as the customer's Social Security number. RackCo stored this information to track customers who returned merchandise without a receipt, a practice that is not uncommon in the retail industry.

The hackers accessed RackCo's system sporadically throughout a year-and-a-half–long period. Electronic footprints showed that most of the hackers' break-ins were done during peak sales periods to capture high quantities of data.

Facing Legal Action

Roughly one month after the breach was detected, RackCo notified its customers and the general public about the intrusion. In a press release, RackCo stated that the company identified certain customer information stolen from its system but that the full extent of the theft was unknown. The intrusion involved data from credit card, debit card, check, and merchandise return transactions in the United States, Canada, and possibly the United Kingdom and Ireland. RackCo provided lists of affected credit card numbers to credit card companies, who then notified card-issuing banks, who, in turn, were able to notify customers.

The announcement triggered intense media coverage in the United States and abroad. RackCo quickly fell under heavy criticism, mostly for failing to protect customers' data but also for keeping quiet about the breach until mid-January and the end of the shopping season, roughly a month after the fraud's discovery.

Soon after RackCo's announcement, class action lawsuits were filed against the company on behalf of two groups of plaintiffs. The first group's suit, entailed customers whose personal data was stolen. The second group concerned card-issuing banks that incurred costs to issue replacement cards, reimburse fraudulent charges on customers' accounts, and monitor accounts for fraud.

The Federal Trade Commission (FTC), attorneys general from several states, and Canadian regulators also investigated RackCo for possible violations of consumer protection laws.

Thus far, RackCo has reserved a quarter of a billion dollars to perform the internal investigation, upgrade its computer system, respond to government investigations, defend itself in litigation, and pay settlement-related costs.

Elusive Hackers

Despite intense investigations by the U.S. Secret Service, FBI, and others, the main hackers still have not been caught more than one year after the fraud was discovered. But several downstream users of the stolen credit and debit card numbers have been arrested.

Investigators believe the hackers operated in organized rings that sold stolen information on the Internet. They likely sought out middlemen to buy large quantities of the pilfered data, who in turn resold the data to others in smaller, more customized batches. The credit card information was probably packaged based on credit limits, expiration dates, issuer bank, and other factors.

A 24-year-old Ukrainian man was arrested in Turkey for pushing some of the card numbers. He allegedly obtained the data from the hackers of RackCo through online forums and anonymous Web sites commonly used to traffic stolen information. He then sold the data to end users using similar Web sites. The prices he charged for the cards ranged from $20 to $100 each, depending on various factors. The card numbers were sold in batches of up to 10,000.

Months before the Ukrainian man's arrest, a group of end users in Florida were caught using certain card numbers stolen from RackCo. Some of the card numbers they held were purchased from the Ukrainian man. Their method of operation was to transfer the data onto credit card blanks made to look like real credit cards using printing and encoding equipment that is relatively easy to legitimately obtain. Then, in a modern-day version of money laundering, they used the fake cards to buy gift cards as high as $400 at various big-box stores throughout Florida. The gift cards enabled them to purchase store merchandise such as jewelry and electronics. In some cases the crooks later returned the merchandise for cash.

Initially, their plan was quite successful, resulting in roughly $8 million in fraudulent charges. But the group was caught when attentive retail employees became suspicious of the high volume of gift card activity. One staff member wrote down the license plate number of a car driven away by three members of the group, and investigators traced the number to one of the fraudsters. Employees also retrieved video images of two of the men from store cameras, both positively matched to driver's license photos and photos in a database of store club members. In all, eight people in the ring were arrested. Several of them have pleaded guilty to fraud-related charges. Their leader was sentenced to five years in prison.

The Incompetence Within

An investigation at RackCo reportedly revealed the following:

- RackCo failed to comply with parts of 9 of the 12 items in the Payment Card Industry (PCI) Data Security Standard, the core set of security measures required in the credit card industry.
- The company used deficient and outdated wireless technology like WEP wireless, rather than the more secure Wi-Fi Protected Access (WPA).
- RackCo improperly configured its wireless network.
- RackCo stored and retained cardholder data in violation of regulations. For over a decade, merchants have been forbidden from storing Track 2 data because, if stolen, the data makes it relatively simple to create a counterfeit card.
- RackCo did not segregate from the rest of its network the devices it used to store, process, and transmit cardholder information.
- User names and passwords used by RackCo employees were not secure—in some instances passwords matched user names.
- Intrusion detection processes were improper.
- Firewall protection was flawed.
- Software patches were inadequate.
- Computer access and activity logs were not properly maintained and reviewed.
- Antivirus protection was not up to date.

Notably, RackCo knew about its problems for years but failed to address them. More than two years before the data breach was detected, the company reportedly received a report outlining its noncompliance with several data security standards. Some of the shortfalls were major security risks, but the company still did not take precautions.

The decision to forgo suggested improvements to RackCo's wireless technology was made at the company's highest ranks. More than a year before detecting the breach, RackCo's chief information officer (CIO) sent an e-mail to IT staff acknowledging that "WPA is clearly best practice." Nevertheless, the CIO said, "I think we have an opportunity to defer some spending from [next year's] budget by removing the money for the WPA upgrade."

Shortly thereafter, another RackCo employee circulated an e-mail stating: ''[T]he absence of rotating keys in WEP means that we truly are not in compliance with the requirements of PCI. This becomes an issue if this fact becomes known and potentially exacerbates any findings should a breach be revealed.''

Despite the known security risk, RackCo refused to upgrade from WEP to WPA. The decision proved devastating.

The Canadian Regulators' Investigation

Canadian regulators investigated the data breach at RackCo for eight months. Afterward, they published a report of their findings and recommendations.

Regulators found that, at the time of the initial breach, RackCo used outdated WEP wireless encryption technology in its retail stores. At least two years before, computer security experts began widely criticizing WEP as an insecure wireless technology. In fact, the organization that originally developed WEP technology recommended it be upgraded to WPA. Several months after the initial breach—before it was discovered—RackCo finally decided to upgrade to WPA wireless technology. However, the upgrade took two years to complete, during which time the hackers continued to access RackCo's system.

At the investigation's conclusion, regulators deemed the recording and storage of customers' driver's license, state, and military identification numbers as excessive and unnecessary. Alternatively, RackCo should have used less sensitive identifiers, telephone numbers being one possibility.

Lessons Learned

The significance of complying with industry security guidelines, namely PCI standards, cannot be understated. Many retailers do not adhere. However, RackCo pushed the line, failing to comply with parts of 9 of the 12 PCI standards.

RackCo knew of its noncompliance long before the data breach was discovered. The company should have been more aggressive in its efforts. Had it been so, one of the largest data breaches in history might have been avoided.

Businesses should be mindful when weighing the cost versus benefit of upgrading data security. As a starting point, decision makers should consider the likelihood of a data breach, its sensitivity, its quantity, and its possible consequences. In this instance, the probability of a breach was high due to the number of violated PCI standards. RackCo's security shortcomings occurred continuously for several years, increasing the window of opportunity for an intrusion. Because RackCo had a high volume of credit card sales and stored much of its customers' data for lengthy time periods, the quantity of stored data was massive. Consequences for RackCo included investigation costs, litigation expenses, and loss of customer goodwill.

Decision makers at RackCo should have weighed these concerns against the financial costs of upgrading data security. RackCo's CIO expressed budgetary concerns about upgrading security; however, the costs were negligible in light of RackCo's strong financial position. The company's net income exceeded $500 million—*half a billion dollars*—in each of the five years before the breach was discovered. Furthermore, the company's assets far exceeded its liabilities in each of those years. Money was not an issue. A more careful cost-benefit analysis should have led to the decision to improve data security.

Another lesson learned is that hacking and lax data security cast a wide net. Victims included RackCo, its customers, card-issuing banks, and credit card associations—among others. RackCo suffered financial harm and damage to its reputation. The company reserved a quarter of a billion dollars to fund its internal investigation, computer system upgrades, response to government investigations, litigation, and settlement-related costs. Also, its reputation suffered as customers, understandably, became wary about shopping there.

RackCo's customers spent considerable time and money dealing with the breach. They were forced to closely monitor their credit card accounts and credit reports for fraud. They also spent time disputing fraudulent charges, canceling compromised credit cards, and switching electronic payment links such as utility bills and other monthly services from old card numbers to new ones. Customers suffered out-of-pocket damages for things like fraudulent charges on their accounts (to the extent these were not reversed by banks), credit-monitoring services, identity theft insurance, the cost of opening new checking accounts, fees for reordering checks, etc. Moreover, emotional harm such as stress, anxiety, and the continuing fear of identity theft affected customers. This is especially true for those whose personal ID information, which sometimes contained their Social Security number, was stolen.

Other victims included the banks that issued credit and debit cards to RackCo's affected customers. Those banks incurred costs to reimburse fraudulent charges on cardholders' accounts (federal regulations generally limit cardholders' liability to $50 for unauthorized purchases—banks are forced to reimburse the cost of the fraudulent charges); replace compromised cards, which generally costs $5 to $20 per card; and monitor cardholders' accounts for fraud.

Recommendations to Prevent Future Occurrences

Comply with Industry Regulations

Complying with industry regulations is often easier said than done in light of inevitable budget concerns, limited personnel resources, and a host of other obstacles. However, at a minimum, companies should objectively assess their greatest security risks to identify and prioritize key areas for improvement.

Periodically Examine the Data Security Environment

Companies should consider a policy of periodically examining their data security environment. Perhaps an annual or semiannual examination could be set with reviews scheduled at times of the year when operational and personnel resources are at their peak. Alternatively, a rotating schedule might work best where different substantive or geographical areas of security are examined on a rotating basis. At the very least, some type of periodic review system should be implemented because computer hardware and software can become obsolete quickly.

Limit Data Collection and Storage

Companies should limit data collection and storage to the minimum information required for business purposes. For example, is a Social Security number or driver's license number necessary? Would a phone number be a safer and equally effective alternative? Is a complete date of birth necessary, or would a birth year and month be sufficient? Sensitive identifiers and other information should be abandoned in favor of less risky ones.

Take Data Security Seriously

In a nutshell, businesses should take data security seriously. Granted, the best hackers in the world can probably find a way to penetrate even the strongest data security environments, but that does not mean businesses should treat data security as a low priority. Here, perhaps, a PCI-compliant system would have blocked access to RackCo's data or at least convinced the hackers to move on to a more vulnerable target.

About the Author

Jon Lambiras, CFE, CPA, Esq., is an associate at Berger & Montague PC, in Philadelphia. He represents plaintiffs in class action litigation primarily involving consumer fraud and securities fraud. He has published and lectured on various fraud-related issues. He is a graduate of Pepperdine University School of Law (2003) and Bryant College (1996).

CHAPTER

Bad Education

RUSS ALLEN

It was a wet and windy October afternoon in Gloucestershire, England. With lunch now behind us, Chris and I looked forward to a quiet journey home to our wives. Chris McDermott and I go back a long way together: first, as detectives on the same investigation team in the Fraud Squad at Scotland Yard; then, after our retirement from operational police duties, as forensic auditors with the Internal Audit Department of the Metropolitan Police. Now, both of us having left that job, Chris works with me on various assignments for my own forensic auditing company.

Our current assignment was drawing to a close, so when my cell warbled at about 2:30 p.m. I assumed it would be my wife with hints as to what gourmet delight she was planning for the evening meal. Alas, it was something totally different—a call that was to launch me into another two-year assignment.

"Is this Russ Allen?" the caller asked. "You won't remember me, but I was in the audience when you lectured to the Internal Auditors Association last year. You kindly listed your phone number at the end of your presentation, saying that if we had a problem, we could give you a call; well, I have a problem and could use some help."

I learned that Sean Jefferson was the audit and assurance manager within the Ministry of Science, a government department responsible for auditing a number of academic sites throughout the United Kingdom. Sean explained that they had received a letter and compact disk from a whistleblower making allegations of corruption, theft, and fraud against a head of IT at a university in Rutland specializing in medical research. He had my attention. "Where are you based, Sean?" I asked, secretly hoping that it would be close to home.

"We are in Salisbury, Wiltshire," said Sean. "Is that near you?"

"Sure, just a mile or so down the road. How urgent is it?"

"Nothing desperate—yesterday will do," he said.

"How about if I drive down now on my way home? It won't be too much out of my way," I responded.

I lied; it was at least a couple of hundred miles out of my way. But when you have the prospect of a new assignment, who is bothered with the odd mile or two? Leaving Chris to tidy up the Gloucestershire office, I headed in a southerly direction to Wiltshire.

Sean was an avuncular gent, but I was soon to learn that beneath his somewhat casual, laid-back approach and appearance there lay a very sharp brain and a very professional internal auditor. "Thanks for coming down so promptly," said Sean. "We didn't want to mess anything up evidence-wise, so I thought we had better call the experts in as soon as possible." After an introduction to the rest of his team, I was given a cup of scalding hot tea to nurse and Sean brought me up to speed.

Anonymous Revelation

St. Joseph's University in Rutland, England, has a major research facility in medical science and therefore must collect and store large amounts of data. The massive quantities of information garnered from such a research-oriented institute require expensive mainframe computers to manage the records and a highly qualified computer manager to take care of both the hardware and software for a university with over a thousand staff members, all inputting relevant data. Dr. Bernard Braithwaite was such a person. He was the backbone of IT and, after almost 15 years with the department, he had recently been appointed the head. Well liked and trusted, he could always be relied upon to come up with viable solutions to the computer system's inevitable myriad of problems. Dr. Braithwaite acted as the safe and steady pair of hands that any institution would want at the helm of a key department.

That is, until an anonymous letter and CD dropped through the door of the Ministry of Science in London cast a shadow of doubt on the integrity of Dr. Braithwaite. The ministry immediately called in the audit and assurance unit. Sean presented himself to the London office where he met the undersecretary of state.

"I want you to leave no stone unturned, to establish the truth behind this spurious allegation by someone hiding behind a veil of anonymity against such a loyal and respected member of staff," the undersecretary told Sean. "I know Dr. Braithwaite personally, as he sits with me on the Interuniversity IT Working Group, and I rely on his expertise a great deal. I guess he has ruffled someone's feathers. I want you to identify the whistleblower at all costs and establish their motives so that we can take the appropriate action against them."

I read the letter. Basically it alleged that over a substantial period of time Dr. Braithwaite had been giving away large quantities of surplus IT hardware to a particular individual named George Sayers. He had either charged Sayers a nominal fee or had just given the equipment to him for free. The letter further claimed that both Sayers and Braithwaite were engaged in a project in Wales that involved the IT hardware. The whistleblower was seemingly upset by the waste of public money and the fact that Dr. Braithwaite was apparently personally benefiting from the scam. The CD contained copies of e-mails between the two men that supported the allegations.

"What is your first impression, Sean? Do you believe them?" I asked.

"It's hard to say yet; we revisited our last audit report a year ago. We made a few recommendations on controls but nothing significant in the asset area. We stayed away from the university itself until after we spoke to you. What do you suggest?"

"First things first—we must have a plan and we need to make some initial decisions. I suggest that we ignore the view of the undersecretary and not identify the whistleblower at this stage because we'd be wasting valuable time and might well alert Dr. Braithwaite of our activities. Even if we did find out who it is, I doubt if it would advance our case one bit. What is far more important is corroborating the information given, and if it turns out to be true, then we won't ever need to identify the whistleblower."

Sean asked, "How do we do that then?"

"By some old-fashioned due diligence," I replied. "Why don't we start right here and now?" I fired up my laptop and started quizzing some of my favorite research Web sites. I soon got a hit and could show that both men had been directors of the same IT consulting company, Saythwaite Co. Ltd. It had ceased to trade two years ago.

"Well, we've crossed the first hurdle," I said. "We can prove a link between them, so there probably was a conflict of interest when he was selling or giving away the hardware; we're in business."

My thoughts turned to the next step. "First, someone needs to go to Rutland and start ferreting for evidence, ideally without alerting Dr. Braithwaite. I suggest someone go under the cover of a follow-up audit; who do you have in mind for that, Sean?"

Sean looked at Desmond Smithers. "What about you, Des? A fresh pair of eyes on our findings could be useful. Plus, as you aren't known at the university, asking a lot of extra questions would make sense for a new guy."

Desmond Smithers, a lanky gent well over six feet tall, had apparently only recently joined the department after some 20 years auditing in the private sector for Extol Oil. "That's fine by me," he replied.

I was to work closely with Des over the next few months and became increasingly impressed by his commitment, shrewd auditing skills, and willingness to take on a new investigative mantle; if he didn't know, he would ask. He turned out to be a wonderful assistant who could be relied upon to do the job properly.

Sean disappeared to a meeting while Des and I began work. I said, "We'll need to get hold of the latest copy of the university policy document spelling out the correct procedures to follow concerning the acquisition and disposal of assets from the actual site. Human Resources should have it; they usually issue the document to all staff on appointment and update it annually. Next, and probably most important on the list, is to secure the main piece of evidence, which is the backup tape from the IT system covering the past year. So what I would like you to do is to speak with the director of IT, within the Department of Statistics, to establish what backup system each university research facility has in place, and they may well have a copy of the IT working practices manual which covers these issues. Whatever you do, please do not mention St. Joseph's by name. Keep it to a general audit inquiry and secure a copy of the manual if you can. Maybe it's on their intranet; I'll leave it to you to find out."

Des and I beavered away for another hour or so, with me pointing out that the thrust of our investigation was to find confirmation and verification of the contents of the e-mails and thus prove the validity—or otherwise—of the allegations in the whistleblower's letter. Des also printed off all of the e-mails on the CD and prepared a spreadsheet of the contents, including each e-mail's sender/receiver and topic area. We were still engrossed when Sean entered the room, clutching an armful of papers.

"We're nearly finished for today," I said. "I've given Des a to-do list that he'll explain to you. I'll come back next Friday and see how much progress has been made." Sean was happy with this and even agreed to my fees without a whimper. I left with Sean's words ringing in my ears. "I'll get on to Procurement to make sure your contract is ready for you when you get here next time."

A Deceitful Donation

On my arrival at the audit offices the following week, I was welcomed with a cup of tea and my contract awaiting signature. I dealt with them in strict order of importance, and before the ink was dry on the contract I was quaffing my tea.

Des had done a superb job; he presented me with a fully indexed folder containing all of the e-mails with an Excel-based summary of their content. He briefed me on his findings and could say that the crux of the e-mails had been succinctly enumerated in the letter by the whistleblower. The scam centered on the "donation" of a Sunblade brand mainframe computer by Dr. Braithwaite to a George Sayers and his company, Crosstitch UK Ltd. The e-mails also demonstrated that Sayers had made an application to the UK Development Agency for funding of a project that involved Crosstitch opening up offices in a deprived area of Wales.

"We need to get hold of information about that grant application," I said. "Any ideas?"

"Sure," Des replied. "I'll speak to the agency's audit department; they must be able to access the file."

Within an hour we confirmed that in Crosstitch's application they had stated that they spent some $250,000 on the purchase of a second-hand Sunblade brand mainframe computer from Semester Dataset Ltd., a company based on the island of Jersey (a tax haven offshore the United Kingdom). The application had been successful and Crosstitch was given a $150,000 development grant from the British government.

"Well, well," I commented. "The plot has thickened. I don't suppose the folks in Wales saw the Sunblade did they?"

"Funny you should say that," said Des, "but the grant officers did go to Crosstitch's premises and inspect a Sunblade but did not see it actually working. Are you thinking what I'm thinking?"

"I most certainly am; we must get the serial number from St. Joseph's and then somehow check out the one in Wales."

"That is not all," said Des. "Have a look at this." He showed me his e-mail analysis sheet with the entry against an e-mail sent by Braithwaite to Sayers. Braithwaite had written: "What are you going to use this kit for, analysis or just as a doorstop to impress the grant inspectors?"

Sayers had responded: "Must make it look good; otherwise we won't get the funding. And when we do, I'll give you our agreed $10,000 for giving me the kit."

"Fraud, theft, corruption—this case has got it all; best we get out there and get the evidence we need before it goes missing," I said. "It seems our whistleblower is a very public-minded individual indeed. I suggest we do a complete audit of the IT hardware at St. Joseph's. The only way we can do that is to get Braithwaite out of the way. I suggest that you, Sean, and I visit the dean on Monday and give him the news. I don't think he's going to like it."

"So," replied Sean, "it seems like our Dr. Braithwaite has really got his fingers in the cookie jar. I'll call the dean straight away to make sure he will be available, as we don't want a wasted journey. I'll just tell him that it's a confidential matter and that it can't wait; 2 p.m. sound OK with everyone?''

We all agreed and then split up to make our own plans. In my case, I headed home to file away all of the paperwork from the previous assignment. I also needed to dig out the templates to create a new database for this case on my laptop and do some serious research into George Sayers. It was going to be a busy weekend; there was no time to waste. With all the activity of the auditors at the university our cover might have already been blown, so I wanted to strike quickly as a damage limitation exercise.

The Dirt Is in the Details

Driving to Rutland, I reflected on the new information I had discovered about George Sayers; he had a Ph.D. in computer sciences which meant we weren't dealing with an amateur. I needed to complete the circle where Braithwaite was concerned. To do that I had to prove that the Sunblade computer was not at the university, that its disposal had been carried out in the manner suggested by the whistleblower, that no money had been received by St. Joseph's for its "sale" to Crosstitch, and that Braithwaite had been the author of the relevant e-mails to Sayers. I would also need to persuade the dean to suspend Braithwaite immediately on the grounds of gross misconduct and to allow the auditors to escort him from the premises. It was going to be a challenging couple of days.

To say that the dean was not happy has to be the understatement of the year. "Mr. Rapley, how dare you make outrageous allegations about our most respected senior member of staff—all on the whim of some faceless individual?" the dean stammered.

Sean interposed, trying to defuse the situation. "That is not quite right, Dean," he said. "We have been able to corroborate several points, plus we have found new evidence that looks quite damning. We cannot possibly do our work effectively while Dr. Braithwaite remains on the premises, so I must recommend that you use the discipline procedure to suspend him from duty while we sort this mess out."

We waited while the dean tried valiantly to contain his anger, which did little to help his condition, but he did eventually, and somewhat reluctantly, agree to Sean's request with the proviso that we have the whole issue resolved within 72 hours. I knew full well that that was not enough time for this type of investigation, but at least it gave us a window to get the extra evidence that I was convinced would be found in the IT department and particularly in Braithwaite's office. I made a tactical withdrawal to the refectory while these domestic issues were attended to. When all the paperwork was done, I would need to act with precision to steer the investigation forward with speed. Time was of the essence.

The audit team, under the direction of Des, was soon at work digging out the asset register and doing a physical comparison with all of the hardware on site. Following the quarantining of Braithwaite's office and the seizure and depositing of the relevant backup tapes in the dean's safe, Sean and I busied ourselves debriefing Jonathan Dwyer, the deputy head of IT, who was similarly shell-shocked at the turn of events. On one hand, he wanted to be loyal to his existing management; on the other, he wanted to be helpful to us. He was able to fill us in on the practices within the department, especially with regards to the disposal of the IT kit. There was a culture, apparently, that believed that there was "no point in wasting time in trying to find a buyer for an extra kit because it was just not cost-effective." In many cases the kit was thrown into a dumpster.

I honed in on the Sunblade and asked Jon what had happened to it. He replied, "We had replaced that computer a couple of years ago and it had been gathering dust in the corridor ever since. We had even taken bits off of it to use on other machines, so it was not in a working condition when Dr. Braithwaite suggested that he had found a buyer for it. I can't remember if he said how much he had been offered for it, but I know that when I came into work one Monday morning it was gone. I, for one, was pleased to see it go."

"Did you ask him where it had gone?" I asked.

"Oh yes, he said his friend, Dr. Sayers, needed it for a project in Wales—we often give extra hardware to Dr. Sayers."

"Who could authorize disposal of an extra kit?"

"Only Dr. Braithwaite himself. He always insisted that it was his responsibility alone and I was not going to question it."

"Is that what the manual says?" I asked.

Jon replied, "No, I don't think it is, but Dr. Braithwaite can be insistent when he wants to be, and I was not interested in arguing with him."

"What about remote access—can he access your system from home?"

Jon answered, "Yes he can; I suppose you will want me to change the passwords to deny him from now on."

"You got it."

This seemed to indicate that the missing Sunblade had found its way to Wales. Now all we had to do was to prove it, but that could wait for the moment because I had a more pressing matter to attend to: searching Braithwaite's office and checking out his computer for traces of the telltale e-mails. First, I needed to hire independent computer forensic experts, so I made a call to some trusted and reliable ex–police officers who specialized in this field. Their reply was prompt, "Dan, we will be with you later this evening. Book us a couple of rooms in a hotel and we'll make a start in the morning." They were a great couple of lads who never let me down.

At a little after eight o'clock on Wednesday morning, with my full English breakfast now only a memory, Ivor and Frank, the computer technicians, were busying themselves stripping down the array of computers in Braithwaite's office and using Encase software to copy the hard drives' contents. After a full day's work, they eventually packed away their equipment and headed north, back to their offices and laboratory in Birmingham. I had given them a list of key words lifted from the whistleblower's e-mails to run them through their working copy of the downloaded data as a matter of urgency. "Should be done by lunchtime tomorrow—I'll give you a call," said Ivor as he sped off.

The next day we were all busying ourselves on our respective tasks. The audit team was doing the asset audit and finding numerous anomalies, which would need further investigation and explanation. Sean and I were documenting paperwork we had seized from the office. It was nearly noon before my mobile chirped urgently in my pocket; it was the long-awaited call from Ivor. "What do you want first, the good news or the bad news?"

"How about the bad?" I responded.

"OK, only a few of the keywords showed up on our initial trawl on Braithwaite's computer. But now for the good news: I got a stack of hits within the hidden files. It looks as though the user did a dump of a hundred or so e-mails during Monday."

That was good evidence for us, especially as we could retrieve the originals from the backup tapes we had squirreled away in the dean's safe. The case was looking stronger by the minute and the criminality aspect seemed conclusive. I recommended that we report the case to the police immediately and began preparing a comprehensive report on the evidence and findings that we would first submit to the undersecretary before handing it over to Scotland Yard.

So after only four days, I was being ushered into Detective Superintendent Jake Arnold's office on the fourth floor of the Yard. "Welcome back, Dan. Good to see you again. The last time you were here was in this very office when I came to see you for advice; how times have changed. What can I do for you?"

I introduced him to Sean and we briefed Jake about the investigation. I was grateful that he accepted the allegations, and Sean and I were taken to the duty squad's office, where we spent the next couple of hours going through the fine details with Detective Sergeant Trevor Jones, himself a native of Wales, and his colleague Detective Constable James Barnett.

Within the week, Sean and I were back at Scotland Yard for a further briefing. Sgt. Jones said he had read the report and accepted our recommendation to apply for search warrants for the home addresses of both Braithwaite and Sayers and the business premises of Crosstitch in Wales. We decided to use a multiskilled team led, of course, by the police. So we settled on three teams, one for each address, consisting of police officers, forensic auditors, forensic computer experts (I again called on Ivor and Frank to assist), and internal auditors. The names of participating individuals were left with Sgt. Jones so he could make the application to the courts for the warrants.

I drove some 250 miles to Wales and met up with my team, led by Detective Barnett, in the Holiday Inn. Sgt. Jones was leading the Braithwaite search team in Rutland. Following a run-through of each of our roles for the forthcoming raid, we all opted for an early night.

We arrived at the offices at 8 a.m. only to be met by the cleaner, who told us that most of the staff would not be in for another hour. On Dr. Sayers's arrival, Detective Barnett went through the formalities and introductions. After his initial outrage and protestations of innocence, Sayers realized that we were not leaving without gaining access, so he calmed down. While Detective Barnett and colleagues interviewed Sayers, the audit team started checking all of the hardware in the offices. We were delighted to make the acquaintance of the missing Sunblade; now we had clear evidence of the theft. The police also seized other items of hardware identified by the audit team from St. Joseph's asset register. Using Encase, the computer forensic guys ran a copy of the remaining computers on site. We eventually left a little after six o'clock. Sayers had been arrested and taken by the police to the local station to be processed and bailed before they continued on to search his home, about 10 miles away.

Our team reconvened at the hotel at 9 p.m. to discuss the day's events and have a celebratory drink for a job well done. There was also good news from the Braithwaite team because, apart from retrieving imaged copies of his own computers, they had found six brand-new boxed Sunscope laptops hidden under his stairs and another in the study. They also recovered the delivery note for the seven laptops from the supplier; it had been made out to St. Joseph's about five months beforehand. Seven laptops did appear on the asset register, but they had different serial numbers; we would need to get to the bottom of that later. Braithwaite, likewise, had been arrested and bailed to reappear at a later stage.

With the police now in effective control of the investigation, my involvement was reduced drastically. I prepared the discipline papers that would be required if St. Joseph's decided to prosecute Braithwaite. The case progressed satisfactorily over the ensuing months, with the police also identifying the personal assets of both Braithwaite and Sayers, enabling the court to seize them in order to recompense the lost revenue to the university and the government.

The computer forensic experts proved that the Sunblade had never worked while in Wales, as some key components were missing, and therefore it had been used by Sayers solely to dupe the grant officers into giving him the $150,000. Sayers's funds were traced to New Jersey in the United States, where he had embarked upon a tax evasion scheme as well. He had committed a check cross-firing scam through several of his own shell companies, which resulted in a bank statement showing an alleged transaction of $350,000. This had been presented to the grant officers in Wales as evidence of the purchase of the Sunblade.

As for Braithwaite, he had negotiated the supply of the seven Sunscope laptops directly from the manufacturer, in apparent recompense for an incidence of bad service by them. He had not put these seven units through the university books, but he did make an identical order a couple of weeks afterward, for which the university paid in full, that was correctly recorded. This explained the anomaly of the different serial numbers on the asset register.

The two men eventually stood trial many months later. Both pleaded guilty to a variety of offences including theft, corruption, and fraud, and each was sentenced to a term of imprisonment. Compensation orders were made by the court; the police are now actively pursuing the recovery process. Braithwaite and Sayers stand to lose their houses as well as their bank balances. They have destroyed their reputations and, in Braithwaite's case, an otherwise respectable career. He was dismissed from St. Joseph's for the disciplinary offence of gross misconduct.

Lessons Learned

Though we never identified the whistleblower, he or she was a vital part of setting the investigation in motion and uncovering the fraud. Statistically, more fraud is discovered as the result of such information than by the work of auditors. It is important to acknowledge and follow through on tips. Without the whistleblower, Braithwaite and Sayers would not have been brought to justice.

Recommendation to Prevent Future Occurrences

Checks and Balances

No authority challenged Dr. Braithwaite's decisions, allowing him to become a loose cannon and enabling him to steal the computers. In many organizations, CEOs fail to hold directors accountable, choosing to rely solely on their perceived competency and integrity. Lack of checks and balances for the accurate maintenance of the asset register and the disposal of surplus equipment, as well as failure to adopt audit recommendations, made this fraud possible.

About the Author

Russell Allen gained his extensive investigative experience in fraud and corruption as a senior detective at Scotland Yard and in Botswana. He now works as a consultant forensic auditor investigating and lecturing on fraud for national and international clients in both the public and private sectors.

10

If Only His Nose Could Grow

BARRY DAVIDOW

Word around the office was that Martin Thomas was one of the fastest male athletes in the world. I am not a sports fanatic, but I do recognize big names, and Martin Thomas did not ring a bell. I wondered aloud where my colleagues got their information, but my suspicion was always shot down with reprimanding looks. Questioning Martin Thomas was considered borderline blasphemous.

His coworkers maintained that Martin was brilliant and had obtained his degree from one of America's top universities. According to them, he had made millions in the financial markets and only continued working because he enjoyed it. Impressive for a man in his early 30s.

Martin had the physique of an athlete. His suits, shirts, and ties were expensive and his hair was styled at the best salon in town. He won people over with his charisma and welcoming smile. In short, the image of Martin Thomas was immaculate.

He was also, as I came to understand, a pathological liar. Cunning and ambitious, Martin was gifted at cultivating deceit. He had built an entire life around dishonesty—and a successful one at that. Martin fooled everyone. After all, his reputation was sterling.

Russett Financial Services Inc. is a USA-based multinational corporation. The business model was to provide financial services and contractors to a wide range of corporations. Under the inspired leadership of Steven Masters, the Australian founding CEO, the company had grown rapidly into a thriving, highly profitable business. As far as Steven was concerned, it was still only a fraction of the size he envisioned. When I began the investigation, Martin had been the financial controller for about two years.

Don't Tell Me What I Won't Find

Frank O' Toole, a colleague, former police officer, and one of the best fraud interviewers I've ever known, received a call from Bill Wiggins, the director of finance at Russett, one Tuesday morning.

"I'm sorry to worry you over such a small matter," began Bill, "but our holding company has instructed us to solicit external advice. We found an unusual transaction. We'd appreciate it if you could check it out. I'm absolutely sure it's nothing, but we'd still like you to deal with it immediately."

Bill showed us the printout. Evidently, $14,000 had been transferred via computer from the general balance of staff income tax deductions to the tax deductions account for Martin, enabling him to claim the $14,000 from the Australian Taxation Office without it having been deducted from his pay. The transaction was indeed unusual. It was not entered as a journal entry, which would leave an audit trail, but instead as a plus $14,000 next to Martin's income tax and a minus $14,000 next to the general balance. If this was truly fraud, it was a clever way to bypass internal controls and obtain a payment without being detected. It was purely by chance that John Kent, the IT manager, had found it. He had been in the process of sorting out another anomaly in the staff income tax system when he stumbled across the odd plus and minus amounts.

I spent the rest of the day with John, sifting through computer logs and analyzing times and patterns. Unfortunately, we could not identify who made the two entries.

The next morning I arrived early to speak with Steven Masters, the CEO, with my report and the evidence in hand. While waiting, I sat at Martin's desk, where I noticed a company bank reconciliation. As an auditor, I could see at a glance that there was an error in the additions. Curious, I compared the cashbook figure to the balance on the cashbook software program, as well as the bank balance to the bank statement. He had transposed two numbers in the bank reconciliation statement, yet it still balanced. Something was wrong. Either Martin had done the calculations elsewhere and copied them across incorrectly or he had force-balanced the reconciliation.

About 20 minutes later Martin arrived. He had been told that I was an auditor on a routine visit. I introduced myself and said: "Martin, I don't understand this bank reconciliation. You've transposed two figures. You typed 53,000 instead of 35,000, yet it still balances. Can you explain that?"

"Barry, you won't find anything wrong with the bank reconciliations," he replied.

Oftentimes, people actually reveal the truth through their deceptive, omissive statements. Martin didn't say, "There is nothing wrong." He said, "You won't *find* anything wrong." The subtext could easily be, "Barry, you're an idiot. I have fooled people far smarter than you, so I'm confident that you won't find my fraud.''

I wanted to double-check to ensure that my suspicions were reasonable, so I asked, ''Martin, it seems as though there is an error in the bank reconciliation. Are you telling me that it is not wrong?''

''Barry, I'm telling you that you won't find anything wrong.''

Again, he did not deny that there was an error or that the bank reconciliation was incorrect. I now had two reasons to believe that there was a serious problem. With surprisingly little persuasion, Martin agreed that I could look further into the bank reconciliations.

The Intimidation Factor

Martin then requested a few days off to spend with his family. Steven consented to the leave so that the office would be free while we proceeded with the investigation.

Frank and I agreed to a two-pronged approach. He would look into Martin's background and personal asset acquisitions and I would investigate the bank and cashbook transactions. As Australia's foremost fraud investigator, Jeff Williams provided investigation advice and technical expertise.

I was shocked to find that five separate bank accounts had been combined into one cashbook in the computer. Merging all of the accounts meant that we had a mammoth task trying to ascertain whether the bank reconciliation was accurate and whether or not any questionable activity had occurred.

Mary Wong, an external auditor, was assigned to assist me with the reconciliations. We were faced with a quandary. Bank reconciliation is most efficient if completed annually. Doing so month by month is advantageous in that it offers 12 opportunities to check for accuracy. However, many transactions that are cleared the next month end up on more than one reconciliation, resulting in a great deal of wasted effort.

I designed a system that would allow us to check each month's, if necessary, while still doing the year's reconciliations in one go.

When we completed the bank reconciliation for the last financial year, our results were dramatically different from Martin's. The only common figures were the bank and cashbook balances. Unfortunately, our reconciliation still did not balance. Mary spent her whole weekend and a few days at the office reworking it. She found minor errors but still could not force it to balance.

We performed bank reconciliations for the entire time that Martin had been in charge of banking transactions. We had hoped that they would enable us to accurately calculate the true cashbook balance and identify bank transactions that had been entered inaccurately or omitted altogether.

I was given a copy of the external auditor's working papers for the bank reconciliation. One of the items, close to $5 million, had been labeled as "timing." The explanation for it was long, convoluted, and nearly incomprehensible. I arranged to meet with Martin to request clarification.

He offered the same long and complicated explanation that appeared in the working papers. At one point I interjected, "Martin, I apologize for being so thick about this, but I still don't understand. For something to be in the bank reconciliation it must be in the cashbook but not in the bank statement, or in the bank statement but not in the cashbook. If it's not in one of those, it shouldn't be in the reconciliation. Could you show me where this item is and where it eventually appears after the end of the financial year?"

He explained that sometimes there were delays in clients' payment for the services provided, but the corporation was still required to compensate its providers on time. And then he repeated the long explanation. I again asked him to show me where in the records.

He responded crossly: "Barry, I have explained it to you and explained it again. If you cannot understand, there is nothing I can do. The auditors from one of the Big Five international accounting firms looked at this and they accepted it. The audit senior and the audit manager examined it. They understood my explanation. If you cannot, I can't help you." He was trying to intimidate me into not auditing the figures further.

I met with Frank to compare notes. It turned out that our suspicions had proved correct regarding Martin's background. There was no evidence of Martin winning any races in the United States, as he had claimed. There was also no record of him being a licensed CPA, obtaining the fancy degree, or working several of the jobs documented on his resume.

Frank had researched Martin's property ownerships at the land titles office and prepared a list of the properties he had purchased and the amounts paid for them. We were able to trace all of the property payments back to the embezzled funds from the company's bank accounts.

Martin had been an astute player in the property market. The insurance company that insured Russett Financial Services Inc. sold all of the properties at fire-sale prices to recover their money as quickly as possible, fearing a downturn in the property market. If the properties had been held for another three or four years, they would have received more than double the prices for which they had been bought.

I prepared a schedule of all Martin's bank transactions and collected the supporting documentation. Some proved legitimate while others were rather suspicious. I conducted interviews and gathered all the available evidence for the suspect transactions, including copies of all of the paid (canceled) checks from the bank. When all had been collected and analyzed, Frank and I formally interviewed Martin.

No Concept of Truth

We started off by asking him about a particular check. Martin claimed that it had been a legitimate payment. The check was made out to him but had been entered in the cashbook as a payment to a contractor. Frank paused, looked at him, and said: "Martin, you said that you wanted to cooperate. We know that check was paid into your bank account and that the funds were later used to purchase a property in Randwick. Please do not lie again." Martin's face turned pale; he asked for a break and phoned his lawyer from another office.

We asked him about another check. Again he claimed that it was a genuine payment. Then we showed him the evidence that it was clearly not. Visibly shaken, Martin requested another break to speak to his lawyer.

This happened with every transaction we asked about. After each break, he seemed to have lost more of his composure and confidence. By the end of the interview Martin was hunched over and mumbling his replies. I suspect this had been the first time in many years, possibly ever, that he had been forced to face the truth and consequences of his deceptions.

Martin knew that I was interested in the subject of ethics. During the interview, he looked me directly in the eyes and said proudly: "Barry, as far as ethics go, I did the right thing. I put half the money I took in my wife's name."

I asked Martin why he took the money.

"Because nobody checked the bank reconciliations," he replied.

"I know how you got away with it, but why did you do it?"

"Because nobody checked the bank reconciliations—I don't understand the question. Surely anyone in that position would have taken the money."

Martin did not understand that most people would have chosen honesty when faced with that sort of temptation.

We suspected the frauds amounted to over $10 million.

Martin pleaded guilty to fraud—larceny as a servant—in New South Wales. Before being sentenced, he admitted to the judge that he had lied throughout his entire life. Martin claimed that he was ashamed to have deceived his wife. His situation had recently forced him to reevaluate himself. Newspapers reported that he promised to try to change into a person of substance rather than the veneer he had always been.

When I read this, I was pleased that perhaps some good might come for Martin and his family. I remarked to a friend—a psychiatrist—that I believed that Martin would grow and become a better human being from the experience. "That depends on whether or not he is a psychopath," he replied. "If he *is* a psychopath, then he was just saying that because it's what he thinks the judge wants to hear. Chances are he's lying for a lighter sentence."

Martin was sentenced to three and a half years in prison.

Lessons Learned

The external auditors used the electronic bank transactions downloaded from the company as the documentation for their audit test. Based on the outcome of the case, it seems likely that some items were removed before the transactions were given to the auditors. An important lesson for both internal and external auditors is to obtain the electronic bank transactions directly from the bank and not from the audited. That way information is not manipulated.

Furthermore, not everyone adheres to simple honesty or the idea of integrity. Those crooks make it important to implement proper controls and balances to prevent gross misconduct. Some people lack morals and will cheat if given the opportunity.

Recommendations to Prevent Future Occurrences

Simplify Computer Processes

The more complicated the computer process, the greater the risk of fraud. In this particular case, we cannot be sure, but we believe that the system of reconciliations was designed to be overly complicated by Martin in order to hide his fraud. Simplify computer systems whenever possible.

Don't Succumb to Intimidation

Auditors should never accept explanations because they are too embarrassed to admit they don't understand them. I suspect that the auditors in this case were intimidated by Martin, which is why they did not question him sufficiently, allowing him to continue to perpetrate his crime.

Segregation of Duties

The risk of this fraud would have been greatly reduced if there had been adequate segregation of duties between cashbook and performance of the bank reconciliations.

Employees Living Beyond Means

One of the most widely known but often disregarded fraud indicators is the sight of employees living beyond their means. In this case, Martin's lifestyle was extravagant for anyone, but especially when compared to his income. He claimed that he was already rich and only worked for fun. Nobody questioned his unconvincing explanation, even though Martin would wax lyrical about his vacations and time off work, and he complained frequently about being overworked.

Corporate Culture

There was a culture of attending to business strategies and operations at the expense of sound internal controls at Russett. This case highlighted the importance of incorporating solid internal control management in order to reduce or prevent fraud.

About the Author

Barry Davidow, CFE, B.Com, B.Acc, M. Tax Law, MIIA, CA, is a director of Fraud Prevention and Governance Pty. Ltd., a company specializing in all aspects of fraud control. He has over 20 years' experience in preventing, detecting, and investigating fraud and corruption in a wide range of industries and the public sector.

CHAPTER 11

Keeping Up with the Jamesons

MIKE ANDREWS

Frank and Evelyn Jameson were happily married and lived with their two young children, Simon and Alison, in a beautiful country home in England. On warm summer evenings the children could be seen playing in the tree house their father built, while Frank and Evelyn enjoyed a game of tennis on their court in the back garden. They had a dog, a Red Setter named Charlie, who took great pleasure in chasing rabbits and stray tennis balls. Being a sociable fellow, Frank met regularly with friends at the local pub to tell of his latest family holiday or to boast of his two children, who continued to excel in private school. Being a bit of a braggart, he drove a brand new BMW sports car and enjoyed showing it off. Life in the Jameson household seemed idyllic, a portrait of what any family might hope to achieve through diligence and good fortune. But Timothy Blevins, an acquaintance of the Jamesons who knew Frank from the local pub, didn't believe they'd earned their wealth honestly. He developed nagging suspicions after Frank made several off-the-cuff remarks about spending days on the golf course or afternoons at the gym, indicating he rarely, if ever, completed a full day's work. These comments raised doubts as to how the Jamesons had acquired their lifestyle. So Timothy contacted Peter Wilson, an investigator with over 20 years of experience examining fraudulent state benefit claims for an agency called the Department of Work and Pensions, to determine whether or not his suspicions were warranted, and Peter agreed—something didn't add up. So he summoned his colleagues and commenced an investigation.

The Tip of the Iceberg

Timothy alleged that Evelyn was claiming state benefits for a relative who had died some years back, information he gathered through a mutual friend. With a quick inspection of the records, Peter established where the checks for the benefits were being cashed. Not wanting to alert the

Jamesons at this point, Peter decided to use surveillance cameras to obtain confirmation and installed them in the post office where Evelyn supposedly cashed the checks.

It did not take long. In just two days, Peter had hard evidence documenting Evelyn's fraudulent claims.

"We've got them!" exclaimed one of Peter's colleagues.

"Not quite," Peter replied. "There's still work to be done."

Peter's intuition led him to believe that this was only the beginning, the first glimpse of more deception to come. It seemed improbable that a family could afford a life of luxury just from fraudulent state benefit claims. Neither Frank nor Evelyn was gainfully employed. Either the government had become quite generous of late, or the Jamesons were using more than one means of supplementing their lifestyle. The question continued to bother Peter for several months.

By now it was winter. The days were cold and nights even colder. Peter remained undeterred. The investigation had moved into a new phase. Day in and day out, the team Peter had assembled braved the freezing cold, armed with binoculars and hiding behind trees for cover, trying to a catch a glimpse into the Jamesons' world—anything that might reveal a vital clue to break the case wide open. At the very least, they wanted to establish if either Frank or Evelyn appeared to be working for a living. During the past few months, Peter had uncovered a web of deceit trailing the Jamesons like a dark cloud. Yet somehow Frank and Evelyn had kept it hidden from their family and friends. After all, why doubt the Jamesons? They lived life like it was one big happy ending. But Peter knew better. He had talked to previous landlords that rented to the Jamesons, landlords that had been left with thousands of pounds in rent arrears. He also spoke to utility companies that had been trying to track the Jamesons down for years in order to collect unpaid electricity and gas bills.

Individually, the fraudulent state benefits claims, the rent arrears, and the outstanding electricity bills were relatively small sums of money, but when combined, they added up to quite a substantial amount—over $200,000. Peter had more than enough evidence to arrest the Jamesons, yet he remained unsatisfied, still plagued by niggling doubts. Although the fraudulent state benefit claims were high dollar, it still didn't seem to be enough cash to support the Jamesons' lifestyle. Peter suspected another form of fraudulent income.

No Stone Left Unturned

Winter was drawing to a close and spring was just around the corner. I was busy with my typical workload of cases as a computer forensics investigator working in a local government office. Dave, one of my colleagues, walked into the office, closely followed by a man I didn't recognize.

"I've got someone here who wants to talk to you," Dave said as he brought me my usual morning cup of coffee. "This is Peter," he explained, "He's an investigator who might need your help on a case."

I sat down with Peter and we spent the next hour or so chatting. He filled me in, starting with the Jamesons' lavish lifestyle leading up through where the case had progressed. It all sounded interesting, but I couldn't see where I fit in. Peter explained.

"They've got computers," he said, "and we want them searched from top to bottom."

During the surveillance operation, an investigator on Peter's team had established that there were multiple computers in the Jameson residence. Surely nothing suspicious about that. After all, nearly everyone has a home computer in this day and age. But Peter wasn't convinced. Experience taught him never to discount a possible source of evidence; no stone would be left unturned. I agreed with him and offered to assist.

"I'll be in touch," said Peter, "We're planning to raid the Jamesons' house soon, so I'll let you know once we have a date."

Weeks passed. It was now early May and I had heard nothing further from Peter. Perhaps the trail had gone cold. Or maybe the Jamesons had pulled another disappearing act. It wouldn't be unusual; I had witnessed multiple investigations dry up. Sometimes there's just not enough evidence to go on, or the witnesses won't come forward, or maybe the hunch led to a dead end. Then out of the blue, the call came.

"Peter here," said the voice on the other end of the line. "We're ready for the raid. Are you available in early August?"

The delay, it seemed, had been one of logistics. During the investigation, Peter had identified a number of individuals who were potentially in collusion with the Jamesons. This new discovery compounded an already complex operation. Peter wanted to round up all the suspects in one fell swoop. With police officers, search officers, and forensic experts required at each of the three different locations simultaneously, the operation presented an organizational nightmare. But everything was now in order. Plans were made, search orders obtained, personnel assigned, and the date was set.

The morning was crisp. The three teams assembled at the back of the local police station at 5:30 a.m. It was going to be a long day. We ate bacon sandwiches and readied ourselves for the raid. Everyone received a last-minute briefing and then we were off. A convoy of cars and police vans made its way through the countryside heading for the Jamesons' house. The traffic was light at such an early hour, so we made swift progress, approaching our destination ahead of schedule. As we neared the house, the police van heading the convoy signaled for everyone to stop and pull over to the side of the road. Several police officers changed from t-shirts and trousers into full body armor. Based on a risk assessment, the police had reason to believe that Frank Jameson could become hostile. Every precaution would be taken.

It was nearly 7:30 a.m., the designated hour of entry. The officers wearing body armor would go in first and secure the scene, followed by the rest of the search team and forensic support. The other two addresses identified in connection with the Jamesons were receiving similar visits.

I sat in the car with my colleague, Carol Stevens, and waited. We anxiously wondered what would happen during the raid. Would Frank become violent? Would the situation get out of control? Would the family even be in the house? Perhaps, as with their previous properties, the Jamesons had left already. Then the call came; Frank and Evelyn had been arrested.

We drove down a long, graveled drive lined with trees to reach the house. We parked next to Frank's BMW and entered. The scene was a bustling hive of activity. Police, detectives, and search officials were all going about their business. I sought out the individual in charge.

"We're here to examine the computers," I said as I shook hands with Paul Fielding, the chief officer. Paul directed us through a maze of corridors to an elegant living room with oak-paneled walls. Charlie, the family's Red Setter, was curled up on a leather sofa in the corner. He didn't seem at all bothered by the invasion of strangers in his territory.

"There's a laptop over in the corner," said Paul, pointing to a rickety antique table next to the sofa occupied by Charlie. "There are three more upstairs when you're done with this one," he added.

We set about our work, trying not to disturb Charlie, just in case he suddenly decided he didn't approve of strangers in his house after all. I watched as Carol carefully removed the hard disk drive and connected it to the analysis equipment. We always carry the necessary tools with us in the field to perform on-site forensic examinations; that way, if we find immediate evidence, it can be used to our advantage before the suspect has time to regroup. I can recall several instances where we uncovered a particularly damning e-mail or memo that was then presented to the perpetrator during the first interview. The hope is such evidence will foster an early admission of guilt. This time, however, there was nothing that immediately caught our eye, so the laptop was reassembled, placed in an evidence bag, and sealed up, ready for removal from the scene.

We made our way up a winding staircase to the first floor landing where Paul directed us to one of the bedrooms containing another computer. I quickly got to work, removing the side panels and connecting our equipment to the hard drive. Again, nothing particularly interesting popped up. Perhaps the computers had no incriminating evidence after all. Nonetheless, it was bagged up and sealed, along with two more found in adjacent rooms.

Word filtered through from other raids. More arrests had been made and more computers confiscated. The search teams had also uncovered documents linking the occupants of those houses with the Jamesons. Overall, it turned out to be quite a successful day. Now we just needed to find relevant data on the computers.

It was late in the afternoon and the search of the property was winding down. All the evidence had been secured and moved to the vans for transportation. I took custody of the four computers and headed back to the forensic lab. It had been a long day. The analysis would have to wait until tomorrow.

I was in the office early the following morning with Carol. We were eager to get started on the computers. There were now seven in total, with three from the other two raids added to the four we collected from the Jamesons. We had other cases to work on, but this investigation was just too intriguing. Our first task was to image the hard drives; we had to make copies to maintain the integrity of the original evidence. This process took us two days, after which we were ready to get to work in earnest.

Piecing It Together

The initial analysis produced nothing particularly useful. However, we did find one puzzling document. We recovered a letter that appeared to confirm the employment details of Evelyn Jameson: employer, Ward & Willis Advertising; job title, Sales and Marketing Director; salary, $140,000 per annum; length of service, three years. The document verified that Evelyn was a trustworthy person and a model employee. As far as we were previously aware, neither Frank nor Evelyn was employed. But analysis of the document's metadata (which is, essentially, records information such as the document author, the date it was last amended, the date it was last printed, etc.) revealed another anomaly: the document was created by Evelyn. We marked this file as potentially relevant, although at the time we couldn't quite figure out how it fit into the overall investigation.

In addition, we discovered accounting software on one of the computers; perhaps the Jamesons were running a legitimate business that required the software. But we had a duty to analyze everything, even what might appear, at first glance, to be relatively innocuous. Examining the software revealed details of the same business we'd found on the hard drive: Ward & Willis Advertising. Apparently, the business had only one employee, Evelyn, the sales and marketing director on a salary of $140,000 per annum. It still didn't make sense, so we relayed this information to Peter.

Peter had been busy since the raid, buried under a mound of paperwork. I passed on the information relating to Evelyn and her apparent employment.

"That's incredible," exclaimed Peter. "We've got a copy of a wage slip here for Evelyn matching those details."

"OK, I'll do some more digging and get back to you," I replied.

Carol and I set to work on pulling apart the accounting software. Sure enough, it had been configured to act as a payroll system that allowed the user to print pay slips. Evelyn had created an apparently fictitious job reference, company accounts system, and pay slip. But why?

Days passed as we sifted through masses of computer data trying to find a lead. We received a call from Peter.

"Evelyn's been applying for multiple bank loans," explained Peter. "We've found copies of credit agreements that go back years; the amounts are staggering. We've also found records of the other houses they've rented." Peter went on to explain how he'd asked the Jamesons' previous landlords what documentation the couple had used to secure their leases. In most cases, copies of pay slips and employer references were provided by Evelyn.

It started to make more sense. False job references and false pay slips—all that was needed to secure a lease on a property, to open a bank account, to apply for a bank loan, or to purchase a new car. But there were still unanswered questions: how had they managed to get away with it for so long? Why hadn't the banks caught up with them? How could they continue to obtain loans with no evidence demonstrating that their previous loans had ever been repaid? These questions were soon answered.

We had been working on the analysis of the computer evidence for just over a week. I was seated in an office next-door to the lab when Carol burst in.

"I've found it," she said excitedly. "I think I know what they've been doing."

I followed Carol next door and sat down at the analysis workstation where she had been scouring through tens of thousands of key-word search hits. For the next several hours, Carol and I analyzed the information she believed would complete the picture. What we uncovered was a timeline of Internet activity documenting a series of searches. They were conducted using both generic Web search engines and very specific Web sites. The information sought was the one constant: persons with the same name as the Jamesons, or more specifically persons with the same first and last names as Frank and Evelyn. And not only were they looking for people with the same names, they were also looking for their addresses and dates of birth.

Once again, we fed this information back to Peter. He had been following leads from the bank loans the Jamesons had been applying for. After we put our heads together and discussed our different sides of the investigation, it all became clear.

A Case of Stolen Identities

The computers had been examined, the paperwork completed, and the reports prepared. Peter and I met one final time to review all of the evidence, to ensure that we were comfortable with the complete picture before the case went to court. What had been uncovered was a web of deceit carefully spun for many years. Aside from the fraudulent claim for state benefits, which is where the investigation began, significant frauds against several banks and credit card companies had been discovered along the way. Evelyn and Frank Jameson used the identities of other individuals with the same names to make fraudulent applications for bank loans, credit cards, and even the purchase of their BMW. They used similar methods to secure leases on the various country properties they had occupied over the past few years. Each time the modus operandi was the same. They would rent a house using the false job reference and wage slips as proof of identity and sound character. They would next apply for bank loans and several credit cards, listing their newly acquired property as their current address. Then, having searched the Web for the personal details of another ''Frank Jameson'' or ''Evelyn Jameson,'' they would give the individual's address as their own previous place of residence. Provided the other Frank (or Evelyn) Jameson checked out OK and had a sound credit record, the real Frank (or Evelyn) Jameson would be approved for the loans and credit cards. Armed with their new-found wealth, they would abscond from their recently acquired property and move on to the next one, then repeat the process and leave behind yet more unpaid rent arrears and utility bills. Finally, the case was cracked.

Almost two years passed before the full investigation was completed. It had proven very difficult for the police to piece together the numerous loans, credit cards, and mortgages the Jamesons had acquired over the years. In all, over $3.5 million of fraud was uncovered. But the suspicion remained that this was merely the tip of an iceberg that would never be fully exposed. Evelyn admitted to the majority of guilt; she revealed that it had been her idea and she had pressured her husband, Frank, to go along with it. Evelyn was imprisoned for two and a half years, and Frank received a suspended prison sentence. The other individuals in collusion with the Jamesons played minor roles in a number of connected frauds. Eventually, the charges against them were dropped.

Lessons Learned

Carol and I learned quite a bit from our investigation. Most importantly, without interagency cooperation, this job would never have come to such a successful conclusion. Each team involved in the case worked independently, but only when the full body of segregated evidence was integrated did the full picture materialize. When we first uncovered Evelyn's reference letter, we had no idea what significance it would bear. Without it, we would not have comprehended the accounting software's relevance, and Peter wouldn't have known the significance of the printed wage slip he recovered or the various records of bank loans and credit cards. It was the identity theft, the final piece of the puzzle, which tied the loose ends together.

This case demonstrated the ease with which a fraud can be committed. Armed with only a standard home PC, an Internet connection, and some readily available accounting software, the Jamesons were able to defraud banks, credit card companies, estate agents, and car dealerships out of a lot of money.

Recommendations to Prevent Future Occurrences

Identity theft has been a hot topic for a number of years now. This case occurred before the popularity of personal networking sites such as Bebo, MySpace, and Facebook, and before the explosion in job search sites where people freely upload their résumés. These Web sites are rich reservoirs of information for would-be fraudsters. Evelyn Jameson had to rely on less obvious sources of information, such as Web sites like 192.com, which can be used to locate information about people. Still, she could find what she needed to perpetrate her fraud. The risks are even greater today, as the Internet is saturated with personal information.

Be Aware of the Risks

Three key pieces of information required to apply for a bank loan online are name, address, and date of birth, all of which were readily available to Evelyn Jameson on the Internet. This data is even easier to find today for would-be fraudsters. In a matter of minutes, perpetrators can go online and find what they need to falsely apply for a bank loan or a credit card.

Protect Your Information

While it can be argued that the Web sites that require information have a duty to protect users' privacy, we are all responsible for protecting ourselves. Indeed, many of the social networking sites do have privacy settings whereby users can restrict what is publicly available. However, there is no guarantee you will be safeguarded. A better practice would be to not place sensitive personal information, such as full name and date of birth, on these sites.

Similarly, we should all be conscious of the information we include on résumés that we post on job search Web sites. Does a would-be employer really need to know your full date of birth and address in the early stages of the recruitment process? The answer is probably not, so why not omit that information from résumés posted online?

Alert the Authorities

Should you learn that your information is being used to perpetrate fraud, contact the proper authorities immediately and take the necessary steps to prevent further damage.

About the Author

Mike Andrews has been a computer forensic investigator for the past seven years and spent the earlier part of his career in the IT industry. Having previously worked in law enforcement and for an international risk consulting firm, he now runs his own independent computer forensic consultancy in the United Kingdom.

12

Imaginary Satellites

GEORGE KYRIAKODIS

In Benjamin Franklin's letter to Jean-Baptiste Leroy in 1789, Franklin wrote, "Our new Constitution is now established, and has an appearance that promises permanency; but in this world nothing can be said to be certain, except death and taxes." That is, unless you're a fraudster with a desktop publishing program and a quality printer.

Seve Stein was an avid golfer. He enjoyed flaunting his expensive country club memberships and boasting of the courses on which he had teed off around the world. But such extravagance wasn't uncommon for someone in his position. He owned and operated a successful employee-leasing company, Seve Stein Inc. It had multiple Fortune 500 clients for whom it provided talented engineers and other technical professionals for interim projects and other endeavors that did not require a full-time employee. Seve Stein Inc. had done quite well for a small business.

Once a year, Seve made his annual delivery of tax returns to our office, during which time he'd make small talk, usually to brag about the success of his company, before thanking us for taking his money. Occasionally, he informed us of significant accounting problems, like the purported embezzlement that took place when his controller was found to have stolen several thousand dollars. At the time, the remarks seemed like professional gestures to keep me informed of cash flow issues and possible legal proceedings to encourage transparency.

Having founded the business in 1985, Seve experienced significant growth just before and during the "tech bubble." When that bubble burst and the industry slowed, many companies collapsed and a lot of jobs were lost. Seve Stein Inc. felt the impact, but they weathered the storm and avoided insolvency. In fact, the downturn may have helped the corporation solidify its status as a premier engineering outsourcing agency for those struggling companies that could no longer afford fulltime staff. And now they had even fewer competitors. However, a lean approach to expenses was the call to order as the tech slump reduced Seve's margins and put a dent in free cash flow.

Suspect Satellites

Lower Weston Township is a Pennsylvania municipality with an annual budget of approximately $16 million. Revenues are comprised of wage taxes, real estate taxes, and business taxes, as well as certain fee-based services and grant money. With over $4.5 million in business tax collections, my department is a significant source of income for the township—and a headache for local business owners who don't understand why a gross receipts levy at the local level costs them more money than their combined federal and state dues on net income. But the business taxes imposed by the township are a necessary evil because they evenly distribute the tax load among residents, employees, and companies in the community.

As a true gross receipts tax, the more a company earns in revenue, the more tax is due regardless of any accompanying expenses or the ultimate profitability of the enterprise. For startup firms and those companies with razor-thin margins, the business tax on gross receipts can be a hardship if they fail to exercise due diligence and learn about the levies prior to moving into the township. Companies that base their locations on rental charges rather than the entire cost of doing business in a specific municipality, inclusive of tax consequences, are sometimes caught off guard by the imposition of the gross receipts tax and have a difficult decision to make. They either can pay or move to a location where the overall cost of conducting business is less expensive.

Seve may have based his original decision to move into Lower Weston Township solely on the cost of his rent. The office space was the perfect size for his administrative staff. Located close to the train station, it allowed smooth travel to downtown Philadelphia and offered quick access to the Pennsylvania Turnpike for commutes. It was convenient for both employees and Seve. Plus, the rent was free! Seve had purchased the building years before as an investment. With 7,200 square feet of prime office space, the use of only 2,000 square feet for his business still left him with ample room for tenants who helped defray the cost of the mortgage.

When Seve filed his first tax return, he learned that convenience has its price. In this case, it was an annual business tax exposure on his $1.8 million gross receipts in the amount of $6,300. As sole shareholder of the corporation, he would see his disposable income directly affected by this unanticipated expense. An additional $6,300 per year could pay for another country club membership or several golf trips. So Seve decided to move several miles away to a municipality that didn't have gross receipts taxes and relied instead on its real estate taxes to fund operations. While the savings on the business taxes were real, rent expenses were higher and the conveniences were gone.

Three years later, Seve relocated his business back to Lower Weston Township, a surprising move considering his business had grown from $1.8 million to $3.6 million in gross receipts. But I knew that the 2,000-square-foot space he had previously occupied remained vacant after he moved out of the Township and had not generated any income for his property investment. So it made sense for him to return, even with the additional fees. However, his taxes were not as high as I had expected. Although the volume of his receipts had increased significantly, his taxable volume had actually decreased. Seve said he had opened up satellite offices that were accountable for over $3 million in volume. The allocation of gross receipts to these satellites significantly reduced his business tax exposure in Lower Weston Township, which helped justify his decision to move back into his former office space. It seemed reasonable.

Seve happily dropped by my office to give me his annual return and make full payment of the business taxes due. He made it a point to explain the specific exclusions he was seeking with the allocation of gross volume to his satellite offices; he described in detail how these were completely accountable for their volume. For years, our exchange was the same, almost as if by rote memorization. It was déjà vu each time, except for his description of the repeated accounting turnovers within his administrative office. His first controller had allegedly embezzled from him. Since moving back into the township, he had been through three other controllers in a three-year time frame. Each of the previous controllers had left his or her position under a specter of improprieties ranging from embezzlement to incompetence. Luckily, he told me, his current controller was sharp as a tack, personable, and truly appreciated her job. Maura Alory was a perfect match for Seve's business, and I would later see why.

In his last visit to my office to make his annual delivery, Seve was as cordial as ever. He offered the usual spiel, but added a quick comment regarding the Easton office, one of the satellites to which he was continuously allocating significant receipts, saying, ''Greg Sandich's Easton office is really growing like gangbusters.'' I guess he felt compelled to justify the exponential escalation of his allocation of receipts to these offices. But Seve misspoke. He referenced an employee who I knew was situated in the Lower

Weston office, not the one in Easton. Since I also review the wage-withholding tax returns that his corporation filed, I was already aware of the seven administrative staffers that were in our township, and Greg was one of them. I collected Seve's payment and bid him good day until next year. Little did he know, I was beginning my investigation into whether these satellite offices actually existed.

Hit with an Audit

At the time, my investigation tools were somewhat limited. Since this was a tax case first and foremost, confidentiality issues constrained my investigation and prevented me from divulging critical details of the case to parties not in privy. At the same time, there was a limit to the detailed tax information I could gather from other official federal, state, and municipal sources regarding these alleged satellites. My most important lead was Seve's own tax filings and backup documentation. Several phone numbers appeared, identifying offices in Lower Weston, Easton, and Phoenix, while the only address listed on the letterhead was for his Lower Weston office. I proceeded to call all of the phone numbers and asked for Seve by name, identifying myself as a township employee with some basic questions about the business. I hit the jackpot.

Seve's staff was most helpful on the phone. When Seve was available and I was transferred to him, I always had an excuse for calling: I found a mathematical error on his recent filing, or maybe a withholding tax was coming due and my call was a friendly reminder to make sure he didn't miss the due date. I could do this almost indefinitely without raising any suspicions. But there was no need to continue. On the occasions I called the Easton and Phoenix phone numbers, I was automatically transferred to the Lower Weston office. The receptionist confirmed my suspicions; there were no satellite offices. Seve Stein Inc. was bumped to the top of the audit list.

Several months passed before I was able to issue the formal audit notification. A few weeks after the notice was mailed, Seve called. He was not as cordial as he had been in my prior dealings with him.

"Why do you want to audit me? You don't need to audit me!" Seve exclaimed over the phone. "When I dropped off my tax returns and you looked them over, you never had a question—nothing's changed."

Seve proclaimed that he could not meet the stipulated deadlines and needed to postpone the audit. While it is common for audit dates to be pushed back for short periods of time, it's quite another for the postponement to last two months. Maybe Seve thought that if he laid low for a while, this whole ordeal would just blow over. No chance of that. Perhaps he needed some time to gather the documents, since my audit notice required copies of all in-force leases during the audit period, municipal returns from the satellite office locations, and canceled checks as proof of payment of the rent and taxes. Or maybe he needed time to fabricate them. I would soon find out that it was the latter.

Think Before You Fabricate

Eventually, I made my way to the Lower Weston office to conduct the audit. I met Maura for the first time and she was a big help in the general review of the company's financial statements and payroll. She led me to an ample office space where I could comfortably set up. All the pertinent records were in filing cabinets and other appropriate binders, and Maura assisted me in tracking down the necessary information. I reviewed the internal controls in place on their system for invoicing clients and found that they were adequate and that they accounted for all gross receipts. Maura was very accommodating until I began asking questions regarding the satellite offices.

"Maura, where are the rent expenses for the satellite offices shown?"

"You're going to have to ask Seve about that," she replied.

I asked about the leases and the municipal returns that may have been filed for gross receipts taxes or withholding taxes, and she responded again that Seve would need to answer those questions. Maura was smart not to get involved with Seve's illicit activity, although she might have known about it. She never blew the whistle and called into question her boss's motives, which is why she remained gainfully employed, unlike her predecessors.

It was now time to meet with the man himself. Maura escorted me into Seve's office and left the room, closing the door behind her. The place was cluttered with paperwork and golf memorabilia, including a scorecard hanging behind his desk with what I guessed was his lifetime low score or a hole in one. Hanging on the walls were desert scenes from various golf courses, as well as a picture of Seve and several friends. I looked at his photo and asked him if he liked desert courses more than the traditional wooded ones nearby.

"I love the desert because it gives me a break from work. When I'm at the country club, I still feel like I have to put out fires at the office. When I'm in Arizona, I'm so far away that I can truly take a break," he replied.

I thought this interesting, considering that one of his satellite companies was supposedly in Phoenix. But I proceeded with my line of questioning as if I had no suspicions. "Maura said you had the documentation regarding the satellite offices. May I see the lease for the Easton office?"

Seve opened a nondescript box sitting on a chair and rifled through its contents. After he handed me the lease, I reviewed it to gather some basic information. I wrote down the address of the office, the duration of the lease, and the square footage of the property being rented. The most important fact, the name of the lessor, immediately raised red flags. It was Greg Sandich! I continued with my questioning and asked to see rent payments made to Greg. Seve went back to the nondescript box and produced a series of photocopied checks. The stub portion included the term "rent," but there were no indications that the checks were used for any other purpose. The variation in the amount of each check was dismissed as being other variable costs in running the satellite office, costs that had been included as a reimbursement.

When I asked him to provide the reimbursement requests that Greg would have submitted, so I could isolate the rental amounts, he said he didn't have them. Surely, even if the older records were purged to save space, Seve's accounts payable history for a recent check drawn to Greg would have provided the evidence needed to support his claim that some portion of the check was used to pay rent in Easton. I came to realize that Seve had fabricated a certain amount of supporting documentation ahead of time, but not enough to anticipate my inquiries.

I knew at this point that I would need to expand my interview to include Greg. I asked Seve if I could speak with him regarding the expense reimbursements and was told that he wasn't at this office. "He's at the Easton office," Seve snarled. "That's Greg's office. But I'm not sure he's in today."

I pointed out to Seve that I had heard Greg's name called several times over the office intercom to answer his phone, had even heard Seve speaking with him while I was in Maura's office. Seve turned white as a ghost.

He quickly returned to the nondescript box and provided Easton's letterhead as further evidence, as if to say that Greg's input wasn't necessary and we should move forward. While Seve watched, I called the phone number listed on the letterhead, expecting to be bounced directly to the receptionist down the hall from me. Instead, I heard an official phone company recording stating that the line was being checked for trouble. "You know, your Easton office phone is having some trouble. I think it's been disconnected."

Seve responded with a somewhat muted "Oh." Someone who had a legitimate company in Easton would have asked an assistant to immediately get the phone company on the horn to find out what the trouble was. But Seve didn't even flinch.

The letterhead proved to be more useful than just providing me with the fake office phone number. It was good quality, 25%-cotton Strathmore bond, similar to his Lower Weston office's prestigious letterhead. I asked if this was what would be used by Greg and his staff, to which he responded in the affirmative. I asked to see something else, such as a quote or an invoice that used the Easton letterhead. It wasn't in the nondescript box, which means Seve hadn't thought far enough ahead to fabricate it. "You had indicated in a prior tax return that the sales responsibility for General Amalgamated Dynamics International rested with the Easton office," I remarked. "But does any documentation exist to verify this relationship?"

"No," Seve responded.

The letterhead I was holding was obviously printed on a laser printer. It still had the pinch-roller mark on top and a hazy residual toner image along the entire right margin. I was able to match it with other original documents Seve had previously provided and concluded that this letterhead was printed specifically for me using regular office blank stock. When I asked outright if he had printed this letterhead purposely for me, he quickly denied it.

I attempted to defuse the interview by looking at a different satellite office. Seve regained his color, at least for the moment. The lease for the Aston office was in the name of an entirely different party, Metro Tech Staffers Inc. Seve's business was not mentioned either as a lessee or a sublessee. But before I could ask the obvious question as to why this lease had any relevance, Seve provided a stock purchase agreement for this Aston business and said the lease was never updated. "There aren't any lease payments for this office, since it's part of the stock purchase agreement," he added.

I then asked Seve for Maura's assistance. I wanted her to show me where the financial statements listed this new asset—that is, the affiliate entity being purchased—and to show me the payments made to Metro's shareholders.

Before I could finish my statement, he answered that Metro's sole shareholder was being paid out as an employee. He turned white again. I think he immediately knew what my next question was going to be. "What's the name of the employee and how can I get in touch with him?" I asked. He wouldn't answer.

Another Trick Up the Sleeve

I'll never forget the parting words we exchanged at the conclusion of the audit. As I walked to my vehicle, a stripped-down police cruiser, he walked alongside and asked me what to expect. For a split second my mind wandered and I had a vision of Seve sitting in the back of my car wearing knickers, a tam-o-shanter cap, and handcuffs. I explained that I would complete a report and provide an assessment that would need to be paid within 30 days. Seve's final words to me before entering the car were "Please be gentle."

Though not an admission I could use in court, it also wasn't an outright denial and made me feel as though, at least to Seve, I had established a solid case against him. I replied, "I can only do what the law allows and requires me to do." With that, I went on my way, and Seve went back inside his office.

While I was in the compilation phase of my investigation, I was lucky enough to have my colleague, Helen, travel through Easton on her way back from visiting family up north. She offered to swing by Seve's Easton office and see what was really happening there and maybe take pictures and talk with the staff. As it turned out, the "office" was nothing more than a single-family dwelling with no commercial indicators on the exterior. Further research would show that it wasn't Greg's house but that of his mother, who had lived there for over 60 years. I went through the appropriate channels to my counterparts in Easton and determined that the property in question had never been zoned for commercial use, nor had Seve secured the required licenses to operate within the City of Easton.

I completed my assessment and reported the findings to Seve, much to his dismay, well within the 30 days that I was allowed. The result: a balance due of $119,018.96 that was owed to the township because of Seve's fraudulent claim of nonexistent satellite offices. But collecting on this assessment would prove difficult, even with the clear indications of the fraudulent filings. It seemed that Seve, while postponing the audit for two months, had also taken steps to form an alter ego company, Can't Catch Me LLC. When the township sued Seve Stein Inc. for the unpaid money, Can't Catch Me immediately went into operation with the same staff, line of business, and headquarters location as the old company.

With litigation now approaching the fifth year since the fraud was discovered, no defenses have been raised regarding Seve's fraudulent reporting to the township. Instead, the focus of the defense's case has been the insolvency of the original entity. Seve has since sold his property and moved his business to a locality that doesn't have business taxes but does have much higher real estate tax exposure, which is more difficult to elude. As for me, I fully expect my next investigation will be against Can't Catch Me to determine whether we have enough evidence to pursue this entity's assets in satisfaction of the predecessor company's liability, which continues to increase as interest accrues. At present, Seve's liability is over $179,000.

Lessons Learned

I learned through this case that some of the most successful frauds are the simplest. It was clear that he fabricated the Easton lease and the stock purchase agreement for the Aston office on his computer, using nothing more than a word processing program. The letterhead was a simple cut-and-paste job printed on the company printer. Not only did Seve use the computer at the start of his scheme, to file the fraudulent returns and generate false statements regarding the allocation, he also tried using it to fabricate the documentation needed to keep his scheme going. Since business taxes are self-assessed, as are most taxes, it's easy for someone to present false figures. Questioning taxpayers and requiring third-party verification of key exemptions have greatly reduced the amount of fictitious exclusions being claimed by taxpayers. For those who continue to make unsupported claims, auditing is the only route the township has to protect its interests and build the case necessary to recover the correct tax due.

Recommendations to Prevent Future Occurrences

Computer Forensics

It's important to maintain an adequate arsenal of computer forensic tools. At the time of Seve's interview, the township did not have the imaging software, data analysis tools, or quick access to experts in the field of document analysis such as the Montgomery County Detectives Economic Crimes Unit, which slowed the investigation.

Follow Your Instincts

After Seve accidentally revealed that an employee who worked in the central location was supposedly operating an office elsewhere, I followed my instincts and pursued the audit. It's crucial to stay alert and follow your suspicions. Lay the burden of proof on dubious claims; an honest person will be cheerfully transparent.

About the Author

George J. Kyriakodis, CFE, MS, MBA, has been employed as a business tax officer and auditor for a southeastern Pennsylvania municipality for over 19 years. He also served as the municipality's management-information systems director for several years, combining his talents for forensic accounting and his love of technology.

Never Pass Your Password

JAMES MARTIN AND HARRY CENDROWSKI

The phone rang. John Balczak answered, "Help desk, this is John."

"Oh, hi John. It's Carol in the lab. I'm trying to print a report but it's not working. I'm really under the gun—I have to get this out right away."

"Great," John thought, "another stupid problem from a person likely making three times my salary. She probably couldn't even fix the simple things that most college freshmen could handle without breaking a sweat." But Carol was a nice person, and it was, after all, his job to help her. "OK Carol, I'll stop by and take a look."

John had worked in the information technology department of Mistretta Labs eight and a half years as a help desk technician. He was responsible for supporting computer users throughout the organization. That included handling application support, hardware issues, and security and log-in problems. Over the past few years, he also spent quite a bit of his time supporting users with their personal digital assistants (PDAs). Everyone seemed to be getting one, and they all experienced problems synching and transferring data. John still was just a technician, although he thought he was going to be promoted to a supervisor of tech support on several occasions. But that never happened. He believed that the current company management was inept, and that passing him over for promotion was just one more demonstration of that incompetence. When he was overlooked the last time, he wrote the CEO a scathing letter that clearly explained the shortcomings of company management, along with several examples of issues facing the organization's IT controls. Of course, they did not even take the time to respond to his suggestions, but sooner or later they would realize he was right.

John grabbed a pad and pen and prepared to go help Carol with her printer problem, when the phone rang again; the caller ID read "Janice Watson." Janice was the director of human resources, and John had helped her with computer issues on several occasions. "What could she be calling for at 4:50 on a Friday afternoon?" John wondered aloud as he reached for the phone.

"The company has to make cutbacks, John," said Janice. "I'm sorry, but you have to go."

■ ■ ■

Mistretta Testing Labs Inc. was started in 1924 by Antonio Mistretta, an immigrant originally from Rome. He was a chemist and scientist and started the company to study new food-preservation techniques. While the industry was difficult during the Depression, the fledgling business received several wartime contracts to develop preserved rations for ground troops. During World War II, Mistretta Labs experienced a period of rapid growth.

In the late 1940s, Antonio's son Matthew identified several new business opportunities, including using the labs to validate marketing and advertising claims. By this time radio had become an established commercial medium, and consumer demand pushed the development of new and innovative products, each with a unique claim regarding quality, longevity, or other specific benefits. Antonio realized that a scientific basis to support such claims would help make an advertising campaign more successful. "It is beneficial to say that this new chewing gum is less harmful to the teeth," Antonio stated in 1950, "but wouldn't it be better to gather a panel of dentists, perhaps five or six, and have them state a claim of improved dental health? Perhaps this could lead to an outright recommendation for this new product."

By 1965 the product-testing division had grown to become the largest division of Mistretta Labs, providing scientific studies for food, drugs, consumer products, and durable goods.

In 1986, Matthew's son Mike joined the company and left his own mark on the organization. Mike was fascinated by advances in computer technology and especially by the new personal computers that provided increased productivity and lab capability. He developed several virtual testing methods that were patented and allowed the company to continue to provide innovative service to their customers. By the early 2000s, Mistretta Labs, under the leadership of Mike, was a highly technical company with dedicated internal data centers serving the labs and a full information technology (IT) staff. Of course, given the sensitive nature of information handled, robust security protocols were implemented, including semiannual testing of security procedures, an annual review of authorized user IDs by each data owner, and an annual audit. The combination of tremendous laboratory-experiment capability and cutting-edge technology made Mistretta Labs a leader in the industry and helped establish their reputation as an innovative and reliable firm.

Information Leak

"Mike, its Justin Sand," stated the voice at the other end of the phone.

Justin was president of SandMan Products, industry leaders in sports drinks and a new entrant into the promising market of low-carbohydrate alcoholic beverages. SandMan was a major client of Mistretta, and Mike and Justin were friends. In fact Mike was personally overseeing the testing of SandMan's new product.

Justin's voice sounded stressed and gritty: "I have just been handed a printout of a Web site and also a printout of a blog. Both contain verbatim e-mails between your lab director and one of our product development specialists. They also include a number of e-mails that appear internal to your company. Worst of all, the e-mails are dated within the past week. They relate to our new products that you're testing—stuff that hasn't even been announced yet. I can't tell you how harmful this is to our future products and to our relationship. I can't believe your company is so careless. I need you to explain to me how this happened—and how much of this stuff is out there."

Mike asked Justin for the addresses of the Web sites containing the suspected information and hung up the phone. He knew it was unlikely that someone had broken into their e-mail system, but the fact that Justin mentioned the internal e-mails concerned him. Mike immediately called his IT director, Dick Morgan. He also called me.

Acting Fast

I first met Mike Mistretta several months prior to this call. At the time he had received a complaint from an employee making allegations of problems with key internal-control procedures. Given the important role of control procedures at Mistretta Labs, Mike was adamant that the claims be immediately vetted to determine what, if any, changes should be made. He wanted the work done by an outside firm to ensure that the results were objective; he believed in his people, but he also wanted to independently verify the outcome. Based on my interactions with Mike, I knew he was a stickler for details and truly committed to appropriate conduct. From the tone of his voice on the phone, I could tell he was worried. I agreed to meet him in his office, packed my briefcase, and started out on the crosstown trip.

"Jim, glad you could make it on such short notice. Thanks for clearing your schedule," Mike said as I entered his spacious yet understated office.

"I think you remember Dick Morgan, our IT director, from your earlier assignment."

Mike was friendly and professional as usual, but there was an underlying air of tension in the room. "Frankly, we just don't understand how this happened," he said. "As you know, our security controls are evaluated every year as part of our financial reporting process, including our password change procedures. Also, on a semiannual basis every data owner has to review the user accounts with access to that data and approve their continued use. Our e-mail system is set such that the user must change their password every 60 days and the password has to contain at least eight characters, with both letters and digits. This sort of thing isn't supposed to happen. Thankfully, Dick's team has found some interesting leads already."

Dick Morgan was seasoned and thorough, "We called up the Web sites that Mr. Sand sent over. Here are printouts of the content," Dick said, handing them to me. "Interestingly, you will note, all the e-mails are either to or from Jay Birdsong, our marketing director. Unfortunately, a number of the correspondence is with privileged contacts, so they contain sensitive information. Jay is on his way from the airport, and should be here in about 30 minutes. Also, we looked up the Whois record for the Web sites. As you probably know, Whois is an Internet database listing the registered owner for a domain name. Most significantly, one of the Web sites is registered to a former employee."

"You might remember the name John Balczak," Mike interjected. "He was one of the technicians in IT support. Good worker, bright, but he was always sending letters and correspondence about how things should be improved, that we didn't know how vulnerable our systems really were. We had to lay him off due to staff cutbacks about 45 days ago, which is just about two weeks before the date of the earliest e-mails posted on these Web sites. I sure didn't think he would do something like this though."

I thought for a minute about the severity of the situation and how to best prevent additional damage. Clearly, the organization needed to cut off further access to confidential information, to quickly remove any of it that had already been posted on the Internet, and to determine, if possible, who had obtained and posted the information. Sure, it initially looked like the perpetrator might be John Balczak, but there was a lot of work to do to prove it. Also, Mike would eventually need to explain to his client how this happened and the steps taken to prevent this situation in the future.

"First, I recommend you expire every password in your e-mail system— ask each user to change their password," I began. "Second, we will need to speak to Mr. Birdsong. It might be that his e-mail account was hacked. On the other hand, he could be involved. Also, check the e-mail server access log for the records to Mr. Birdsong's account—note the IP address of the access point and see if you can determine if it was reached from inside or outside the building. And lastly, Mike, I recommend we call the FBI. They have a cybercrime unit and they take this sort of thing very seriously."

Dick left to begin his research and Mike called Birdsong's assistant to request that he stop by when he arrived. We called the local FBI field office and asked for the assistant special agent in charge (ASAC), whom I had worked with on several panel discussions for the local Association of Certified Fraud Examiners chapter.

Mike explained the situation and the potential for loss to his company: lost revenues, lost business opportunities, and most importantly the loss of jobs if their major customer discontinued the business relationship. If Sand pulled their account, the company would likely need to close the lab and administrative office in town, which would result in the loss of several thousand jobs.

The ASAC reiterated that the FBI takes such cybercrimes very seriously and, in fact, had a dedicated cybercrime unit to work on cases exactly like this. He said that the Web site registration linked to the former employee might be good enough to obtain a search warrant for his house, but it would be helpful if we could establish a positive link verifying that the former employee had actually accessed the information. I explained the current steps of the investigation and agreed to provide an update when we learned more.

Birdsong hadn't arrived yet and Mike needed to give an update to Justin Sand, so I went downstairs to check on the progress in IT. Dick was quite excited when I arrived.

"Hey, look at these log records," he said. "I used a database to extract records that show when Birdsong's account was accessed. The e-mail system logs the IP address of each access request. We can see from the first segments of the IP address—the network ID—where the communications are originating. First, look at the network ID of these access requests. That's the local network; they're here in the building. That's probably Birdsong in his office checking his mail. Then there are many with a second network ID—I looked that up and it's assigned to the wireless phone company. It's probably Birdsong checking his mail on his PDA. Then there's this other group with a third network ID. That's assigned to the cable company and is probably a high-speed home connection. Look at the time stamp; it's all during odd hours of the night. This one is at three in the morning! I called Birdsong on his cell phone and asked him about his home connection. He still uses dial-up and doesn't have a high-speed connection. I looked up the IP address for the cable connection, and it covers the area where John Balczak lives. Doesn't really prove anything, but it's in line with our theory."

I complimented Dick on his work and took notes to update the FBI. The records available to the general public do not identify the specific house, only the general area of coverage. But maybe that was enough to help them in their investigation. I headed back upstairs to Mike's office.

"Well, I spoke to Birdsong," Mike explained, seeming rather annoyed. "He said he remembers John Balczak, that he was the tech support analyst assigned to the marketing department a couple of years ago. He said he hasn't spoken to John since he left. He did admit, after I pressed him, that he had given John the password to his e-mail account, he thinks about 18 months ago or so, because they were testing his new PDA. And, yes, he admitted that when he has to change his password, he uses the same root word with an incremental number at the end."

"So all John would need to do," I chimed in, "is guess how many times Birdsong has needed to change his password in the last 18 months and change that password incremetally." It appeared that Birdsong was likely not an accomplice—at least not a willing participant. "I'll call the FBI and give them an update; you might do the same with Sand," I said.

The ASAC noted that the information regarding the IP addresses and the suspect's access to the password information was helpful, and that the FBI would likely be able to pull a warrant to search his home the following day. In the meantime, the FBI cybercrime unit contacted the Internet companies hosting the Web sites and asked that the materials be removed from the sites and from search engine caches.

Justin Sand told Mike that he was impressed and grateful that we had moved so quickly to remove the information, and that within several hours of the initial discovery the FBI cybercrime unit was investigating the case. He was still concerned, but he voiced relief that the breach seemed to be an isolated incident and not the sign of an outright technical failure.

Mike and I agreed that we would regroup the following day to discuss the status of our investigation as well as the FBI actions. In the meantime, Mike asked IT to continue to analyze the access logs for any suspicious activity, either by IP address or by access time.

A Bitter End

The next day, the FBI served a search warrant on the Balczaks' residence. The ASAC noted that John was calm and cooperative with the investigators. It appeared that he had not been working; it was midday during the week and he was unshaven and his clothing wrinkled. He showed the investigators his home computer, which was subsequently taken into custody by the FBI. He also provided several CD-ROMs that he stated contained information downloaded from the company servers during his employment. John then provided the passwords to access the Web sites and he agreed to remove any remaining confidential information.

When questioned by the FBI, John admitted that he had accessed the Mistretta Labs e-mail system after he left his employment. He stated he was bitter at his discharge and wanted to "get even" with the company. He reviewed the content on Birdsong's account, including the inbox, sent items, calendar items, and notepad items, and specifically looked for information that was controversial or confidential. John corroborated that he had been given Birdsong's password several months previously, and that he realized Birdsong simply changed the password's numerical suffix by a set increment whenever a new password was required by the system. John said that Birdsong did not know he still had the password and he hoped that his actions would not get his former coworker in trouble.

Acting Alone

Based on the evidence gathered, prosecutors noted that John would likely be charged criminally under the federal Computer Fraud and Abuse Act (CFAA). The CFAA has various provisions that apply in cases involving computer crime: for example, when someone "knowingly causes the transmission of a program, information, code, or command, and as a result of such conduct, intentionally causes damage without authorization to a protected computer." This provision would apply if an employee used a disk scrubber program to remove information from a computer without authorization. More to the point in this particular case, the act also covers when someone "intentionally accesses a protected computer without authorization and as a result of such conduct, causes damage." The CFAA charges are important as the prosecution is under federal jurisdiction and accordingly such trial would occur in federal court.

By the end of the second day following the discovery of the confidential information, all of it had been successfully removed from the Internet, the perpetrator identified, and the confidential information recovered from the possession of the perpetrator.

To ensure that John had acted alone, Mike Mistretta asked that all the employees within IT and the marketing department be interviewed to determine if they had been contacted by John, and if so, when. Also, during the interviews, employees were asked if they understood the company's security policies and procedures and if they had any ideas regarding how to improve the systems. The interviews did not lead us to believe that anyone else had been involved with the security breach. Mike was satisfied that the incident was isolated, that it was the result of an error on the part of one employee that was then exploited by another.

Lessons Learned

The first and most important lesson learned from this case is the importance of the human element in any security or control system. Mistretta Labs had implemented robust security devices and performed regular reviews of the functioning of those controls. And the controls were in place and functioning when the incident occurred; management fully expected that such a system compromise wasn't possible. The weak link in the system, the one that eventually failed and allowed the incident to occur, was a simple human control: A user did not keep his password confidential, and he chose password alterations that were easy to guess. In any system, the actions and behaviors of people will always be a wild card—you don't know how they are going to act. Internal control procedures and cultural expectations help create a guideline, but at the end of the day some may stray from the expected norm, either intentionally or because of a lack of attentiveness.

The case also highlights the importance of a strong control environment, including a culture of security awareness. The role of the control environment in every organization is to provide consistent reinforcement of the expectations of appropriate behaviors. The culture of the organization is part of the control environment; when it comes to security, the culture should remind employees of their continuous responsibility to safeguard confidential information. Over time, there is a natural tendency toward complacency with job duties and responsibilities, and employees can lose sight of important control objectives. People need to be reminded that the confidential information they deal with on a daily basis needs to be protected. Also, they need to be aware of why procedures are in place and why they are important to the success of the organization.

User passwords are an inherent weakness in organizations due to the sheer number of passwords that users need to maintain. In some organizations, a user may have four or five different passwords for different systems or resources. Procedures to change the passwords over a set interval add to the complexity. To try to remember them, users may use a common root with an incrementally changing suffix; worse yet, maybe they write down their new passwords on a list. Another threat happens when users store their system passwords in a PDA; if the PDA is ever lost or stolen, another person could gain access to the passwords.

The uncertainty involved with human decision making is why monitoring procedures are so important. Monitoring must constantly evolve to check for emerging risks and threats that were not previously identified.

Recommendations to Prevent Future Occurrences

Awareness

The primary recommendation was for Mistretta to implement a cultural initiative reminding employees of the need to safeguard confidential information. This does not just relate to passwords and e-mail content, but also to printed material and other electronic content as well. There is tremendous opportunity for compromise of confidentiality in pages sent to a printer and not immediately retrieved, pages left in the copy machine, facsimile pages, and confidential information thrown in the trash or an unsecured recycle bin. Employees should be aware of confidential information displayed on their computer screens, especially when others are around, and always secure their workstations when they leave the area. All employees should understand the obligation to safeguard confidential materials and be aware of opportunities where that confidentiality could be breached.

Track Log Information

The organization should develop reports to highlight system log information that could indicate a threat. New threat identification software can automatically monitor log information and identify communication through or to suspicious locations. The risk environment of Internet communication is extremely volatile, with previously unknown exploits and threats emerging literally every day. The traditional methods of monitoring just won't cut it anymore.

Establish Relationships with Helpful Firms and Agencies

In the end, Mistretta Labs was lucky in the sense that they already had a relationship with an independent investigative firm that could quickly respond to an incident. Having such a relationship in place, and already approved and coordinated by outside counsel, means that vital time is not lost in the early hours and days of a crisis. In this case, we had contacted the FBI cybercrime unit within the first six hours of discovery and the perpetrator was apprehended the following day, which greatly affected the perceptions of Mistretta's client. If Mistretta had to initiate a new relationship at the onset of a problem, the response time would have been slowed by at least several days. As part of their crisis management plans, organizations should have a standing relationship with an independent investigation firm that is engaged through outside counsel.

About the Authors

James Martin, CFE, CMA, CIA, CFFA, has performed forensic examinations of numerous business arrangements to determine the accuracy of recorded transactions, including the health-care, durable-equipment, real estate, and construction industries. He is a coauthor of *The Handbook of Fraud Deterrence* and *Private Equity: History, Governance, and Operations*, published by John Wiley & and Sons, Inc.

Harry Cendrowski, CFE, CPA/ABV, CVA, CFFA, is the president and founding member of Cendrowski Corporate Advisors, and provides consulting relating to business valuations, mergers, due diligence, complex commercial litigation, forensic accounting, and fraud examinations. Harry is coauthor of *The Handbook of Fraud Deterrence* and *Private Equity: History, Governance, and Operations*, published by John Wiley & Sons, Inc.

Why Computers and Meth Don't Mix

STEPHEN R. MENGE

Jason Harner was a 32-year-old high school dropout living with friends in an area known for its high crime rates. He shacked up in a single-wide mobile home that served as the neighborhood drug hangout. His criminal background included a number of petty theft convictions and several arrests for narcotic violations, but after our run-in, counterfeiting and identity theft would be added to the list. It was later discovered that Jason had ties with two other individuals who helped take his commitment to crime to new levels.

Michael Neyholm was 33 years old and had recently moved to Florida. His girlfriend, Chrissy Kissler, was a Florida native. She was also 33 but the lines in her face showed the wear and tear of a hard life. At the time, both Michael and Chrissy were staying with his mother in a two-bedroom condominium in a retirement community. As their love affair with one another grew, so did their appetite for methamphetamine. Their addiction eventually led to their expulsion from his mom's residence, so the pair relocated to area motels. Both had previous arrest histories, mostly involving drug possession. These two would become the Bonnie and Clyde of counterfeit checks and stolen identities in our community.

Trailer Treasure

As a detective, I was assigned to the Polk County Sheriff's Office Fraud Unit and tasked to handle a broad variety of fraud-related cases. Fall had just begun, and over the summer my unit had been inundated with identity theft and check fraud complaints. Each week seemed to bring a new stack of reports fresh off the streets. Many of the cases were similar, mostly instances of counterfeit checks that had been written with fake identification. I was the only one in the office when we received our first major break. The call came from dispatch, "You're not going to believe this, but . . ." The deputies had raided a house where they found a subject in the act of making a counterfeit driver's license. I wrote down the address and charged out the door. Having just finished logging in five new fraud cases, I had a feeling that this was going to be a productive day.

I traveled to Jason's rundown single-wide mobile home and met with deputies Plumley and Bright. The trailer, complete with bedsheets for curtains, sat on a lot overgrown with weeds and littered with beer cans and other debris. At the rear of the property stood a dilapidated shed that consisted of a single broken door and two rooms separated by a flimsy wall. Deputy Plumley had been dispatched to this site in response to a disturbance in progress involving a male and female who were seen throwing objects at each other. As Deputy Plumley stepped into the shed, he found several people huddled around a computer. The monitor displayed an image of a Florida state driver's license in the making. Watching the suspect type in the last character on the keyboard, Plumley loudly cleared his throat. The counterfeiter turned around and dropped his jaw in shock. He was arrested immediately, before he had time to delete what he had entered. Later identified as Jason Harner, the suspect said: "I wasn't making a fake driver's license. I was only trying to help print what was on the screen."

All of the subjects in attendance were separated and detained until my arrival. Two of them, including Jason, were in possession of meth-amphetamine. This would prove to be a common denominator for most of the identity theft or fraud-related crimes we uncovered for the months to come.

After receiving a brief rundown of the situation from the deputies, I entered the shed to examine the crime scene. A monitor and keyboard sat perched on a small table next to a lime-green computer tower with a printer resting on top. The area was strewn with paper, more beer bottles, an assortment of mismatched, broken chairs, and an old couch. Displayed on the monitor was the layout of a Florida State driver's license that would include the name, number, and address copied from a stolen checkbook that lay next to the keyboard. In the printer tray I found clear plastic laminate with the same information printed on it. Additional clear plastic overlays of driver's license templates were found near the chair where Jason sat sulking with his head down. A purse next to Jason's chair contained an altered driver's license for Jennifer Bumler, who was one of the individuals standing beside the computer when Deputy Plumley entered. The ID had been switched so that her real name, number, and address were removed and the newly created overlay could be fitted over the face of it to change her identity. Jennifer could have then taken those stolen checks and used them nearly anywhere.

I collected a number of overlays with different names as well as the computer equipment as evidence. Statements made by Jason indicated that he had passed other checks with different identifications over the past month. He also provided the names of several associates whom he dealt with on a regular basis. After talking with Jason, I realized that there was no telling how many overlays had been created by just this one computer alone.

We obtained a search warrant to analyze the hard drive for further evidence. I took the computer to Glen Hayes, who conducts forensic examinations for the sheriff's office computer crimes section. Upon examination, Glen was able to identify numerous driver's license templates and their print dates. Receiving his report, I reviewed the information with my partners, detectives Reichert and Lyon. Sitting in our tiny office, we each took a stack of templates and began sifting through the mountain of cases dating back to the start of the summer. The rustling of paper was interrupted intermittently with "Here's one!" or, a few seconds later, "I got one!" Since the printed information was dated, it matched within a day or two of the cases involving counterfeit checks. And because Jason was willing to divulge the names of his closest associates, we now had suspects and leads.

One by one, we began to solve pending cases. Our bulletin board filled up with photos of those recently arrested for having passed fake identification and fraudulent checks. Our newly dubbed "Wall of Shame" grew so fast that we ran out of display space. Every day, the deputies working the street came into our office and asked, "Well, who do you want picked up today?" Each day, we armed them with warrants and the names of potential suspects. After several months of solving cases, it was clear that Jason had been a main supplier of the false IDs. Now he was incarcerated, but we knew it wouldn't be long before someone else filled his shoes. By December, two new faces had emerged to replace Jason as the identity theft king.

Meth and Motels

As the phone rang, my eyes squinted toward the alarm clock that displayed 4 a.m. Detective Lyon was calling. "You're not going to believe this," he began.

Rubbing my eyes and smiling, I told him to proceed with his news. Deputies had uncovered a thieves' den at one of the local motels just off the interstate. They had found a mountain of stolen IDs, drugs, and mail. Additionally, there were suspects willing to tell their side of the story. Upon arriving at the half-star motel, I met with Deputy Dunn who had two subjects under arrest for narcotics violations. The room contained an assortment of stolen mail and checks. I talked to Maggie Beutel, who was in handcuffs. "None of this is mine. It all belongs to Mike and Chrissy," she swore.

"Mike and Chrissy who?" I asked. "And where are they now?"

"Mike Neyholm and Chrissy Kissler. They're staying a couple of doors down. Room 203. None of this is mine!"

Both names had recently come up in discussions with other subjects arrested from the "Wall of Shame." Borrowing Deputy Dunn's laptop, I checked the driver's license of Michael Neyholm and compared his picture to the photocopy of the identification used by the person who checked into room 203. It was a match; however, the motel information showed another name: Bill Chapman. The ID was a fake but the subject was, in fact, the man we wanted. I went to his room and knocked. Michael answered, surprised to find several deputies at his door. He invited us in and said, "Excuse the mess."

The room looked as if a bomb had been set off. Clothing, tools, and garbage were everywhere. A computer was conspicuously set up in the middle of the room. Next to it, we found the familiar clear plastic laminate used to produce overlays. I interviewed Mike and told him I was interested in searching his room and that I would be looking for counterfeit materials or anything else illegal. He consented and indicated that not all of the contents were his—a familiar response by now. Mike said that a lot of the junk strewn about the room belonged to his girlfriend, Chrissy Kissler, but she was nowhere to be found. I later learned that she had argued with Mike and thrown a rock through his car window before leaving. My search revealed a large volume of mail, credit card information, counterfeiting materials, and meth. It was going to take time to sort through and identify all the new victims. Mike was soon taken to jail and booked on drug charges and possession of a counterfeit ID.

After just a few weeks in the slammer, we had to release him. The charges were not sufficient to keep him locked up, so once he made bond Mike was back on the streets. During that time, the evidence collected from the motel room began to yield new victims and new charges. Finally, I was able to issue several warrants on him and send my shift deputies out on the hunt again. The following morning I received a call around 10 a.m. from Sergeant Rauch. He informed me that his deputies had located Mike at the Publix parking lot in a stolen vehicle. Before I could hang up, Rauch said, "Oh, by the way, there's more." I smiled and headed out the door.

Upon arrival at the Publix parking lot, I met with Deputy Wright. He had Mike in the back of his car, both for the warrants I had obtained some days earlier and for additional charges of auto theft.

"Hi, Mike. Good to see you," I said with a wave. Mike scowled.

"What do you want me to do with this?" Deputy Wright asked, showing me an additional fake driver's license with a picture identification of Mike under the name of Ryan Payne. Along with the ID, Mike had a stack of checks under the same false name. I looked into the stolen vehicle and in the backseat I found a local shopping center bag with newly purchased items. The receipt had been printed 30 minutes prior. By this time, Sergeant Rauch had arrived and I requested that he send another deputy to the store and find the clerk who printed this receipt. I wanted to see if they had a "Ryan Payne" check in their register. Overhearing our conversation, Mike just shook his head. Approximately 10 minutes later, Deputy Wright pulled up with the clerk who had waited on "Ryan Payne." I turned to the young clerk and asked, "Can you tell me who made this purchase from you earlier today?"

"Sure, he's sitting in the back of that cop car."

He pointed to Mike. Almost instantly Sergeant Rauch started singing, "Oops, I did it again . . ." in his best Britney Spears voice. Through chuckles, I asked, "Mike, do you want to give a statement about all this?"

But he was not nearly as enthusiastic as Sergeant Rauch and offered no response. These new charges violated his pretrial release. Mike would be going away for awhile.

First Clyde, Then Bonnie

The mail recovered from the motel room occupied by Mike and Chrissy was identified by local homeowners. Most of the checks had been taken from their mailboxes and "washed" in an attempt to cash them. "Washing" is the process of removing the ink from the face of a check and rewriting it to whomever. Chrissy had taken one of the checks and created a fraudulent driver's license. Then she took the items to a local bank where she attempted to cash the check. Growing suspicious that the transaction was taking too long, Chrissy fled the bank and left the fake identification, check, and her fingerprints at the teller window. Her image was also captured on surveillance video. We issued a warrant for her arrest and it took only a few days for Chrissy to surface. The computer seized from the motel room was submitted for forensic examination to Glen Hayes in the sheriff's office computer crimes section. Searching the hard drive revealed images of known identifications that had been recovered, as well as others not yet discovered. New electronic evidence emerged in the form of computer-generated checks. Copies of these were collected and matched to similar ones that had recently popped up in local stores. During the three weeks that we sifted through the evidence and matched the new information with pending cases, Mike and Chrissy were still wandering the community.

It would not be long before I received an evening call from Deputy Eppel, who was patrolling a known drug area, and had found Chrissy. He placed her under arrest for the active warrant related to the information stemming from the motel room. And he made a new discovery. When I answered the phone, Eppel happily greeted me with "I got your girl, and I have something else you're not going to believe."

By this time I was a converted believer in the unbelievable, so I said, "Try me."

Eppel had found an outline for a counterfeit check in Chrissy's possession, but this wasn't earth-shattering news. "And?" I replied.

"I'll just surprise you when you arrive."

With that, I was out the door and on my way to the Sheriff's Office substation to interview Chrissy. When I arrived, Eppel handed me a clear evidence bag containing a single yellow sheet of paper. A closer inspection of the document revealed that it was a hand-drawn duplicate copy of a Polk County Sheriff's Office inmate account check.

"Unbelievable," I replied.

"I told you so," said Eppel with a grin.

That evening at the jail, Chrissy looked like a broken woman. Eyes watery from crying, she was in disbelief at the course of her life these past several months. I read Chrissy her Miranda warning, after which she consented to an interview. I placed a stack of folders containing her pending cases on the desk in front her. On top lay the clear plastic bag containing the fake Sheriff's Office check. Chrissy began to sob again, head dipped down, pressing her chin into her chest. She confessed to a number of cases that evening and admitted that she created the check outline. She was taking it to the counterfeiter when she was stopped by Eppel. She and Mike had intended on creating a number of counterfeit checks to clean out the inmate bank account belonging to the sheriff. But she'd had enough of this dishonest lifestyle and wanted out—out of the drugs and the lies. Chrissy blamed meth for ruining her life and spurring the fraudulent activities with her boyfriend. The fake Sheriff's Office checks were supposed to be their ticket to a better life. Cash enough checks, get enough money, and they would get out of the state altogether. I closed nine active cases that evening, along with an additional charge of counterfeiting a payment instrument, before contacting Judge Prince to obtain a bond of $100,000, hoping to ensure Chrissy's stay at the Polk County Jail.

Time to Face the Music

Jason Harner, as a pioneer in the fake identification market, ended up with five felonies and two misdemeanors. He knew that the forensic evidence recovered from the computer could, in fact, bury him in charges. Not wishing to drag those out, he pleaded straight up to all of them. He was adjudicated guilty and sentenced to 15 months in Florida State Prison. All subsequent information gathered from Jason's computer was tied to other fraud cases and people who used the fake identifications. Those individuals faced individual counts of forgery, utilizing forged instruments, and theft.

Over the following months, additional charges were filed against Mike and Chrissy. Mike had requested a bond reduction from the court. Coincidentally, new charges were filed the morning of his hearing. The sergeant received calls from Mike in jail, and when those went unanswered, Mike's mom began phoning him, begging for the charges to stop.

From the mountain of documents recovered from Mike and Chrissy's motel room, as well as what was found on them, the physical evidence was overwhelming. Additional evidence recovered from their hard drive tied many of the crimes together. The images stored on the computer had not been deleted or overwritten. Most of them were shown to have been used by either Mike or Chrissy, who were subsequently charged with passing counterfeit items. After all the paperwork was in, Michael Neyholm faced 59 felony charges and Chrissy Kissler racked up 62. Neither of the defendants took their cases to trial. A deal was struck between the defense attorneys and the prosecutor. In exchange for multiple charges, they consolidated the majority of identity theft and fraud charges and Michael entered a plea of guilty. Michael Neyholm pleaded guilty to all counts against him. He also pleaded guilty to the drug charges. All in all, Mike was sentenced to 51 months in Florida State Prison. Chrissy also pleaded guilty to all fraud charges and she received the same deal with her drug counts. She received 50 months in Florida State Prison.

Lessons Learned

These three individuals were an eye-opener for me and detectives Lyon and Reichert. Computers infinitely expand the potential for fraud. As part of our efforts to stay ahead, our unit attended training that taught techniques regarding how to properly collect and handle electronic evidence. That training further enforced my belief that crime will escalate to evolve with technology.

In light of the large number of counterfeit check cases we had worked, it seemed rather odd that the Sheriff's Office would issue checks to counterfeiters. In response, we met with the administration and requested they issue money orders to inmates in lieu of checks. By doing so, the office could avoid the compromise of any future account.

Recommendations to Prevent Future Occurrences

The Whole Picture

As an investigator on the lookout for people in possession of fraudulent materials, one should try to avoid tunnel vision. Investigate *any* potential source of information, specifically items such as portable storage devices or electronics. A personal computer or laptop might not be the only place to look for pertinent data; other portable storage devices such as CDs, memory cards, and thumbnail drives could yield new leads.

Preserve Evidence

Any collected items should be maintained and handled as potential evidence. Even information deleted from a hard drive may still be recovered if the images haven't been erased or overwritten.

Know the Law

The laws of the State of Florida require a search warrant for investigators examining the hard drive of a personal computer. Check your state's laws as they relate to data recovery and the forensic examination of these types of devices. The information gathered might not only strengthen your case, but it could expand it to other areas as well.

About the Author

Stephen R. Menge, CFE, has been a law enforcement officer for the past 17 years with the Polk County Sheriff's Office and the office of the state attorney. He has actively conducted fraud and economic crime investigations for the past 14 years. He holds a masters of business administration from Saint Leo University.

Fishing in Dangerous Waters

JOE DERVAES

Frank Johnson wanted out. He was tired of his desk job and the endless spreadsheets, and he was sick of having to decide which tie to wrap uncomfortably around his neck each morning. Just because you don't stop breathing in a day doesn't mean you're not being strangled. Frank needed fresh air. An avid outdoorsman, he loved to fish and he'd always dreamed of owning and operating a charter fishing boat in western Washington.

So Frank approached his good friend John Parkinson with the idea. He and John worked together and they also fished together, which meant they probably spent more time with each other than they did with their wives. Without hesitation, John agreed to the plan. The friends became equal partners in the venture and began their search for a boat, setting the wheels in motion.

At the office, Frank was a big fish in a small pond. For the past 14 years, he had worked as the deputy treasurer-controller responsible for managing the accounting department at a public utility district (PUD). He lived in a quiet town in eastern Washington. His second wife, Mable, was employed in the purchasing department of the PUD. Their combined income was $120,000. On the surface, Frank appeared to be well off. But as he celebrated his fiftieth birthday, a financial crisis loomed in the distance.

John was financially stable and would have no problem obtaining a commercial loan for his share of the down payment on a boat, but personal debt was running Frank's life. His monthly expenses included two house payments, one for his family home and a second for his mother's. He paid child support for children from his first marriage, and he foot the bill for his daughter's lavish wedding and his father's recent funeral. Frank wasn't impoverished—there weren't holes in his socks—he simply didn't have the money for a down payment on a fishing boat. But he wasn't sharing the bad news with anyone, particularly his partner.

Frank and John continued their search for a suitable vessel. They discovered a four-year-old Sabreline Flybridge Cruiser moored at a marina in western Washington. It was a beautiful yacht powered by twin Detroit Diesel 8.2-liter engines, each producing 250 horsepower. Reasonably priced below its estimated market value of $190,000, the 36-footer was a steal at $182,860. It certainly had potential. With a combined net worth of approximately $500,000, the partners were able to finance the yacht at a local bank, turning their dream into a reality. Each partner contributed $10,000 for the down payment to seal the deal. Frank and John were now in the charter fishing business!

Their goal was to ensure that the business generated enough revenue to pay all operating expenses, marina moorage charges, and the monthly payments on the loan. They were quite successful during the first summer and met their financial expectations. John went about his life as usual. Frank, on the other hand, started blowing money right and left. His family went on extended vacations, including one overseas. He had mounting credit card debt, yet managed to purchase several outdoor recreational "toys," like vehicles and accessories for the boat. Frank even started remodeling his home, when he should have remodeled his finances.

The revenue for the charter fishing business declined during the first winter. The monthly boat loan, insurance, and marina moorage fees still had to be paid even in the off-season. Always a step ahead, Frank had failed to adequately plan for the idea of an "off-season." He was in dire straits. No matter how much income the family earned, there never seemed to be enough money to pay all the bills. Desperation has a way of undoing people. Frank became careless at work. He was slipping toward disaster. What he did to stay afloat ultimately led to his downfall.

■ ■ ■

The public utility district where Frank worked is consumer owned and serves a predominantly agricultural region of eastern Washington. It provides low-cost power to customers and is a regional leader in Washington's economy. Managed by a five-member board of commissioners elected by the citizens who live within the district's geographic boundaries, the PUD is the second largest energy-producing agency in the United States, right behind the Tennessee Valley Authority.

The PUD has approximately 1,200 employees and generates over $300 million in operating revenues each year, offset by approximately $230 million in operating expenses. Large dollar expenditures are relatively common. Operating an electric system and two dams on the Columbia River, the PUD serves approximately 42,000 retail customers and distributes power to 22 long-term purchasers in three states, using 404 miles of transmission power lines and 3,740 miles of distribution power lines. It sells over 3 billion kilowatt hours of electricity each year and delivers services to residential customers at an average cost of just over four cents per kilowatt hour.

Don't Write Checks You Can't Cash

Frank, the deputy treasurer-controller, left the office one morning to meet with the contractor remodeling his home. Meanwhile, Marcy Doolittle, the district's check redemption clerk was processing the redeemed checks that had cleared the bank the previous day. She accessed the electronic file and began reconciling the information against the computer file of outstanding checks. The computer prepared an exception report identifying one check that had cleared the bank but was not listed as outstanding in the PUD's records. Marcy sorted the batch of redeemed checks and identified the suspect. To her surprise, it was payable to Frank Johnson for $7,148.53. He had personally endorsed and deposited it into a Seattle bank account.

Alarmed, she handed the computer exception report and check to her supervisor, Linda Bates. "Something is very wrong here," Marcy said.

Linda was shocked and agreed that the check was irregular. They needed to get to the bottom of this situation, and fast, so she marched down to the treasurer-controller's office to discuss this matter with Sam Mayfield, Frank's supervisor. She wasted no time: "Sam, Marcy discovered an irregular check in yesterday's bank activity."

She showed him the documents. "Frank has somehow found a way to issue an unauthorized check to himself. He also cashed it, which makes things even worse. We need to talk to him about this transaction. He's at home working with the contractor remodeling his home. Should I call and ask him to come back to the office?"

After catching his breath, Sam said, "Yes, right away. Tell him to report to me as soon as he returns. If he asks you what's happening, tell him I have some important documents for him to sign."

Linda called Frank. "Hi, I'm sorry to disturb you at home, but something urgent has come up," she told him. "Sam wants you to come to the office immediately to sign something."

"I'm just wrapping up my negotiations with the contractor; I'll leave in a minute."

Frank was a bit unnerved by Linda's telephone call; he wasn't aware of any urgent activity at the PUD. He drove back to find out what was happening. He went to Linda's office, who hurriedly escorted him down the hall to see Sam.

"Sam, what's this meeting all about? What documents are you talking about?" Frank asked.

"Frank, sit down so that I can go over this material with you."

He took a seat and Sam placed the computer exception report and the redeemed check on the conference table so that he could see them both. The color in Frank's face drained. His irregular activities had been detected. He needed to come up with a plausible explanation to defuse the situation.

Sam continued, "Frank, we discovered an unusual check in yesterday's bank activity and need your help to understand what it represents."

Frank started talking and talking fast. "I know all about this check. Let me tell you what happened. The internal auditor and I were testing our disbursement system. We processed this transaction to determine if our internal controls would detect a payment like this. As you can see, our procedures in the accounts payable department didn't stop this check from being issued. But from these documents, I can see that our check redemption procedures have identified it for further review. This is the answer to our testing, and we can now work on changes in our internal controls to ensure that these kinds of transactions don't slip through the disbursement system in the future."

Frank's explanation certainly sounded plausible at first. But Sam responded, "I'm not aware of any such test."

"I'm sorry I didn't tell you about this earlier. I tried, but you were out of the office. So the internal auditor and I prepared the test transaction and processed it anyway. I was going to tell you about it today, but something came up at home and I had to spend time with the contractor remodeling my house."

Sam replied: "Frank, I am already aware that you and the internal auditor have *not* been testing our disbursement system. So why did you issue this check and then cash it? Besides, cashing the check is never part of an internal control test—*never*. I want the money back right now!"

Frank took out his checkbook and wrote a check to the PUD for $7,148.53, the amount detected. Handing it to Sam, he said, "Here's the money for the test transaction. I can't stay any longer because I have to get back to see the contractor. We can talk about this situation more tomorrow if you want."

Frank left immediately, without even visiting his office. Instead of going home, he drove up into the foothills outside of town and twice attempted suicide. Thankfully, he was unsuccessful in both attempts, so he drove back home. He knew that any further investigation of this matter would prove he had violated the trust the PUD placed in him as the deputy treasurer-controller. He prepared a resignation letter on his home computer and went to bed. He would be ready to face Sam again tomorrow. But it was a sleepless night.

Frank entered Sam's office first thing in the morning, placed his resignation letter on the desk, and said: "I'm sorry. I have no excuses. Your investigation will uncover more transactions. I just got greedy."

He then left the PUD for the last time, still not even visiting his own office. Sam's suspicions about the circumstances of this situation were accurate. Frank's confession and resignation were all the proof he needed.

Check, Please

Sam immediately called the State Auditor's Office to report the situation, as required by law. This agency is the external audit firm responsible for the audit of all public entities in the state of Washington. Sam talked with Janice Walker, who had performed the PUD's last annual audit.

"Janice, we have a very serious situation on our hands. The deputy treasurer-controller issued at least one unauthorized check to himself for $7,148.53. When confronted about the matter, he made restitution and resigned. But as he departed the office, he apologized and said that we would find more transactions. I need your help to investigate this matter further. I've already briefed the PUD's executive staff. They want to know if you can start work immediately."

"Yes, I can," Janice replied. "I will clear my schedule and be right over. In the meantime, ask the staff to secure all of the accounting records related to this transaction. I'll also need some work space near the finance department. Can you make all of these arrangements for me this morning?"

"Everything has already been taken care of by my staff. I'll see you shortly."

Janice contacted me because I managed the agency's statewide fraud program. We went over the known facts of the case. Realizing the gravity of the situation, I told Janice: "This is urgent. It could potentially result in a significant loss. In fact, it's so serious that I'm going to notify the state auditor today and then join you at the PUD tomorrow morning."

Janice drove to the PUD's office to begin the preliminary investigation. First, she interviewed the staff to obtain a full understanding of the procedures and controls in the disbursement system. She analyzed the process and studied the documents the staff had assembled, and then spent the rest of the day and most of the night reviewing all of the PUD's redeemed checks for the prior year, finding nothing unusual.

After briefing agency officials about this new case, I went home and packed my bags for the trip across the state. I lived in western Washington, while the fraud occurred in eastern Washington. Upon arrival, I checked into a motel and prepared myself for the upcoming meetings. I met with Janice and PUD officials early the following morning. We discussed the sequence of events over the past two days and reviewed the accounting documents for the irregular disbursement transaction. Janice and I then spent time alone analyzing the situation and then went to lunch.

Upon returning to the PUD, we asked to meet with the staff again. Linda had spent most of the morning sifting through the files in Frank's office.

"I have some great news!" she said when she entered the room. "I found a check in one of Frank's filing cabinets that I believe is related to the case. It's payable to one of our vendors for $7,148.53, the same amount as the irregular check Frank issued to himself. But this one hasn't been endorsed yet. Frank is the representative for a personal services contract with this vendor. But, that isn't a valid reason for this check to be held in his office. And the same amount on these two checks must be more than just a coincidence."

"Linda, that's great investigative work," I responded. "I think you've found a piece of the puzzle that will certainly help us solve this case."

We brainstormed the facts again. If Frank misappropriated funds from the PUD by issuing two checks for the same amount, one to himself that was not recorded in the accounting records, and one to a valid vendor that was recorded in the accounting records, our challenge was to determine how he planned to conceal the false transaction.

We summarized what we already knew. Janice had reviewed all of the redeemed checks for the past year and found none issued to Frank other than for his normal payroll. We knew that at least one unauthorized check was issued to him for $7,148.53 and that he cashed it. We could review the bank's electronic file of redeemed checks to identify any others made payable to Frank that had cleared the bank, but that would be labor-intensive and costly. To conceal the irregular payment, Frank would have had to manipulate the check redemption process. The question was how? Linda and Marcy confirmed that Frank had access to the check redemption records.

Marcy informed us that Frank had performed the daily bank reconciliation recently. When she and Linda looked at the records, they found that the computer exception report for that date was missing from the file. Marcy then reviewed the files for a week when she had been on vacation last year. She was shocked to find that another computer exception report was missing during that period. Linda and Marcy returned to discuss these latest developments with the auditors. The staff confirmed that there was no way to reproduce the missing exception reports and they knew of no legitimate way to modify these records for personal benefit.

"Let's look for an unauthorized way these records could be altered," I said. "The information systems [IS] department could help us by identifying any computer software changes that might have been made, particularly on the days where we have missing computer exception reports."

Linda responded: "There were cuts in staff a few years ago, and Frank is the only person authorized to make computer software changes to the check redemption program. John Parkinson is the chief of the IS department. But that complicates matters because I don't think he can help us on this investigation. He and Frank are partners in a charter fishing business. We need to talk to Sam before we proceed any further."

These new disclosures were a big concern. I contacted Sam and arranged for a meeting later in the afternoon to discuss our plan. Reviewing all computer software changes to the check redemption program appeared to be the most cost-effective way to identify any unauthorized transactions Frank may have processed through the disbursement system. There was also a possibility that John might somehow be involved.

Sam contacted a programmer in the IS department and asked him to report to his office immediately without disclosing the nature of the meeting with John. Once the programmer understood our predicament, he agreed to review the check redemption program software later that evening.

The following morning, he asked us to meet him in a conference room. We arrived to find the table covered with papers. The programmer began his presentation by explaining what he had done overnight, giving us the good news first.

"Frank made five unauthorized computer software alterations to the check redemption program. However, the coding changes for three of these alterations had not yet been activated. One of these changes included coding to manipulate the $7,148.53 unauthorized check the staff found payable to him. The other inactive changes might have been for test purposes or could represent future unprocessed transactions. Now for the bad news. The coding changes for the remaining two computer software alterations have been activated. But that means that the potential for unauthorized disbursement transactions is limited to those two changes."

Everyone was relieved at first. However, this elation would soon diminish when, through our research, we discovered the amount of these two unauthorized transactions.

The programmer translated the code changes to the check redemption program into English for us: "When processing the check from the bank file payable to Frank Johnson, change all of the check identification information to a check payable to a legitimate vendor and then reprocess the disbursement transaction normally."

We thanked the programmer for his outstanding and timely work. The meeting adjourned, the staff returned to work, and we began our audit to document the amount of the loss in this one-year case. It had been an amazing three days. Our research confirmed Frank's admission to Sam when he resigned. There were more transactions, two in fact, for $215,846.00 and $13,930.70. The total loss for this computer fraud case was $236,925.23.

Breakdown of the Scheme

There were three components of this scheme. First, as a personal-services contract representative, Frank prepared false invoices to pay three legitimate vendors. He then processed three vouchers through the accounts payable section to create checks for these fictitious payments. He placed Post-it notes on the vouchers asking the accounts payable clerk to return the checks to him after processing. The note indicated that he was either going to deliver the checks to the vendor at a meeting or attach additional documents to the check before mailing the payment to the vendor. The accounts payable staff complied with Frank's requests because deviation from normal operations was a fairly routine practice. This U-turn in the accounts payable section was a subtle compromise of internal controls in the disbursement system. Frank retained these checks in his office. They were never mailed to the legitimate vendors.

The printer used to create checks in the disbursement system rendered several blank checks useless at the beginning and end of each run. While these voids were recorded on a log, the documents were not properly labeled. The staff wrote "void" across the top of the document reserved for the description of the transaction, leaving the check at the bottom of the document untouched. Frank removed some of the improperly voided checks from the vault and used them to create three checks payable to himself, always in the same amount as the transactions in the first part of his scheme. He also took redeemed checks from the vault and used an optical scanner to copy the facsimile signature-plate information to a file on his office computer. Then he used his computer and printer to create the unauthorized checks payable to himself. Finally, Frank endorsed the checks and deposited them into a Seattle bank account he had established for this purpose.

When the daily bank reconciliation was performed, the computer prepared an exception report identifying the unauthorized checks Frank had issued to himself and deposited in the bank. He altered the computer software for the check redemption program by changing the information on the bank file, essentially replacing the details on the unauthorized checks payable to himself with check information from those payable to the legitimate vendors recorded in the PUD's accounting system. He used a regular and color copier to record the bank endorsement information from the back of prior unrelated check payments to the legitimate vendors to the back of the current fraudulent check to this same vendor. He then switched the checks, destroying the check payable to himself and placing the check payable to the legitimate vendor back in the redeemed check file. Finally, Frank removed the computer exception report so that there would be no record of his manipulation.

During this investigation, I subpoenaed all financial information from the Seattle bank account identified in the endorsement on the unauthorized checks issued to Frank Johnson. I confirmed that the opening deposit in the account was for $215,846, the amount on the initial unauthorized check in this scheme. The first withdrawal from the bank account was a $10,000 check for the down payment on the yacht. The initial disbursement check in this scheme went unnoticed for a year. Frank got greedy, which led to its detection.

Agent Orange?

The PUD had an employee-dishonesty bond policy covering the loss in this case, and the insurance carrier promptly reimbursed the total amount plus audit costs.

This case would normally fall under the jurisdiction of the county prosecutor and be brought before a superior court in the state of Washington. However, the prosecutor transferred the case to federal authorities to increase sentencing.

Frank Johnson entered into a plea bargain agreement with the U.S. Attorney's Office, pleading guilty to state charges of misappropriating funds from his employer and federal charges of money laundering and counterfeiting. The prosecutor requested a sentence of 31 months in federal prison. But Frank's defense attorney advised the court that his client was a Vietnam War veteran who was exposed to Agent Orange during his military service. Frank was also under a psychiatrist's care for the strain induced by the crime. The U.S. District Court judge, believing the defendant's mental and physical health would deteriorate during incarceration, imposed a lenient sentence of only 15 months in federal prison. He also ordered Frank to complete 150 hours of community service and three years of supervised probation. In a rather unusual twist in the case, the judge further penalized Frank by ordering him to pay a fine equal to the amount of his equity in the 36-foot yacht that he purchased with the stolen money, as well as interest on the misappropriated funds.

Once he was convicted, the State Board of Accountancy revoked Frank's CPA certificate, barring him from future work in his chosen field.

Frank received an early release from prison and reentered society. He was subsequently employed as a counselor in a state social-services agency. To my knowledge, he's still there today. Life goes on after fraud; it's just different!

Lessons Learned

The audit team learned the value of brainstorming during the preliminary phase of the investigation, a step that has since been added to audit standards.

Managers need to look for a "straight line," one that starts with the initiator requesting payment for the transaction, continues on to accounts payable and the checks' review and production, and then reaches the individual in charge of the checks' distribution. The risk of fraud increases when a check makes a U-turn in the accounts payable system or doesn't follow its normal course. Such transactions automatically become exceptions to the internal control structure, requiring intense scrutiny and monitoring by managers and proper documentation. These compromises include the use of written communication (such as Post-it notes), any verbal communications employees have with the accounts-payable or check-distribution staff, and a practice that was a fatal flaw in this case, namely picking up checks outside the organization's normal procedures.

Recommendations to Prevent Future Occurrences

Segregate Duties

The duties of employees must be properly segregated; lack thereof proved to be another fatal flaw in this case. While assigned in the accounting office, the deputy treasurer-controller was the personal-services contract representative for several vendors, usually the purchasing department's responsibility. He also performed computer programming duties for the check redemption program, a task normally left to the IS department. In addition, Frank was a member of the committee that determined priorities for information systems changes. During committee meetings, he understated the importance of corrections needed in the check redemption program. Segregating duties and creating a system of checks and balances are vital in preventing fraud and abuse.

Staff the Proper Personnel

An auditor with electronic data-processing skills should be assigned or available on all complex audits. This individual should determine whether computer software changes have been properly documented, authorized, and approved for critical operating programs.

Do It in Ink

All organizations need to ensure that they properly store both blank and redeemed checks. Checks should be properly "voided," and the check issuance log should be completed in ink, never in pencil.

Sealed and Delivered

The bank file of redeemed checks should always be delivered unopened to the individual who performs the daily reconciliation. The staff should secure these records to preclude any compromise before the reconciliation is performed.

About the Author

Joseph R. Dervaes, CFE, ACFE Fellow, CIA, of Vaughn, Washington, is a retired Washington State Auditor's Office Special Investigations Manager. He managed the state's fraud program for 20 years and participated in 730 employee-embezzlement fraud investigations of losses totaling $13 million. He graduated from the University of Tampa and has over 42 years of audit experience.

The Man Who Told on Himself

ALAN GREGGO AND MIKE JESSEE

A small-company owner, Johnny Peedler achieved success through a keen temperament and hard work. He had his hand in numerous financial endeavors and bragged about his business savvy. Johnny and his wife were mainstays in town, attending the local church and volunteering in the community. But Johnny's ethics were less than faultless. Making a buck was the name of the game. And if circumstances required, he would gladly play out of bounds for cash.

The Foster Group is the leading manufacturer and retailer of luxury watches in the world. Its founder and current CEO, whose passion for making quality timepieces remains unmatched in the industry, created the company in the mid-1950s. Through vision, hard work, and unrelenting focus, the Foster Group continues to grow today as a global entity.

The success of the loss prevention department for the Foster Group began with its leaders, two individuals with years of experience and willingness to adapt and evolve. Wanting to stay ahead in the field, they created a division within the department to focus on external theft, Internet sales, and the counterfeiting of Foster Group product lines. I left law enforcement after eight years to lead this division.

I was immediately impressed with the professionalism, experience, and work ethic throughout the entire department. But I also quickly recognized that we had an uphill battle to fight when it came to illicit Internet sales. We make and sell the best watches on the market, and the high demand increases the likelihood of knockoffs or other counterfeit schemes online. As a detective, my focus had been centered on computer crimes and mandating cooperation with Internet companies through subpoenas, court orders, or written requests. In the private sector, voluntary cooperation is typically not part of the vocabulary, especially for Internet auction sites.

Isn't Greed Grand?

Johnny Peedler's complaint reached me after a few months on the job. Prior to his contacting us, Johnny's Internet auction site wasn't on our radar. But that soon changed when he called one of our retail stores and angrily complained that the Foster Group hadn't shipped him the watches he was promised by our associates. Irate, he demanded that he receive the goods for which he paid. Knowing that we do not sell our watches in bulk to individuals, the store manager smelled a rat and immediately contacted Brian Kym, her loss prevention manager, to relay Johnny's concerns and accusations.

Brian eagerly contacted the suspect customer to find out more. The first conversation was full of grievances. Johnny claimed that the Foster Group failed to supply him with the product he had purchased, saying he paid for bulk amounts at reduced prices. He didn't realize that he had also just told on himself. Brian ascertained that we had both an internal theft issue and a case of unauthorized sales of our product, so he contacted me to help substantiate Johnny's complaint, pull information for an internal investigation, identify how he was selling our product, and possibly seek criminal charges against him.

Having only spoken to Brian a few times since I began working with the Foster Group a few months prior, I wasn't sure what to think when he informed me of an interview where the "victim" admitted to receiving hundreds, possibly thousands, of our stolen product from company associates. He laid out Johnny's claims of a middleman who obtained the stolen watches through his sister, a district manager supervising 10 Foster retail outlets, as well as his sister-in-law, a store manager. After obtaining the product, the middleman sold it to Johnny to then sell on the Internet.

Brian had interviewed Johnny on several occasions and had developed a solid relationship, which would help mollify our subsequent interactions. It also didn't hurt that Johnny was willing to tell all about his dilemma to anyone who wanted to listen, whether it was self-incriminating or not.

Sure enough, the salesman was open and honest with me about the predicament. Apparently, $100,000 worth of our product sold for a mere $15,000 was just another deal—nothing out of the ordinary. He'd been selling our merchandise for the past two years and was angry that his middleman would fail to send the product after he paid for it fair and square. He assured me he was a good businessman, had been dealing with this guy for years, and had only been ripped off once or twice before. Several hundred watches were sold on the auction Web site, but Johnny had taken his middleman to court and sued him civilly a few years prior to this incident. Issues began when the middleman found himself in financial debt and began pocketing the money without bringing Johnny the product. The wheels of their business relationship began to fall off.

During the weeks these interviews were taking place, we scoured inventories, incident reports, and various other tools in place to catch these types of errors, but we found no red flags.

How could the Foster Group be missing such a large amount of product without knowing anything about it? We needed the names of the associates involved before we could move forward. At that point we had a lot of unsubstantiated claims and very little hard evidence.

In what would be my final interview with Johnny, I asked multiple questions that made him very uncomfortable. It became apparent that he didn't like where this investigation was heading. He eventually relented and named our associates and his middleman, and he gave me the name of the Internet account where he was selling the watches. Johnny also provided a list of the merchandise he still had in his possession but hadn't yet listed on his auction site. *Jackpot,* I thought to myself, but we needed to prove the loss to the company and confirm Johnny's story through internal reporting and interviews with the suspect associates.

Damaged Goods

Both associates, the middleman's sister and sister-in-law, had been with the company for years and knew our system backwards and forwards. We spent hours reviewing inventory results for clues on how the product was stolen. Expecting to discover higher shrink results or more incident reports, we found neither. The stores were well within the average. The review of incident reports did uncover a few thefts of our product that could be linked back to items Johnny had sold on his auction site, but it wasn't enough. For us to terminate the employees, the interviews were going to have to produce results. We needed admissions of guilt and for the associates to explain how and what they were stealing.

We chose to interview both associates at the same time, which was a challenge in itself. They worked in separate cities and had different roles within the company. The only fact we gathered from the interviews was that they knew we were coming. There were no confessions; no one admitted to knowing how the middleman was obtaining his product, and they denied ever speaking with Johnny.

It was interesting to note, however, that the associates were well aware of their inventory results. One even mentioned that her store had never been higher than the average and that reported thefts were always on par with her region. These facts confirmed our suspicions that the associates were involved. They knew that by keeping the stores' shrink and incident reports within range, no red flags would be raised. Also, by removing product labeled as damaged, they could keep the stores' levels within par and allow a lot more product to be removed without causing alarm.

There were other telltale signs of their guilt. After the interview with the middleman's sister-in-law, her husband showed up in a fit of rage, admitted that his wife knew what was going on, but asserted that she wasn't the mastermind. During the interview with the middleman's sister, the investigator walked her to her car and found a bag full of our watches. Her boss indeed permitted her, as a district manager, to drive to local stores and collect damaged watches for review, but there was no reason why she should have that kind of bulk. It was later determined that she was making special, unauthorized trips in order to recover damaged product behind her boss's back.

When the interviews were completed, we wrapped up the review of internal reporting and compiled as much evidence as possible regarding sales from the Internet auction site. Johnny did not take off the product tags, which differentiate the items we sell in our stores from those of other retailers. He also replied to most buyers with a description of the merchandise sold, so we were able to identify sales older than 90 days. Attempts to work with the auction site went nowhere, and the outfit had to be subpoenaed by law enforcement before they would supply any additional information.

I discussed the case with our legal department. It was determined that prior to alerting law enforcement, we needed to place Johnny on official notice that the product he was selling was stolen, that he was to return our product, and that he had to immediately stop selling it over the Internet. We received a notice from Johnny's attorney that any additional contact would need to go through him.

Jurisdictional Limbo

Immediately after the interviews, both associates abruptly resigned from the Foster Group. Though we didn't obtain an admission from either one of them, we were able to identify the middleman when his sister revealed his name in an interview. We also confirmed thousands of dollars' worth of Internet sales through Johnny's auction site. With the large amount of circumstantial evidence against him, the middleman and the associates, along with the solid evidence from the auction site and incident reports, I felt comfortable approaching law enforcement with this case.

Prior to meeting with local law enforcement, we needed to eliminate any holes or questions. We drafted an outline of events along with captured screenshots of our product on Johnny's auction site. A copy of the agreement between he and his middleman explaining what product he was going to deliver was also included.

When I advised Johnny that we were going to discuss this case with the police, he wanted to talk with them first and explain his side of the story. His viewpoints had not changed. He was still the victim and he saw nothing wrong with buying and selling our stolen watches. Johnny was confident that the police would see it his way. I had to reach law enforcement before he did.

Prepped and ready, I reached out to the local police department in the town where Johnny lived. However, after my initial phone conversation, I knew things would not be as smooth as I'd hoped. I spoke with the department's captain and provided a brief history of our company and the Cliff Notes version of the investigation. He let me speak with the detective who would be looking into the case. After recapping and laying out the evidence we had gathered, the detective's first comment set the stage for things to come. He'd had issues with the middleman before, he said, but to him Johnny was a "good man and most certainly the victim."

I laid out the case against Johnny and his middleman to the detective over four conversations and several e-mails, providing what I thought would be enough information to spur an investigation—Johnny's admission, his knowing that the product was stolen, the Internet sales on his auction site, the list of 50 watch SKUs (codes that identify inventory) he had in his possession ready to sell. The one thing missing was a subpoena to the Internet site confirming the number of sales, the identity of the auction site's owner, and an exact dollar figure that could be used to calculate the total amount stolen. This required action from the detective, but it never came.

Everyone in the town knew Johnny Peedler, and the detective was no exception. I requested that we keep our conversations confidential until he was given all the paperwork and facts in the case, but it didn't happen. Johnny contacted me immediately after I spoke with the detective. He was irate that I tried to incriminate him and said he was no longer going to cooperate with the Foster Group.

"I'm going to sell the product on my auction site, whether it is stolen or not," he yelled.

I made several attempts to get Johnny or his middleman interviewed by law enforcement. I spoke with the captain and assistant chief, expressing my concerns about their refusal to open an investigation. Jurisdictional issues were the given reasons why the local department wouldn't proceed. It boiled down to the fact that we hadn't filed a theft report against the associates with their local departments. After several failed attempts to file theft reports, due to the lack of physical evidence and admissions, we reached out to both the county and state law-enforcement agencies. The county said the city needed to investigate, and the state wanted the case to originate in a local community before they would consider getting involved. The case was stuck in jurisdictional limbo.

Several months after the end of the investigation, the middleman robbed Johnny in another deal gone bad. The local detective reached out to me and wanted to discuss the middleman's arrangement with Johnny. Our conversation ultimately aided in the arrest of the middleman. He spent the next five years in prison. The local police department still refuses to interview Johnny.

Lessons Learned

As a newcomer to the private sector, I learned that there are no sure cases. Local law enforcement will not always accept investigations, no matter how convincing the evidence. Being prepared and outlining the work you've done is an important step in garnering police support. But again, there is no guarantee.

Jurisdiction is the next hurdle that typically needs to be cleared in Internet cases. Oftentimes, the crime may fall within several jurisdictions. Partnerships within all levels of law enforcement are critical. This case drove home the importance of cooperation and what can happen without it during an investigation.

Furthermore, it's important to remember that not every interview will result in an admission of guilt; however, key facts should still be gathered to keep moving forward. By spending the time and reviewing each interview with the investigator, important statements were identified that added evidence to support our case against Johnny, the middleman, and his associates.

The Foster Group learned from this case as well. Internal measures were taken to eliminate loopholes the associates had exploited. It raised our awareness regarding a new form of Internet fraud and showed the extent to which some associates can exploit weaknesses within company policies and procedures. The loopholes in the processes we closed were critical, but a policy is only as good as the manager enforcing it. We've strengthened antifraud training and created new reports with additional indicators to identify internal theft.

Internet investigators have an uphill battle to fight due to numerous obstacles. Jurisdictional issues are a key area that needs to be addressed, as is the problem of gaining cooperation from law enforcement and the auction sites.

But, in the end, criminals will push the envelope until they're caught. Greed is a powerful motivator.

Recommendations to Prevent Future Occurrences

Recognizing Internet Risk

The Internet will continue to present problems, especially within the retail environment. Companies should recognize the growth of Internet auction sites, list serves, and third party vendors and prepare for the risks. Acknowledgment of the problem is a necessary and important first step.

Garner Support of Upper Management

Once a company recognizes their vulnerabilities, action needs to be taken immediately. The Foster Group was fortunate and had two forward-thinking leaders who recognized this growing issue and spent the money to investigate and manage the problem. This case forced us to recognize critical loopholes that had allowed it to take place. If a fraud occurs, it is important to garner the support of upper management to change policies and close gaps in controls. In order to enforce the new policies, the Foster Group established accountability and more reliable tracking of damaged and returned products. The company also implemented software to monitor Internet activity; associates have been hired to focus on enforcing Internet-auction sales regulations.

Be Proactive and Prepared

The Internet is a new tool for fraud. It provides criminals with the perfect venue for committing their crimes anonymously. Be proactive, recognize this growing trend, review your company's policy, and take steps to eliminate the opportunity. As the saying goes, "The best defense is a good offense."

About the Authors

Alan Greggo, CFE, CPP, is the AVP Loss Prevention for Luxottica Retail based in Cincinnati, Ohio. He has a bachelor of science degree in law enforcement administration from Youngstown State University. He serves on the Retail Loss Prevention Council of American Society for Industrial Security as chairman of the Organized Retail Crime Committee.

Mike Jessee is a LP manager of Organized Retail Crime for Luxottica Retail. His team's focus is on combating the effects of ORC proactively through internal and external partnerships, training, and investigations. Mike has been a Mason Police Department detective focused on computer, Internet, and financial crimes. Mike has also earned a Master of Science degree in criminal justice from Xavier University.

CHAPTER 17

Triple Threat

JEAN-FRANÇOIS LEGAULT

MPO is a telecommunication company providing cell phone services to its many subscribers, both on prepaid and postpaid plans. Prepaid plans, also known as "pay as you go," require subscribers to pay for their minutes in advance, while postpaid subscribers pay after the minutes have been used, with the bill most often arriving at the end of the month. Industry analysts and investors have always placed a higher value on postpaid subscribers, many of them not even considering prepaid accounts as genuine subscribers when evaluating wireless companies. Because employee bonuses were based on the number of postpaid subscribers at MPO, the staff was under pressure to secure this type of plan. An incentive of this nature left the company wide open for fraud.

MPO employed a dedicated team of call center agents responsible for handling incoming calls from would-be subscribers interested in acquiring cell phone service plans. The team's new manager, Anne McGee, was intent on running a tight ship. As a strong-minded outside hire with solid call-center management experience, she was primed to identify issues requiring attention. As part of an ongoing reorganization, she had signed on to get the call center back on track.

Not long after she started at MPO, Anne reviewed monthly sales bonus reports for her team. Her assessment of the payouts raised some questions. The numbers seemed unbelievably high. She had never seen agents surpassing sales goals by such a lofty margin. The bonuses were not much, only a few hundred dollars per month at most, but an above-average number of call center agents appeared to be reaching double what they should be, which raised a red flag.

Suspicious, Anne contacted the corporate security unit, charged with handling all internal investigations. I had previously collaborated with them on a variety of technical investigations, so the director called on me to assist with the case. At the time, I was working as an information security analyst for this organization. Coming from an IT background, I was initially involved in technology-related investigations ranging from the downloading of illicit content to attempted security breaches. I later became frequently solicited to assist in investigating technological fraud allegations due to my information security background. Anytime a call came through from the corporate security unit, I knew I would need to tell my manager I would be off the radar for a couple of days.

This time the call came from a retired police officer, Randy Smith, from whom I learned a lot, especially regarding interviews. Having worked major crimes for the last part of his career, he was fazed not one bit by internal investigations. After working murder and rape cases, the world of corporate security was a welcome change of pace. He was a good-natured guy, but when it came time to work he was all business. Randy carried out his investigations with great preparation and great attention to detail. He was always willing to share his experiences to help me become a better investigator and interviewer.

Although we were both familiar with most aspects of the telecommunications business, the call center functions were a bit of a mystery. So we sat down with Anne and listened as she clarified how, exactly, the bonuses were calculated for employees.

Anne explained that upon purchasing their activation package, these soon-to-be subscribers were presented with the options of activating their new phone in the store, contacting our call center to activate the phone, or using the Web-based activation system. As postpaid accounts provide a guaranteed revenue level, MPO implemented a program to provide employees with a bonus as incentive for securing postpaid plans. This benefit was determined by the ratio of postpaid accounts compared to the total number of activations handled by an agent. Once an agent reached a certain threshold, he or she was entitled to a bonus—the better the ratio, the better the bonus.

The potential for an additional payout led these agents to seek out schemes to increase their commissions. When the bonus reports came out, Anne said she was immediately skeptical.

"Individuals are reaching percentages in the high 80s, which in my opinion is nearly impossible," she explained.

Unsure of how employees might have been boosting their sales ratio to such an extent, we had to keep an open mind. Anne was our sounding board. At the onset of the investigation, we brainstormed and ran ideas by her to see if she thought they were possible. We suggested a variety of possibilities such as fake subscribers, phone system manipulations, and insiders manipulating reports, changing the agent's ID for the activation, and performing the activations under someone else's name. A couple of ideas were met with laughter or comments like "That's preposterous!" but we ultimately found a starting place.

Scheme One

Our first step was to listen in on calls being routed to the activation department. Like any other call center, we ran a standard disclaimer when anyone phoned in, a recorded message stating that calls might be monitored for quality assurance purposes. We used the recordings to document accurate information in the case of an incident and also to assess the quality of our employees' performance.

Through listening to the calls, we uncovered the first of a few schemes being used by agents to boost their sales ratio. It was rather simple and did not require any technical skills. Customers would contact the activation department after purchasing their startup kit in order to activate their new service. Upon receiving the call, the agent would inquire as to what service type the subscriber desired. If the customer requested postpaid, the agent would gladly activate the account in accordance with standard policy. But if the customer asked for prepaid, the agent would often try to sway the caller by explaining all the benefits of postpaid service. If this method failed, the agent might claim there was a system malfunction and request that the client call back later, or drop the customer back in the phone queue after saying he or she would be placed on hold for a few moments, or simply hang up in hopes that another employee would take the call if the subscriber tried again.

This behavior generated complaints from other agents as well as from customers. The team leaders did not respond to the problems in a responsible manner as they did not want to affect personal relationships with their fellow employees. Those involved in the first scheme were fired; they were advised to repay the bonuses if they wanted to avoid legal action, which they did.

Thinking Outside the Box

But we didn't stop there. After analyzing the omissions reports, Anne believed that other employees were manipulating their sales percentage due to the unusually high number of peak performers, something she had never seen in her experience. Either her team had been eating their Wheaties or they were exploiting a loophole to bolster their sales numbers. To avoid skewing the investigation, Anne didn't provide us with the names of any of the agents she believed were manipulating the system.

At the beginning of a shift, agents log into a system that keeps track of activations based on their account. This allows the system to generate a commissions report based on each employee's record. Expanding on this notion, we had to identify other ways in which agents could activate new subscribers outside of the customer care application. From activating the account to reviewing payment information, this function permitted creation, modification, and viewing of subscriber profiles. We considered two plausible schemes and began investigating both.

Scheme Two

The first involved using a second user account to activate prepaid subscribers. By using a second user ID, one not assigned to him or her, the agent could perform prepaid activations without affecting his sales ratio. When the sales report was generated, only the activations the agent had performed while logged in under his own user ID would appear under his name, and the rest would not be tied to him.

As part of the bonus calculation method, agents were required to activate a certain number of accounts per hours worked in order to demonstrate substantial progress. An employee using a second user ID would have to find the proper balance to avoid upsetting his own profile's activation tally. After reviewing the calculation method, we concluded that an agent could achieve his efficiency goals and still activate prepaid accounts outside his profile. It was a balancing act. And since these fraudsters could simply stick any prepaid accounts on another profile, they didn't waste time trying to convince subscribers to select a monthly plan. This enabled them to perform more activations in less time, which hid the fact that they weren't activating all the subscribers under their own user ID.

But there were two flaws with this prospective scheme. First, how could an agent access another system without the appropriate privileges? Surely no coworker would lend an account for prepaid activations, as it would directly reduce his or her sales mix percentage. So how could a fraudster set up a valid account? The answer was revealed by chance a few days later when one of the Windows network administrators happened to come to me to discuss a new security standard that we were implementing, and a rather simple one at that. He told me that generic user IDs would now require a high-level sign-off in order to be granted. A generic user ID is simply a user account not associated with an individual employee. They can be test, application, or temporary accounts.

The network administrator mentioned that the call center management had requested that a number of these generic user IDs be created for agents who had forgotten their passwords and been locked out of their accounts.

This privilege was granted under the premise that the call-center support team would contact the help desk each time one of the IDs was used, at which point the password would be changed so that the temporary user could not freely access the account again. But this rule was seldom followed.

I sat down with the Windows network administrator to examine account usage. We learned that many of these generic accounts, which enabled users to activate new subscribers, had been used frequently from multiple work-stations. And the passwords had not been reset in months.

I quickly set up a meeting with the leader of the call-center process support team who controlled the accounts. He explained that when an agent forgot an account, they would give him or her one of the generic user IDs along with the password. I then asked why his team wasn't having the passwords reset after use, as policy stated. The answer wasn't much of a surprise: Due to lack of resources, they had not been keeping track of who had been using the accounts over the past several months. And they didn't even bother to contact the IT help desk to reset the passwords. I was frustrated that they had failed to follow policy, but at least we had a lead.

I asked the team in charge of producing the commission reports to pull out a detailed list of all subscribers activated over the last three months using these generic accounts. No surprise there: They were almost all prepaid. My next objective was to find which employees had been using them. I began by testing out whether it was possible to start up two customer-care applications on a single computer simultaneously. It was. My theory was that agents were starting up the application twice, once under the agent's rightful username and the second time under a generic account from which he or she would activate prepaid accounts. The complicated part was finding out whom. We had two issues there, the first being that the application did not keep track of the workstation from which a user had logged into the generic account. The second problem was that even if I were able to identify the workstation, call center agents did not have assigned seats. They could sit wherever they wanted within the area reserved for their team. Some even moved around during their shift to sit closer to friends. The only way to track account usage was by actually watching them.

We enlisted the assistance of the application development team and the operations team who were responsible for maintaining the customer care application. The work gave them access to control logs that showed who was logged in from where and at what time. With their help, we began monitoring concurrent log-ins by reviewing the access control logs for duplicate log-ins from one workstation. Once we identified instances of a single computer that was logged in twice using different user accounts from a single workstation, we needed to determine whether one of the accounts was generic. Through prolonged monitoring, we identified agents who were using this scheme to increase their sales bonuses. But we wanted clear proof of their involvement, so the investigators monitored calls being handled by each of the identified agents. We listened in on calls where prepaid subscribers were being activated by the suspected agents. Using this information, we examined the activation log to determine which agent had activated which subscriber. Many had been activated under generic accounts. Once again the employees involved were terminated, with no legal proceedings undertaken provided the funds were paid back in full.

Scheme Three

While we were investigating the previous scheme, I began digging into the second scenario we had identified during our brainstorming session. I suspected that agents had taken advantage of our online activation platform to "hide" prepaid account activations.

In the months prior to the beginning of the investigation, we had launched an online activation platform that allowed new subscribers to activate their accounts independently as well as select their own options using our transactional Web site. Some of the employees decided to use the service to activate prepaid accounts instead of using their own application, so that the prepaid accounts did not affect their ratio.

This transactional platform was hosted in a separate computing environment. Due to security risks, the company had decided to host all of its online applications on a different infrastructure. In the unlikely event of a security breach of an online application, it would be limited to this separate computing environment and would not impact the rest of the organization's internal systems. This network architecture made it so that anyone on the corporate network would connect to the distinct online platform as if they were communicating to a particular location on the Internet. Network traffic would thus flow out of the internal corporate network as if it were going out to the Internet, but it would be redirected to the online application platform by a networking device that connected both the corporate network and the online transaction platform to the Internet.

The first step in investigating this scheme was to identify any access coming from the corporate network and going to the online activation platform. Like many organizations, we had implemented an Internet proxy server that acted as a relay between internal resources and the outside world. Before allowing the Web request to go out, it would be filtered and each request logged. This allowed us to ensure that the sites visited by employees met the company's Internet access policy; it could also tell us every Web site they had visited, from which workstation, and at what time.

It was time to start crunching some logs. I had to identify every workstation that had completed the activation process. However, simply identifying workstations that had accessed the first page of the online activation process was not going to provide me with the information I needed. A lot of people view that page for legitimate reasons, from call center employees walking a client through the steps for activation to the marketing department looking at the layout. So I sat down with the Web application developers to understand the online infrastructure, including the URL of the Web page displayed once the activation process was completed.

Any time this URL showed up in the proxy logs meant that someone on the corporate network had used the online activation system. This was against policy since it could hide prepaid activations—these would appear to be coming from the subscriber themselves, unless someone took a closer look. I would need to sift through the millions of log entries generated each day to determine whether anyone on the corporate network was activating subscribers this way. I proceeded to write a short search script that identified each of the workstations that accessed the specific URL, as well as the time and date for each. This simple script would parse the logs, recognize every instance of the pattern, identify the actual URL, and would send the specific line from the log file to a separate file. In the end I had a much smaller file to review, one containing only the hits and log entries for access to the specific URL I was looking for. Using the IP address that was logged in the proxy, I could only tie the action to a workstation, not a specific agent.

In light of this, I had to find an alternative way to determine who was sitting where. I needed to match up three pieces of information: my search results, the access logs for each workstation, and timekeeping information for each agent I identified.

The process I used to identify the perpetrators was methodical and tedious, but worth it. First, I sorted the results generated by my script by workstation and by day. This provided me with a list of the time of day at which an online activation was completed from one of the workstations in the call center. Then I identified the first "result" of the day for each workstation and used the access logs to ascertain which particular agent was on that computer. To verify the culprit, I examined the timekeeping records to make sure no one else had logged on or off the workstation. Next I recorded all the "hits" for each workstation in a given shift for each employee.

This process was repeated each day for our three-month data set. It was painstakingly long and, well, a little boring. In hindsight, I should have attempted to automate this process using a database and some scripting, but I had no idea what anomalies I might find while processing the information. And I did find a couple, such as agents logged onto two workstations and access logs reporting there was no one logged in while someone was clearly activating accounts online. It ultimately made sense to do everything manually even though the techie in me wanted to find a way to automate it.

Finally, I identified a list of employees whose calls should be observed. We applied the same process we used for our investigation into the abuse of generic user accounts: monitor calls taken by the agents for prepaid activations, identify the subscriber, and determine who activated the account. The online application had its own username that allowed us to identify if the account had been activated online. If someone was not aware of the scheme, it would simply look like the subscriber had activated the account from his or her own computer.

As in the other two schemes, these individuals were fired and no legal action was taken as long as they repaid the fraudulent commissions they received. As for the team leaders, many of them were reassigned and given a second chance. There was no hard proof that they were aware of the agents' deception.

Lessons Learned

As someone who dealt with the world of hackers during a time when hacking was about the challenge and not financial gain, I was surprised by the ingenuity of these individuals. They put their jobs and personal reputations on the line for just an extra couple of hundred dollars per month.

Computer fraud, as I learned, is people fraud. I have yet to witness a PC boot up in the morning and decide to commit fraud on its own. There is always someone behind that keyboard. You can be a computer guru but fail in the field of computer fraud investigations if you don't grasp the human element. This became clearer to me as I delved into criminology and interview techniques after performing such investigations. One thing still remains clear: A good investigator is a good investigator, no matter what. It's all a question of adapting to the evidence we must review.

I learned that a fraud examiner must be extremely thorough. If we had not been painstaking throughout this investigation, we might have stopped after discovering the first or second scheme. Our brainstorming sessions allowed us to identify and pursue a number of plausible scenarios that we flushed out fully, all of which turned up perpetrators.

Recommendations to Prevent Future Occurrences

Limit Generic Accounts

Organizations should limit generic accounts that provide a multitude of opportunities for fraud and security breaches. Certain situations require them, but it is essential that an owner be named for the account and should be held accountable for all activity. Furthermore, a strong password should be used in conjunction with these accounts.

Limit Web Site Access

Limit access to certain Web sites in call centers. Ideally, a "default deny" policy should be applied for frivolous or potentially dangerous sites. Although difficult to implement in most contexts, these safeguards would be easy to establish in a call center, where job descriptions are usually narrow and delimited.

Track Log-Ons

Proper logging is critical to most computer fraud investigations as they link people, systems, actions, time, and date. In this case, the customer care application documented who logged in but did not indicate where the log-on took place. Furthermore, the Internet proxy server only kept track of the workstation that accessed the URL, not the user. Having had this information would have allowed us to concentrate on the investigation instead of adding time-consuming steps.

About the Author

Jean-François Legault, CISA, CISSP, is a senior manager with Deloitte & Touche's Forensic and Dispute Services Practice in Montreal, where he specializes in computer forensic investigations and the prevention and detection of computer-based fraud. He is also a frequent guest speaker on topics relating to forensics, technology-based fraud, and information security.

18

Swiped

PETER BELLOLI

Ever since he was a boy, Ron Toppell craved esteem and power. Years of hard work paid off and he was eventually promoted to account manager for one of Ashmont Maintenance Co.'s larger job sites, a position with a significant amount of authority. While most would view this as an opportunity for positive change, Ron saw it as a weakness to be exploited.

Growing up in a lower-middle-class neighborhood where he was teased by classmates had left Ron with a chip on his shoulder. As a result, he developed an obsession with getting ahead. His drive, whether born from a desire for authority over his peers, avarice, or pure ambition, led him to a fateful decision—one that would cost him his job.

Ashmont Maintenance has been in business for 60 years, created by a hardworking husband-and-wife team shortly after they immigrated to America from Lithuania during World War II. The husband held a factory job during the day and cleaned nearby office buildings at night. The wife raised their children and handled bookkeeping during the evenings.

Starting as a cleaning service for businesses in their neighborhood, Ashmont expanded its client base to include nearby schools, colleges, and small banks. By the time the torch was passed to the next generation of the family, in the 1960s, the company was a solid regional player in the building maintenance field. The sons cultivated Ashmont and it grew into a nationwide facilities-management provider, whose services included janitorial, mechanical, heating ventilation and air conditioning (HVAC), and landscaping.

We're Going to Overtime

As an internal audit manager for Ashmont, I see allegations of fraud, theft, misappropriation, and malfeasance cross my desk on a regular basis. Only one other auditor works for me, so with our limited resources we tend to be more reactive than proactive, meaning that most of our cases reach us through tips, hunches, or complaints. And that's how I first came to hear the name Ron Toppell.

I received information from the finance department regarding procedural breakdowns at a particular job site. One of the finance directors expressed concerns that Ron was consistently failing to submit vendor invoices to the corporate accounts payable department before the close of month-end. These lags caused her to accrue significant amounts to the general ledger every month as she waited for Ron to send the actual vendor invoices. Although delaying expense recognition is certainly counter to company policy, it is usually considered a minor infraction.

Over the course of my tenure with Ashmont, I have seen several cases where account managers purposefully held on to expenses. Often, they will not submit them for entry because they need their job site's profit-and-loss record to improve. Basic accounting principles dictate that when you under-report your expenses in any given period, you are improperly inflating your profit (or decreasing the extent of any loss).

Issues like this were generally handled with a low-key approach. The next level up in management would be notified with specifics about the situation. The offending manager would be reprimanded if the amounts were relatively small. Rarely would it lead to termination. But this time what developed from a routine matter surprised even me.

In order to validate the finance director's concerns and determine the volume of any irregular activity that was occurring, I ran several reports on Ron's account. Such reports come directly from Ashmont's mainframe and represent the actual revenue and expenses associated with a particular job site. When we notice significant variances in actual versus budget amounts, those discrepancies become a high priority.

The initial review of the reports on Ron's account did not identify any specific indications of fraud; however, there was enough anecdotal evidence to warrant a trip to his office for further investigation. Located in a particularly fetid section of Philadelphia's dock and shipping waterfront, Ron's job site was a decrepit manufacturing plant. In retrospect, it's likely that the rundown state was a contributing factor as to why this fraud was not uncovered sooner. Nobody in their right mind would want to visit that site. So by natural aversion to squalor, Ron was left largely undersupervised by upper management and worked essentially below the radar of the finance department.

Under the guise of a standard operational audit, I arranged for a three-day review of back-office functions at the plant. The initial thrust was to determine why the expenses were being postponed. The effect on the job's reported profit may induce some managers to delay expense recognition, but I didn't see any proof of it occurring willfully. Of course, Ron always had explanations for the delays, often placing the blame on others—usually the client. This made an investigation of his claims politically difficult. However, I decided to continue with the review for two reasons. First of all, even though he had plausible excuses, Ron's tone, cadence, and mannerisms when responding to questions did not engender any trust with me. Secondly, employees who were willing to cut corners in one area could very well be breaking policy elsewhere.

While undertaking the various audit programs, I noticed several instances of sloppy procedures, incomplete files, and ignorance of company policies. While poor management is not ideal, it's not illegal either. The audit revealed several areas that needed improvement. Although this revelation alone would have made the trip worthwhile, what I discovered next was even more compelling.

Ashmont uses an electronic time clock to record employee labor hours. All workers must swipe upon entering and leaving the plant. The time-recording system then calculates the hours worked as the basis for their payroll. While the software for this labor-recording system resides on Ashmont's mainframe, several onsite computers had access to the program as well, to allow for adjustments should someone forget to swipe the card, accidentally double-swipe, and so on.

Standard procedures call for job sites to review the employee swipes every two days in order to ensure that they are entered properly and that any errors are corrected in a timely manner. The company mainframe polls the clocks at the end of the workweek and the data is fed into Ashmont's payroll program, then the checks are issued.

Normally, an administrative assistant at the job site is the one who monitors and makes pay adjustments. Due to frequent office staff turnover, the site manager also had access to the computer and was able to change, add, or delete card swipes. Ron would be between assistants for three to four weeks at a time, giving him ample opportunity to fraudulently alter the time cards in the system.

As part of my analysis, I ran a report from the time-recording system that logs all changes. For any given date range, it listed the employee for whom the alteration was made, who made the adjustment, and the total number of hours worked per day. This standard audit procedure also recalculated payroll entries for every employee during the week of the review. I performed a complete payroll history review of anyone who had the access needed to enter or change clock data, and I found that Ron had altered his own swipes nearly every single day. He was using his computer to change his actual swipe-in to one hour earlier and his swipe-out to one hour later. These changes resulted in the system recording 10-hour workdays instead of the standard eight hours, thus giving him 10 hours of overtime per week.

When asked about the alterations for the five days during the review period, Ron had no explanation, nor did he seem upset. He merely shrugged his shoulders and his nonchalance reinforced my belief in his guilt. By the end of my visit to his plant, Ron probably felt he had dodged a bullet. Although he didn't have the access to change past data in the timekeeping system or Ashmont's mainframe, I wanted to keep my investigation a secret, lest he try to destroy documents or clean house.

Usually, salaried employees at Ashmont (account managers and some supervisors) are not obliged to punch, swipe, or record their hours. They are paid a standard 40 hours per week. Unsalaried employees, conversely, always record their hours using whatever system exists at a particular job site. Ron was a salaried manager, therefore not required to swipe his hours on a time clock. His administrative assistant would simply make one manual entry of 40 hours into the system for him each week.

Upon returning to the corporate office, I dug more to verify my findings. I ran additional payroll reports from the mainframe and presented the results to the director of payroll for confirmation. Ashmont does not take fraud lightly, so when he corroborated my findings I was confident in my investigation.

As a salaried employee, Ron was ineligible by policy for overtime pay, but the results of the additional reports indicated that this malfeasance had been occurring for nearly the entirety of his two-year period of employment. Ron took advantage of the control deficiencies in the payroll system. Although policy prohibited overtime for salaried employees, over the years Ashmont had allowed numerous exceptions, so payroll personnel no longer questioned aberrant entries. The missing funds amounted to $33,700 in fraudulent overtime.

When I sent the draft audit report to Ron and his boss, the regional operations director, Ron's responses to the accusations were weak and hardly credible. He stated that he extended his swipes to "show accountability" to the customer for his actual time onsite. But this was illogical: An employee wouldn't swipe in one hour before coming to work, nor swipe out one hour after leaving. He acknowledged that he was not eligible for overtime, but blamed the timekeeping system for not being set up properly. Ron also stated that he was unaware of being paid the additional money. Yet overtime hours were clearly stated as such on all of his check stubs.

See You in Court

The regional operations director notified Ashmont's legal department of the findings. After conferring with human resources, the chief counsel advised operations that they should interview Ron. Again, he offered no credible explanation as to why he used his computer to change his swipe times. The regional operations manager showed Ron copies of e-mails directing him to eliminate overtime hours at his site. Not only had he disregarded that directive, but the overtime being incurred was false hours for his own benefit.

Ron was terminated from Ashmont at the end of the interview. The company filed a complaint with the local police. Copies of payroll documents and reports from the timekeeping system were forwarded to the lead detective.

The police arrested him several months after his termination. Due to the nonviolent nature of the crime, he was released on his own recognizance and the case was referred to the district attorney (DA). Educating the assistant DA on how the electronic time-clock system operated and how Ashmont's payroll policies and systems worked was a lengthy task. I put exhibits together, explained our payroll reports, and forwarded copies of canceled checks and check stub reprints.

At the recommendation of Ashmont's chief counsel, the company engaged a collection agent as well as a private outside counsel to file civil charges against Ron. Once the DA's indictment came down, it was decided to hold the civil case in abeyance until an outcome was reached criminally. Since civil charges require a less stringent burden of proof, Ashmont could pursue the civil charges at a later date if things fared poorly on the criminal side.

With the overwhelming amount of proof facing him, Ron Toppell finally pleaded guilty a week before his trial date to a felony theft pursuant to a scheme. He was granted probation before judgment, which includes five years' probation and mandatory restitution.

An underlying mistake Ron made (aside from falsifying hours) was not recognizing that computer programs in today's world almost invariably keep logs of changes to crucial data elements. For Ashmont, employing 20,000 workers made payroll records critical information not to be simply discarded or archived. The preventative and oversight controls were insufficient, but thankfully the data-tracking systems were well established.

Additionally, the contract with this client was a fixed-price agreement that covered specified maintenance procedures. Ashmont would be paid the same amount each month to perform the specific functions listed. Any work requests not covered in the contract were considered "out of scope" and charged on a cost-plus basis. Any employee overtime was billed to the client on a cost-plus basis.

With a strict, fixed-price contract employee, theft is borne by the company. As long as performance isn't compromised, clients are generally not concerned since their cost structure won't be affected. However, all the illegitimate hours Ron entered were billed to the client. Ashmont had to tell the client what occurred and refund the overbilling. They hoped the client would appreciate their vigilance in uncovering the fraud, but it was a precarious moment in their working relationship.

The fact that the problem existed for nearly the entire two years of Ron's employment with Ashmont pointed to several internal control weaknesses in their policies and procedures. Now the chief financial officer and other senior managers are working with the internal audit, finance, and payroll departments to strengthen internal controls.

Lessons Learned

The discovery of Ron's malfeasance led Ashmont to query its payroll system for all other salaried employees who were paid either straight time or overtime for any hours over 40 per week. It turned out that several salaried managers were being paid for extra hours. The reasons are currently under investigation and will be used to help formulate a clear, precise policy. Neither the electronic time-clock system nor the main payroll had sufficient controls to prevent salaried employees from being paid over 40 hours per week.

Centralized accounts-payable systems can provide important safeguards in expense recognition. Ashmont is instituting corporate purchasing cards for small amounts as well as an online purchase-order system for large dollar-amount items. These measures will redirect accounts payable invoicing away from the individual job sites and centralize it at the corporate office, thereby reducing the ability of local site management to cause delays in expense recognition.

Recommendations to Prevent Future Occurrences

Institute Proper Controls

Ron was able to exploit the payroll system because, as site manager, he had the ability to change his own payroll records. To avoid this scenario, management should implement systematic controls in both the time-recording system and the payroll programs to preclude employees with data entry access from changing, adding, or deleting any entries related to themselves.

Clear-Cut Policies

Establish clear guidelines as to when a salaried employee may earn overtime. Conventional wisdom is that only hourly, not salaried, employees can earn overtime.

Periodic Reviews

Regional operations directors should review payroll reports on a periodic basis. By examining the weekly check registers during site visits, regional management would have discovered the overtime codes and caught on to Ron's scheme. This task needs to become part of the standard operations site-visit criteria.

Stable Staff

Frequent changes in office staffing levels masked the fluctuations in Ashmont's overall labor expense. These peaks and valleys caused a lot of "noise" that made trend analysis difficult, and the incorrect conclusion was drawn that the fluctuations were caused by turnovers. Take the necessary steps to maintain a stable number of office staff.

The Importance of Audits

Although the auditor's initial concern was timing of expense recognition, the most significant problem was detected when the standard audit program was followed. Auditing can be repetitive and even tedious sometimes, but internal auditors should avoid tunnel vision when on assignment. In this case, performing standard review steps led to a big win for the internal audit team.

About the Author

Peter Belloli, CFE, CIA, CAFM, is based out of the Boston area. A graduate of Merrimack College, he has been in the auditing field for over 18 years. Currently, he manages a small audit shop for a facilities management company. He specializes in payroll fraud and asset misappropriation.

Have Computer, Will Video

DOMINIC A. D'ORAZIO

Ray Rocchet was the type of worker that employers cherish. Having served in the U.S. Army for nearly a decade, he decided to continue his service by becoming a government employee with the American Logistics Agency. Drawing upon his experience in the military world, Ray was able to "talk the talk" with other officers, convincing them that he could get the job done. He was also a longtime volunteer firefighter and a member of several township first-aid squads. A pillar in his community, he was always working to improve the neighborhood. He and his wife proudly reared four children, one of whom always chose her father as her favorite dance partner at family parties and weddings.

Ray's home was located in a typical middle-income neighborhood. The house, which underwent numerous renovations, would eventually contain a wide array of electronic gadgetry, including monitors and video cameras that were purchased with revenue from Ray's various private enterprises. He also owned a few high-end sport utility vehicles and some boats.

After working for American Logistics Agency for several years, Ray rose to the position of supervisory computer specialist and was responsible for outfitting soldiers with equipment on a moment's notice. He dealt independently with contractors for this reason, without needing approval from anyone. Ray was considered likable. He was known for getting the job done under rapid deployment conditions, which earned him unwavering trust.

The American Logistics Agency is a federal government entity located in the northeast region of the United States. The agency develops, acquires, fields, and sustains an array of systems—tactical, strategic and base command and control, communications, computers, intelligence, surveillance, and reconnaissance—for the joint war fighter. The agency deals with the research and development, management, acquisition, and distribution of equipment to support U.S. soldiers who are fighting overseas. It employs about 10,000 people worldwide and works with thousands of contractor personnel.

Although the agency shares a site with other federal agencies, one covering over a thousand acres of prime real estate, ALA is a self-sustained community with its own fire department, police department, post office, supermarket, gas station, health clinic, church, liquor store, thrift shop, credit union, and motor pool. The area also provides a child care center, three swimming pools, a physical fitness center, tennis courts, softball fields, a bowling alley, a golf course, an athletic complex that contains a football field and a running track, and a picnic area complete with a pavilion, barbecue grills, and a scenic brook to enjoy the mild seasons. In addition, houses are provided to married military soldiers, while apartments are provided to single soldiers and rented to single employees. The grounds include walking trails and historical monuments honoring fallen soldiers.

Like many federal bodies, the agency employs not only its core professionals—researchers, developers, procurement officials, logistics specialists, and item managers—but also lawyers, internal auditors, criminal investigators, an inspector general, and a public affairs officer. Additionally, the agency has a resource management office and a personnel office to ensure that it is properly financed and staffed, and an information technology office to make sure the computers, servers, and information systems are working properly. It's one of the state's largest employers and produces $3.4 billion for the state's economy, especially for towns along the agency's boundaries.

Despite Ray's spotless reputation, his director, Orson Whipple, had an uneasy feeling about him. Not receiving any information about Ray's operations, he requested that someone from the resource management office conduct a quick review. Mary Hansen was put on the job. Not long after she began evaluating the situation, Mary came across something fishy: an unauthorized administrative fee was being charged to every customer's order. Mary knew that these charges were improper because the agency already paid for Ray's office expenses, but she did not have the expertise to dig deep into the financial transactions. She reported the findings to her superior and recommended that the internal auditors do an in-depth search of the records to determine the whereabouts of the money collected for the fees.

At the same time, Whipple had established a group of four people to go down into Ray's operations to determine whether they were in compliance with regulations. Regina Martino was responsible for reviewing all monthly bills submitted by SEI to the American Logistics Agency. She had come across telephone charges ranging from $5,000 to $6,000. Regina asked Ray, the branch chief, to justify the telephone charges.

"They were for a T1 line that served as a backup line to Kuwait which his branch supported," he explained.

Regina then inquired as to why the telephone charges were for a location other than where SEI's home office was in Newton, New Jersey. Since Regina did not receive a satisfactory answer to her question, she informed her supervisor, Francine Hamilton, who agreed to visit the address listed on the telephone charges.

Regina and Francine arrived at the site, a small one-story building located in an industrial complex in Teterboro, New Jersey. After obtaining a key, they entered the facility and found monitors installed on the walls across the perimeter. The monitors were hooked up to computers. As their research progressed, they found out later that Ray had set up a private organization, Double R's Computer and Video Co., that ran a subscriber-based pornography site using the agency's high-speed Internet capability. The transmission line allowed subscribing members, who paid Ray to access the Internet and search pornographic sites, to view and be viewed using two-way video cameras. Double R's had been in business for almost a year and a half prior to its discovery. The agency had disbursed over $100,000 for the T1 line billed through SEI. With the identification of the pornographic site and confirmation that the agency was paying for it, Regina and Francine summarized the results of their review and presented them to Whipple, who in turn called criminal investigators to conduct an investigation.

The criminal investigators asked Regina to research the monthly invoices. She discovered that the agency paid for 17 months' worth of billings, with the monthly amounts ranging from $5,000 to $6,000. Regina also found out that their share of the billings was 75%, while the contractor (SEI) paid the other 25%.

At the same time the criminal investigation was being conducted, the local internal review office was asked by the agency's chief counsel to look at some of Ray's other operations, including a private enterprise (Ray's Renovations Inc.) on contract with the agency to renovate an existing building, a private enterprise (Ray's Moving and Storage Inc.) on contract with the agency to deliver computers and monitors to the various departments of the American Logistics Agency, and eventually the purchase of computers by Ray's branch for Ray's personal resale. The computers being purchased were billed through SEI as if they were for a particular customer, and were paid for by the agency.

Before I actually started my internal review, Ray found out that I would be looking into his other operations. He quickly resigned from the agency. Ray thought that once he quit, the criminal investigators would drop the investigation. He thought wrong. In fact his resignation facilitated our search. Furthermore, the findings did not have to be handed over to the attorney(s) representing Ray.

As the director of the internal review office, I began conducting an internal review and asked for office space to perform a search of Ray's records. Ironically, Francine provided me Ray's former office, which was vacant at the time.

I was looking through his computer for any files that pertained to requisitions made through the contractor, SEI. One day I happened to click on a program and the monitor screen changed from a file to a movie screen. As I focused on it, I realized I had opened a program that allowed the user to visually talk to the receiver at the other end. In essence, it was a video camera that happened to be taking pictures of me sitting at Ray's former office. Hurriedly, I shut it off, but not before I was observed by the personnel servicing the server who realized that it was I who turned on the program.

At the start of my review, I met with the criminal investigator, Special Agent Stone Harrington, to make sure that I would not impede his investigation. Agent Harrington went over the basis of his inquiry (mainly the T1 line) and what he was looking for. He told me that my review would not necessarily impinge on his investigation. If I found any fraud, he said, he would add it to his list of charges against Ray.

My review focused on the list of customers who bought services or equipment from Ray, purchase orders made by SEI and eventually billed to the agency, and monthly invoices for any other discrepancies or oddities.

At one point, I interviewed Paul Moronelli, who was the representative for the contracting officer for the SEI. Paul was responsible for making sure that the SEI employees performed their services. Paul, in his role as the representative, was the "eyes and ears" because he was on the job site and could easily attest to the work done by the contractor.

As the internal review evaluator, it was my job to interview personnel to obtain the information needed to build my case. Paul was responsible for approving all purchase orders made by SEI personnel. As we spoke, he told me that he had run across several suspicious transactions that were not approved by him and instead had been made by Ray. Although Ray was his supervisor, Ray did not have the authority to approve any purchase orders.

"Did you approach Ray about those questionable purchase orders?" I asked Paul.

"Yes, but he told me to mind my own business."

Paul appeared nervous. I looked at him and asked, "How many purchase orders are we talking about?"

With his head down, he responded, "Multiple purchase orders."

"Did you inform the contracting officer about this potential problem?"

Paul shook his head.

I pressed further; "What were you waiting for? Why didn't you inform the contracting officer?"

Paul responded, "I wanted to be absolutely positive that there was something wrong with those orders that Ray had approved before I informed the contracting officer. And because Ray can be a very vindictive man, I didn't want to get on his bad side. Also, I know him from my Army days. I considered him to be a friend and a visionary for the department. On the one hand, I respected Ray for the great things he has done for the Army. On the other hand, I couldn't believe that he was approving purchases for no particular customer and telling me that it was none of my business."

"When you found the first instance of a purchase order not being right, you had a fiduciary responsibility to immediately inform the contracting officer," I replied.

He looked me right in the eye and said, "I wanted to be certain before I acted."

I asked Paul to give me some examples. He showed me several, all of which contained computers or computer parts where the mailing address showed a "Colonel Aaron" in San Diego, California, or a "Sergeant Thomas" in Salem, Oregon. I asked Paul what was wrong with these purchase orders. On the surface, they looked legitimate. The computers were being shipped to military customers. Moronelli informed me that he had no customers in San Diego or Salem.

After that startling revelation, I decided to take another look. I gathered all of the orders that listed any or all of the following information: Colonel Aaron, Sergeant Thomas, San Diego, California, Salem, and Oregon. The orders totaled over $220,000. Looking at the batch of purchases that I found, I noticed that the vendor was located near the SEI office in Newton, New Jersey. I visited the vendor and asked to see the shipping invoices. After persuading the owner that I was involved in a criminal investigation, one involving his name, he agreed that it was in his best interest to cooperate with me.

I went back to my office and searched the telephone directory and the Internet to see if I could find a "Colonel Aaron" in San Diego. I did not locate anyone. Then I decided to use the name Rocchet in a search. There was an Aaron Rocchet in San Diego. When I compared his address to the one on the shipping invoices, it matched! I tried following the same procedure with "Sergeant Thomas" in Salem, Oregon, but to no avail. I turned my findings over to Agent Harrington with the hopes that he had more resources to find the supposed "Sergeant Thomas."

We discovered that Aaron Rocchet was Ray's brother and operated a business located in Salem, Oregon, which turned out to be the other address.

Ray enlisted ex-Army buddies as "investors" on his private enterprises, some of whom footed the bill for strippers that performed in front of cameras in the small, rented office. In turn, he allegedly promised his friends that he would pay for the installation and maintenance of a high-speed Internet connection. That alleged promise would come back to haunt Ray during his trial. Instead, he placed the orders through the SEI Corp., a Newton company with which he had worked, and had them submit the bills to the American Logistics Agency. The irregularities weren't easily recognizable because they were buried within $60 million worth of communications contracts with three firms.

When a junior employee questioned the contracts, Ray tried to bully the employee into ignoring them. According to Agent Harrington, "Rocchet went way over his authority."

Ray Rocchet was charged with 68 counts of mail and wire fraud and submitting false claims to the Agency in two separate schemes: for running the T1 line (a high-speed Internet connection), and for ordering computers and computer parts from a Newton store using Agency money and reselling them through his brother's electronics company in Salem, Oregon.

In his opening statement at the trial, Assistant U.S. Attorney Giovanni Falcone told the jury that Ray's first scheme used more than $100,000 in agency money, and his second scheme $220,000. Falcone also told the jury that, "This case is not about Mr. Rocchet's larceny, it's about the elaborate schemes he concocted to cover his larceny."

What's worse, Ray had justified the purchases by telling contractors they were supporting the troops in Kuwait. It left everyone with a bad taste in their mouths.

During the trial, Ray's three former partners in Double R's Computer and Video testified on behalf of the prosecution and stated that Ray concocted the idea for the interactive pornographic Web site and that they never saw any profits from the business venture. Two of the partners claimed that they let the company run two live sex shows out of their offices in Sparta, New Jersey, with exotic dancers dressed in lingerie or togas and engaged in erotic behavior for viewers over the Internet. The two partners were also told by Ray that he was paying $3,000 a month for the T1 line and supplying the computer equipment. The third partner was also under the impression that Ray was paying for the T1 line out of his own pocket. One of the partners also testified that, after an agency supervisor had become suspicious of the T1 line, Ray told him to go to the Teterboro office and remove all but one computer.

During the course of the trial, Ray tried to place the blame on another individual, George Goner. Poor Mr. Goner could not offer any defense; he had died before the trial started.

Rocchet was found guilty on 68 counts of fraud and was sentenced to 39 months' imprisonment. He was ordered to pay restitution in the amount of $383,605 and a special assessment of $6,800. Mr. Rocchet was debarred for 15 years.

Lessons Learned

Although most of the employees of the American Logistics Agency are hardworking and conscientious, there will always be a bad seed, someone creative who tests the system. And if he or she succeeds, the action becomes magnified over a period of time. Ray saw several areas where he could support the American Logistics Agency using his entrepreneurial skills to establish various companies that contracted with the agency. However, ambition has a way of clouding the conscience. Ray crossed the line and lost his job and his friends' respect in the process.

Ray was providing a good service to the American Logistics Agency by filling a need to order computers, assembling the parts to make whole computers, and shipping them with a quick turnaround time. The customers were quite satisfied; they were receiving the finished product within one or two months instead of waiting the normal 8 to 12 months. And though this seemed like great customer service, Mr. Whipple should have delved into Ray's operations sooner to see how and why he was so successful.

Employees and employers need to differentiate between friends and those "friends" who are not following the Agency's policies. Sometimes it's a simple common-sense test that must be applied. In this case, Paul did not use the common-sense test. Otherwise, he would have notified the contracting officer about the questionable purchase orders.

Recommendations to Prevent Future Occurrences

Segregate and Rate the Employee

Require that employees be rated by someone other than their immediate supervisor, especially if they have significant fiduciary responsibilities. Ray should not have been the only one to rate Paul. As it turned out, Paul was hesitant in reporting Ray to the appropriate officials because he was concerned with his own job welfare.

Establish Proper Oversight of Managers

Ensure that there is a level of oversight from the top of the agency down to the bottom, and that each level performs its oversight responsibilities. In this case, there was a supervisor between Ray and Mr. Whipple, but the supervisor did not have the time to properly oversee Ray and his operations.

Require and Check for Appropriate Documentation

Review all purchase orders that are approved without the required signature of the contracting officer's representative and match them to an existing customer. If there is a mismatch, alert someone.

Use Common Sense

This is sometimes easier said than done. If things don't seem or smell right, check it out. If things are not right, inform the appropriate officials. All too often, employees only focus on their area of responsibility and prefer not to get involved. They should.

Take the Time to Review the Operations of Each Department

Directors should cover all departments under their responsibility during regular managers' staff meetings. The hope is that this would give them a good feeling as to how their departments are operating.

Establish and/or Utilize a Cross-Communication System within the Organization

Establish a system that ensures all departments are notified and capable of reacting when an unauthorized purchase order has been made, so that proper actions can be taken to minimize damage and weed out those individuals responsible for the fraud.

Follow Up on Any Flagged Items

Once an area is flagged to the appropriate officials, make sure the appropriate action is taken in response.

Coordinate with All Program Directors

Make sure that all directors review and verify that their internal controls are in place and working. If not, correct them. It's not a lack of trust, it's merely a good control measure.

Check All Employees

All employees' performance should undergo a managerial review process.

Inform the Employees of Consequences and Maintain a Watchful Presence

Ensure that all employees are made aware of the consequences of approving purchase orders that are not required by your organization or any of its contractors.

Maintain Appropriate Documentation

Records needed to justify for the reimbursement of the department's operating expenses should be properly documented and retained for at least three years or until the records are audited, whichever comes first.

About the Author

Dominic A. D'Orazio, CGFM, is the director of the internal review office within a U.S. Army installation in the northeastern United States. He has assisted criminal investigators toward their successful prosecution of cases involving white-collar crime. Mr. D'Orazio is a graduate of the Philadelphia College of Textiles and Science (now Philadelphia University) and has over 29 years of auditing experience.

Server, We Have a Problem

MARTY MUSTERS

Even as a little boy, Joe Damien exhibited a natural aptitude for computers and quickly learned their language. By the time he entered a local community college, Joe was a real whiz, fluent in programming and troubleshooting. Other students looked to him for advice and help with their computer problems. After graduation, Joe was hired by Wylan, a local tech store that offered network and computer support for small and medium-size businesses.

The Always on Time Transportation Co. (AOTC) was Gabe Sunderland's vision. A former truck driver, he had always wanted to own and operate his own trucking company. He worked hard, like most entrepreneurs, and built a profitable business with offices across Canada, the United States, and Mexico. AOTC is heavily reliant upon computers to manage the trucking routes on a daily basis. The transportation industry is highly competitive. A quarter of a penny per mile can be the difference between winning and losing a bid to haul goods.

AOTC was one of Wylan's clients. Joe had been assigned to the job and for a number of years he maintained and serviced the AOTC network. But the working relationship came to a sudden halt when Gabe decided that Wylan no longer offered the level of service that he needed. So, with proper notice, he canceled their contract and switched over to Best Service Computers, a local competitor. Best Service had a reputation for responding quickly when called, but they lacked the network expertise of Wylan.

Server Down

It was a cold and dreary February day at the AOTC headquarters, located in a small community just outside of Toronto. Gabe, always one of the first to arrive at the office, noticed that the computer systems were down again.

Usually this meant the server was hung and simply needed to be rebooted. Karen Johnson, one of Gabe's employees, managed most of the computer maintenance. But this time, when she tried to reinitialize the server, she noticed that something was terribly wrong. Karen entered the normal administrator user ID and password and received a message reading "Invalid." This was odd—the password hadn't been changed in years. Next, she tried her own user ID and password. Again, the server showed "Invalid." Karen moved to her desk and tried to log in through her personal computer, and again she was denied.

More employees started arriving at the office only to find that they, too, were unable to log on. Their computer screens should have displayed the log-in name, such as SMITHJ for Jackie Smith. Instead, the displays read ADMINISTRATOR. Alice, the company comptroller, bypassed the server and signed on to her computer with its local account so that she could continue working on the books. To her surprise, the entire financial folder had been deleted from her computer!

Best Service was called to find out what had happened. They responded quickly but stalled when it came time to proffer an answer. They were perplexed. Best Service only managed to determine that someone had changed the administrator password and disabled the other accounts, leaving everyone locked out of the system.

Best Service devised a recovery plan. If they could access the location on the server where the user accounts and passwords were stored, then they might be able to crack the password and restore the system. They booted the server from a CD, copied off the SAM file, which holds the user accounts and passwords, and took that file back to their offices to attempt to crack the password. For three days they tried with no success.

Gabe was more than a little concerned about the lack of progress. A trucking business lives and dies on its ability to transport shipments to the right place at the right time. All of the routes, orders, and billing were dependent upon the computer system. So each day the server remained down was another severe blow to AOTC. After the initial discovery, Gabe implemented a paper system to keep track of all of the truck routes and schedules, but this was far from ideal. Invoicing was lagging, payables were late, and the truck drivers were looking for their checks. Business operations were looking bleak. So Gabe called Best Service and told them that he needed his systems repaired without further delay.

Best Service switched to plan b. They took the original hard drives out, put in brand new ones, and started rebuilding the server from scratch. Unfortunately, the backups only had the company's data and not the applications, so it would take time. Finally, after seven days, the system was back up and running.

A Silent Attacker

Ten days after the initial incident, Gabe called me. As an expert in the area of computer forensics and investigations, I had seen this kind of case before. I sent one of my technicians to retrieve the original hard drives from the server and take an image of the comptroller's computer and bring them back to me for a quick analysis to confirm my initial suspicions. I sent the following note back to Gabe:

> I reviewed the two disk drives from the server and the one drive from the comptroller's machine and I can report the following: an intrusion occurred between the evening of Feb 7 and the morning of Feb 8. There is evidence to suggest that the attacks occurred on multiple computers including, but not limited to, the comptroller's machine, the server, as well as a few others. I have noted that a program called VNC viewer was installed on one of the machines during the attack, which is allowing the attacker continued access to your network.

Gabe and I met immediately and devised a plan to protect his network. I imaged several other key computers that I suspected were part of the attack. In total, two servers and seven computers were imaged in an attempt to collect enough information to determine what had happened, how it happened, and most importantly, who was responsible.

My first priority in analyzing the data was to determine exactly what occurred, based on the evidence. With this in mind, all of the data was reviewed to determine what had brought the server down on the morning of Feb 8, as well as what files (if any) had been deleted from the comptroller's computer. I began by trying to piece together the sequence of events starting at 5:00 p.m. on the evening of February 7, when the server had been logged on remotely by someone using a program known as Remote Desk Top (RDP). The user log-in was "admin."

It's important to note that the server log did not contain any failed log-in attempts at this time. The password was alphanumeric, had 14 characters, and contained both uppercase and lowercase characters, so whoever broke in knew the password. It was starting to look like an inside job.

Activity restarted on the server using the connected account at approximately 7:56 p.m. on February 7. The deletion of files began at 7:56 p.m. and lasted until 8:50 p.m. At 8:45 p.m. the comptroller's computer was accessed remotely from the server. Again, the logs did not note any failed log-ins at the time, indicating that the attacker knew the password.

The administrator's password had never been used before on the comptroller's computer, so I knew that the administrator profile must have been created within Windows during that time frame. After the attack, the assailant went back to the server and deleted the Internet history at 8:46 p.m. At 8:50 p.m. the deletion of files on the server stopped. At 9:00 p.m. the folders C:\Financials and C:\Alice Files were erased from the comptroller's computer. From 9:01 p.m. until 9:11 p.m., the assailant deleted a series of files, this time with the target being folders of information. From 9:32 p.m. until 9:35 p.m., additional files were erased on the server. The active directory was then disabled, which resulted in the log-in fiasco that nearly crippled Gabe's company.

And then I found the critical piece of information that helped me solve the question of who did it. An analysis of the comptroller's system log records showed that our assailant initiated a print job accidentally and then immediately canceled it. However, the action left a trace in the logs naming the attacking computer as JOELAPTOP. Now we were getting somewhere. Ten seconds after the print job was canceled, the log-in stopped in an attempt to cover the mistake. I searched for the string JOELAPTOP in all the evidence seized. The results of this search found two e-mails linking it with the name Joseph Damien.

Escape Into a Trap

Joseph Damien worked for Wylan, the computer company Gabe had cut ties with six months prior to the attack. Everything now made sense. Joe would have known the passwords, as Best Service didn't bother changing them when they took over. He knew what information was stored and where, and how to wreak the most havoc.

Gabe and I were sure we had identified the right person. Now we had to catch him. But the crime was puzzling. Why did he do it? Was he paid? Or did he get drunk and decide to be a vindictive idiot? Gabe consulted several lawyers and formulated a plan. We would apply to the courts for an Anton Pillar order, which in Canada is a civil search warrant, and then legally confiscate the computer identified in the attack: JOELAPTOP. Finally, we could determine whether this assault was part of a bigger corporate-espionage scheme or, as I said, simply Joe retaliating against his former client. I filed an affidavit and presented it to the lawyers who, in turn, filed a motion with the courts for the Anton Pillar order.

By the end of April we had the court's permission to proceed. But the execution wasn't going to be as easy as we had hoped. Joe's schedule was irregular. He had a girlfriend named Alana, and he split his time between her apartment and his. Joe didn't always go directly to work; sometimes he went to his first service call instead. We didn't want to tip him off and, by doing so, give him time to destroy any crucial evidence, which he certainly had the expertise to do. A private investigative company followed Joe for two weeks, tracking his every move. It was determined that each Monday morning he went directly to his office for the weekly company briefing. The following Monday, I waited with two lawyers, one who represented AOTC and one appointed by the courts to represent Joe. He arrived at 8:30 a.m., right on time, at which point the AOTC lawyer served him with the Anton Pillar order indicating that we could seize any and all electronic evidence in his possession. Specifically, we were looking for the computer called JOELAPTOP.

Joe was shocked. He immediately asked to call his lawyer, even though he had one present to represent him. His lawyer simply advised him to cooperate with the Anton Pillar Order. We checked the laptop on Joe's desk first. He turned it on and I looked at the name. The display read, "JOENEWLAPTOP."

I turned to Joe and asked, "Where is JOELAPTOP?"

"You're looking at it. I had problems with it, so I had to reformat the computer and start over again."

His answer didn't make sense. If I were to reinitialize my hard drive and reload the operating system, I would still call the computer the same name. Now, if I had purchased a new computer to replace an old one, chances are I would call the new one NEWLAPTOP. My intuition told me Joe was lying. I was convinced of two things at this point: first, we had the right man, and second, I couldn't trust a word he said.

Next I took his Blackberry. He protested: "I need this to do my current job. Customers will be calling and expecting me to respond."

This brought about an interesting dilemma. Joe's current employer had nothing to do with his alleged criminal activity, so we did not want to negatively affect Wylan. Joe had a point. Should we disrupt their business beyond what's deemed reasonable, we could be liable for lost revenues.

I decided to take an image of the Blackberry by using its desktop manager and create a backup that I could analyze later. This decision proved to be both a mistake and a blessing. As part of the order, Joe was not allowed to speak to anyone (except his lawyer) about the case until all of the evidence had been seized. By leaving Joe with his Blackberry, we gave him the means to communicate with others.

After seizing all of the evidence at his place of employment, we went to his apartment where I confiscated two tower computers. While searching Joe's place for more digital evidence, I noticed him feverishly typing on his Blackberry.

"What are you doing?" I asked, my eyes narrowed in suspicion.

"Just looking after my customers," he replied with a nervous shrug.

"Let me see the message."

"I can't; I deleted it."

I grabbed the Blackberry from Joe. The message that he just sent had indeed been deleted. However, not five minutes passed and a message popped into his Blackberry from Alana, his girlfriend.

The title read, "RE: URGENT—YOU NEED TO DO THIS NOW."

Alana had included the original text in her reply. It read like this: "Alana, you need to go to your apartment. Remember that laptop that I gave you? Take it and hide it on the neighbor's balcony. Leave work, do it now, they are coming—Joe."

Alana responded: "Joe, what have you gotten yourself into? Are people coming to my apartment? How will they get in? I am not going to do anything unless I know what is going on—Alana."

I smiled at Joe. His shoulders slumped and he shook his head, cursing his bad luck. The laptop was in her apartment. The Anton Pillar order allows you to follow the evidence, and since Joe had also sent the e-mail to Alana at her work, we now had two more locations to search: her home and her office.

It was close to midnight before we finished gathering all the evidence. Everything had to be properly catalogued with the lawyers. In all, over 1.5 terabytes of data had been seized. Now just the analysis remained. I confirmed that the computer JOELAPTOP had logged on to the AOTC computer systems; however, it was not the source of the attack. One of the two tower systems seized had been the source. The best evidence was found in the log of a key logger. As it turned out, Alana had suspected Joe of having an affair. In order to spy on him she had installed a key logger that she checked regularly. The key logger was active the night of the attack on the AOTC computer systems and each and every step had been documented, including the changing of the password on the AOTC systems. At approximately 11:53 p.m. on the night of the attack, Joe had changed the password to "UPYOURS."

Corporate Espionage or Petty Revenge?

Thorough analysis of all the evidence seized revealed no link between Joe and any other party in the attack on AOTC's computer systems. In the end, only Joe can answer as to why he attacked AOTC. Did he harbor a grudge against AOTC? Was he just a link in the chain to a bigger scheme? Only he knows.

The case was initially taken to civil court as AOTC sought damages for the disruption and loss to their business. Unfortunately, Joe has limited assets, so even a successful judgment would mean little in the way of restitution. The case has been turned over to the authorities for prosecution in the criminal court system.

Lessons Learned

I learned throughout this investigation to trust my instincts. Joe lied to me about the laptop when I first met with him. I went with my instincts and didn't trust anything he said from that point on. If he gave me a piece of information, I treated it with a dose of healthy skepticism. I also learned to expect the unexpected. I never thought Joe would use his BlackBerry to try and communicate with someone else in efforts to destroy critical evidence. I will be more vigilant in the future, even though what I overlooked turned out to be a blessing in disguise. Without this bit of luck, things could have turned out differently, and not for the better.

Recommendations to Prevent Future Occurrences

Update Passwords Regularly

As a precaution, passwords should be updated frequently and changed whenever someone leaves the company. In this case, simply changing the password on a regular basis might have prevented the security breach.

Firewalls and Detection Systems

It is imperative to secure your network properly with firewalls, intrusion detection systems, and network monitoring. They were not in place at AOTC. These preventative measures can help stop fraud before it starts.

Know Your Capabilities

Understand your company's capabilities and weaknesses. It is especially important to know the capabilities of those who tend to your computer network. Find out if they have experience working with network security. If they don't, then have them work with someone who does to help safeguard your company.

About the Author

Marty Musters, CFE, CISSP, CISA, is the Director of Forensics with NCI (NetCyclops) and a licensed private investigator in the Province of Ontario. He is a member of the High Technology Crime Investigation Association of Ontario (HTCIA). Marty has written numerous articles on computer forensics and is a sought-after speaker. He works for both law enforcement and corporate clients.

CHAPTER 21

Do It for the Kids

MICHAEL AMMERMON

Though small in stature, Anita Buck had the energy and work ethic of a Fortune 500 executive. A happily married mother of two, she was the associated student-organization bookkeeper at Desert View High School, where her daughter was a sophomore. Anita was well liked and familiar with most of the students; she volunteered countless hours to help with prom, dances, and various fund-raisers. Recognized for her tireless efforts, Anita made sure every school club was accounted for properly. In fact, when any of them was low on funds, Anita was even known to offer financial support from her own pocketbook.

In the first year of her employment with the school district, Anita was assigned an assistant to help with her many duties. But it wasn't long before the aide began complaining that she didn't have enough to do—Anita refused to give her any accounting responsibilities. After a six-month strained working relationship, Anita told her district office that an assistant wasn't necessary, that she slowed the process. The district listened and again allowed Anita complete control of the accounting records, cash, checks, and deposits, with the entire office to herself.

Desert View High School is located in the Washington Unified School District, which includes 13 elementary schools, five junior high schools, and three high schools. With an annual budget of $140 million, the district employs over 1,800 teachers and 890 administrators and support staff. The student clubs at Desert View are largely self-sustaining; they earn money through yearbook and snack bar sales in addition to other fund-raising activities, often in excess of $160,000 annually. Since there are over 23 student clubs at Desert View, the school uses an electronic bookkeeping system specializing in student organization accounting.

Sue Blanton, an imposing woman and the district's internal auditor, was responsible for training all student organization bookkeepers. She knew the accounting software front to back and took her job seriously. As part of district policy, all student organization bookkeepers were required to submit monthly bank reconciliations, bank statements, and student-organization financial reports to be reviewed by Sue, as well as the district's chief business officer. Sue expected the timely production of these documents and demanded strict adherence.

Along with reporting to the internal auditor, the student organizations had a certificated, credentialed teacher, Diane Tomkins, who served as the official adviser. Diane worked closely with Anita—they started off with a positive and productive relationship. In fact, Anita, Sue, and Diane all became good friends, meeting for lunch once a month and shopping together. Sue and Diane never suspected a thing. After all, the school district is audited annually by an outside firm, and in the three years Anita had been in charge, the auditors had uncovered nothing irregular. But that would soon change, thanks to the persistence of a gut feeling.

A Snake in the Grass

Although each year's annual audit had followed the proper procedure, with squeaky-clean results, after three years Sue became concerned that Desert View's student-organization financial reports were falling behind. Whenever she raised her concerns with Anita, they were met with a barrage of excuses—*I'm overworked, I have a lot of personal problems, I'll have it tomorrow*—followed by profuse apologies and promises to improve.

Diane was running into the same problems whenever she tried to talk to Anita. As weeks passed, Sue began e-mailing Diane to discuss their mutual concerns. What they didn't know was that Anita had been intercepting Diane's e-mails. Diane taught several classes during the day, during which time Anita would covertly access her computer and delete her e-mails from Sue. Before long she had fostered a strong animosity between her two supervisors, gradually cultivating feelings of distrust. Anytime a conversation was directed toward her own shortcomings, Anita would stoke the fire between her two managers to avert the unwanted attention; the secret to a good magic trick is a well-timed distraction.

Another month passed before Sue determined that something was amiss in Desert View's student-organization accounting books. She telephoned the audit firm and requested a special audit of Desert View's student organization accounts. The firm sent out a team immediately.

When the auditors arrived, they found Anita Buck looking very distressed and her office in disarray. Once they explained the purpose of their audit, Anita cooperated skillfully. Having prepackaged the proper bank reconciliations and financial reports, she showed the auditors how the financial data components tied together. She even admitted to many of her own errors, requesting that they write up her poor performance. From time to time during the audit, Anita shed a calculated tear or two while guiding the team to selected files where they could sample and confirm the accuracy of her reports.

The audit was a success, or so it seemed. Numerous management recommendations were offered and Anita promised to do better; everything appeared copacetic. Sue, however, was not convinced—she believed that Desert View's student-organization club cash balances should have been higher for that time of year. So she began reviewing each individual club account and financial statement dubiously, questioning every club adviser about fund-raising events. To Sue's surprise, she found that most simply dropped off their cash and check receipts to Anita, who then counted the money, created the receipt, and updated the accounts. District policy clearly states that funds must be double counted by two individuals at an event and a copy of the sales deposit sheet must be retained by the club adviser to ensure accurate records.

Sue was not happy. She was a stickler for the rules, and the fact that several district policies and procedures were being circumvented really pushed her buttons. She began to personally go to Anita's and Diane's offices every few days. Some of the visits were emotional and stressful, often resulting in tears from Anita as she walked away saying: "Nobody will help me! I'm doing the best I can!"

The district's fiscal year-end was right around the corner. Anita had been the student organization bookkeeper for three years now. Sue approached the superintendent and chief business officer and suggested that they bring the district's legal counsel into the matter. She remained unconvinced that Desert View's student-organization accounting problems were merely minor errors that simple management recommendations could correct.

The district's legal counsel, Charles Allen, was a seasoned attorney with a military background. He set up a meeting with Anita, during which he witnessed her teary-eyed apologies—routine, by now. Charles suggested that the district place Anita on paid administrative leave while her office was inspected thoroughly. When Anita received notification about the move, she seemed relieved. She told Sue that she would be happy to assist in any way possible and that now maybe everyone would understand the difficulty of her job.

Next the district IT staff copied Anita's computer hard drive and hired a computer information firm to analyze the data. They promptly found an irregularity. For some reason, Anita had eight copies of the student organization's accounting program data file. This was a red flag.

Anita tried to skillfully deflect the situation as she had done in the past, explaining that the extra files were merely backup data or old experimental files. She said the extras served as a guide for how to properly apply and post transactions. But this time the internal auditor was not convinced and sent the miscellaneous files to the accounting software company for their opinion.

The software company issued a preliminary report indicating that they had uncovered quite a few irregularities. Among the problems, they found that some of the specialized financial data-tracking features on the software had been disconnected. They recommended that a forensic auditor be hired to investigate. That's when I received the call.

Spread Thin

For the past 12 years, I've specialized in governmental and organizational fraud and forensic examinations. I met with the school district legal counsel, superintendent, assistant superintendent of human resources, and internal auditor. After the meeting, Sue and I drove over to Desert View to take a close look at Anita's workplace.

Her office was in complete disarray. Documents, files, and invoices were stacked everywhere haphazardly. I videotaped and digitally photographed them for evidence. Then we found a large safe in the backroom. Sue knew the combination and opened it to discover deposit bags containing cash and checks. The cabinets contained outdated files, and we found a small jar with approximately $200 in cash.

When we opened the cash register drawer, under the tray we discovered checks to organizations that were undeposited and several months stale-dated. So far we had uncovered eight sets of electronic accounting records, a messy room, and some outdated checks. Nothing stood out as solid evidence of financial fraud.

But at the end of Anita's desk credenza was a drawer we had not yet opened. Inside we found a complete mess—vendor invoices, Post-it notes, to-do lists, everything stuck together without a trace of organization. We reviewed each item meticulously; this time nothing would be overlooked. At the very bottom of the drawer we discovered numerous checks written to vendors and other payees. They were all computer generated and contained original-ink double signatures, some of them backdated over 15 months, and not one had ever been mailed out. Sue was baffled; she couldn't fathom why these checks were still in the drawer, unmailed. But I knew why. I explained that these checks might represent the amount of cash possibly being diverted. This also clarified the multiple accounting records, which were necessary to manipulate bank reconciliations and conceal the scheme. Things were beginning to come together.

Sue turned pale. She slowly sat down, clearly frightened at the implications. I looked at her and calmly said: "Don't worry; it's not your fault. If it is what I think it is—using multiple sets of books—Anita has duped everyone and done an outstanding job."

Sue turned to me anxiously and whispered, "I'm going to be fired."

"Sue, if it had not been for you, your gut feeling and persistence, this might never have been detected by anyone."

We continued our search, sifting through the rest of Anita's office, and discovered more evidence. Lodged behind cabinet drawers, we found fund-raising deposit bags with cash and more stale checks made out to the Desert View student organizations. Ultimately, we uncovered $114 in coins and $200 in cash scattered in seven locations, 21 stale checks payable to student organizations spanning 31 months totaling $5,974, club fund-raising deposit bags containing cash and checks spanning 30 months totaling $1,475, and 58 checks payable to vendors spanning 33 months totaling over $12,727.

Sue and I prepared a deposit for the bank totaling around $1,100, comprised of the uncovered cash and the checks that were still valid. In addition, we found nine cash-advance envelopes with receipts and balances that fell short by $6,127.

I obtained a complete working copy of the electronic accounting program and a backup copy of each of the eight databases of accounting transactions. Returning to my office, I opened each of the eight sets of accounting books. This process was going to take time. Fortunately, one of the book sets was a demonstration file, which I quickly eliminated. I compared transactions, bank reconciliations, and numerous journal entries entered within and spanning each set of books. I discovered that the "Tracks" program, used to track student sales, fees, and deposits before they were integrated into the accounting program, was disconnected and that student cash transactions were being directly entered. Using this method, the identity of the student transaction was lost. I examined checks written, endorsed, and prepared for mailing to the vendors, finding that the majority were written using three of the accounting databases. The bank reconciliations were spread out among four of the databases, and in many instances, checks were duplicated in some sets of books and omitted from others. The individual club accounts were full of journal entries without description. The journal entries were primarily records of transferring money from one club to another. No wonder Anita felt overworked! I couldn't help but to think that clubs probably complained that the total in their accounts did not measure up to the amount of money earned, and in response, Anita simply moved funds back and forth between accounts in an attempt to cover the holes.

The Road to Coming Clean

When I finished my analysis, I knew that the electronic accounting records were not sufficient to explain the amount of cash that had been pilfered over the past three years. So far I'd only determined Anita's methodology.

The cash and check deposits that school organizations submitted could be placed aside or hidden. In time, if the club failed to notice that their deposit wasn't recorded on their account report, then Anita could remove the cash undetected. Many of the clubs did not retain their records because they trusted the bookkeeper.

While reviewing the different versions of the accounting records, it was interesting to note that some clubs had fewer journal entry transactions than others. It is likely that certain clubs retained their own logs and records of the deposits and expenditures they incurred and were able to inquire about any irregular activity. Upon questioning, Anita was probably forced to correct some records, so she adjusted other clubs' accounts in order to keep the cash shortages from being discovered.

As more cash was removed from the system, fewer funds were available to pay for the checks that were written. In order to maintain the facade that the account activity was normal, checks were prepared and signatures obtained by three signers, as was required; however, Anita never mailed or distributed these checks.

The use of cash advances seemed to be prevalent, although not allowed by the district. Unmonitored advances gave Anita ample opportunities to alter the advance and subsequently remove any unspent cash for personal use. With control of the accounting records and few clubs reconciling their account activity, she could adjust the advances of each club as she saw fit.

As the losses and the scheme grew, it became more difficult for Anita to manage so many sets of books. Accounting for the actual records became confused and mixed with the false accounting records. Insufficient-funds checks started to pile up and the accounting got further behind. More and more clubs began to question their accounts. Club activity reports that once reflected simple transactions became cluttered with journal entries, and that just inspired more inquiries.

The district mandates that the transactions recorded in the Tracks student sales system be imported into the accounting software. With Tracks disconnected from the accounting program, Anita could alter deposits at will. After analyzing records and reviewing what the software company provided, we determined that more than $24,000 worth of student cash transactions was missing.

Since much of it was unrecorded cash, bank reconciliation discrepancies were used as another component of quantifying potential losses. In total, these discrepancies were just over $10,000.

Considering that the entire loss was attributable to cash removed from the electronic accounting system prior to recording, the total was quantified at slightly more than $50,000. What I needed next was a face-to-face meeting with Anita Buck.

One Admission Please

Before I met with Anita, I wanted to know everything about her. I spent several days on background analysis, researching her favorite Web sites, learning about her family members, her pets, and her hobbies. By the time I was finished, I even knew how much Anita tipped her hairdresser. I also developed a theme underlying the motivation for embezzlement. It became clear to me that Anita loved luxurious purchases: expensive purses, limo rides for her children's events, equipment for the student organization office. She made it a priority to keep up appearances.

I also requested that Sue supervise the complete organization of Anita's office. That was Anita's home territory and where I would conduct the interview. I wanted her to be comfortable. It took three days to clean her space to perfection. It looked dramatically different from the mess that once surrounded us.

The stage, the theme, and the evidence were set. We scheduled an interview for Anita to meet me at 9:00 a.m. on a Friday in August, during summer break when very few people would be at Desert View High School. Thirty days had passed since I started the examination. As we entered the office, the first words out of Anita's mouth were "Wow, this office looks so different."

We moved to a table, where I made sure Anita was comfortably seated closest to the unlocked door. The opening conversation was light. We had a few laughs as we discussed common areas of interest, family, friends—wherever I found a connection. Anita mentioned that I knew a lot about her and her family.

"Yes, I'm very thorough," I replied. "I like to try to understand situations before passing judgment."

"You're not like anyone I've talked to," she responded.

When the moment was right, I took out a large binder, placed it on the table and said, "I'm not like any other accountant or auditor you have worked with; I'm a forensic accountant specializing in financial fraud examinations."

The expression on Anita's face changed. Her jaw dropped and she suddenly became very serious. I sympathized by saying, "I understood how difficult it must have been for you to see others always owning nice things." I watched her body language and facial expressions, again waiting for the right moment, and then I said, "Anita, based on the evidence I have compiled, I have reason to believe that you have stolen around $98,000 over the past three years."

I purposefully quoted a much larger figure than the actual potential loss. She sat quietly not saying a word. After a full minute passed, her eyes welled with tears and she said, "Mike, it can't be that much."

I looked at Anita and told her how proud I was of her for coming clean. As Anita and I talked, she continually expressed remorse for taking the money. She reiterated that she could not possibly have stolen $98,000. The truth of the matter was that Anita really did not know how much she had pilfered. As we discussed the evidence, she agreed to write an admission letter and return $50,000 to the school district from her home equity line of credit. She also agreed to meet with the economic crimes detective with the local police as long as I attended the meeting with her.

As Anita and I reviewed my findings, I asked her to tell me, in her own words, how she orchestrated the scheme. Anita revealed that all of the money she had stolen came from the cash deposits. She stopped using the Tracks system because it downloaded the student deposit information directly into the accounting records, which would have shown that her deposits were incorrect. Anita also explained that, by the third year, she had so many sets of electronic books that even she became confused and lost track of which books she was using.

Expelled

As a result of the entire examination process, which included carefully documenting the crime scene, correctly preserving the electronic evidence, performing a thorough background check, developing the proper theme justifying the embezzlement, altering Anita's work environment, and treating Anita Buck with respect and kindness, the stage was properly set. The outcome unfolded according to plan, resulting in an admission of guilt by interview, an admission letter signed by Anita, the return of $50,000 to the district, and a secondary interview with the local police department detective. At the station, Anita confirmed everything she told me and established that she wrote the admission letter of her own free will.

The admission letter, among other things, included a promise to make restitution by reimbursing the district $50,000 within two days, a resignation effective immediately, a vow not to use the district for any job reference, a forfeiture of her vested vacation balance, and an apology to the district for her actions.

Eleven months later, Anita Buck pleaded guilty to felony embezzlement. Since she had cooperated and paid restitution, she was sentenced to only 180 days of weekend incarceration, 1,500 hours of community service, and five years' probation.

As a result of the examination, the accounting software company has modified their own accounting program to prevent the copying and creation of multiple sets of accounting data files.

Lessons Learned

After the examination ended, I met again with district management. Sue made a keen observation. She said that, after having gone through this entire process, she learned to follow her gut feeling. She realized that no matter how much you like someone and trust them, professional skepticism must be maintained.

Recommendations to Prevent Future Occurrences

Although it's impossible to eradicate the possibility of fraud, the following recommendations were offered and adopted by the district.

Update Software

Update electronic accounting software to a version that eliminates the ability to copy accounting data files. Make sure employees have an understanding of the software so that irregularities will not be disregarded. In addition, it would be beneficial to activate certain features that allow the district office headquarters to monitor the accounting software from the district office location.

Enforce Timelines

Add a district policy that provides specific timelines for reporting to the district and specific penalties should someone fail to meet those deadlines. That way everyone is on the same page and everyone is held accountable.

Surprise Inspections and Employee Rotation

Perform surprise inspections as a method of deterrence. Also, bookkeepers should rotate schools within the district so that one person does not have complete control over any accounts.

Employee Education

Reinforce your policies by making sure all employees are aware of the rules of ethics. In a case such as this, make sure that Tracks cash receipting is the only method allowed, and reinforce the fact that the direct recording of deposits within the electronic accounting records is not acceptable.

Budget for Auditors

It is important to budget sufficient funds for the district internal auditor. Auditing is an essential aspect of maintaining a clean system, and funds invested in fraud prevention will save money in the long run.

Hotlines

Establish a fraud-reporting hotline with an external reporting service so that individuals can come forward anonymously with reports of illicit activities.

About the Author

Michael Ammermon, CFE, CPA, is a sole practitioner in Laguna Niguel, California. He has 17 years of governmental, nonprofit, and private sector financial, forensic, fraud, audit, and litigation support experience. Having performed numerous financial fraud and abuse examinations in the public and private sectors, he makes his primary focus governmental organizations such as K-12 school districts, community colleges, and other agencies.

Moving Money

NEIL HARRISON

At 24 years old, David Rushe had his whole life ahead of him. He graduated from high school at 18 with aspirations of becoming a DJ. After spending a couple of years bar-backing at local night clubs, he put his dreams on hold and took an office job at an insurance brokerage firm in Bristol, west of London. His administrative role was a far cry from being a DJ, but it helped keep him solvent.

After four years, David was stuck in a rut—tired of work and bored with life. He needed a fresh start in a new city, and Birmingham was just the place. Within six weeks David had found himself a new job as a credit controller with a respectable blue-chip company, Burnell Property Management (BPM). He also moved into some new digs, a small one-bedroom apartment in Newtown. It wasn't the nicest area, but it was cheap and only a short bus ride from the pubs and night clubs of Birmingham City Center.

BPM is one of the oldest and most respected property management firms in the United Kingdom. It has advised property owners, developers, investors, and landowners for 80 years. Primarily, the company manages commercial properties, a service that includes finding tenants, collecting rent, and handling maintenance programs. Over the years it has expanded and now employs surveyors, property lawyers, and even environmental scientists.

A $40,000 Dilemma

I was reading the local newspaper at lunchtime one Tuesday when the phone rang.

"Hi, is this Forensic?" a rather flustered voice asked.

"Yep, Neil speaking, how can I help you?"

"It's Tony from the audit department; we've got a problem. One of our clients just called. They've had some cash stolen and need advice. Any chance you could drive out tomorrow for a meeting?"

"No problem, Tony. E-mail me their address and telephone number and I'll be out there as soon as I can."

After several years of tax and audit work as an accountant, I found myself in the fraud investigation field. I work in the forensic accounting department of a large international accountancy firm and there is no end to the number of clients in need of our services. Investment fraud, check fraud, credit schemes—we'd seen it all.

I checked my e-mails and found a new message entitled "Burnell Property Management." It explained that BPM had lost $40,000 to a suspected fraud. They were not certain of the facts but guessed that one of their employees was involved. Forty thousand dollars was a small sum compared to our typical investigations, but occasionally more is uncovered when we begin turning over stones.

The following day I strolled through the crisp morning air to the client's offices from a nearby parking lot. They occupied a new office block in a fashionable part of the city.

I walked through the main doors into a large atrium with marble floors and tropical plants. In the middle was a reception desk. A security guard pointed to the elevators behind him and directed me to the third floor. At the top I was greeted by Malcolm, the company's financial controller. A tall man in his mid-30s, he wore a casual gray suit with a collared shirt.

"Good morning. You must be Neil."

"Pleased to meet you. You are Malcolm?"

"Yes. Thanks for coming on such short notice. I've set up a meeting with Mark Yates; he's the finance director. If you follow me I've got a room booked and some coffee brewing."

Malcolm led me down a corridor and into a small meeting room. Mr. Yates was already there, seated and waiting. He was in his late 40s and a tough-looking fellow. He stood up and introduced himself. His confident and slightly aggressive manner told me he wasn't a man to be crossed.

"Here's the problem," he began. "Three days ago Malcolm had a call from a cashier at Northern Bank. A scruffy teenager had tried to withdraw $40,000 from an account at a local branch. The cashier was suspicious. The account had recently been credited with $40,000 from BPM and the lad didn't look like one of our landlords. The cashier asked him for evidence that he was entitled to the money received from BPM, but the kid replied that he had lost the relevant paperwork and would forward it at a later date. As the dialogue continued, he became nervous and fidgety. The cashier told him she was going to call BPM. With that, he bolted."

"OK, Mr. Yates, what do you know about this payment?" I asked.

"Malcolm, maybe you should take over now," he replied.

"It's all to do with David Rushe. He's a credit controller in our finance department. A few days ago he approached me with a payment request to the account in question. I'm afraid to say I authorized it," explained Malcolm.

"Tell me about the payment," I said.

"Well, a couple of weeks ago we received some money in our office bank account—$40,000, to be precise. It was from Banchor Consulting, a former customer. I guessed that Banchor had paid the amount in error, so I asked David to give them a call and sort it out. He came back about 10 minutes later and told me he had spoken with them and the amount had indeed been paid by accident. Later that day he came to me with a request for a payment to a Mr. Steve Agar, explaining that Banchor wanted the money refunded to this individual."

"So the refund to Banchor was paid to an account in the name of Steve Agar. Didn't that strike you as strange?" I asked.

"It did, but David showed me an e-mail from Banchor. It definitely indicated that the money was to be refunded to Steve Agar. I sent the payment and thought nothing of it until this week when the cashier called, at which point I immediately telephoned Banchor. They had never heard of Steve Agar and denied sending the e-mail. I called David to my office and told him about the cashier and my phone call. We agreed that the situation didn't make sense; after all, the bank details supposedly came from Banchor. When I asked him to retrieve the e-mail so we could double-check it, he appeared uncomfortable. David claimed that he had thrown it away and deleted it from his computer. I inquired as to why he would do such a thing when policy requires that the e-mail be stapled to the payment request form. He became angry and accused me of calling him a liar. 'No one is calling you a liar,' I said. Anyway, yesterday, he called in sick and now refuses to answer his phone."

Mr. Yates straightened in his chair. "I'm certain David is involved, but the bank account details came from Banchor. Neil, I need you to sort this out before we discipline David. I also need to know if any other funds have gone missing."

"No problem, Mr. Yates. I'll get to it."

Impotent Controls

Following the meeting, I returned to the office. I sat back and thought long and hard about the job. Banchor denied sending the e-mail, but Malcolm was sure that he had seen it. Maybe David was colluding with someone at Banchor. After all, why did they pay the money in the first place? Maybe

Malcolm was lying about the e-mail to cover his back for authorizing the payment. To start, we needed to review all of David's e-mails, both outgoing and incoming. I called Josh, one of my firm's forensic technology specialists and a former IT security consultant, in hopes that he could recover the deleted e-mail from Banchor.

We met at the BPM offices later that afternoon. He was a large chap, probably a result of his sedentary lifestyle.

"Josh, I need you to extract a copy of David Rushe's e-mails from the server. I also want you to image his desktop computer."

A computer hard disk is like a textbook. The beginning of a textbook includes a table of contents indicating the whereabouts of each chapter. The equivalent on a hard drive is called a file allocation table, or FAT, and it tells the computer where on the hard disk each file can be found. When a file is deleted from a hard disk, the relevant FAT entry is deleted. The computer then thinks the file is gone. The reality is that the file will remain on the hard disk of the computer until the space it occupies is overwritten with a new file. A typical hard disk will be full of deleted files and fragments of deleted files not yet overwritten. I had asked Josh to image David's computer, a task that copies every last bit of data on the hard disk. This enables the forensic IT specialist to recover and read deleted files, often containing crucial evidence the suspect thought had been deleted.

Leaving Josh to complete his work, I decided to catch up with Malcolm and find out some more about BPM's accounting systems. The finance department was located in a large open office on the ground floor. I found Malcolm hovering around a pretty secretary.

"Hi, Malcolm. May we have a quick chat about your accounting systems?"

"Sure, follow me."

He led me out of the room and into his personal office, which was piled high with files and paper. On the wall was a picture of Malcolm with the D-list celebrity soap star Leslie Eacock.

"I see you mix with the stars," I said, with a hint of sarcasm.

"Ah yes, I met Leslie at a charity bash. He was a nice guy. I played golf with him last year," replied Malcolm. "Now, how can I help you?"

I requested that he take me through business operations, how BPM recorded income, and how they processed purchase invoices. When he finished, I asked him how BPM paid its suppliers.

"We don't use checks very often anymore. Our suppliers and employees are paid by BACS, a form of direct deposit. The BACS machine is a computer that links to the bank. We've got high-level control over these payments. When we want to make a payment, we put a creator card into the

BACS machine and enter a PIN number and the account details of the recipient. The final step is to authorize the payment, which is done by plugging an authorizer card into the system and typing the authorizer PIN number."

"Who has these creator and authorizer cards?" I asked.

"Angela and Jake in accounts payable both have creator cards. My assistant, Lisa, and I have authorizer cards," he replied.

"And where do you keep the cards?"

"In the finance office safe.""The safe that was open when I walked through the office earlier?" I asked.

"Er . . . yes."

"When a payment is made, how do you know which bank account to send it to?"

"We use the bank account details stored on the supplier information file. It's part of our computer accounting system."

"And who can update those files?"

"Uh, anyone with access to the accounting system."

"And who has access to the system?"

"Everyone in Finance," he replied. Malcolm sat back, his face contorting uncomfortably as yet another weakness in his accounting system was revealed. "That's not good, is it?" he asked.

"Well, anyone in Finance can change supplier bank-account numbers," I said. "That means the high-tech controls over BACS payments are easily circumvented." I moved on. "What about the Banchor refund? How was that paid?" I asked.

"We paid the refund by BACS. As I explained, David gave me the payment request form. Jake used his creator card to raise the payment and I authorized it. But I checked the account number to the e-mail from Banchor."

The meeting carried on for another half-hour while I questioned Malcolm about all parts of the business. Upon finishing, I walked over to IT to find out how Josh was getting on.

Josh explained that he had imaged David's computer. With regard to the deleted e-mails, we were in luck. The client's system archived everything that had been sent or received regardless of whether it was deleted from the user's computer. All Josh needed to do now was extract David's e-mails from the server.

Over the next couple of days, I interviewed all of the finance staff. The first one of real interest was Laura. I had learned from previous conversations that she had dated David for a while. Laura was a pretty girl with long black hair, dark brown eyes, and a fresh complexion. When she entered the room she seemed nervous, ready to burst into tears. But as the interview progressed, she began to relax. Laura explained that she had dated David for a couple of months but now regretted it.

"I feel so stupid," she said. "He used me like a piggy bank. He still owes me $600. I don't suppose I'll ever see it again. I should have known better."

"Have you spoken to David since he left?" I asked.

"Yes, he called me and asked what people were saying about him. He tried to convince me that he hadn't stolen any money. I just don't trust him anymore. I should never have trusted him. He's got a past, you know."

"What sort of past?"

"Well, I know that he had to do community service every Saturday. He wouldn't tell me what he had done, but he'd been sentenced to 300 hours of service."

I sensed anger in Laura toward David.

"I should never have dated him. I just know everyone is talking about me now."

She continued for another five minutes but added nothing more of any interest. After Laura, I interviewed 15 more staff members. As the talks progressed, it became apparent that David owed money to most people in the department. Only small amounts to each person, but it added up to a couple of thousand dollars in total. A picture of David was building, but the real answers would come from his e-mails.

Forge Ahead

Later that week I met with Josh again. He was sitting in an office that resembled a futuristic battleground. His desk was covered with cables, various computer components, and other pieces of technology.

"Hi, Neil. I was wondering when you'd be back. I've put the image of David's computer on to an external hard disk and I've put his e-mails on a DVD."

"Thanks, Josh."

"Oh, and Neil, when I was out at the client's I managed to grab electronic copies of all BACS payments reports from the BACS computer."

"Great," I replied. The payment reports would list every payment made through the BACS system, which might provide useful evidence.

I went back to my office and loaded David's e-mails onto my laptop. One by one I read everything sent or received by David over his six months at the company. After several hours I had found nothing of interest other than some messages in which he begged colleagues to lend him money. One coworker had even allowed him to borrow funds from the company's petty cash. Still, there was no e-mail from Banchor. I began to wonder if it actually existed. Maybe the e-mail was an embellishment added by Malcolm to cover his back. Following my unsuccessful review, I turned my attention to the image of David's computer. I took the external hard disk given to me by Josh and plugged it into my laptop. There were so many files on the computer that it would take months to review all of them. I decided it would be best to use a software tool that enables vast quantities of electronic data to be sifted through in seconds using key words. My first key word was Banchor. Straight away it brought up a local copy of an e-mail saved on David's computer. Excited, I opened it and reviewed the contents. It read as follows:

> From: asifkhan@banchorconsulting.co.uk
> Sent: April 19 2:02
> To: david.rushe@BPM.co.uk
> Subject: Re: Payment
>
> David,
> As per our discussions, please pay the $40,000 that was paid to you in error into the following account:
> Sort Code: 70-44-44
> Account No: 07663411
> Account Name: Mr. Steve Agar
> Northern Bank
>
> Hope this okay.
> Regards,
> Asif

I read the e-mail again, sat back and thought hard. Why hadn't I found this message when I reviewed the contents from the server? I had been assured by the client's IT manager that the server held every e-mail, even deleted ones. Maybe it was there and I had missed it. I loaded up David's e-mails and scrolled to April 19. That's when the plot unraveled. On that day at precisely 2:02 p.m., David received another e-mail from Asif Khan. It read as follows:

> From: asifkhan@yazoo.co.uk
> Sent: April 19 2:02
> To: david.rushe@BPM.co.uk
> Subject: Re: oi!
>
> U alrite mate? How have u been? I just been busy with work and college.
> We shud meet up, gangsters leavin next week
> Asif

The e-mail from Banchor was a fake. David had typed over an old message from a friend and printed it as support for the client's refund. That was why I couldn't find the e-mail on the server. It had never been received; it was a forgery. I thought back to my conversations with Malcolm. Controls over BACS payments could be easily circumvented by changing supplier bank-account numbers in the supplier master file. My concerns grew. Was $40,000 the full extent of BPM's loss?

Thankfully, Josh had obtained the BACS payment reports. Each time BPM made an electronic BACS payment, the computer generated a report listing each bank account where the funds had been transferred. Josh had compiled these reports into a single file, which I loaded into my data-mining software. It contained 48,000 records representing payments to the value of $196 million. My first test was to compare the bank account numbers on each of the 48,000 payments to the Steve Agar bank account number. Fortunately for BPM, the $40,000 Banchor refund was the only payment made to this account. Given the wide scope for fraud, I decided to extend my testing. I loaded the BPM electronic customer files and the BPM payroll files into my data-mining software. They contained the bank account numbers of every BPM employee and supplier. Again I was quickly able to cross-reference each of the BACS payments to either a supplier or employee bank account. The only payments made to David's own account were those of his monthly salary. I reviewed the rest of the output. More than one hundred payments with a total value of more than $1.96 million went to unmatched accounts controlled by neither suppliers nor employees.

I called Malcolm and arranged a meeting with him and Mr. Yates. I showed him the two e-mails and explained that the file times showed that the second one was modified after being received.

"So he was a thief!" exclaimed Yates.

"That really disappoints me. He was a nice lad and a decent worker. But what could we have done?" asked Malcolm.

"I've had a look at David's personnel file. Your human resources department didn't check his references. My investigation revealed he's got a criminal record," I replied.

"Bloody HR!" yelled Yates.

For the remainder of the meeting, I explained the control weaknesses I had found and listened as Yates explained the many things he would like to do to David Rushe given half a chance. The following day, Yates and Malcolm set up a meeting with Northern Bank. They reimbursed the $40,000 to BPM and the matter was referred to the police. The $1.96 million of payments made to accounts outside the purchase ledger and payroll were found to be deposits refunded to property tenants. The paperwork seemed in order.

David was soon invited to a disciplinary hearing, but shocked no one when he failed to show up. His employment contract was terminated immediately. Much to the chagrin of BPM, the police never picked up the case. As a result, no further investigations were undertaken.

Lessons Learned

Forging an e-mail is very easy in this day and age. Simply by typing over the original contents, one can then print the fake or forward it to an unsuspecting party. Malcolm had relied on the message presented to him by David despite an obvious red flag—the refund was directed to a personal account, while the payment was originally from a business.

Furthermore, it's important to remember that a chain is only as strong as its weakest link. The total lack of control over the supplier master files rendered sophisticated controls over BACS payments impotent. BPM was lucky. David had not capitalized on this major flaw. The situation could have been much worse.

Recommendations to Prevent Future Occurrences

Verify Suspicions

Malcolm should have acted on his suspicions and verified the transfer with Banchor before authorizing the payment. Instead, he relied on an e-mail with suspect information. Don't dismiss gut feelings; always verify your suspicions.

Limit Access

Limit access to supplier master files. The creation of new suppliers and the modification of existing supplier details should be off-limits to employees who process payments and invoices.

Background Checks

David's history was never verified before he began work at BPM. If a background check was administered, his track record of dishonest behavior would have been revealed, hopefully preventing his employment in the first place.

About the Author

Neil Harrison, CFE, FCCA, is an assistant director at Deloitte & Touche LLP. As a senior member of their United Kingdom Forensic and Disputes Services team, he has led many high-profile investigations into fraud, bribery, and corruption. He has been a court-appointed expert witness in the field of accounting and has lectured on fraud risk, forensic technology, and asset tracing.

CHAPTER 23

Operation: Overnight Identity Theft

BRUNO PAVLICEK

Keith Evans and Jerry Straiser grew up on the wrong side of the tracks. Like so many of today's urban and susceptible youth, the two young men faced some of life's toughest challenges while coming of age on the hard-core streets of Newark, New Jersey. But Keith, the aspiring 18-year-old with a taste for the fast-paced life, decided to embark upon adulthood and a criminal career with a bang.

As a minor, Keith already had various encounters with the law, collecting a repertoire of offenses such as resisting arrest, burglary, attempting to elude police, receiving stolen property, manufacturing and distribution of controlled dangerous substances (CDS), and possession of CDS on school property. And now, leaving his days as a juvenile delinquent behind him, he embarked upon a new level of crime as the leader of an identity theft ring.

Jerry, the only kid in the neighborhood whose family owned a computer, decided to join Keith as his right-hand man and accomplice. Several years Keith's senior, Jerry had just finished a three-year probationary sentence for possession of drug paraphernalia and hindering apprehension—nickel-and-dime offenses when compared to Keith's resume.

The two boys maintained a friendship. Jerry's family wasn't very fond of Keith, but the devious duo managed to break both state and federal laws right under the unsuspecting noses of the elder Straisers. Over several months, the boys utilized the Straiser family computer to pilfer the personal information of 159 unwitting victims and make fraudulent Internet purchases totaling over half a million dollars.

The Prosecutor's Office

The Harris County Prosecutor's Office (HCPO), located in Brookville, New Jersey, serves as one of 21 New Jersey county prosecutor's offices. Staffed with prosecutors, agents, and sworn detectives, the HCPO serves as the chief law enforcement agency in Harris County and is empowered to investigate and prosecute any and all state crimes of a felonious nature. The Economic Crimes Unit of the HCPO employs several detectives, a detective sergeant, and a prosecutor, all of whom investigate other municipal departments and train them in investigating crimes concerning theft by deception and fraud.

I was one of two detectives assigned to the HCPO's Economic Crimes Unit for the entire county of Harris. In my position I worked with various municipal police departments and several federal agencies, either jointly or in an assisting capacity. Although some of the cases were ultimately prosecuted on a federal level, most were charged and prosecuted in state superior court.

With limited manpower and shrinking budgets, our unit was relegated to investigating crimes of a second-degree nature. According to New Jersey statute, second-degree theft-related crimes require a minimum of a $75,000 loss. Also, a second-degree crime in New Jersey translates to a presumption of incarceration in state prison between 5 and 10 years. But that's just "paper justice." The reality of the sentencing process means that the perpetrator's criminal background, as well as his or her status in life and whether he or she is able to pay back the money, quite often dictates the severity of the criminal sentence. That's why at times it was satisfying to work a street level case such as this: The criminals had no political connections, and they almost never had the ability to pay the money back.

A "Winner" of a Case

This particular case came across my desk as a request for assistance from the Johnson Township Police Department and U.S. Secret Service. While the HCPO had a good working relationship with various departments and agencies throughout the county, we particularly enjoyed working with the U.S. Secret Service.

It began when my sergeant called me into his office one day and told me he had a "winner" of a case for me. Whenever he said this, I knew long hours and hard work were ahead. This "winning" assignment was no different; for the next several weeks, my entire life would be devoted to this case.

A week before contacting us, the Secret Service and the Johnson police had attempted to bring down an identity theft ring. It was after their attempt went south that they decided to bring us in. My response to the news was lukewarm at best. I thought, "Great, now I have to pick up someone else's pieces." However, once I found out that this particular ring was responsible for victimizing 159 people throughout the United States, of which about 50 were Harris County residents, to the tune of half a million dollars in stolen computers and other electronic items, I was all ears.

Later that afternoon I met with Special Agent Harmony of the Secret Service and Detective Sun of the Johnson Township Police, who proceeded to bombard me with details of the case: suspect names, victim names, monetary losses, and jurisdiction issues. At the end of the hour, I must have had 10 pages of notes. Already in full investigation mode, I tried to connect the dots between the names of suspects being hurled at me. We had a long road ahead of us, but the case had piqued my interest. After all, it was an opportunity to take down a street-level identity theft ring, and the stolen money was fairly big—in excess of $75,000, which would be considered a second-degree felony punishable by 5 to 10 years in state prison. For the next several weeks, all three agencies took the ball and ran with it, with the HCPO assuming the lead. Eventually, the Harris Township and Henderson police departments and the U.S. Postal Inspection Service also joined our make-shift task force.

At the outset of the investigation, we discovered that the financial victims were two companies: Hewart Package, a large computer manufacturer, and Photo Street Co., a California-based electronics retail distributor. Both companies reported to us that laptop computers and other high-end electronic items, such as digital cameras, palm pilots, and DVD players, were being fraudulently ordered through their company Web sites. These items were then shipped overnight via the National Courier transport company.

A review of the shipping logs and delivery records of National Courier revealed a pattern of shipping addresses within the cities of Henderson and Newark, New Jersey, where the stolen goods were being sent. Additionally, confirmation was made that the route used to ship these items was handled by a National Courier employee named Roger Barrington.

During our background investigation of Roger, National Courier's corporate investigators revealed to us that he was generally defensive and arrogant. Furthermore, several months back, the FBI had surveilled Roger, suspecting that he was involved with another street-level identity theft ring. They attempted to interview him and he basically told them to go "pound salt." Since the FBI had no probable cause to arrest Roger at the time, nothing was done and their investigation had subsequently fizzled out.

As we were conducting our investigation, the identity thieves continued to make fraudulent purchases reflecting this same pattern. One such purchase flagged by the Photo Street Co. revealed a suspect e-mail address that was traced to a large online service provider. A grand jury subpoena was served upon the Internet service provider by the HCPO's Computer Forensics Unit, and within 24 hours we finally had our first substantial lead. The subscriber information on the e-mail account came back to Jerry Straiser of Newark. A search warrant was then obtained for Jerry's residence.

By the second week of the investigation, we were working around the clock. Over the next several days, we planned a coordinated operation between the HCPO, U.S. Secret Service, Harris Township Police Department, and Johnson Township Police Department, with assistance from National Courier.

We had two plans of attack. One was to initiate a control delivery operation by following a National Courier driver to the address linked to the e-mail address the boys used to fraudulently purchase packages; the other was to search Jerry's computer.

The planning phase had reached an end, in that we received word that another package had been ordered by the bad guys and was being delivered to a Henderson address via National Courier. A drive-by of that address revealed it to be a real apartment building—right in the middle of a drug-infested neighborhood. Nevertheless, we had to now step it up a notch.

The Chase

On the day of the operation, our first goal was to accompany National's driver on his route to the suspect address. National's corporate security team, however, was skittish about us commandeering one of their trucks. As a result, we were relegated to surveilling the National truck and its driver, who incidentally had no idea he was in possession of a stolen package. He also had no knowledge that a team of undercover police cars would be tailing him.

Now, inasmuch as Roger Barrington was found to have previously delivered most of the stolen packages and was a viable suspect, we specifically decided to trail the package on board with a different driver. Our intention was to save Roger for later in our investigation rather than risk exposing ourselves to a target who could potentially give warning to the rest of the gang.

As the surveillance operation commenced that morning, we followed the driver zigzagging through various streets around Henderson. At the same time, I had another team of officers assigned to Jerry's residence in Newark, where they were conducting a concurrent surveillance of his house. They were also awaiting my word to hit the house, since our intention was to conduct the two operations—the delivery of the fraudulent package to the apartment complex in Henderson and the execution of the search warrant at Jerry's residence in Newark—simultaneously.

However, like any other mobile surveillance, we started encountering variables while driving. We didn't know exactly when the driver was going to approach our target street. To make matters worse, we also knew that our target street was littered with drug dealers and their juvenile sentries on bikes. So by constantly following the driver, we ran the risk of being noticed by one of these lookouts and scaring the mule—the low-level person hired to sign for the stolen package. As a result, we ended our pussyfooting and stopped the driver. He was more than willing to assist us. One of the Secret Service agents jumped on board and became our eyes and ears.

Murphy's Law, in the meantime, descended upon us as the Newark team reported to me that Jerry was leaving his residence and getting into his car. "Damn it, why can't anything go right?" I asked in frustration. But there was absolutely nothing we could do other than tail him. We had no arrest warrant on Jerry—our warrant was for his computer.

Some quick brainstorming led me to instruct one of the detectives to make a call to Jerry and arrange to meet him at his home. The detective called him, stating that he just wanted to speak to him about the possibility that his computer was involved in a crime. I hoped that even if Jerry knew he was caught, he'd rush back to his house to destroy the evidence. Once we had him, we'd be able to execute a search of both his residence and his computer. Ideally, we'd elicit a confession and arrest him on the spot, killing two birds with one stone. In order to hit his house and execute the delivery simultaneously, we had to get our hands on Jerry as soon as possible. But there were no guarantees.

Despite this minor setback, my primary goal was to successfully make the control delivery. From there we would, hopefully, obtain a confession from the mule who was signing for the package. Then we could get him or her to positively ID Jerry from a photo lineup.

No Honor Amongst Friends and Thieves

The time had finally arrived. The delivery driver was slowly approaching the corner, with our agent carefully stowed in his box truck. All of the drug dealers buzzed outside while their lookouts were circling the block like vultures. One premature drive down the target street by any one of us would have caused a chain reaction of people scurrying like cockroaches. Needless to say, that would cause our operation to fold. We had no choice. We were blind as to what was going on, as our teams were now strategically parked around the corner away from the peering eyes of the lookouts.

Seconds felt like minutes, and minutes felt like hours as our ears were glued to the radio. But, sooner than we imagined, the agent radioed in and said the mule had just come out of the apartment and was signing for the package. All the teams converged and, within seconds, the block was covered with a dozen cops and federal agents who seemed to come out of nowhere. The entire street suddenly emptied itself of the dealers and lookouts, leaving only the mule—a young man by the name of Joe Timms—who was now in the prone position, cuffed, and under arrest for simply signing his name to the package.

Immediately upon taking Joe into custody, I instructed the Newark team to commence their search warrant. In the meantime, upon speaking with Joe, he consented to have us conduct a search of his apartment, where we met with his sister, Crystal. She wasn't in custody just yet, but was nevertheless told her Miranda rights and immediately questioned.

Within the next 15 minutes the Newark team advised me that the search of Jerry's residence appeared to be successful, in that we were able to seize his personal computer. But what was of concern was that his bedroom contained no other items of evidentiary value. There were no paper slips with victims' names or identifiers on them, no stolen or counterfeit credit cards, no false IDs—nothing. All we had was Jerry's computer, as well as a local outstanding traffic warrant on him.

Thankfully, back in Henderson, the Timms siblings began confessing. Crystal indicated that a woman named Tanya had actually recruited her into the role of accepting packages shipped by National Courier. She would then turn over the parcels to an individual named Mark. The physical description Crystal provided of Mark was similar to that of Jerry, but she was unable to positively identity him from the photo lineup.

Crystal also stated that on several occasions, her brother, Joe, had helped her with this endeavor by signing for the packages, as he had done on this particular day. Altogether, Crystal indicated she made approximately $400 for acceptance of three to five packages. When her brother assisted, however, she would pay him a cut of $20 to $30 dollars.

The Timms siblings were released on criminal summons complaints. Phase one of the days operation was finished, but we weren't out of the woods yet. The most important phase was only beginning: the interrogation of Jerry Straiser. Our other team had made contact with Jerry and was in the midst of transporting him back to Harris County.

Back at Johnson Police headquarters, Jerry became an open book. At one point he became so emotional he even started crying—a very good sign when someone is confessing. Our suspect started off by telling us how his neighborhood friend, Keith Evans, was the leader behind this identity theft operation. He also stated that Keith had paid him to utilize his family's home computer to make all of the fraudulent purchases. The names and credit card numbers of the identity theft victims were being gathered by Keith via retail credit card receipts stolen from two popular clothing stores in the local mall. Often Jerry would observe Keith inputting this information on the retail Web sites of Hewart Package and Photo Street Co. from a stack of credit card receipts he had in his pocket or in a brown paper bag.

Jerry eventually decided to take on a more active role in the operation, as he began assisting Keith in also picking up the National Courier packages. These packages were arranged to be delivered at addresses where mules would sign for them. Jerry also admitted that he would find mules in the Henderson and Newark area on behalf of Keith to accept these packages. He had helped Keith recruit a National Courier driver to participate in the operation. The driver was paid to put aside the fraudulent shipped items and then meet Jerry or Keith at a predetermined location to turn over the packages.

Jerry finally admitted that he was, in fact, going to pick up the same package on which we were conducting the control delivery in Henderson that day. At the conclusion of the interview, Jerry provided a sworn taped statement and was charged with identity theft, theft by deception, and conspiracy-related charges. He was subsequently lodged in the Harris County jail.

The next day we came across the nail that would seal Jerry's coffin, thanks to the forensic analysis results of his seized computer. Over 900 pages of evidence were generated and analyzed, revealing voluminous Web sites that Jerry visited, including Hewart Package, Photo Street Co., and National Courier. Further analysis also revealed that the computer was used to conduct various searches of zip codes and addresses, as well to make online purchases using some of our victims' credit cards and names.

Despite all of this evidence, there was still much work to be done. We didn't have Keith Evans in custody; an affidavit for his arrest warrant still had to be prepared. Additionally, even though Jerry fully described the duo's collusion with the National Courier driver, he never knew the true name of the corrupt delivery man. Further compounding our difficulty in nabbing the deceitful deliverer, we had no photo for Roger Barrington—the driver we suspected was the ID thieves' accomplice—because he had never been arrested before, which made a successful photo lineup improbable.

Another Thief and a Lucky Break

Three days after we had nabbed Jerry and the computer evidence, I received a phone call that broke yet another lead for us. Secret Service advised me that they had detained an individual identified as Reston Beander, a stock boy employed at a clothing retailer—one of the two from which Keith had obtained the receipts—at the local mall. The agent informed me that Reston was under arrest for identity theft. He was being held at Weberville police headquarters, and had identified a coconspirator named Keith who drove a white Mercedes Benz.

That evening at the Weberville police station, Reston said to us that he met Keith on the streets of Newark. Keith proposed to him a "business deal" saying, "I know a way to make some easy money."

The scheme involved retrieving peoples' names and credit card numbers from store receipts, then conducting a general Internet search to cross-reference the names collected to actual addresses and phone numbers. This information would later be used to make fraudulent Internet purchases.

Reston explained that he did not hesitate in joining Keith's operation. He sought out employment as a stock boy at two clothing retail stores just to gain access to customers' credit card receipts. Day after day, he would pilfer the receipts from the stock room and turn them over to Keith.

Much like a bank vault, the stock rooms at these stores represented small gold mines that, for the next several months, netted Reston several thousand dollars tax-free, courtesy of Keith, his new partner in crime.

But Reston decided to go above and beyond the call of duty for Keith. Much like Jerry, he offered to pick up some of the fraudulently purchased merchandise as well. On several occasions, Reston determined ahead of time through the National Courier tracking Web page when a certain package was being delivered to a particular address. He would then drive to that residence just before the driver's arrival time and hide in the backyard of the residence. As the delivery driver approached the residence, Reston would casually walk out toward the front of the house, making it appear as if he were the actual homeowner, and sign for the package. Then he would go back to his car and leave, and subsequently meet up with Keith to make the exchange.

As we were concluding the interview, the moment of truth finally came around as Reston was shown a photo lineup with Keith's picture embedded within the array. The last nail had been driven into Keith's coffin as Reston without hesitation positively identified his photo.

Now all we had left to do was snag up Barrington and hunt Keith down.

You Can Run, but You Can't Hide

We all knew at this point that Keith Evans must have been on to us. Word on the street travels fast. So in an attempt to lure Keith into our hands, we leveraged Reston by having him phone Keith and request a meeting to discuss ordering up another package. But as young as Keith was, he wasn't stupid. Unfortunately for us, he never returned any of Reston's calls. So we had to resort to old-fashioned police work and started pounding on some doors.

The next day we broke up into four teams and cruised the neighborhoods around our suspect's stomping ground. We covered all of Keith's hangouts, displaying his photo and inquiring as to his whereabouts—to no avail. We knew that looking for him out in the open like this was akin to revealing a hand during a poker game, but this was our method of last resort, which at day's end, left us to believe that Keith was basically dust in the wind.

It was rush hour and we were stuck in some inner-city traffic. I decided to contact the rest of the teams to tell them to start heading home. As I picked up the radio to call my colleagues, the Secret Service agent riding shotgun in my cruiser interrupted me. "Don't look now, but I think that's Keith sitting on the passenger side in the car next to us."

I was pretty pessimistic at that point, thinking, "What are the chances?" But we had nothing to lose, so we followed the vehicle until we came to a safe area away from the gridlock. As soon as we signaled for the car to pull over, it stopped. I got out of my car and slowly approached the passenger side. As I opened the car door, my eyes fell upon a kid weighing all of 150 pounds. Although my gut told me we had him, I had to confirm my suspicion. "Are you Keith Evans?" He knew at that point it was over and just nodded yes.

After we took Keith back to Brookville and Mirandized him, it took less than five minutes for him to tell all. He began by stating his motive for committing these crimes, which was his lack of employment and his related need for money. With that problem at hand, Keith sought out assistance from an individual with the street name Ice, who also resided in Newark. Ice, the leader of another local identity-theft ring, told Keith he could help him by instructing him on how to compromise victims' credit card numbers and make fraudulent purchases over the Internet. The credit card numbers would be obtained from Ice's cousin, who apparently worked as a stock boy at a store in the same mall where Reston worked.

As time passed and Keith gained more confidence in the finer points of his "new trade" that he'd gleaned from Ice, he branched off on his own. Keith initially recruited Jerry because he was the only individual in the neighborhood who had a computer. According to Keith, Jerry eventually immersed himself more into the scheme by finding drug addicts who would allow their home addresses to be used as mail drop locations for the National Courier packages. Keith, on the other hand, was responsible for recruiting the National Courier driver that helped the twosome execute their scheme. He confirmed the identity of the corrupt driver as Roger Barrington, and stated that he was introduced to him by Ice, who used Roger to deliver his crime ring's fraudulent packages as well.

Keith further advised us that, upon receipt of the fraudulently purchased packages, he would pawn them off throughout electronic store front locations in the New York City area. The managers of these stores would usually pay him 40 percent of the retail value of the item he had stolen. That 40%, Keith confessed, would then be split evenly between himself and Jerry. Overall, Keith estimated that he was netting about $3,000 a month just for himself.

The last individual who was arrested in this case was the National Courier driver, Roger Barrington. We arrested him at his workplace and brought him back to Harris County for questioning. To our surprise, obtaining his confession did not present a challenge. But unlike Keith and Jerry, Roger wasn't a street criminal with a record. He was just a delivery man living with his mother and said he had fallen on hard times. He was struggling to make ends meet when the opportunity to illicitly supplement his income arose. Ultimately, he succumbed to the financial pressure.

Do the Crime, Pay the Time

After all the arrests were made and the confessions were obtained, three of the defendants—Keith Evans, Jerry Straiser, and Roger Barrington—were prosecuted federally. Roger received a federal probationary sentence due to his cooperation and lack of any criminal record.

Jerry Straiser, however, who during the course of this investigation was also being investigated by the FBI for trafficking narcotics, was subsequently sentenced to serve 10-plus years for his roles in the identity theft scheme and in the narcotics distribution case that the FBI had just finished. Ironically, Keith Evans, who had a more extensive criminal history than Jerry, was sentenced to serve only a three-year sentence. The Timms siblings, on the other hand, received state probationary sentences due to their minimal role in this operation.

Lessons Learned

Fortunately, this case was cracked in an extremely short period of time. Identity thefts generally take months to solve because the perpetrator is rarely determined. A large part of the success is a result of the cooperation of all of the agencies involved, including assistance from the two victimized companies.

At the same time, there was intense pressure to keep this case in house, rather than turn it over to the U.S. Attorney's Office. In the end, we decided that justice would be better served federally because the resources of the HCPO had already been overexpended and some further investigation was still required. Moreover, the punishment would be more severe with federal charges.

Recommendations to Prevent Future Occurrences

Identity theft is a crime that is difficult to hamper. Nevertheless, we made the following recommendations to the companies who were impacted by this case:

1. Organizations should conduct proactive and random audits of all consumer Internet purchases, paying particular attention to questionable shipping addresses that are either in high crime areas or are believed to be mail drop locations.
2. Retail stores should initiate better controls over sensitive customer documents instead of leaving them in the open in their stock rooms.
3. Corporate security departments must advise their retail staff to maintain customer receipts under lock and key in file cabinets, accessible only to management and/or senior sales employees.

About the Author

Bruno Pavlicek, CFE, M.S., is a veteran New Jersey police officer and county prosecutor's detective. In the private sector today, Mr. Pavlicek serves as a part-time adjunct faculty instructor with New York University, where he teaches fraud investigation and interview and interrogation principles. He is also a senior investigator with a major telecommunications company.

24

The Karma of Fraud

DAVID CLEMENTS AND MICHAEL CERNY

Larry Jones was recruited to be Affirm Bank's head dealer for the foreign exchange market (also known as Forex), where one currency is traded for another. It's a risky business, even for banks, but Larry had been headhunted into this role. In his mid-30s, married with no children, and living in a fashionable downtown area, he'd already proven his worth as a trader in another establishment. His aggressive, forthright, no-nonsense attitude set the tone for the trading transactions. He was also a gambler and known to bet on anything—an addiction that crossed over to his work life. He didn't mask his habits, openly communicating his activities through e-mail and telephone conversations with other team members.

Like Larry, Danny Philips had been recruited to be a senior trader from a similar role at another bank. A strange and complex character, he frequented rave parties, subscribed to various fads including a nut diet, and claimed to be a practicing Buddhist. Even after being busted for fraud, Danny commented that, ''There was no real loss; mankind hasn't actually lost this money. It's just been redistributed.''

Victor Olivetti was the junior trader on the Forex market. He had been recruited as a graduate and had shown an aptitude for options trading. Now in his mid-20s, he was earning a significant salary and, like most traders, a considerable bonus. He enjoyed the trimmings that accompanied his income, including fast cars and a high-quality lifestyle.

Although the Forex market was headquartered in Australia, the bank also had a subsidiary operation in London in order to provide a 24-hour global trading service. This was run by Grant White together with a junior trader. Grant attended college with Larry, and now, in his early 30s, he was a respected senior trader. Unlike his peer, however, Grant was focused and reserved.

Two additional team members completed the desk in Australia. One was a junior trader and the other was an analyst. The desk was overseen by the head of foreign exchange.

These traders were making the bank a heck of a lot of money—on paper, anyway. They earned big bonuses and treated the bank's risk area as a speed bump. If they hit it hard and fast enough, they barely noticed it. Their culture oozed testosterone. In the end they all went to prison, undone by an inside whistleblower.

Affirm Bank of Australia was one of the largest in the country, with Asia Pacific and European subsidiaries. Its established trading center offered a range of services in addition to foreign-exchange options trading. The bank's Forex trading market target was split into two categories. One was made up of retail trades, deals done on behalf of clients for a small commission; normally these deals made up the majority of the bank's Forex activity. The other category was proprietary trading; these deals were done for the bank and used the bank's money. Traders were allocated a small sum with which they could trade currencies if the risk was considered low. By effectively betting the bank's funds on the rise or fall of specific currencies, they stood to make money for the bank.

The value split between these two types for the Affirm Bank was supposed to be approximately 80% retail trades to 20% proprietary trades. However, when the dust had settled, it was discovered that the traders had actually reversed the split and were gambling with the bank's money for 80% of the trades.

Affirm used a proprietary IT trading system, which was constructed specifically for its individual requirements. Normally, these are developed either in-house or by a consulting software engineering firm from the ground up and tailored to meet the bank's needs. Although the systems are beneficial for their customized qualities, they often have vulnerabilities due to the lack of extensive security testing. These weaknesses are typically ''patched'' as they're exposed, but in some cases they're simply discovered too late.

The Falling Dollar

During the second half of the year, the Australian dollar had made significant gains against the U.S. dollar. The traders, known betting men, decided to back a downturn in the Australian dollar, just as gamblers back red hoping that the run of black will end. But the Aussie currency value continued to rise and the wrong bets began piling up. After a series of losses, the traders were faced with the possibility of forfeiting their annual bonuses. With this in mind, they decided to conceal the damage by exploiting weaknesses in Affirm Bank's trading system and processes.

By December, the now significant losses began to make the junior traders nervous. In January, Grant had an argument with his assistant in London and mentioned the specifics of the Forex team's financial predicament. The junior trader was aware of some losses but hadn't known the actual amount. Realizing the extent of the damage, he felt uncomfortable and called Victor to discuss. Two hours later he called the other junior trader in the Australian office and told her of his concerns. She went for a coffee with the Forex analyst and told her about the situation. The analyst quickly decided to blow the whistle.

The head of foreign exchange convened a meeting with Larry, Danny, and Victor over the weekend, called up Grant, and discussed the state of affairs. The following Monday, the traders went through their books and determined that the loss totaled $180 million. All of them were suspended on Tuesday. But after a revaluation of the portfolio, a final figure of over $300 million in losses was declared.

Big Loss Leads to Big Investigation

After the suspension of the four traders, our firm was appointed by Affirm to investigate the events and trading activities that led to the losses. Our team, recruited from all over Australia, comprised over sixty people: market analysts, ex-traders, systems analysts, trading risk experts, forensic investigators, and forensic technologists. The team also included administrative assistants who spent hours transcribing taped interviews.

The initial phase consisted of gathering a vast quantity of evidence. We used the records of Affirm Bank's Forex trading system, which recorded details such as dates, counterparties, currencies, values, and other properties. Several copies of the trading system were made from backups over the four years leading up to the event. We also undertook a forensic examination of the traders' computer systems, including their e-mail and Internet activity over a four-year period. Finally, we checked their telephone conversation history with brokers and other Affirm Bank employees.

With over two terabytes of electronic information, it was necessary to adopt automated processes for effective analysis. Our computer forensics specialists compiled e-mails and electronic files from the Affirm Bank servers and employee computers into one central repository. This process revealed that Larry had deleted 14,000 e-mails on the Friday prior to the fraud's exposure. All data was loaded into a central database repository, where the duplicate e-mails and files were suppressed. Here we could execute search terms, which saved time by ensuring that only the relevant information was reviewed. Our analysts then prepared a brief on each suspect in the case, giving the investigators sufficient background on each of their interviewees.

An analysis was conducted of the taped telephone conversations, for which a two-phase approach was adopted. The first phase involved one of our investigators reviewing the tapes for conversations that discussed inappropriate activity and recording the times that those occurred. The second phase involved another investigator reviewing these conversations and profiling each suspect to be included in the brief.

Our forensic accountants and trading experts then engaged in an extensive review of the Forex trading system to understand how the traders were able to manipulate and cover their losses.

With such a complicated investigation, communication between the various team specialists was crucial. We had catch-up meetings every morning to discuss what new information had been obtained. This allowed us to plan and prioritize what was further required by each specific team. Equally crucial was our robust case-management system linking into all the exhibits we had gathered and identifying all actions undertaken. Law enforcement would be eventually involved, so we had to ensure that the evidence we gathered met criminal prosecution standards. We employed analysts to update and disseminate knowledge on a real-time basis.

The Forex team's mandate was to grow both customer business and proprietary trading income. In recent years the strategy had been to increase the percentage of customer-based revenue. Contrary to the strategy, that year risk-based proprietary trading activity grew significantly. So too did the size of the team's trading book. At the time of our investigation, Affirm Bank's currency options business consisted of a large and complex portfolio. Prior to the fraud being discovered, the notional principal of the currency options book was some $253 billion.

The first part of the investigation was to determine how the traders were able to conceal such large losses for so long without Affirm Bank's risk group being notified. This involved analysis of the Forex trading system, review of the reporting structure within the trading room, analysis of e-mails, correspondence between front, middle, and back offices, and 50 interviews—all of which had to be completed in three weeks.

Our investigation revealed that the perpetrators had been smoothing trades for at least four years. Options dealing is notorious for significant swings in profits and losses. Banks are conservative organizations and prefer less volatility. So the traders gave management the smooth version, altering profits and losses, by exposing loopholes in the Forex trading system.

We used the electronic discovery-review environment to examine e-mails and accurately determine the timeline in the daily reporting structure, in addition to examining the relationships each trader had with middle- and back-office operations. As a result, we were able to confirm how the traders had used more devious methods of concealment that exploited a weakness in the end-of-day procedures. The Forex trading system end-of-day process was run at approximately 8:00 a.m. the following morning (Australian East Coast Time) to allow transactions executed in the New York time zone to be captured. The traders entered false transactions in the system just before the end-of-day close. The profits and losses arising from the system were then posted to the daily management reports.

The back office commenced their procedures at about 9:00 a.m. in order to process the previous day's transactions. During this one-hour window the traders had time to reverse the false transactions they had entered into the system before the end-of-day close to ensure that their frauds went undetected. Up until October the traders had been reentering false trades and reversing them on a daily basis. Information made available by chance to the traders allowed them to streamline their concealment. They initially assumed that the back office was checking internal options transactions, which were internal bank dealings between desks. For this reason, they were surrendering the false options in the one-hour window to avoid detection. However, we learned from a recorded phone conversation that by October the traders had realized that these did not have to be surrendered each day. Since the back office was not checking internal transactions, one-sided transactions (not involving another party) would not be identified.

By using options with longer maturity dates there was no need to surrender and roll forward the false trades every day. The fraudsters still had to keep an eye out to make sure the trades didn't reach their maturity dates, because if they did show up on the system's finalized trades report, a cash settlement would be required. And that would effectively end their fun.

The principal objective of the false one-sided option transactions was to obscure some of the risk measures used to monitor trading. A total of 78 were identified between October and January.

Unjust Bonuses

The next part of the investigation was to determine the traders' motivation. Why were they going to great lengths to hide their true positions? An answer, at least in part, was revealed in one of the taped telephone conversations on September 18 between Larry, Danny, and Victor. The bank's year-end was September 30, which was when their performance would be assessed.

Near the end of the month, Larry called Danny and Victor and said, "I want to make sure we're above 37 million when they rule the line, but it'd be good if we could say on the end-of-year report that we made budget, or exceeded it, not just 98% of it. It just sounds a lot better for bonuses. We deserve to claim that we made budget this year. Everyone's done a good job—well, except me. The beautiful thing is, it's our choice.''

At the end of September they reported a profit of over $37 million. In reality, they were down by about $5 million, meaning they overstated their profit by $42 million. By falsely reporting, the four traders received bonuses totaling $790,000 for the year.

Then things really started to go downhill. For reasons unknown, Larry was convinced that the Australian dollar was about to fall against the U.S. dollar. He continued taking risks by entering large unhedged deals that significantly increased the bank's exposure. As the Australian currency rose, so did the losses.

The stress was starting to tell on Victor. During one phone call, Larry was telling him which false trades to enter into the system.

"You don't like the sound of this, do you?'' Larry asked.

Victor replied, "It's always really hard doing this stuff.''

At one point in December, after they had incurred losses of over $5 million on three separate days, Larry called the desk from his phone. There was a discussion about the situation and how they needed to hide the losses. It was at that time he made the prophetic statement, "Don't worry boys, it's only money. If we pull it off, we're kings. If we don't—well, guys, we're all going to jail.''

They didn't pull it off, and between the end of December and January 12 they lost another $100 million.

The Enlightened Way Out

Our report on the trading losses was published in March, two months after our investigation began, which was run parallel to a separate one by the Australian Prudential Regulatory Authority (APRA).

We had follow-up meetings with Australian Securities and Investment Commission (ASIC) investigators and provided them with all the information we had gathered. The most valuable parts were the interviews we had with Larry Jones and Grant White. ASIC subsequently charged the four traders with a number of criminal offenses.

Larry Jones was the leader and major cause of the losses. As the head trader, he instigated the false trades to hide the true losses. He also organized the manipulation of the September results to ensure that everyone received bonuses. It became apparent from the interviews that the other traders were going to blame him for the frauds in order to mitigate their own involvement. Larry pleaded guilty to all charges and was brought before the court prior to the other three fraudsters. As no other evidence had been heard against him previously, Larry was able to put his own spin on the events in order to minimize the penalty. He was sentenced to 29 months in prison with a minimum term of 16 months.

Grant White was the next to face court. He also pleaded guilty. His defense counsel said that because Grant was in London he was not part of the team that undertook the falsification of the trades. As such he was sentenced to 16 months in prison, with a minimum term of 8 months.

Danny Philips represented himself throughout his trial. He was found guilty on 17 of the 19 charges against him, which included gaining financial advantage for himself and others, along with one count of gaining financial advantage by deception. He was sentenced to 44 months in prison with a minimum of 30 months.

Victor Olivetti pleaded not guilty, using the defense that, as the youngest of the four traders, he had been coerced into the scheme through fear. He was found guilty of all 12 charges, including gaining financial advantage for himself and others, and one charge of gaining financial advantage by deception. He was sentenced to 28 months in prison with a minimum of 15 months.

Danny ended up writing a book about the fraud. When interviewed by one of the media about his Buddhism, he said: "Now, I was obviously spending a lot of time studying and practicing for enlightenment and stuff like that, and some of my colleagues said along the way, you know, 'If that's all you care about, why don't you go and live in the mountains?' And basically, I was like, 'If I do that, that's making a decision which is not following the natural way. For me to leave, something will happen and I'll leave.' And, yes, something obviously has happened and I've left."

Lessons Learned

So why did it happen? The official reports, which came out in the months following the fraud, indicated that there were a number of failures in the risk management process and the bank didn't pick up on the red flags.

There was also a bit of luck involved, good for the traders but bad for the bank, when an internal e-mail caused the back office to stop checking and matching internal bank trades. This provided the perpetrators with the opportunity to hide the true nature of their position in an ongoing manner rather than having to undertake a daily fraudulent process.

Recommendations to Prevent Future Occurrences

Adequate Supervision

The fraudsters took large, complex, and risky positions, and their immediate supervisors only reviewed headline profit-and-loss reports. Because the traders concealed the losses, they gained their immediate supervisors' confidence, who were led to believe that the risks were tolerable. Multiple risk-limit breaches and other warnings were not treated seriously, and no effective steps were taken to restrain the traders. Warnings from the market about large or unusual currency transactions were not properly investigated. Not everyone is honest, which is why proper supervision is paramount.

Risk Management Communication

There were flaws in the design, implementation, and execution of risk management. The middle office knew about and recorded but failed to respond to persistent risk-limit breaches effectively. They raised warnings about the currency options desk's breaches and other exceptions, but these were not reported to the CEO or the board. The board received risk management information that was incorrect, incomplete, or insufficiently detailed to alert them to limit breaches or other matters related to the currency options desk's operations. By failing to communicate effectively, the middle office put the bank at risk for fraud.

Implement Financial Controls

There were insufficient procedures to identify, investigate, and explain unusual or suspicious transactions. Normal month-end processes lacked adequate cut-off procedures and did not restate results to adjust for canceled or amended transactions. There was no review of the percentage of client trades to proprietary trades. It is important to implement proper controls to limit the potential for fraud.

Watch for Gaps in Back-Office Procedures

The back office did not detect false transactions. This failure was caused in part by the one-hour window between close-of-day for reporting purposes and back office checking, which enabled the traders to falsify the true position of the desk. Starting from a particular date, junior back-office staff discontinued checking internal currency-option transactions. As a result, the traders were able to process false one-sided internal options transactions without being detected.

Governance

The division's management was aware of significant trading-limit breaches and failed to investigate and take action. Value at risk (VaR) reports, which should have formed a significant control, were effectively ignored by the perpetrators' supervisors because of ongoing systems and data issues. There was no sense of urgency in resolving the VaR calculation issues though they had been a problem for a period of two or more years. It is important to resolve issues as quickly as possible to minimize vulnerabilities.

About the Authors

David Clements, CFE, is a director in the Melbourne, Australia, Forensic Services Practice of PricewaterhouseCoopers. He has over 23 years of law enforcement experience with the Metropolitan Police in London, the Victoria Police, and the Australian Securities and Investment Commission. He is a graduate of Monash University and has worked for PricewaterhouseCoopers since 1997.

Michael Cerny is a director in the Melbourne, Australia, Forensic Services Practice of PricewaterhouseCoopers and specializes in computer forensic technology. He has experience in the analysis, extraction, and migration of data, major forensic technology investigations, assistance with law enforcement search warrants, and large-scale electronic discovery. He is a graduate of the University of Tasmania and has worked for PricewaterhouseCoopers since 2001.

Secret Shopper

JAY DAWDY

Polished, intelligent, energetic, and a marketing whiz, Linda Capri-Knoxville had achieved a high level of financial success in her career. Her lifestyle in adulthood was a stark contrast to her destitute youth. Linda's accomplishments had afforded her financial freedom—and she wasn't afraid of showing it off.

She drove the newest-model BMW sports sedan, wore the latest fashions, and accessorized with every season's must-haves, including her favorite Gucci handbag and an iPhone. Attractive and in peak physical condition, Linda competed in triathlons to stay in shape. She fit the model of a high-powered businesswoman.

Linda's personal life wasn't quite as successful. Trouble brewed beneath her shiny veneer. She and her husband, Marty Knoxville, were going through a messy divorce and custody battle. Marty was also a partner in the company that they had both helped form years earlier, Expert Consultants International (ECI). ECI was struggling for the first time since its inception. Revenue growth had experienced a sharp decline in the past three years, and the company's profit margins had plunged because management was failing to keep expenses in line with the decreased revenue. Linda felt her work at ECI was no longer inspiring; her career path was uncertain and she didn't even know whether she had a future with ECI—especially since she and Marty were getting divorced. She was driven by resentment now, rather than ambition.

ECI was a marketing consulting firm that had generated millions of dollars in income for Linda. But recent years had brought change. Linda's aggressive business development skills weren't as valuable as they once were. She had become increasingly bored with her work and disenchanted with the level of credit she was receiving for the company's success. She had helped her husband and two other partners build ECI from the ground up.

But now their lack of appreciation coupled with her marital problems and the financial stress at the company painted a bleak future. Linda wanted to get what she deserved before they pushed her aside completely.

ECI had been in business for over 12 years. It started as a small advertising company formed by four young, hard-charging colleagues who left a large Madison Avenue advertising firm after learning the business. In just 12 years, the outfit had grown into a multimillion-dollar marketing research company with several Fortune 100 clients. ECI now employed over 100 people and had developed multiple new lines of advertising and marketing research services.

Given the energy and drive of its partners, it was no surprise that ECI's revenue and profits soared from its inception. The business growth led to significant financial rewards for all of its partners, including Linda and Marty, who married shortly after the firm was established. Their fourth partner had left the firm about four years prior in a buyout deal struck by Marty and the president of ECI, Shepherd Jenkins. Linda was a little peeved about the way the deal went down, but she'd gone along with it and now she had to face the fact that her control was diminished. And she didn't function well without control.

ECI's headquarters was based in an upscale northern New Jersey suburb where Linda and Marty also built their home. The office was located inside one of many homogenous buildings grouped together in a sleek suburban office park, which also housed several other consulting companies and corporate headquarters.

Although ECI had grown rapidly, annually adding new clients and growing their revenues year after year, those days were over. Of late, ECI had had its first down year in both revenue and profits, and the company had started making some changes and more closely examining expenditures. As part of a recent "restructuring," Linda had been put in charge of "special projects," where she felt her skills were being wasted.

The firm continued to produce high revenue and profitability, but ECI was suffering in part because the company had been very loosely managed since its inception. It lacked organization, structure, and good accounting policies, and it had no internal controls. During the boom times, when Linda was out front leading the charge, no one cared about internal controls, separation of duties, human resources, or any other policies and controls—it was all about revenue growth and putting numbers on the board. Linda was aggressive and she knew how to use her powers of persuasion to develop business for the firm. She did this very successfully for a long time. Since ECI had emphasized new areas of growth in more recent years and had become a more mature company with repeat business, Linda wasn't making quite the impact she had in the past.

Although clients loved her, she had a reputation inside the company as being difficult and combative. No one dared cross her or challenge her authority. She could do whatever she wanted inside the company, but it was very hard for her to accept being marginalized by the other partners. She let it be known that she wasn't happy.

Since her job was now less demanding—and because, frankly, she cared less about the business—she began spending more time outside of work, building her dream home, and buying the latest tech gadgets for her own use. About three years ago, while ordering some new equipment for the company, she decided, "What the heck; I'll order a few laptops and PDAs for myself too," reasoning that, "No one here will know any better and no one will dare question me—they owe me, dammit."

Big Spender

Shepherd Jenkins was the president and majority shareholder of ECI. He'd been with the company since the beginning and he was the logical choice to head it. From outside appearances, he was CEO material from central casting—tall, smart, sharply dressed, and filled with business acumen. With his Ivy League education and keen understanding of numbers, he'd kept a close eye on the company's profitability over the years. He was especially upset by the declining margins in the past few years, in large part because it directly affected his paycheck, and he certainly didn't like seeing his annual income decrease.

Shepherd had questioned the large expenditures that Linda had been making for some time. He was also suspicious of her enormous expense account reimbursement requests. They seemed to grow with each passing month. Although this had been a sore subject with him, he hadn't cared too much in the past because business had been booming. Besides that, it was a pretty awkward situation since Marty and Linda were his partners and Marty had been one of his best friends since their early days in the ad business. He and Marty had always been close. Shepherd was secretly overjoyed that Marty was finally taking his advice and divorcing Linda. As far as he was concerned, the marriage termination was long overdue.

In light of the recent separation, Marty was spending some nights on Shepherd's couch, providing Shepherd an opportunity to privately air his concerns about Linda's spending habits. Besides that, ECI and its partners weren't making as much money as they were previously, so it was necessary to take a close look at all their expenses and see where they could cut back.

The latest incident with Linda's purchases had arisen three weeks earlier, when the manager of the company's IT department was looking for two new laptops and two new color printers that Linda had purchased and charged to his budget. They were nowhere to be found in the offices. Upon further research and inquiries with the vendor, the IT manager discovered several other recent purchases by Linda—laptops, printers, and other equipment—that could not be located on company grounds. The vendor confirmed that the items had been shipped to Linda's home address. He then brought the issue up with the head of operations, Kendra Macintosh, whom he knew he could trust.

Kendra wasted no time taking this issue to Shepherd. She also took the opportunity to share some other rumors with him about large purchases Linda had been making. They agreed that these orders warranted additional investigation.

Aside from the incident with the laptops and color printers, there were other expense reimbursements that had concerned Shepherd in the past, but any time he mentioned the expenses to Marty or Linda, it only caused friction. Shepherd thought things might be different now that their divorce was in motion. And there was another considerable expense that Linda had been submitting for years—reimbursement for her chiropractic treatments, which he suspected were inflated.

"Hell, Linda is one of the fittest people I know! She's a freaking tri-athlete—why on earth would she need a chiropractor?" Shepherd exclaimed. He had never understood what those treatments were for and why they weren't covered by the company's insurance plan. And, he wondered to himself, "Why the heck did we, did *I*, ever make an exception and agree to pay those expenses directly?"

He realized that agreeing to reimburse the expenses directly to Linda was not smart, but when she was booking new business he really wasn't that concerned about how much money she spent. He wanted to keep her happy and the business flowing. In retrospect, he realized he'd made a mistake, but he expected that any expense submissions she made would be legitimate. Now, Shepherd was determined to figure out, once and for all, if the company—*his* company—was getting bilked. He and Kendra took a few days to research and put together a list of Linda's suspect reimbursements. They concluded that there was certainly a problem that would require professional investigation. Kendra then recommended calling their attorneys for some guidance. Shepherd replied, "Yes, but let me talk to my old friend Marty first."

After a couple of beers with Marty that evening—and once Marty stopped complaining about his wife, his divorce, and those damn legal fees—Shepherd realized that it was time to address the issue. He explained the abnormalities, showed Marty the documents that he and Kendra had compiled, along with the list of questionable items, and said he wanted to hire someone to investigate this further. He was surprised at how easy it was.

"I guess their marriage was worse than I thought," he confided to Kendra the next day. Marty had agreed with Shepherd on the spot. When Shepherd explained the situation and said they wanted to investigate further, Marty simply replied, "Go for it. I think she's been up to no good for some time now." Shepherd consulted with legal counsel the next day.

ECI's outside law firm agreed that the situation should be examined and recommended bringing in an investigative firm to lead. That's where my firm came in.

A Call for Experts

We had handled several prior cases for the law firm: everything from complex fraud schemes to litigation support to background investigations. ECI knew we had the expertise and the skills to get the job done.

When the call came in from counsel that next morning, I was sitting at my desk finishing up a batch of pre-deal background investigations for an investment banking client, itching for a good fraud case. After counsel explained the situation, we made an appointment to meet with the client the following day. I briefed some other investigative personnel in the office and we brainstormed the case based on what we had learned from counsel. The next morning we went to ECI's offices for our first of several meetings.

The other investigative team members included two fellow CFEs (one of them the president of the firm) who had investigated numerous fraud cases, and our primary forensic accountant, who was fully equipped with financial skills as a CPA, CFE, and MBA. We later brought in one of our best field investigators and interviewers, and perhaps most importantly, a computer forensics expert.

Our first step was to interview the client and obtain as much information as we could upfront. We interviewed Shepherd and Kendra Macintosh for a few hours that day. Kendra knew everything about the day-to-day activities of the firm. Kendra and Shepherd outlined a number of suspicious purchases and showed us some of Linda's expense reimbursement submissions and the supporting invoices. We also discussed some of the other problems that Linda had been involved in over the years, including the excessive reimbursement of her chiropractic treatments. Based on that conversation alone, it was clear to us that a detailed investigation was necessary.

Kendra Macintosh was a no-nonsense administrator, a chain-smoker, and a good source for information and investigative leads. She took frequent breaks outside for one of her many cigarettes and we learned that these were the best times to get her undivided attention. She had been with the firm for a number of years, knew everyone there and all of the gossip. She got things done and was well respected for it. As a result, a number of employees confided in her.

During our first meeting, after Shepherd laid out the basic facts in a businesslike manner, Kendra said flatly, "Linda's been stealing from this company for years and it's time we did something about it." According to her, Linda's spending habits had been the subject of employee gossip for years.

It was clear that Shepherd wasn't crazy about Kendra's frankness, but he trusted her, had a great deal of respect for her, and knew she was right. Kendra would be an important ally in our investigation. We loved the fact that we got straight information from her—even if we did have to breathe in a little secondhand smoke during some of our interviews and discussions.

Shepherd and Kendra described some of Linda's questionable purchases, which they had uncovered during their review, and asked us to investigate everything closely. We made special notes to examine those suspect purchases and requested immediate access to all of Linda's expense account records.

Shepherd explained that a number of years ago they had made a special exception to reimburse Linda's chiropractic expenses directly because, apparently, they weren't covered by ECI's insurance plan. He couldn't explain why they weren't covered and he seemed a little embarrassed that they had been paying her directly for those expenses. "I thought it would be a temporary situation," he said, "but it turned into an ongoing deal—almost every month for the past four years." He and Kendra both questioned whether she was still actually receiving the treatments, although they both believed the invoices looked legitimate.

"I knew that it was a big mistake to make that exception, and it really didn't make much sense, but we did it anyway because Linda was a producer back then." Shepherd said. Kendra replied, "Yeah, I think I told you so."

Problematic Payback

After submitting our initial plan to counsel and obtaining a signed engagement letter, we commenced the investigation. To begin with, we collected the actual expense account records and documentation for Linda's purchasing activity. It was clear from our initial review that Linda's expense reimbursements, across multiple categories, were significant. There were also several duplicate expense requests.

The first in-depth step of our investigation was to have our forensic accountant carefully analyze Linda's three years of expense account submissions that we had obtained from ECI. We categorized the data and dumped all of the information into Excel spreadsheets for further analysis. In Excel, we were able to put a timeline on the expense submissions. We also arranged the reimbursements in columns by category so we could sort the data by multiple fields and highlight questionable activity. We were looking for patterns in behavior, duplicate reimbursements, and recurring expenses for the same amounts. We were also flagging the material items so we could focus our subsequent investigation on the most problematic and suspicious items first.

It didn't take long to notice that the chiropractor expenses that Shepherd mentioned were in fact major items, averaging close to $3,000 dollars per month. Additionally, when we reviewed the supporting documentation, we saw that the chiropractic invoices for the treatments were almost identical for each session of treatment—except for the dates. We knew these invoices warranted additional scrutiny and we expected that a computer forensics examination of Linda's computer might yield valuable evidence as the investigation progressed.

The other major issue that stood out during our review of the expense reimbursement spreadsheet was a large number of purchases for supposed business items that could also be used personally, such as laptops, printers, and PDAs. The fact that she often purchased the same item multiple times did not help her case.

After careful analysis, we highlighted the questionable items and came up with a list of expenses for additional investigation and a list of interview subjects. Some of the people we targeted for interviews were internal to the company, while many others included vendors and merchants from whom Linda purchased the various products. Most importantly, we wanted to interview the chiropractor Linda was supposedly visiting a few times a month. However, we needed more evidence that we could use during the course of those interviews, so we called in our computer forensics expert and obtained mirror images of the two computer hard drives that Linda had been using at the company.

The computer forensics operation was conducted at night, so as not to alarm any other employees and to avoid any run-ins with Linda. After the initial part of this examination and data capture was complete, we ran several searches on the data using the names of the vendors and of the chiropractor to see if any of her documents contained those terms.

We discovered that Linda had copies of both the invoices from the chiropractor's office (dating back some four years) and those from some of the merchants where she had purchased items for reimbursement on her computer hard drives. The original versions of these invoices had been scanned in and copies of the receipts had been converted into Microsoft Word documents. We later discovered that the Word invoices had been duplicated into separate folders for each month. Although it was the exact same file, it was copied over several times and the dates had simply been changed to correspond with the times that Linda claimed reimbursement for chiropractic treatments. We then matched those dates and the invoices with the expense accounts and they corresponded with the submissions that Linda had made for the same amounts and dates.

It was clear to us that Linda had scanned an original invoice from four years ago and then converted the document into Word. She simply duplicated the same invoice over and over—just changing the dates—and submitted those for reimbursement on a continual basis. There were also other invoices that had been copied, and we wanted to confirm with the chiropractor and the merchants what had occurred in each of those individual situations.

We noted the vendor names on each of the questionable invoices and made a list of people that we wanted to interview. We started with the chiropractor. We presented him with the invoices and explained the nature of our inquiries. He was taken aback and was very surprised, exclaiming: "Linda Knoxville? I haven't seen her in four years."

While he was careful not to reveal any medical or confidential information, he confirmed that the receipts we had (the same ones Linda used for her expense reimbursements) were not actually from his office. He was upset that they had been fabricated. He said they looked like versions of his invoices, but that he hadn't seen Linda during any of the months corresponding to the dates we presented. In total, the reimbursement Linda received for chiropractor treatments that were not actually received was over $90,000.

Our field investigators paid visits to many of the other vendors that we had obtained invoices for during the computer forensics examination. We targeted those that looked suspicious both in our review of the computer documents and in our initial expense account analysis (e.g., duplicate submissions, similar amounts, and so on).

Upon conducting interviews with several of those vendors, most of whom were cooperative, and presenting them with the invoices obtained from the expense accounts, we learned that Linda had used many scams to receive bogus reimbursements. With some vendors she simply duplicated invoices and changed the dates, much like with the chiropractor invoices (the vendors had no record of multiple purchases). Occasionally, she made legitimate purchases but later returned the merchandise, so no actual expense was incurred even though she submitted for and received the reimbursement.

The additional bogus reimbursements that we discovered totaled several thousand dollars. And that was without investigating every suspicious transaction. It was now evident that Linda had engaged in multiple methods of obtaining money for expenses that she never incurred.

Tying It All Together

Our investigation had included interviewing company employees, collecting submission forms, categorizing Linda's expense account activity, analyzing

the computer forensics and documentation, and interviewing the chiropractor and the vendors, who confirmed that the reimbursements were improper.
Upon completion of the aforementioned steps, we tied our investigative
findings together in a comprehensive report to counsel.

The improper expense account submissions that we unearthed totaled
well over $100,000. And that didn't even include any personal purchases she
had made and kept for herself, such as the laptops and color printers that the
IT manager initially brought up.

At that point, the client decided they had enough evidence. Although
the company chose not to pursue a criminal case against Linda, they had
all the evidence they needed to end their business relationship with her.
They set up a meeting with her attorney, arranged for her severance, and
negotiated a very favorable buyout of her remaining ownership in ECI.

Lessons Learned

Linda's fraud was a classic case of a disenchanted executive who felt like the
company owed her. In order to snatch up her "fair share," she abused her authority
by stealing. This behavior was fueled by a total lack of controls at ECI and a very lax
attitude toward reimbursements, as well as making a special exception to policy for
Linda's chiropractic appointments, which came back to haunt the company.

The business was declining, Linda was being marginalized, and she was
unhappy. She was in a position of authority and was allowed to override controls
and do whatever she wanted. She felt a sense of entitlement and invincibility, so
she rationalized her scheme. Allowing exceptions to an expense account policy—
whether a person is a partner or not—is a mistake that Shepherd lived to regret. All
three elements of the fraud triangle—pressure, opportunity, and rationalization—
were in full force.

Very few preventative internal controls were in place. The aggressive mentality
of the partners (tone at the top) and the rapid growth of this company created an
environment where no one cared about controls—they simply wanted to keep
growing. This all contributed to an environment where fraud could occur and did.

Perhaps the most significant lesson learned was the value of the computer
forensic evidence that we collected from Linda's computers. Her computer was
not only the technological device she used to perpetrate the fraud by creating
realistic-looking invoices, but also the primary tool that we used to prove that fraud
had occurred. The combination of this, along with our forensic accounting and
good old-fashioned fieldwork and interviews, provided the right combination of
investigative skills necessary to solve the case.

Recommendations to Prevent Future Occurrences

Tone at the Top

One of the major reasons fraud occurred at ECI was due to the poor tone at the top. Because the company was focused almost solely on revenue growth, there was no attention to procedures or controls during that growth phase. Senior management must let employees know that they are keeping an eye on them and are taking the control environment seriously. Codes of ethics and employee training can help create the perception of detection.

We recommended prosecution of Linda in order to set an example and show their employees they took fraud seriously. ECI declined, but realized that they needed to change the culture of the company. They accepted several more detailed recommendations.

Employee Fraud Hotline

If this procedure had been in place earlier, it is likely that some of the employees, particularly those who were intimidated by Linda, would have anonymously blown the whistle earlier.

Strict Adherence to Company Reimbursement and Accounting Policies

When Shepherd made an exception to the rules regarding Linda's chiropractic expenses, she took advantage of the situation and exploited their lack of oversight and controls. Policies exist for a reason and it's important that they be followed.

Set Procedures and Approvals for Purchasing

Linda should have been prevented from making purchasing decisions on her own and potentially ordering and keeping company products for herself. Also, a more detailed monthly financial review process, including variance analysis and investigation of any significant financial occurrences/changes, would have been an effective means to discover the fraud earlier.

About the Author

Jay Dawdy, CFE, CMA, is a partner with Gryphon Investigations in New York City, where he runs a wide range of financial investigations, fraud cases, due diligence inquiries, and complex litigation-support cases, work that has given him extensive experience in conducting occupational fraud investigations. Jay also serves as an instructor in financial statement fraud at Baruch College.

Would You Like a Receipt?

SHIRLEY QUINTANA

Personable, full of energy, and blessed with the gift of gab, Jesse Guerrero was a fantastic sales representative. He worked with his sales assistant, Marie Lopez, who also happened to be his ex-wife, at the largest title-and-escrow insurance company in southern California. They made a great sales duo. Their marriage wasn't quite as successful, which resulted in divorce a few years back, but the pair stayed together as a business team. Diane Guerrero, Jesse's favorite sister, wanted to work with her brother. She had watched him and his ex-wife rake in the dough for years, and was delighted when she was hired as Jesse's administrative assistant.

Jesse and Marie had landed their positions shortly after John Zielbauer, an effective employee aggressive in his pursuit of business, was promoted to regional manager at Dependable Title & Escrow Co. Senior management at Dependable wanted to expand in southern California. With the pressure to increase revenues and find new markets, John knew he needed to recruit strong, successful sales representatives. He heard about Jesse from a friend and invited him out for dinner one evening. John was impressed. Jesse was fun, affable, could talk up a storm, and claimed to have a long list of clients in Orange County, the market John wanted to cultivate.

When John offered Jesse the position of sales representative at Dependable Title & Escrow, he was surprised when Jesse requested a sales assistant. However, John knew that if Jesse could bring in the business as he claimed, the revenues would more than cover an additional salary. So John hired Marie. The new office was going to need an administrative assistant as well, so he hired Diane on the recommendation of Jesse. Although these three employees were related, John felt that they'd work well together. If they could produce what they promised, he would be way ahead of the game in Orange County. Company policy required him to disclose the relationships, which he did, confident that the new team would be successful. But John never suspected just how ambitious they would be.

Dependable Title & Escrow is a subsidiary of a national insurance company. About 1,600 employees, two-thirds of whom are escrow officers and sales representatives, run 22 county operations covering California, Washington, Nevada, Arizona, Alaska, and Hawaii. The business is extremely competitive, particularly in southern California, where historically Dependable had trouble expanding. The regional managers scouted for new sales reps in the hope of "stealing" them away from the competition, enticing them with guaranteed salaries for the first three months (sales reps are normally paid on commissions), sign-on bonuses, and big expense accounts. These types of maneuvers are typical in the industry, which leaves it vulnerable to mass movements in staff. When a sales rep is lured to another company, the customers usually follow, and oftentimes so do other sales reps. That's how Jesse and his team came to work at Dependable.

Fishy Receipts

Late one February evening, I strolled past the accounts payable (AP) department, when Veronica Waters called me over.

"Shirley, may I speak to you for a minute?" she asked. I walked to her desk, where Monica Hall and Mary Carter, also AP clerks, were standing. Veronica showed me three different employee expense reports, setting them side by side.

"Take a look at the receipts attached to these," she said, pointing to one from Joe's Crab Shack, another from a restaurant called The Claim Jumper, and a third from the chain Black Angus.

"See how these receipts look alike?" Veronica asked me, "The font is the same, yet the receipts are from different restaurants. And the reports were submitted from three different employees."

The three clerks peered over my shoulder as I examined the reports. Their assessment was a good one. "The Joe's Crab Shack receipt looked particularly 'fishy,'" I remarked. We all laughed at my feeble attempt at a joke.

"I called the restaurant and asked them if I could fax this receipt, just like you taught us," Veronica explained. "Joe's Crab Shack took a look and said that this is not their receipt."

Veronica had received similar replies from Black Angus and the Claim Jumper.

"Have you taken the expense reports to Lisa Cates, your manager?" I asked. She had, but Lisa was leaving for the day and had asked Veronica to bring them back again tomorrow to review in further detail.

"And then I saw you in the hall and I wanted to get a second opinion, just to make sure," Veronica said.

Following company protocol was important, so I was glad she had already shown the reports to her manager, albeit briefly. I also appreciated the fact that Veronica sought me out. Having handled several investigations in the past, I knew to make AP aware of the various indicators to look for when processing invoices. We had developed a good working relationship over the last eight years I had been with the firm.

I looked at the other receipts and quickly noticed a pattern: All three employees were submitting for reimbursements from the same restaurants. Additionally, the receipts looked suspiciously similar. All used dark bold print and the same font size and type. The clerks were certainly onto something. I suggested that they discuss their findings with Lisa first thing in the morning.

Monday afternoon Daniel Cortez, the controller, came by my office. He had recently seen the expense reports and was unhappy to have another potential fraud on his hands. After he had reviewed the receipts with Lisa, they both realized that Internal Audit needed to be involved. Dan formally requested our assistance and notified the president of Dependable, as per company protocol. Dependable has a very detailed process for reporting and investigating suspected fraud. Now that we had completed all of the initial steps, it was time to formally start the case.

I picked up the phone to call my boss, Jim Gerwin, who lives in Minneapolis and works that region. He is the director of the internal audit function and I report to him directly. Having a long-distance relationship with your supervisor is sometimes difficult. Since he wasn't right down the hall, we couldn't review the receipts together, so we discussed the situation over the phone, per usual. I told him about my initial game plan—to review all three employees' expense reports for the past year and build the spreadsheet analysis we had used during previous investigations. He agreed and said if I needed to send him copies of the reports I could scan them and send them as a PDF file when I was ready (thank goodness for technology!).

I called Payroll to gather some additional information on the employees. I found out that Jesse, Marie, and Diane were related and had all been hired on the same day last October. Interesting. The payroll manager told me that she knew of the relationship between the employees, which also meant that it had been properly disclosed to management.

I called AP and asked for all the expense reports from the three individuals. Having conducted similar investigations, I was ready to conduct the detailed analysis that I knew would be necessary.

Veronica brought me the expense reports that had been submitted to AP, three from each employee. I set up an Excel spreadsheet in order to track the items by individual. I started with Jesse's reports and input each receipt into the spreadsheet, creating columns for the following pieces of information: vendor name (a restaurant in most cases); credit card numbers, including the type of card used (MasterCard, Visa, American Express); date, day, and time of transactions; base amount of the meal versus the total of the receipt (I had learned from another investigation that on occasion, employees submit the same receipt twice, one with tip and one with just the base amount, for additional reimbursement); and number of people in the party. Finally, I made one last column for the average cost per person.

I created different spreadsheets for each employee in the workbook. Patterns began to emerge. Many of the receipts were the expected size and shape; some were even printed on yellow paper (which at first glance looked like carbon copy paper, but was not). However, the font and print type, even from different vendors, was suspiciously similar. In addition, the format of every receipt was nearly identical, which seemed odd given that we were dealing with multiple vendors. We have all been out to eat enough to know that different restaurants use different formats. One restaurant might display the table number on the left side of the receipt, another on the right. Some places include the server name while others do not. Many restaurants list the type of credit card used and others block out the card numbers except the last four digits. The fact that these receipts all used the same format was a definite red flag.

I decided to make copies of every receipt so I could start cross-referencing similar instances. For vendors I didn't recognize, I performed an online search to see whether or not they actually existed. Many of the receipts displayed phone numbers and addresses, most of which I called. Every restaurant was real.

In order to establish the legitimacy of the receipts, I faxed one to a Denny's manager. He called me back right away to let me know that the Denny's logo did not appear on actual receipts. The receipt I had in front of me clearly displayed the chain's familiar logo. I visited the restaurant's Web site and found the same logo that was printed on the receipt.

The restaurants under review were concentrated in southern California—Orange County, Garden Grove, Fountain Valley, and Huntington Beach. I contacted Payroll and learned that Jesse lived in Garden Grove, Marie lived in Fountain Valley, and Diane lived in Santa Ana, which was close to Huntington Beach. Another interesting coincidence.

After combining all the data from the spreadsheet analysis, I took a good look at the emerging patterns. Several receipts from different employees had the exact same credit card number. (*Could they really be sharing the same credit card?* I wondered). I noticed that the same credit card number was listed as a MasterCard in some instances, in others as a Visa. A phone call to Master-Card confirmed that such a situation would be highly unlikely, since each major credit card company uses a different series of numbers. I also discovered that there were about 25 different credit card numbers used between only three individuals. I had to wonder—how many people use 25 different credit cards? I began looking at the approval codes and reference codes and noticed that they were the same on multiple receipts from different restaurants, which I knew was virtually impossible. My instincts were telling me that something was wrong. But all the vendors were real, so how did these potential fraudsters obtain such realistic receipts? I had a breakthrough when I went to pay my personal income taxes.

A Trip to the Golden State

Over a mid-February weekend, I went to have my taxes prepared. I noticed as I was paying for the services that the receptionist had a computer on her desk with a very small printer next to it. She pulled up my account on her computer, typed in the charges due, then the printer spit out a receipt, which was the same size as the ones that I had been looking at for the past week. *Ah ha!* In the past I had uncovered fake invoices, and of course the routine duplicate receipts, but I hadn't seen someone create such a realistic-looking receipt using a computer before! This really took some effort—using the Internet to find real restaurants located in the areas they serviced, copying logos, names, addresses, and phone numbers, and typing this information on a receipt must have taken some time. They even included details such as table numbers, server names, and the date and time of the meal. Amazing! I envisioned a master "shell" document being used to create the receipts, with someone altering the particulars to make them appear real. These schemers probably didn't suspect someone would analyze every detail. They were meticulous and careful, but their efforts still failed!

I contacted my director and informed him of my suspicions. We decided that the best confirmation of this scheme would be to travel to southern California, visit some of the restaurants, and talk to the managers. We wanted to gather as much information as possible before presenting our findings to management.

I took one of my staff auditors with me and we flew to Orange County on February 21. We had copies of all the suspicious receipts and a list of seven restaurants to visit. We jumped in the rental car and took off from the airport to the first vendor, Lucille's Smokehouse in Long Beach. We had mapped out the trip so that the last restaurant we visited was closest to the airport. We ate lunch at Lucille's; the food was excellent. Afterwards, we took the receipt for our meal and compared it to the receipt submitted by the employees. Several discrepancies were immediately apparent. To be on the safe side, I asked to see the manager of the restaurant and informed her of our investigation.

She took a good look at the receipt I handed her, shook her head and said, "No, that's not our receipt. It's close, but there's something off about it."

She excused herself, walked into the back office, and returned a few moments later with an activity report for the date of the receipt. We scanned the report together and could not find the credit card number, payee name, or dollar amount of this receipt that had been submitted by Marie. We thanked the manager, walked to the car, and quickly documented her comments before leaving the parking lot.

We visited several other restaurants and found the same situation. Manager after manager disavowed the receipts and said they had to be from somewhere else. We started noticing little discrepancies: The table numbers weren't legitimate (some managers said the table numbers listed didn't exist), some receipts showed a normal time and others showed a military time (which didn't match the restaurants' receipts), the font or print type was different. Had we not physically visited the restaurants, we wouldn't have obtained that type of corroborative and irrefutable evidence.

Fraud from the Get-Go!

While it was satisfying to confirm our suspicions from the restaurant managers, my work was not yet complete. I knew from experience that before I presented my data to our legal counsel, I would need to make sure all my ducks were in a row. I then started the process of "ticking and tying," making sure all my supporting documents matched to the spreadsheet I had created. Amazingly enough, while Jesse, Marie, and Diane had only been working for the company for a few months, their scheme began on day one. The employees had initially submitted a total of $25,745 in expense reports. Just before we left for our southern California visits, AP received three more expense reports, these totaling $7,595. I added the reports to my analysis and told AP that if the employees called and asked about the delay in reimbursement, to tell them it was in process.

After adding the additional reports to my analysis, we had a total of $33,929 in expenses. I was certain that at least $14,774 were fake receipts and was suspicious of an additional $17,175, based on the format of the receipt, the font and bold type, and the fact that they came from the same restaurants we had visited in southern California. In total, I suspected 94% of the receipts were probably fraudulent.

I drafted a report for my director and made copies of the work papers for my files. I then shipped the originals for his review, along with my spreadsheet. After he reviewed the documents, I presented the scheme to Joshua Sanchez, the company's legal counsel, and walked him through the findings. According to Dependable's procedure for fraud cases, Internal Audit conducts the investigation and then the legal counsel and management conduct the interviews with employees. In this particular instance, Josh wanted to make sure that Jesse wasn't fabricating invoices at the direction of the sales manager or someone else higher in the organization. We had uncovered this type of issue before in our investigations. Per Josh's request, Internal Audit expanded the scope of the investigation and reviewed the expense reports for all sales representatives, sales assistants, and administrative assistants in southern California during the period of October through February. Essentially, we were looking for the same types of issues: same restaurants, bold type and font, format of the receipts, and any other suspicious activity. We were happy to inform Josh that we did not find problems in other employees' reports and concluded that it was unlikely this fraud was endemic.

Josh contacted Jacob Martinez, the southern California regional sales manager, and arranged to have the documents sent to him for review. A meeting was scheduled in the local southern California regional office for Josh and Jacob to discuss the report and the documents. They also arranged for Jesse to come to the office later in the day for a talk, fabricating a reason for the meeting to avoid tipping him off. That afternoon when Josh confronted him with the evidence, Jesse confessed to the scheme, admitting he was also giving fake receipts to his ex-wife and sister to submit for reimbursement. He explained to Josh and Jacob that he used his home computer to find local restaurants in his area, created the receipts on the computer, and used a printer and paper at the local Office Max to print out the receipts. Jesse affirmed that his fraudulent actions were not at the direction of anyone else in the company; however, he said, Marie and Diane were complicit with the scheme. All three employees were immediately terminated.

Lessons Learned

It is important for fraud examiners to cultivate a relationship with the accounts payable department. AP is the last line of defense in any company and should be kept in the loop with each discovery. Spend time teaching AP clerks how to recognize the signs of irregularities. I was sure to let AP know, in a nonaccusatory manner, when I found something that they could have caught—for instance, "Here is what we found, which might be something you guys can look for in the future." I gave them credit in my report for finding the initial problem and returned to tell them how grateful my superiors were for their diligence and attention to detail. While the AP manager was disappointed that they did not uncover this scheme earlier, I told her that she should be proud of how quickly her staff learned of it and that it would minimize costs to the company in the long run.

I learned that it's important to document the issue with all the pertinent details. I was thankful that we visited the restaurants and spoke to the managers to confirm our suspicions. Evidence of that caliber is hard to refute. Make copies and tie the information together for management. Ensuring that the evidence is organized and clear for management to follow will assist them in the decision-making process.

Collaborate with the legal department. I have conducted several investigations, with one even going to trial. You should always assume that the case will go to court. This means clear, concise reports and supporting evidence (think of "just the facts" when documenting the evidence). Obtaining the legal department's advice during the investigation is also wise because there may be other issues to which you are not privy. This information may shed new light on your findings and allow you to conduct a more thorough investigation.

Recommendations to Prevent Future Occurrences

Tone at the Top

Be transparent and promote the right "Tone at the Top." Management did not tolerate the wrongdoers' behavior and immediately dismissed them. To prevent future occurrences, management should openly communicate about the scheme and the results of the investigation. Let the other sales representatives and employees know that they are expected to act ethically and keep the lines of communication open.

Know Industry Practices

Be aware of all relevant industry practices and know the "players" in your company. My first year at this organization, we found sales representatives physically altering receipts they submitted on their expense reports. From then on, Internal Audit routinely scoured the expense reports and repeatedly found problems. Through years of training and audits, we were able to educate management on red flags. Knowing what types of practices are typical in the industry can help you target specific areas to audit and implement a continuous monitoring of that particular area. In monitoring these areas more closely, you may be able to recommend to management stronger internal controls that will be effective in minimizing the fraudulent behavior.

Proper Training

Educate the AP department on the indicators of fraud. As I mentioned earlier, they are the last line of defense and can assist the audit department in identifying potential issues. Had AP not caught this when they did, and if employees kept submitting the reports at the same rate, the scheme would not have appeared on the radar until the next year's expense report audit. The cost to the company could have been much greater because the monthly variances in the expenses were not significant and would have not been discovered during the month-to-month review.

About the Author

Shirley Quintana began her career in internal audit in 1995 while working for a national theatre exhibitor chain. After several years in internal audit, she obtained the Certified Fraud Examiner and Certified Internal Auditor designations. Shirley is an active member of the Institute of Internal Auditors and the Association of Certified Fraud Examiners.

C H A P T E R

The Coupon Code Crooks

DANNY MILLER, MICHAEL ROSE, AND CONOR DONNELLY

As a sales manager at Alpha Computers, Jaymes Daniels had ample authority to offer incentives to his crew, not only to hit their target sales numbers but also to beat the other teams in the company. There was a culture of heated competition and a lot was at stake. One year, sports cars were awarded to managers whose teams boasted the highest sales. Supervisors like Jaymes might earn more than half their total annual compensation in the last quarter of the year just from commissions or bonuses paid out based on their group's performance. Incentives can be effective, but they must come with controls that foster a climate of integrity and limit opportunities for cheating.

Jaymes's team consisted of a close-knit group of seven people. They knew the sales methodology inside Alpha well enough to understand the controls—and the control weaknesses. These seven, some of whom had criminal records, had family and friends scattered across the United States. The group included Danielle Carolyn, a professional salesperson with nearly 10 years of experience; Jayne Ellen, a specialist in small-business vertical market sales; Jonnie Davies, a technical sales lead; Guy Daniels, an intermediate manager just below Jaymes; John Small, a technical specialist with a methamphetamine addiction; and Anne Carthidge, an intermediate manager reporting to Jaymes.

Anne was a particularly ambitious group leader interested in driving sales and achieving metrics to impress the higher-ups. She had a dishonest streak and was well acquainted with Alpha's internal transaction system. But none of the seven were as trustworthy as Jaymes foolishly believed. With the inside knowledge and the criminal experience of friends and family, this team eventually became a scandalous enterprise that would rob the company of more than a quarter of a million dollars.

Alpha Computers, a large manufacturer of PCs, notebooks, and servers, is based in the United States. The business has arranged its divisions under individual, small business, large business, and governmental sales. Each branch has its own managerial team covering planning, forecasting, marketing, operations, accounting, and sales force.

The computer manufacturing business is cutthroat—externally, with company competitors, and internally, against other divisions. Division executives at Alpha have been known to motivate sales managers in critical quarters by offering extravagant prizes in exchange for the right numbers. And in turn, sales managers, hungry for success, will do whatever it takes to drive business.

The largest venue for Alpha is online, where the business spends millions in marketing to drive eyeballs to the company Web site. Sales personnel have various tools at their disposal to encourage potential customers to make online purchases. Coupon codes, which offer discounts, are perhaps the most valuable means and can be given out over the telephone by representatives or by special e-mails sent to targeted consumers. For example, let's say Alpha won a contract for $5 million in computer hardware, software, and services with a school district. To up the ante, it would also offer specials to this client's employees for personal notebooks and PCs at a discounted price using coupon codes. The school district's employees could then access the Alpha Web site, configure their own PC by choosing options on the screen, and check out digitally using a credit card. When totaling the cost of the PC, a special area on the screen requests that the customer enter any coupon codes, after which the price is adjusted to reflect the discount. While the coupons appear to be a simple marketing strategy, they can be fiscally dangerous in the wrong hands.

Coupon Stacking

Regal Consulting, a small company located in Dallas, was owned by a family member of Danielle Carolyn. She set up an account on Alpha's computer system for Regal Consulting and gave it a customer number, fully qualifying them for a small line of credit. To prove that it was a legitimate business, one of Danielle's family members registered Regal as a doing-business-as (DBA) account at a local Dallas bank—under his own name—with a small amount of "seed" money. Again, this was to give the false impression of a legitimate business.

Once a small business is set up in Alpha's e-business Web site and the internal customer-accounting system, the customer can simply log on to his or her account, purchase equipment, and then check out. That is when coupons come into play. In this instance, the perpetrators used a technique called "coupon stacking." The e-business system was developed for ease and speedy use at Alpha, built to be as flexible as possible for maximum customer satisfaction. Because there was no limit on coupon usage, if someone had 10 coupons for $150 each, they could use all of those coupon codes in a single transaction and save up to $1,500. If the customer ordered a system that cost $1,500, he could potentially get it for free.

Sales representatives at Alpha were fast and furiously passing out coupons—and no one monitored them for appropriate use. Danielle and the other perpetrators started conservatively by using codes to discount each of the orders by 50%. But as time passed, they became progressively greedier. The last two orders allowed a discount of more than 90%. When Jaymes looked at the sales reports in detail (more than a month after these last transactions), he asked why the discounts were so large. Danielle, Jayne, and Anne told him it was for promotional activities with a key client—that there were no issues. These same sales representatives were selling to legitimate clients at a fast pace too, so Jaymes ignored his suspicions.

The truth was Regal Consulting was taking the PCs and equipment they'd bought at discounted prices, selling them locally for market price, and sharing the proceeds with Danielle, Jayne, and Anne. Regal was brazen enough to use their line of credit with Alpha to fund the fraud, which allowed them to spend nothing up front and delay discovery.

Warranty Fraud

Jonnie Davies, Guy Daniels, John Small, and Anne Carthidge committed a second series of scams on the East Coast and in a southwestern city. Again, the perpetrators had set up what appeared to be a legitimate business, but was not. Under the leadership of Anne, they were committing two frauds. One was the same coupon stacking scheme as Danielle and her family, which, over a two-year period, had an average discount of 50%. The other involved an internally-known weakness in the parts warranty area.

In particular, John Small, one of his family members, and Jerry Douget, a former technical-support personnel member no longer employed by Alpha, worked together on the details of this scheme. John, Jerry, and Anne met a number of times with John's family member, who showed them how to exploit both the public e-business Web site and the warranty area (which was phone based) for their benefit. The scheme involved claiming that certain parts had failed in systems that actually worked, receiving credit for them, and then purchasing new parts and equipment in order to sell it. John understood that if they moved too quickly, a red flag might be raised. So they eased into it and ran the scheme over a two-year period.

They collected valid part numbers and called warranty representatives. Since the part numbers were legitimate and attached to existing systems that had been sold and appeared to be in warranty, few questions were asked. The perpetrators knew that, for the most part, the company did not require that the failed parts be returned since it was expensive to check in each piece manually. Only hard drives and monitors were screened closely.

Once a credit balance was built over time, John and the others endeavored to claim it. First, they attempted to trade in their credit for a check to the fake company. But Alpha's policy stated that vendors, customers, and consumers may redeem credit only through goods and services unless specifically approved by division management. So, instead, they bought deeply discounted parts using credit that they had fraudulently accrued from the company and resold them.

Trouble in Paradise

As divisional lead, Jaymes did not suspect or detect any of the schemes. He did notice certain anomalies in the sales figures, but he ignored the warning signs. If it had not been for John Smalls, who turned on the others and blew the whistle, the fraud might have continued for years.

A year prior, a whistleblower hotline was implemented at Alpha to comply with the Sarbanes-Oxley Act of 2002, but was also used more broadly within Alpha to handle any misdeeds. John, driven by a growing drug addiction, had completely run out of money and could no longer finance his habit. He had urged Anne and the others to raise the stakes and push for more money, but they resisted out of fear of being detected.

The whistleblower line was monitored by an ethics officer, who recorded and then returned the calls. In effect, this was an ombudsman position meant to be completely independent of the company. The ethics officer was Don Jacobs, who had a long history with Alpha, actually helping to launch the business with the founder. To assure anonymity, the caller was assigned a code number. All activity was recorded for whichever group it was assigned to: the corporate executive group, the corporate compliance group, or the internal audit group. In this case, the vice president of audit was notified by Don that a complaint had been made against certain sales representatives. Initially, it was difficult to obtain information because it became apparent that the informant was an employee probably involved in the fraud. After a brief discussion with the legal counsel and the vice president of internal audit, it was decided that Internal Audit would investigate and keep a representative of the legal group informed.

After Hours Interview

I was a senior member of the internal audit group. My background in both the audit and technology side (as a programmer, database administrator, and project manager) gave me an edge in understanding the mechanics of these frauds. We requested that John, the informant, come in for an interview. Initially he resisted, as he did not want to be identified, but Don made it plain that we knew he was an employee and it was just a matter of time before his wrongdoing was discovered. Eventually, John agreed to sit for interviews with myself and one legal staff member.

The interviews occurred after regular working hours to avoid tipping off anyone involved in the fraud. During our talks, it became apparent that Alpha's e-business systems were being exploited by personnel who knew them intimately. The coupon methodology was not well executed, since all the system did was automatically check for ranges of alphanumeric characters. None of the coupons had expiration dates, and since the divisional business management constantly created new coupon codes, they could be used in ever greater combinations.

John's group discovered the flaw and tested it on a training system with success. Instead of informing someone at Alpha of the potential for fraud, they discussed it among themselves and decided to involve their friends and family in order to exploit the internal weakness. John claimed that they were going to let the IT team know about the loophole after they had reaped the benefits for a while. But greed has tenacity. John claimed that several of the friends and family threatened him and Anne with exposure to law enforcement if they ever blew the whistle. I believed part of John's story was a lie. However, I knew that if I could obtain the proper evidence, law enforcement would determine later if the weak points in his position, like the blackmail, were true. The scheme had gone on for nearly two years before John came forth.

Big Savings Gone Bad

In order to be discreet, our investigation was buried within an already scheduled audit over the warranty process to determine how the fraud was committed. As it turned out, the warranty process did not involve checking to ensure that returned parts were actually valid and linked to the original system sold. Nor did they ensure that, before a credit or part exchange occurred, they first received the exact part that was claimed. I initially pulled transactions related to warranty issues that also used multiple coupon codes on redemption. There were only two customer accounts, each originating in different cities, one in the central Southwest and one on the East Coast. It was determined that the size of this fraud was larger than expected and came to more than $180,000.

If John had not pointed us in the right direction, we would not have detected the additional fraud occurring under Danielle and Regal Consulting. Using the information he provided, we found Regal's suspicious transactions that had previously gone undetected in Internal Audit.

The legal counsel and I began to contact law enforcement authorities. We met with representatives of the district attorney's offices to give them information, answer questions, and walk them through how the frauds occurred. The resulting investigation yielded seven people charged with fraud: three employees (Anne, Guy, and Danielle) and four people on the outside. The personnel implicated in the case but not charged were dismissed from the company, including John and Jaymes. John was not charged in any of the cases since he had agreed to provide evidence against the other perpetrators.

Lessons Learned

Alpha management was determined not to let this type of fraud occur again. Although the financial loss was not consequential in comparison to their revenue, the company reputation was at stake. If investors found out, share prices would suffer, and since value was built on share price, the ordeal had a deep impact.

In addition to the fraud itself, there was an indirect cost in funding a full-fledged investigation. With internal effort, outside specialist legal counsel, outside forensics experts, IT system analysts, and other miscellaneous expenses, the associated cost came to more than $200,000. Together, the total estimated cost of the fraud was just under $500,000.

Alpha conducted an examination of existing controls to address these issues and to minimize future risk. Business procedures were reviewed and system controls were altered and redesigned in vulnerable areas. Automated controls within applications were analyzed and deemed to be the best available and most reliable. Specific checkpoints in the computer applications that were implemented as a result of this case included a review of the business course, exposing opportunities for fraud, and determining if automated controls should be embedded within their supporting applications to reduce the risk profile.

As a result of the review of fraud controls, coupon codes were reengineered. The new structure resembles checks, are single-use only, and each one's value is recorded from one central group in corporate. When a coupon code is used in a transaction, it expires immediately afterwards and the associated order number is recorded. Coupons were also redesigned with a shelf life: If not used within six months, they automatically expire. The e-business Web application that faced the Internet was modified so that the customer could only use one code per transaction and limited the number of coupons by a single user over a defined time period.

I assisted in changing Internal Audit's role dramatically by helping to develop a small group with a focus on external and internal fraud. Eventually, this became an independent entity within the company. With the growth of Alpha globally, the risk of fraud expanded to groups of employees, partner companies, and subcontractors outside the United States, forcing Alpha to reexamine their controls and become more vigilant.

Recommendations for Preventing Future Occurrences

Fraud Awareness and Training

IT and business teams responsible for developing the online software tools were not equipped with the necessary fraud-awareness training to factor in antifraud measures as part of the software requirements. The regional sales manager, Jaymes, lacked this sort of training as well, which might have contributed to why he did not report the red flags to proper authorities. Designing and implementing an antifraud program often serves as a deterrent to dishonest employees.

Governance

At the time of the initial fraud there was no single ownership or accountability for dealing with fraud or the potential for such. Internal Audit was focused mostly on corporate matters. While Alpha had implemented a whistleblower hotline in apparent compliance with Sarbanes-Oxley, it took a major incident and the threat of a reputation crisis for Alpha to take adequate fraud measures. Creating a whole team to focus on fraud prevention and detection with direct links to appropriate internal and external persons was a clear sign of a change in the tone at the top.

Identify Fraud Risks and Determine Effective Fraud Responses

The incidents highlighted the absence of adequate fraud prevention and detection procedures. Two frequently asked questions in a fraud assessment are: How much damage can the company incur in a single incident? And could any one incident of fraud cause significant damage to the assets or reputation of the company? These incidents were above the radar in both respects. On the preventative side there is an opportunity to deploy automated systems that include some element of antifraud controls. These have now been implemented, but the more complex fraud on warranty parts required the collaboration of manual processes with the system tools.

In regard to detection, there remains no substitute for vigilance of staff and management. The antifraud team should communicate that they, as experts, will decide whether or not a red flag should be further explored, rather than the management.

About the Authors

Danny Miller, CISA, ITIL (green badge), is a partner and the Philadelphia practice leader for the business advisory-services practice of Grant Thornton LLP. He has over 21 years of international experience in the information technology and audit fields, has worked as IT auditor, programmer, project manager, database administrator, IT director, and CIO, has led the IT audit function at a major computer manufacturer, and was the author of this case study.

Michael P. Rose, CPA, CIA, CCSA, CISA, CISM, CICS, CITP, MBA, MST, is a senior partner in the business advisory-services practice at Grant Thornton LLP, focusing on governance, risk management, and compliance. Mike is a member of the Committee of Sponsoring Organizations' Oversight Task Force for the development of guidance on monitoring internal control systems. He has over 28 years of experience in internal controls, audit, and fraud-related services, and was the editor of this case study.

Conor Donnelly, BA, MSc, is a senior manager in the business advisory services practice of Grant Thornton LLP. He has extensive experience with both IT and management consulting within a variety of industries, is a member of the Institute of Internal Auditors and the Information Systems and Audit Control Association, and contributed to the recommendations section of this case study.

C H A P T E R

He Fought the Law

CLIFFORD HUNTER

Joseph Foote was an extremely bright and charismatic young entrepreneur who, at 15 years old, was already running his own successful lawn-mowing company and lemonade stands. His business prowess was obvious even from a young age, shown by his use of subcontractors in order to limit his personal involvement but still reap the financial benefits of his endeavors. When he wasn't brainstorming his next enterprise, he enjoyed tinkering with radios and other communication devices. Additionally, Joseph, as with most young people, was an avid computer user and was very comfortable surfing the Internet, where he frequented MySpace and other social networking sites.

Joseph's ingenuity wasn't limited to the business world, however. On more than one occasion, his clever and creative mind was the source of trouble. In fact, Joseph had been expelled from Thousand Oaks High School after he stole a radio from the civilian security guard. Using the commandeered device, he began broadcasting that there had been a shooting and that he needed backup. The Borealis Police Department (BPD) had a school resource officer on the grounds, and the officer rebroadcasted the "information" to the area dispatcher. Police officers were sent to the scene, only to find that it was a hoax by Joseph.

The teen also had run-ins with other authority figures, ranging from an altercation with a security guard over his violation of a mall dress code to transgressions that eventually ended with burglary, trespassing, shoplifting, and assault charges brought against him by the BPD. Each of these situations quickly escalated to further violence, resulting in even more confrontations with the authorities and his parents.

Online Disorder

Founded and owned by Jack Williams, Law Enforcement Suppliers (LES) is a small police-supply store based in rural Pennsylvania that sells police equipment to individual purchasers as well as law enforcement agencies. As there is no public showroom or printed catalog, most sales are conducted via the LES Web site, www.LawEnforcementSuppliers.com, but orders can be placed by telephone as well.

Having just been advised that his company might have been a victim of Internet fraud, Jack Williams called the BPD. Officer Chuck Wilson took Jack's initial report, in which the owner of LES said he had received a purchase order for over $27,000 worth of police supplies and equipment the previous day. The order was received via LES's online ordering site by a company called CL Corp, which Jack believed to be a sham. The request had been placed using a purchase order number that was "not even close" to the regular purchase-order sequence that he uses, which initially raised Jack's suspicions.

He told Officer Wilson that since the requisition was unusual, he tried to call the number that accompanied the order. To his surprise, he was greeted with what sounded like a young person attempting to imitate a company telephone recording. The voice even instructed Jack to press zero if he wanted to speak to an operator, which he did, with no effect. He then tried to contact the person placing the order via the e-mail address provided, but the e-mail was rejected by his server, which said the recipient's address was invalid.

Dressing as the Enemy

Officer Wilson requested that Jack fax him copies of any documents that he could gather from the suspicious online order. The officer kept these faxes as evidence for future reference. As with other matters handled by the BPD, the criminal report was written by the officer who took the initial complaint, was passed on to the officer's sergeant, then flowed through the departmental records system, and finally reached the investigations bureau, where the case was assigned to a detective. As I normally conduct the computer fraud investigations for the BPD, I was the detective assigned.

I began my investigation by making copies of the faxes from Jack. While looking the documents over, I observed that the attempted purchase was extensive and included a number of issues that caused alarm.

Some of the things that had been ordered included several M26 Tasers, devices that use an electrical shock to cause neuromuscular incapacitation; bulletproof vests; handcuffs; pepper spray, an oreocapiscum substance that has replaced Mace, the product formerly carried by police officers or other individuals; and police-style pants, boots, shirts, pistol belts, and security officer badges. Many of these items were ordered in multiples of six, which raised concerns about groups of juveniles dressed in police style uniforms with bulletproof vests and nonlethal weapons.

I checked the address provided with the order and found that it was the home address for Joseph Foote and his parents. The cell phone number on the order form belonged to Joseph as well. I reviewed the young suspect's criminal history, which was already rather extensive for a 15 year old. Based on what I had learned, I arranged for two patrollers, Officers Andrews and Nichols, to meet me at the Foote residence to speak with Joseph and his parents. No one was home, so we left a business card in the door with a note asking them to contact us.

Officer Andrews was a veteran with almost 20 years' experience in law enforcement. Officer Nichols was still fairly young, with only five years' experience, but he had an excellent reputation for outstanding people skills. The two men worked the same beat every day, patrolling the area surrounding Joseph's neighborhood. Consequently, the partners were familiar with Joseph, as they had been in contact with his family on several occasions in the past and had established a good rapport with the parents. Following our fruitless visit to the boy's home, they both agreed to stop by the house later and to try to talk to the parents again.

Back at the station, I called Jack to ask if he still had the original e-mail order from CL Corp, or if his ordering or Web site software could track the Internet protocol (IP) address from the originating computer. This information would allow me to trace which e-mail server had forwarded the order, potentially allowing me to obtain subpoenas for the e-mail service to determine where the order had originated. Unfortunately, Jack stated that his software did not track IP addresses and didn't show the "header" or the routing of the e-mail and its course to him. Though disappointed by this forensic dead end, I had a hunch that speaking with the suspect in person would enable us to uncover a lot of information about the questionable online transactions.

Officers Andrews and Nichols finally located Joseph at his home a few weeks later, and since he was a juvenile, they asked him to call his parents so at least one would be present when they spoke with him. After a few phone calls, arrangements were made for Joseph's father to come home and speak with the officers.

Mr. Foote arrived within minutes, his wife shortly thereafter. The suspect's parents invited the officers into their house, where Andrews explained to them the basics of the case and why he wanted to talk to Joseph. The boy's parents confirmed the e-mail address used for the order as belonging to Joseph, but they said they did not recognize the cell phone number. They repeatedly expressed distress over the incident and indicated that they understood how it could be considered "a Columbine-type warning sign," referring to the school shooting at Columbine High School near Littleton, Colorado, in 1999.

Officer Andrews asked the parents about their knowledge regarding the suspicious transaction or if they had any involvement. Both denied knowing anything about the scheme. According to the Footes, there was only one computer in the house, located in the living room. They consented to having it seized for forensic examination.

The officer then requested to speak briefly with their son. Quickly losing hope for the boy's innocence and wanting to see what he had to say for himself, the Footes agreed to allow their son to be interviewed.

Officer Andrews asked Joseph if the e-mail account from the order was his and Joseph nodded. The policeman then inquired whether Joseph had visited the LES's Web site.

"Well, maybe," Joseph replied.

"These are yes or no questions," said Officer Andrews.

Joseph amended his response to a simple "yeah." Encouraged that he might extract a confession, Officer Andrews continued by asking if he had placed an order for almost $30,000 worth of police equipment. Joseph offered another affirmative answer. The veteran officer knew this minor admission was a key milestone in the investigation. He asked Joseph one last question: "Why?"

Joseph looked down and meekly replied, "I don't know."

Officer Andrews later explained to me that he stopped the interview at this point since he had been able to confirm the identity and location of the suspect, as well as verify that Joseph had indeed placed the order. Further, the officer said he was uncomfortable proceeding with the interview, as it may have required asking technical questions regarding computers and computer crimes that fell beyond the scope of his professional expertise.

Although Mrs. Foote had originally acknowledged that she had no problems with the seizing of the computer, she stopped Officer Andrews on his way out the door to inform him that she was taking online college classes from a local community college and to ask if she could have the computer back as soon as we were finished.

"I'll try," Officer Andrews replied, "but I'll have to forward that request to Detective Hunter. To expedite the investigation, will you ask Joseph for his computer passwords?"

Mrs. Foote promptly provided the passwords to Officer Andrews. When he returned to the station, Andrews placed the seized computer into evidence and asked for it to be held for my review.

Several days after Officers Andrews and Nichols had met with Joseph, I arrived at my office to find a message and report detailing their discoveries. I contacted Detective Larry Michaels, our resident computer-forensics expert, and asked if he would image the drive of the suspect computer. Having recently returned to our fraud unit after a three-year stint as the BPD representative at the local Federal Bureau of Investigation's computer forensic laboratory, Detective Michaels jumped at the assignment, and began imaging the hard drive immediately.

This process involves making a complete and exact copy of a questioned drive onto a clean drive, thus allowing the data to be forensically examined without the risk of altering the original. To image Joseph's hard drive, Detective Michaels copied the data using Forensic Toolkit and a freshly cleaned and swiped hard drive. He further ensured the integrity of the process by running a writeblocker, a device used to verify that no new data was transferred onto the Footes' computer while it was undergoing these procedures.

I called Mrs. Foote later that afternoon and said her computer was ready for pickup. I also requested that we speak briefly when she came by, as I still needed her help in our investigation. Although Officer Andrews had already obtained verbal permission from the Footes to search the computer, a written consent is normally preferred in the event that there are questions at a later date if the case goes to trial. When she arrived at our police station, I had Mrs. Foote sign a written BPD consent-to-search form in an attempt to bypass a search warrant to examine the data on the hard drive.

In addition, I asked Mrs. Foote if she knew her son's friends, since many of his orders were placed in multiples of six.

"I don't know," replied Mrs. Foote, "but I'll certainly try to find out." She mentioned that Joseph had always been more of a follower than a leader but was also very impulsive, frequently acting first and thinking of the consequences afterwards.

Further delving into Joseph's criminal history revealed that he was already on probation. With the evidence against the young criminal mounting, I called his probation officer and notified her of this case as a possible probation violation.

Radioing the Truth

While Detective Michaels was examining the imaged hard drive, he observed another attempted suspicious purchase, from PoliceRadios.com for $22,558, made during the previous year. There was also an associated e-mail from a Richard Frills inquiring about frequency requirements for the purchased radios, as well as a follow-up e-mail requesting credit card information for billing purposes.

The equipment Joseph had attempted to order in this transaction had consisted of six police-type radios; several pairs of ear buds, which are earpieces for cell phones or radios and are designed so that only the user can hear the transmission; lapel microphones, which allow the user to leave a radio on the user's belt or in the radio case; belt mounts and holders; chargers; and extra batteries.

I called Richard, the representative at PoliceRadios.com who had e-mailed Joseph about his order. When questioned about Joseph's order, Richard informed me that his question to Joseph regarding the desired frequencies for radios would have been used to determine whether someone was truly in the business of buying police-type radios or was an impostor. When Joseph told Richard that he would program the radios once he received them, Richard became suspicious, as most agencies prefer to receive them preprogrammed.

Richard said they had not lost any money or equipment on Joseph's fraudulent order but that he would check for related company records or documents. He feared they might not be there, though, as the company had recently rebuilt its records system and would have purged any noncompleted transactions. Richard said he couldn't remember exactly why the order wasn't filled but that he believed he had never heard back from Joseph and that the matter had then been simply forgotten.

A few days later, Detective Michaels finished his examination of the Footes' computer and provided three CD-ROMS of his case findings: one for our police records, one for the district attorney, and one for discovery for the defense. He revealed an additional piece of evidence that was exposed by his forensic techniques: While combing through the data on Joseph's computer, the detective observed the credit card number provided in an e-mail response to PoliceRadios.com, along with the associated card verification value (CVV) code (the three-digit number on the back of a credit card, typically used when the card is not presented for purchase, especially for telephonic or Internet purchases). The e-mail also stated the name on the credit card was "Joe Foote."

Based on this new evidence, as well as my desire to personally interview Joseph, I called Mrs. Foote and left a voicemail asking her to contact me. While waiting to hear back from her, I used the U.S. Secret Service Web site to conduct a bank identification number (BIN) check on the first six digits of the credit card and found it was issued by ABC National Bank.

When I finally spoke with Mrs. Foote, I advised her of the ABC Bank card and asked her what she knew about the account.

"Joseph has an ATM/debit card from ABC Bank. That might be the same one," she replied. At this point, I knew that the evidence was strong enough against the boy that we needed to confront him in a formal setting, so I scheduled an appointment for Joseph and his mother to come to my office.

Mrs. Foote arrived alone, coming from work, and we chatted briefly while waiting for Joseph to appear. When he showed up, all of us went to an interview room, where we were joined by Detective Gregg Kinney, a coworker of mine.

Joseph was advised of his Miranda rights, which he signed off on. I then began my interview by asking him if he owned an ABC Bank card.

"I do," he replied, "but it's not here with me."

"I'll find the card as soon as we return home. I can scan the image and e-mail it to you as soon as possible," Mrs. Foote volunteered. Next, I asked Joseph if he knew why he was here.

"Because of the computer order," he said.

"What exactly did you order, Joseph?" I inquired.

"Tasers and stuff," he replied.

I provided him and his mother with a copy of the order placed on LawEnforcementSuppliers.com. Joseph confirmed that the items listed appeared to be the ones that he had ordered. When asked who was with him when he placed the order, he replied that he was by himself.

"Why did you order these things, Joseph?" I pressed.

He shrugged his shoulders, stating he didn't know. I asked him if anyone had asked him to place the order or had talked to him about it.

"No," he replied.

Detective Kinney chimed in and asked the boy what CL Corp was. To our surprise, Mrs. Foote started laughing. Joseph shot her a defiant glance and admitted that CL Corp was the business he had started to operate cold drink stands in the summers, which he later expanded to include mowing lawns. Since one of the beverages he sold at the stands was Crystal Light, he started calling his company CL Corp. Mrs. Foote then added that her son had started CL Corp several years ago and now had as many as 20 or 30 kids working for him during the summers, selling candy, running drink stands, and performing lawn services.

I again asked Joseph to explain what he needed the police supplies for, explaining that this was his chance to address some of our concerns about the bulletproof vests and Tasers that he had tried to order. He stated that he wanted the items to protect his business, as sometimes people would steal from his employees. Encouraged by his response, I continued my probing about the LES order. I asked the young troublemaker where he got the purchase order number used on the order and he said he made it up. When asked, he denied ever having done anything like this before.

Deciding to switch gears a bit, I approached Joseph about the order that Detective Michaels discovered during the search of the boy's computer.

"Have you ever communicated with a company called Policeradios .com?"

"Maybe," he responded. To help jostle his memory, I handed him a printed copy of the Web-site order form and asked whether he recognized it.

He did. After a few more questions, he finally admitted that he had tried to place an order with the company. He was shown the credit card number on the order and was asked if that was his debit card. He stated it was more likely a prepaid gift card he had.

"Joseph, did you have $22,000 on the gift card?" I inquired.

"No."

I knew we were close to finished, but I had a few lingering questions I wanted to pose to the lad. I asked Joseph what he needed the radios for, and he replied that he had wanted them so he could talk to his employees when they were out working, in case they needed anything or required help. From the corner of the room, Mrs. Foote volunteered that Joseph has always had an obsession with radios, especially walkie-talkie–type radios, and owned numerous models, which he used to talk with friends and neighbors.

Satisfied with the interview and the information I had obtained, and after Joseph and Mrs. Foote confirmed that they had nothing to add, I escorted the boy and his mother to the front lobby, where I informed them they were free to go.

The Outcome of the Investigation

After completing the tedious paperwork process, I filed the case with the district attorney's office, suggesting charges against Joseph of computer crime and attempted theft greater than $15,000. The computer crime charge carried the possibility of 4 to 12 years' prison time and up to a $750,000 fine, and the attempted theft would mean up to 2 to 6 years' prison time and a $500,000 fine. While it is unlikely that a juvenile would be given the most severe penalties in those ranges, Joseph could be charged as an adult at the order of the court and possibly be subjected to the maximum punishment.

To expedite the processing of the case, I hand carried the filings, along with copies of Joseph's other cases with the BPD and the latest copy of his criminal history, to the intake deputy district attorney (DDA). The district attorney's intake unit reviews all incoming cases and then either agrees with the suggested charges or changes them to something more applicable in order to most successfully try the case.

I explained my concerns to the intake DDA regarding Joseph's crimes, describing the types and quantities of equipment he had tried to order and the potential outcomes if he had used this equipment in an unlawful manner. She was alarmed by the youngster's actions as well and agreed to fast-track the affidavit to a judge for his signature so Joseph could be arrested and arraigned.

The DDA's office signed within three days and Joseph Foote was brought before the court for a first appearance, to be advised of his rights, and to ensure that he had a guardian ad litem to represent him in litigation since he was a juvenile.

Nearly three months later I was contacted by the DDA, who reported that he didn't feel the computer crime portion of the scheme had been carried out to an extent that would merit the charge I suggested. He had decided an attempt charge would be more appropriate.

Approximately five months after charges were filed, a plea agreement was reached. Joseph pleaded guilty to a lesser charge of attempted computer crime (felony), with a mandatory mental health hearing and 24 months' intense supervised probation.

After this investigation was wrapped up, the budding criminal managed to rack up a charge from the BPD of assault and threats. Based on the arrest after the plea agreement for his computer crime, Joseph was charged with probation violation. Another visit with the judge resulted in his being sentenced to a maximum of 24 months in a juvenile corrections facility, based on the recommendations of his family, probation officer, the district attorney, and even the boy's guardian ad litem. The outcome of the assaults and threats charge is still pending, but for now Joseph remains in the juvenile facility and is undergoing mental health counseling. Sadly, the bright young entrepreneur's rap sheet is quickly growing longer than his list of business successes.

Lessons Learned

One of our biggest constraints in investigating this case was lack of technically proficient manpower. The BPD, like most police agencies, was limited in both the resources available to work computer crime cases and in the technical skills of the force's officers and investigators. While working this case, I was also working a total of 11 other cases; Detective Michaels, who ran the forensic side of the computer investigation, was working a grand jury case as well as three others. This workload greatly limited the amount of time we could spend on an individual case, regardless of its importance. As a result, one recommendation that has been posed to the BPD is the establishment of a high-tech crime unit, which would employ a forensics examiner and several detectives specifically dedicated to handling all cases like this one.

It is also extremely important to recognize and thank those individuals who go beyond what is expected of them to aid an investigation. In joining this case, officers Andrews and Nichols tackled an assignment that fell outside of their normal duties. Although neither of them has any experience in working the finer points of computer crime cases, I could not have picked two better officers to have interviewed the Foote family. Out of my deep respect and gratitude, I sent to their supervisor a note advising him of the quality of their work. Since that time, both have asked me questions about types of computer crime and about forensic investigation techniques, knowing that they have a friendly ear in this unit.

Recommendations to Prevent Further Occurrences

While law enforcement is typically reactive rather than proactive, there are a number of steps that can be taken at the community level to limit the occurrence of computer crime, as well as at the law enforcement level to improve related investigations. The recommendations in both areas hinge on education.

To help communities guard against these types of fraud schemes, local law enforcement agencies and DAs need to make information regarding computer crime as prevalent as tips for securing your home from burglars and protecting your car or purse. Most areas now have a local-government television station that can be used to get the word out. Public service announcements and interviews with local newspapers are other effective outlets to warn local consumers and business owners. In addition, police officers should go to neighborhood watch meetings and host seminars at local schools to talk to the citizens about helping to prevent computer crimes.

Connecting local police departments with small businesses is especially important in fighting computer fraud at the community level. Unfortunately for most small businesses that find themselves victims of a scheme like Joseph's, most federal agencies simply do not have the manpower to investigate such cases unless the crime involves high dollar figures or a potential terrorism link. Business owners may find a sympathetic ear within those agencies who can direct them to someone that can be of assistance, but typically they must rely on their local law enforcement authorities.

To bring the police and DAs up to speed on computer crimes, education must be stressed at all levels of the justice system. Patrol officers and deputies don't need to be computer experts, but they do need to have a rough idea of what to look for, what questions to ask, and if necessary what equipment to seize.

Likewise, detectives and investigators need to understand the technological issues involved in writing search warrants or arrest warrant affidavits that will be considered by judges and the local DA.

Further, when law enforcement members discover a training opportunity that can enhance their technical knowledge of computer crimes and forensic procedures, they should reach out to make sure they know about the class. It is generally more effective to take a DA—and a judge, if possible—with you to a class than to spend hours explaining.

Finally, police departments should weigh the costs and benefits of establishing a centralized and dedicated computer-crime section or high-tech crime unit. While it does not need to be the top of the line or the best-equipped unit in the country, a core of trained, experienced investigators who can mentor new officers, assist in the technical aspects of investigations, and conduct timely, thorough examinations will help victims, the courts system, and the community by preventing and detecting computer crimes.

About the Author

Clifford Hunter, CFE, has worked for the Aurora, Colorado, Police Department for the past 12 years and is currently assigned to the economic crimes unit as a detective. He retired from the U.S. military after 22 years of service, including assignments in Army Intelligence and Air Force Security Operations.

CHAPTER 29

Eyes on the Company Secrets

TYSON JOHNSON

Freddy Zhang fancied himself a successful engineer on the rise. He lived in a well-appointed basement apartment located in an upscale Toronto neighborhood with his wife, a beautiful young woman working on an advanced degree. Freddy was a computer expert; he believed the world was his oyster.

But the budding engineer rarely thought before he spoke. As a result, he repeatedly created awkward, uncomfortable situations at social functions or with his coworkers. He had a real knack for the inappropriate. That might work for comedians, but Freddy was an engineer. While colleagues put up with him, he was never viewed as a friend, a real team member, or a trusted employee. Freddy was known as an egoist, a man who played only for himself.

TPP Engineering is a successful private company specializing in the building, maintenance, and servicing of power stations across Canada. They also sell proprietary software to utility companies to ensure that power stations run effectively. The particular marketplace TPP operates in is cutthroat, with intimidating barriers to entry and few competitors. Contracts in the industry involve significant dollar values, so maintaining clients and winning new contracts is a high-stakes game. These firms adhere to professional standards in the engineering field and recognize that strong industry reputations are a key to success. TPP Engineering was a well-respected entity.

As one of the smaller firms, TPP Engineering had to be more competitive on service. The employees were known to be some of the smartest and most dynamic professionals in the industry. Not surprisingly, their executive team was highly decorated and full of gregarious individuals. TPP had to run lean operating costs in order to maximize profits, which meant that there wasn't a business unit or employee placed in charge of security—the area wasn't deemed important and didn't represent "billable hours."

Freddy was a former TPP Engineering employee who had followed the mercenary calling of a bigger payday and the potential for more glory with a large industry competitor. TPP had a culture of openness that translated to weak controls, namely as it pertained to electronic information security. Freddy was well aware of that fact.

A Vindictive Lover

I work as the managing corporate investigator for a large firm. We received a panicked call early one morning from TPP's chief operating officer.

"We need to meet with someone right away about a serious security situation," he said.

I introduced myself and informed him that I would be able to meet him in an hour at his office. Before heading out, I briefly researched the company in question.

I was greeted by both the CEO and COO, who quickly ushered me into a meeting room with leather chairs, a mahogany conference table, and a few large plants. The COO, a fit man in his 50s and normally a confident leader with a firm grip, was now bent over in his chair, wringing his hands nervously. He peered over his glasses at me with a look of helplessness. The CEO was heavyset and known for his jovial and fun-loving nature. But he now sat alongside his COO, perspiration on his brow and a quiver in his voice.

"We believe that someone has hacked into our computer system and is stealing our secrets," the two stated in unison.

"What, exactly, led you to this conclusion?" I asked the frightened executives, reminding them to take deep breaths while they walked me through the history. They informed me that an ex-girlfriend of a former employee had come to the office the day before and disclosed that her previous love interest had "trade secrets" at his house, which she had printed off and brought in for them to see. The COO handed me sheets of paper with state secrets—specific technologies.

Some of the documents presented to me included e-mail header information showing the e-mail address of former employee Freddy Zhang. It was clear that information from TPP servers had been sent to Freddy's home e-mail and work e-mail accounts. I knew I needed to dig much deeper.

As a former intelligence officer, I was initially concerned that the security breach was an indication of corporate espionage. Was Freddy simply a tool for a larger competitor to obtain confidential information? Or was he a lone wolf seeking to impress his colleagues, obtain inside intelligence in the interest of his own success, and score points with his new employer? Perhaps an insider at TPP was still sending information to Freddy. Having worked similar operations before (under warranted federal powers, of course), I knew that to run this case properly we needed to call in computer forensic experts and maximize the client's potential for civil actions by starting the investigation under legal counsel. Also, I wanted to ensure that any and all evidence seized during our investigation would be deemed admissible should criminal charges be warranted and an evidentiary handover to authorities required.

What I soon realized was that TPP Engineering had weak controls on employee password protection and lacked a change-of-password policy. It seemed most likely that Freddy used the current log-in and password information to access the system. A search of his residence showed that Freddy had acquired a master list of employee names and passwords for the company while employed by TPP Engineering. He stated he had obtained a hard-copy list of passwords from a file that was kept unprotected in a filing cabinet. He knew the format used for log-in IDs and could access employee e-mails with the list of passwords since they hadn't been changed in years.

Before we knew this information, and immediately after my discussions with the CEO and COO, a major decision presented itself: Should we immediately change the passwords of employees at the company or should we refrain from any adjustments while we investigated the scope of information lost? I suggested that the executives, who appeared to be the main focus of interest in the e-mails I observed in hard-copy format, continue to use their passwords but limit the nature of their e-mail discussions to mundane, unclassified conversations. We proceeded with this strategy. All the while, my legal team was preparing the groundwork for an Anton Pillar order, which is a United Kingdom court statute providing the right to search premises and seize evidence without warning.

I decided to interview and include the senior network engineer in our investigation, as we needed to begin piecing together a timeline of the unauthorized access. We learned that someone was logging into the company e-mail system and accessing e-mail accounts of the CEO and COO with the correct log-in and passwords, which made the access appear legitimate— even when the log-ins were after-hours or on weekends. We observed brazen log-in records. Armed with the knowledge that any dual log-in would have alerted the system administrator, Freddy accessed the CEO's e-mail while the executive was on vacation. Reviews of logs revealed that the accounts were accessed during times when the CEO and COO were away from technology. He just couldn't wait to obtain insight into company information—even before the CEO!

We ascertained that the unauthorized e-mail access had begun prior to Freddy's departure from the company. The information he was privy to included personnel files, competitive bid information, client relationship information, and company financials. Basically, all competitive advantages discussed or exchanged via e-mail were at Freddy's fingertips.

There's No Crying in Crime

To build our profile of Freddy, I began to interview some of the individuals we identified as being on the periphery of the investigation, including two other former TPP employees who had also been observed in the distribution lists of Freddy's e-mail header. I then attempted to interview the scorned ex-girlfriend of the former employee who provided the initial tip. She agreed at first, but then decided not to participate as she feared repercussion from her former lover. I was concerned that Freddy was sending TPP information to other former employees working inside the industry. As for Freddy, we wanted to determine whether his current employer was complicit in the theft. I talked with our legal counsel and TPP executives about what possible legal actions we could take. The computer evidence being collected from the TPP Engineering computer systems was significant. At this point, we were looking at executing a civil search of Freddy's residence to target his electronic media and any hard-copy documents.

Through the interview process, we were able to determine that Freddy was operating as a lone wolf outside the knowledge of his current employer. The other former employees were quick to cooperate when approached. They all knew that any misconduct would be met with serious consequences from the professional bodies that govern the maintaining of engineering qualification, as well as a likely loss of employment and possible criminal and civil charges. These persons informed me that Freddy would constantly send them e-mails to demonstrate his skills and bravery in accessing the TPP e-mail servers. But the former employees just dismissed the communications and never replied to Freddy. For the persons being interviewed, Freddy was a nuisance. They didn't want to encourage him by responding, even to tell him to stop. They stated that Freddy felt superior to the TPP executives and they hypothesized that he was accessing their e-mails out of "morbid curiosity" and "because he could."

Plan of Action

We needed to be sure Freddy would be home when we executed the search warrant. I ordered surveillance to follow him for a few days, determine his travel patterns, and identify any additional issues. We noticed that he carried a laptop with him to and from work. It was crucial that this piece of equipment be at his place when we moved in because we needed to target any and all electronic media as potential sources of evidence.

To avoid inadvertently alerting Freddy of our investigation, we moved quickly and efficiently. Having decided to continue with the operation as a status quo environment, we were worried that he might suspect something had changed since the CEO and COO were no longer discussing serious strategic decisions through e-mail. If Freddy found out he was under investigation, I knew that all the media evidence would be wiped clean. Someone with his computer knowledge would know how to swiftly erase his drives or simply throw them away.

As surveillance continued for a second day, I received the call I had been waiting for—court approval for the civil search. With the good news in hand, I scheduled the search for that afternoon, assuming that Freddy would return home with his laptop, as he'd been observed doing the day before. I had gathered our legal team and computer forensic expert at a local coffee shop to await the word from our team onsite. Local police met with us and were prepared to assist. Legal precedent required a neutral legal counsel to attend the search as an independent witness.

As is always the case, Murphy's Law prevailed. Early during the second day of surveillance, one of our static vehicles with a direct line of sight on Freddy's residence was hit by a neighboring car as the resident was leaving for work. The wreck attracted a crowd to the street as people attempted to identify the owner of the vehicle. Thankfully, our investigator had blackout curtains in his van and did not break cover. The neighbor drove away after leaving a note under the surveillant's windshield wiper. Of all the contingencies I planned for, that was not one of them!

Confessions of an Awkward Engineer

Halfway through my coffee, the surveillance team radioed that Freddy had returned to his residence with his laptop under his arm. We threw out our coffees and what remained of our late lunch before taking off for the scene. After arriving, the lawyers and the local police served Freddy with the Anton Pillar order. From my vantage point on the street where I waited with the computer forensic specialist, it was clear Freddy wasn't forewarned. He was in shock. And then it happened—he started to cry.

After a quick search, I discovered over 600 megabytes of memory on four computers, including his laptop. That's a lot of data to be copied by the forensic computer specialist and would take a great deal of time. I began with the physical search for hard-copy documentation, as outlined in the APO. Meanwhile, Freddy's wife was enraged, forcing local police to keep her under control and creating a tense environment.

Freddy, upon realizing the seriousness of the situation, surprised us all by volunteering information during the search. I listened to his story but continually reminded him that he was not obligated to speak with me and should consult with his legal counsel first. But he stated that he did not want to deal with a lawyer; he wanted to tell me everything right away. This is when Freddy revealed that he found the password list at TPP a few years ago and made a copy for himself. He started reading executive e-mails occasionally out of curiosity and boredom. Then he realized that nobody was auditing this access, so he increased the frequency. Freddy understood that this was competitive information he could use to his advantage. He soon left TPP Engineering for a job with a major competitor. His insight into the industry helped him impress his new boss.

He e-mailed some of his old colleagues who were now working for other companies. One individual, whose ex-girlfriend provided the information that spurred the chain of events leading to this point, would receive unsolicited e-mails from Freddy with insider information on TPP. Freddy admitted that he was sending e-mails to these people in an effort to impress them. In all, a total of four ex-employees who were now employed at competing companies were frequently provided with unsolicited information.

As we searched Freddy's residence, we simultaneously changed all passwords for employees at TPP Engineering. We sent letters regarding the investigation to Freddy's current employer and to the four competing companies where the former TPP employees now worked.

TPP's competitors responded promptly to the official letters and stated that they were launching internal investigations into the activities of the former TPP employees. Freddy faces civil penalties and potential criminal charges.

Lessons Learned

TPP Engineering has implemented new policies and procedures on information security, including password protection and change protocols. Their screening requirements for new hires and exit interviews for departing employees are much more rigorous. They have also strengthened the legal wording of all employee contracts regarding nondisclosure.

Most importantly, TPP Engineering learned that neglect is dangerous and they have taken prudent measures to hire a full-time resource to implement and enforce security protocols at the company. I assisted in writing the job scope for the new position. I have also educated TPP on the nature of fraud and the fact that poor controls lead to vulnerability on multiple fronts. They have implemented a physical-access control system at their office location that will allow entry only to authorized employees and empower TPP to run audit logs on usage. Access to critical and sensitive information is limited, with documents such as password lists being placed in secure storage (both logical and physical).

Recommendations to Prevent Future Occurrences

Hire and Fire Employees Effectively

I call this the bookend approach. Hiring practices should include thorough background screening and actually calling references or talking to former colleagues. Taking these simple steps can save a company serious headaches if done correctly. Surprisingly, this is an often overlooked area of employee screening.

Implement a Culture of Security Awareness

Do employees know what negative behavior looks like? Do they know who they can turn to for reporting such observations? Is there an anonymous forum for calling in complaints and concerns? How does the organization guarantee support and privacy for a whistleblower? Are the punishments for negative actions clearly stipulated and understood? All these questions need to be addressed to create a sense of awareness within the company regarding acceptable behavior.

Strong Security Policies

The responsibility for strong security policies must be designated to a security team, whether a dedicated staff or a committee of managers. Ad hoc security will not suffice. We often encounter organizations with great policies in place but no means to enforce them. This is a serious disconnect from a security perspective. As a simple example, if a company has a "clean desk" policy (no papers on view) but doesn't conduct random audits of workspace to ensure compliance, then what is the incentive for employees to inconvenience themselves by filing away all their work each night? In the constant struggle between convenience and security, a reinforcement mechanism should ensure staff complies with policy.

Take a Step Back

Before beginning an investigation, I make it my normal business practice to take a step back and consider all the possible outcomes ahead. This allows me to determine what types of subject matter experts I will need to ensure the preservation of all evidence, and also how to maintain discretion so that the suspects are not alerted. I recommend this method of thought and planning to any investigator in the field—especially the new recruits, who are sometimes eager to move ahead on a case. Remember, as one of my sage mentors once told me, an investigation is chess and not checkers. Simple mistakes may not cost you the game in checkers, but they most certainly will in chess. Strategy and forethought are paramount to moving ahead in an investigation.

About the Author

Tyson Johnson, CFE, CPP, is the Senior Manager of Security for TD Bank Financial Group. He has worked in the field of intelligence and investigations for both the government of Canada and for private sector institutions. Tyson has tackled fraud from all angles, including terrorist financing support and organizational fraud.

CHAPTER

French Connections

MICHAEL NOTT

■ ■ ■

Mandy French lived with her partner and their two children in a suburb just outside of the Australian capital city of Canberra. Her partner, Daniel Whyn-Stanley, worked for the federal government and earned a decent salary. At Mandy's position with a local furniture removal company, she found that the hours worked for the wages paid did not meet her standards. Her light-fingered habit of helping herself to the odd $20 from petty cash two or three times a week led her to seek employment elsewhere.

Mandy and Daniel's combined income paid the mortgage and provided a good education for their two children, but she wanted better for their family. There was potential for a more lucrative salary as a public servant within the federal government in Canberra, the hub of the Commonwealth Government of Australia. There were always job opportunities within the hundreds of departments and agencies in the capital known as "Public Service City."

■ ■ ■

The Australian Public Service has a code of conduct to which every employee is expected to adhere. Disciplinary matters related to breaches of the code are usually handled in-house. Should the violation involve suspected fraud or other criminal activity, the matter is investigated and evidence presented to the commonwealth director of public prosecutions for possible action before a court of law. The Australian Federal Police usually take on serious high-value fraud cases. However, an increasing number of investigations are being conducted on behalf of government agencies by qualified external contractors.

As various departments developed their own internal units to deal with an increasing number of white-collar theft allegations, the government wisely introduced a fraud control policy whereby fraud examiners are required to be formally qualified to conduct investigations on behalf of the commonwealth, and each department head is obliged to produce a fraud control plan every two years.

I have a background in law enforcement. As a uniformed police officer and later as a detective with the fraud squad of the Victoria Police Force's Criminal Investigation Branch, I investigated my fair share of corporate crime. Upon my resignation from the Victoria police, I entered the Commonwealth Public Service in Canberra and gained many more years' experience working in various internal fraud-investigation units. I studied and obtained formal training recognized outside of the police force. Within a year of earning my qualifications, I left government employment and am now part of a highly experienced team of skilled people who provide clients within Australia and overseas with professional fraud-examination services.

The Benefits of Blandishment

After leaving the furniture removal company, it wasn't long before Mandy had landed a part-time position with a small federal government agency primarily responsible for compliance activity regarding the importation and use of industrial chemicals within Australia. At her new job as human resources (HR) manager, she worked approximately 20 hours a week and earned more than she had as a full-time employee with the removals company. Her reduced hours enabled her to be at home for her children when they finished school.

The first time Mandy tried her hand at manipulating an e-mail, she did so in a big way. The deputy director of administration, Anne Myers, had written the following to her.

> 2 March
> To: Mandy French
> From: Anne Myers
> Re: New Employee—Synda Turnbull—Parking Arrangements
>
> Hi Mandy,
> Our new director, Synda Turnbull, has opted to salary sacrifice parking costs ($140 per fortnight pre-tax). Could you please organize a signed authority from Synda to be sent to salary provider and ensure deduction of salary is pre-tax, as per our salary sacrificing arrangements, commencing next pay?
>
> Thanks,
> Anne Myers
> Deputy Director
> Administration

After forwarding this e-mail to the salary service provider, Jenna Roberts, Mandy revised Anne's e-mail and sent another message to Jenna.

2 March
To: Jenna Roberts APS Payroll
From: Mandy French

Hello again Jenna,
All of my hard work and effort has finally been recognized!!! Yippee, I got my bonus payment! Please, please, please—a big favor—could you pay me my $7,500 bonus in the next pay round? Thanks so much Jenna; you are a champion.
Please find following Anne's authorization attached below for payment of my bonus.

Cheers,
Mandy F.
P.S. Paris looking good again this year—I wonder what the poor people are doing! lol

2 March
To: Mandy French
From: Anne Myers
Re: Your Bonus Payment

Hi again Mandy,
Could you also contact our salary provider and advise them that I have authorized your $7,500 bonus payment? This is to be paid to you in the next pay period if at all possible. This bonus is paid in recognition of the many hours of overtime and hard work you have provided to our agency over the past six months. I thank you sincerely for your efforts and congratulations!

Cheers,
Anne Myers
Deputy Director
Administration

Within 10 days, Mandy's fraudulently obtained bonus was transferred with her normal salary into her personal bank account. For so little work, it had been the easiest money Mandy had ever received. Her rapport with Jenna almost guaranteed that no questions would be asked. Like a drug, the thrill and ease of making extra money was highly addictive. Mandy soon began to defraud her employer in earnest.

Over a period of 12 months, Mandy repeatedly sent reworded e-mails to Jenna and was paid another $18,000 in various amounts as part of her fortnightly salary. In June she sent the following e-mail.

27 June
To: Jenna Roberts APS Payroll Systems
From: M.French@gov.com.au

Dear Jenna,
How are you, hope all is well in cold old Melbourne. I got a pay raise yesterday and was hoping that you could process this increase ASAP. Synda's authority follows.

Thanks Heaps,
Mandy
HR Manager
P.S. If friends were flowers, I'd pick you.

26 June
To: Mandy French
From: Synda Turnbull
Re: Increase in remuneration

Dear Mandy,
In recognition of the valuable contribution you are making to the Agency it has been agreed to increase your hourly rate of pay to $46.50 per hour. This will take effect as of June 2nd this year. Please advise our pay people of this increase and requirement for back pay to June 2nd to take effect immediately. Well done!

Cheers,
Synda Turnbull
Director

About six months before her activities were discovered, Mandy was rated satisfactory by her supervisor in her performance review, meaning she would receive a 3% pay raise—a bonus of up to 15% of salary was reserved for those who achieved a higher rating. As HR manager, Mandy had access to all personal performance reports. Her director asked her to type up a spreadsheet and send it to the salary provider to let her know how much to pay each staff member for salary increases and bonus payments. Not satisfied with her own assessment, Mandy altered her rating on the spreadsheet to read "exceptional" and gave herself a $950 performance bonus as well as the 3% pay raise. She then sent the spreadsheet report to Jenna; two paychecks later, she received the bonus.

Mandy's scheme unraveled when a new company was contracted by the agency to provide salary management and payment services. The new provider ran a series of integrity checks against salary payments made over the past two years and employee details provided by the agency. As pay for a part-time employee, Mandy's $47,000-plus annual income raised suspicions. Her salary for the last 12 months averaged $1,840 per check, not the fortnightly $820 she'd been receiving originally.

A query was sent to the agency's director, Synda Turnbull, who made the naïve mistake of immediately confronting Mandy with what little information she had, demanding an explanation. Mandy's reaction took Synda by surprise. She admitted that she had been receiving extra payments for months but explained that she was under a considerable amount of pressure at home to make a larger monetary contribution to the family. Mandy claimed that her partner would beat her if she failed to put at least $1,000 into their joint bank account each fortnight. She also said that her mental health was in a poor state and that she had been seeking psychiatric help. Mandy turned on the tears and, after confessing to acquiring several thousand dollars, asked that she be allowed to collect her personal belongings and resign. Synda had the sense to escort Mandy to her desk, take away her security building-entry card, and walk her out of the building. Two days later French's partner delivered a handwritten resignation to the agency.

A Case of Manipulation

The agency immediately contacted my then-employer and requested a full investigation into the activities of Mandy French. The extent of her actions were unknown, but it was assumed that she had unlawfully obtained many thousands of dollars in extra pay by somehow manipulating information that would have been accessible to her in her role as HR manager. How she had gone about defrauding the department was a mystery. Some weeks had passed since her resignation, and the agency was full of rumors as to how much money Mandy had left with and what was going to happen as a result.

The agency was also in the process of developing a fraud control plan. Having just been scammed by an employee did not reflect well upon the existing controls and management practices. Synda was keen to ascertain how Mandy had perpetrated the fraud and how much she had obtained. In the process she wanted to identify weak controls and introduce policy and management practices that would prevent a similar occurrence. But first an investigation had to be conducted.

I obtained the agency's consent to have Mandy's desktop computer forensically examined. I wanted to know what was on her hard drive. I also requested a printout of all e-mails sent to and from her address, both intranet and Internet correspondence.

Although Synda had made notes of the conversation when she had confronted Mandy, their acceptability was questionable. However, the resignation letter signed by Mandy did make admissions of dishonesty.

I requested that Jenna search her systems and print out all e-mails received from Mandy. I also asked that she provide a printout of all salary and any other payments made to Mandy's designated bank account. To cover possible ghosting of salary payments, Jenna checked to see if Mandy's partner, her children's names, or any other unknown "employee" was recorded. Each staff member's bank account details were also compared to Mandy's. No matches were found in either of these checks.

Within several days I was in possession of all electronically transmitted and post-delivered correspondence that Mandy had sent to Jenna. I matched the correspondence received by Jenna with that obtained from Mandy's e-mail records at the agency. I isolated any information pertaining to a financial benefit for Mandy, then compared it with the e-mails found at the agency and on her hard drive. That was when the scheme unfolded. I discovered the manipulated e-mails and matched them with the originals. I was also able to demonstrate that Mandy's personal performance assessment had been fraudulently altered so that she received a higher pay raise. The original was still on file in the HR manager's office. The alterations to the spreadsheet received by Jenna were obvious. All assumed fraudulent payments were found and married up to e-mails that were suspected of being fraudulently contrived.

I obtained statements from numerous people, both those unknowingly drawn into the fraud and those involved in the provision payroll services in Melbourne. First, from the purported authors and signatories of the e-mails to prove that these individuals had no knowledge of the fraudulent correspondence. Next, from Jenna to demonstrate that she had received the e-mails from Mandy and had processed them in good faith, unaware that they were fraudulent or contrived. In addition, she signed a statement explaining how Mandy had gained her trust and, through forming an interoffice working friendship over a two-year period, was able to manipulate and dupe her into processing the requests. Finally, the computer forensics expert who sorted the data found on the computer hard drive signed a document verifying that Mandy French was indeed responsible for the alterations.

Had background checks been carried out with former private-sector employers, it might have been revealed that Mandy had resigned from two previous jobs due to suspicions relating to her conduct and allegations of theft. Another employer had dismissed Mandy after she made unauthorized withdrawals using the company credit card. No one had reported these incidents to the police.

Finally, Mandy was presented with the opportunity to take part in a recorded interview with investigators. Through her lawyer, she declined the invitation and made an offer to pay back any monies owed to the agency, which was accepted. The total amount of her fraudulently obtained bonuses and pay increases, $26,000, was repaid to the agency one month before she appeared in court for the fraud charges against her. Mandy, in mitigation, produced psychiatric reports to be considered by the court. Her initial assertions made to her director about being beaten and threatened by her partner were not raised.

Mandy pleaded guilty and was convicted of seven charges of obtaining a financial advantage by deception, a criminal offense under the Commonwealth Criminal Code. The magistrate imposed a six-month suspended sentence and a two-year bond under the condition of good behavior.

A Prolific Liar

After resigning from the agency, Mandy took on the role of full-time mother for a few short months. Even then she displayed her fraudulent tendencies. Within five weeks of her resignation, Mandy was driving her children to school when she was caught speeding as she passed by a traffic surveillance camera situated a mile from her home. In writing a letter to the local road traffic authority, she claimed that her colostomy bag had burst and that she was rushing her children to school so that she could quickly return home to take care of the issue. The local authority withdrew the fine and issued a warning. Mandy had never worn a colostomy bag in her life and later bragged to a few of her friends about her scheme. Within three months Mandy signed on at an employment agency and was soon placed with a large commonwealth governmental department in Canberra. At that point her personnel file from her previous job was clear of bad marks, since she had not yet been convicted or charged of the fraud.

Mandy started out part-time but soon stepped in to fill the role of a full-time HR manager. She did not disclose that she had lost her previous job with the government due to allegations of fraud or that she was making restitution payments, nor did she mention that she was to be summoned to face criminal charges in a court of law.

Since the case was still pending, she was able to answer truthfully two would-be incriminating questions in her application for her police records check. First, "Have you ever been charged with a criminal offense?" and second, "Have you ever been convicted of a criminal offense?" She answered "No" to both questions—both true, albeit not entirely forthcoming, answers that qualified her for the job. These forms have since been revised to include the question "Have you ever been investigated in relation to your involvement in any criminal offense?"

After her court hearing and conviction, Mandy remained at her new job without disclosing her recent criminal conviction to her employer—until a fellow coworker noticed her name in the local newspaper and reported it to a manager, that is. When the court case in the article was put to Mandy, she admitted that it referred to her. However, she claimed that she had only committed the fraud to demonstrate a weakness in her previous employer's systems and that they had misinterpreted her intentions.

I was tasked with providing a forensic investigation service to the department to determine if any fraudulent activity had occurred during Mandy's short period of employment and if there had been disclosure or misuse of official or personal information. This time I felt that I had a headstart because I knew her modus operandi.

First, all departmental claim-for-payment forms that might have been signed by Mandy as a delegate were identified and examined. Forms that were generated during her employment period were viewed to determine if she had signed any and, if so, the legitimacy of those payments. In addition, all e-mails to and from Mandy that were retained by the department were also scrutinized and all electronic documentation stored on the computer used by her were examined. I uncovered records located on her computer showing that in the last few months she had been applying for positions with other government departments. To bolster her applications, she had falsified referee reports purporting to be written by her supervisor and the division head.

Based on her prior history, we also decided to examine all salary payments to her during her period of employment with the department and any e-mails that she may have sent to the payroll office. While nothing suspicious was found, enough evidence existed to justify the department's decision to terminate her part-time employment and discontinue considering her application for full-time employment.

Lessons Learned

Some employers see resignation as a satisfactory result, since the individual in question is off their hands—life goes on, someone else's problem. The lesson learned here was that "the problem" does not disappear, it just moves on to another unsuspecting host. Reporting suspected fraud is a requirement of the commonwealth's fraud control guidelines and prevents people like Mandy from taking a second bite of the apple.

Recommendations to Prevent Future Occurrences

Background Checks

Note the details of a dismissal or resignation in an employee's personnel file when hiring new staff. Recruiters should ask the right questions about previous involvement or association with a criminal investigation, which may go some way in preventing the reemployment of people like Mandy in government positions where they could have access to money.

Verify Payroll Changes

If payroll had verified the multiple raises and pay adjustments with Synda Turnbull, Mandy's deception would have been uncovered much sooner. It is important to check the legitimacy of any payment change request.

Report Incidents

As the old saying goes, "silence is fraud's best friend." It is important to report incidents of fraud to the proper authorities in order to prevent future occurrences. "Out of sight; out of mind" is a dangerous motto when it comes to fraud.

About the Author

Michael Nott, CFE, Dip. Government (Fraud Control Investigation), is currently a fraud investigation specialist based in Canberra, Australia. Names and some locations referred to in this story have been changed to protect the innocent, the guilty, the naïve, and the incompetent.

31

Irreconcilable Differences

JENNIFER BIRTZ

As is usually the case, Betsy Newton was the last person you would suspect of stealing over $300,000 from her employer. A small-town girl, she enjoyed a stable family life with her two rambunctious chocolate Labs and her husband of 10 years, a mechanic. Betsy had none of the usual vices: She never drank, smoked, gambled, or indulged in junk food. An avid jogger and mountain biker, she was tall, blonde, and in great physical shape.

Betsy epitomized ambition; in just one year of high turnover in the accounting department at Westgrove Insurance Agency, she rose from staff accountant to accounting manager, a position she held for several years. From the CEO to the interns, she was liked by everyone. When the accounting function was relocated to Georgia, Betsy made the move along with her husband and their dogs. But after feeling homesick for six months, they returned to their native California. Betsy trained her replacement—a short-term employee—and hightailed it back to her home state to work as a project manager for Westgrove's Irvine office. After the replacement left the company, Mike Rogers, the controller, hired me to work as the new accounting manager. He had always enjoyed working with Betsy and had great respect for her abilities, so he asked her to "download" all her knowledge to me as quickly and efficiently as possible. She spent five solid days trying to teach me everything she thought I would need to know about my new job. During my training, we became quite fond of each other. I noticed her addiction to Starbucks lattes and her passion for her beautiful dogs.

By the end of our week, I had been given a first-class education and was grateful for the opportunity to learn from the best. Everyone, including me, had a great respect for Betsy's abilities and knowledge. She clearly knew the accounting manager's job and Westgrove, in general, inside and out. But too much information can be dangerous in the wrong hands.

■ ■ ■

Westgrove Insurance Agency began writing property and casualty insurance policies for homeowners in 1998. The business started in a corner of a tiny Irvine, California, office building with only seven people. It didn't take long for Westgrove to grow significantly. The agency opened five U.S. branches, moved to a larger Irvine office space, and was soon employing around 650 people. By 2003 the company had written over one billion dollars in coverage and tracked over half a million annual policies using two different software platforms and hundreds of manually maintained Excel spreadsheets. Both antiquated, the software platforms didn't communicate with each other. Accounting personnel had to make do with premium reports that had no check-level detail, causing enormous irreconcilable differences in the premium receivable accounts.

Looking for Buried Checks

Since she was with Westgrove since its inception, Betsy was intimately familiar with the control deficiencies that would enable her to commit fraud. In fact, as a member of the IT project steering committee, she was able to perpetuate her theft by working with IT. Her stealing continued even after I was hired and I had begun performing some account reconciliations that had never been properly carried out. For years prior to my tenure, the accounting group and the escrow group had each taken a crack at reconciling insurance premiums receivable. We all knew there was a gaping hole in the process. The insurance-premium–processing software reports that we used did not provide check details for either the premiums received or the refunds issued. As a result, each month's reconciliation showed varying bulk differences in the millions of dollars, with no hope of identifying them at the check detail level. We could only assume that they cleared themselves the next month, when, of course, additional irreconcilable differences were piled on. We worked out a solution to the program and submitted it to the IT steering committee for approval. Since the committee met in Irvine on a monthly basis, we asked Betsy to participate and push for the project on our behalf. At the time, we had no vote or representation on the committee.

Betsy took advantage of Westgrove's control deficiency. To pass them off as legitimate premium refunds, she recorded her personal checks to her credit union, her mortgage company, and her investment banker to the largest premium receivable accounts. In the meantime, she worked against the company's interest to further her own when she participated in the IT steering committee's project-priority meetings, presumably on our behalf, to argue that the accounting department considered the fix a low priority. In essence, she was able to delay implementing the solution for 18 months before we uncovered her theft. All the while, the accounting department was silently fuming, but we took no action to confront IT.

There was no significant change in Betsy's lifestyle. She continued to drive her 1970s Porsche and flew coach whenever she and her husband were able to go on vacation. She complained about the high cost of living, along with everyone else. Unbeknownst to us, she was just banking the stolen money until she had squirreled away enough for an oceanfront house in the beautiful West Bay area of the Cayman Islands.

Betsy had only been back in California for a couple of years when she announced, out of the blue, that she was moving to Key West, Florida. She resigned from Westgrove and planned to look for a job as a hotel accountant after a month or two of relaxation and jogging on the beach. Her husband intended to open a snorkel and diving business—a nice change from working on vehicle engines all day. We all knew Betsy would make a nice profit on the sale of her Irvine house; the real estate prices in the area had been rising, and the Orange County market, in particular, was off the charts. My only clue that something was amiss was when she gave me her new e-mail address in case we had any questions that we could not answer for our external auditors. It had an odd extension, ''.ky,'' which I researched online. It showed that she lived in the Caymans. I brought this up to Mike, but he was not concerned. We were a little curious, though, as to why she would lie about moving to Key West, but we chalked it up to privacy and had a good laugh about banking privacy laws.

After a few months in the islands, Betsy and her husband became bored with each other. He cheated on her with a Cayman woman. Suddenly their marriage was on the rocks. In a futile attempt to patch things up, the two of them moved back to Irvine, even before they had a buyer for their Cayman Islands home. This time, Betsy was caught up on the wrong end of the housing bubble and needed more money to fund her return. So she turned to her reliable supporter, Mike, the controller who hired me at Westgrove. She knew that if she was reinstated at the company, she could continue to perpetrate her scheme without detection. Mike personally pleaded her case to upper management. In his eyes, they'd be fools not to hire her back— Betsy was critical to the company's success. Management allowed her to return to her former position as project manager with the same computer access she had before she left. We hadn't even changed the system administrator password in Great Plains, the accounting database.

Too Much Trust

Sonja Wesley, a young, inexperienced staff accountant with our insurance escrow department who was located at Betsy's branch in Irvine, was reviewing one of the weekly disbursement reports when she noticed a check that had been written on our largest insurance trust account. The check was for

$9,800 and had been made payable to one of our largest clients, but there was a discrepancy—it had not been issued in the same check run or the same sequence as the 12,000 other checks Escrow had disbursed the previous week. This check had clearly been paid out of the trust account by someone outside of Escrow. Per usual, Sonja walked across the office to ask Betsy, the branch guru, what might have happened. This time, however, Betsy was on vacation. Sonja called our Sun Royal Bank representative to request a copy of the check.

She wasn't worried; this had happened before. She was sure that Betsy simply cut another emergency check for one of the national account managers. Everyone knew client service was critical, so Escrow needed to be flexible and occasionally overlook control violations. They were working 12-hour shifts in order to keep up with the demand while Westgrove continued to add clients and new insurance programs at a wildfire pace. Sonja certainly didn't have time to police what other employees were doing—she was barely treading water herself!

One Bad Check Leads to Another

Eighteen hours later Sonja had the check copy from Sun Royal in her e-mail inbox. But it provided no answers—only more questions. According to the copy we printed from Great Plains, our accounting software, the check was payable to one of our largest clients, Fielding Mortgage. However, the check copy from Sun Royal showed that it was actually payable to Tacit Credit Union. Sonja e-mailed the check copy to me and Betsy to see if we knew anything about it. She still hadn't heard from Betsy since the initial discovery of the rogue check. Sonya had left her two voice messages, and it wasn't like her not to return a call, even on days off.

Betsy soon returned to the office from her beach vacation, Starbucks latte in hand, ready to tackle premium reporting issues with one of our new client implementations. After settling in, she listened to her voice messages from Sonja. Her blood pressure must have skyrocketed. Then she logged into her e-mail and saw the copy of the check she had written to her own credit union; she was certain she would be arrested before the day was over. She had really messed up this time. Betsy knew she shouldn't have printed this check before she went on vacation. If only she'd been available to answer Sonja's question, she could have easily deflected suspicion to get away with yet another incident in her string of thefts.

Looking and feeling genuinely ill, Betsy bluffed her way through her conversation with Sonja, confirming her assumption.

"Nancy Robbies, our national sales support manager, contacted me before vacation; it was late and everyone had gone home. She was desperate for a project manager not in Escrow to issue a large premium refund check and overnight it to a client, apparently one who demands immediate attention every day," explained Betsy.

It was a plausible, familiar explanation—Sonja believed it without hesitation.

Betsy felt quite sick from the stress and fear of being caught and took the rest of the day off to contemplate her next move. Should she hide? Should she wait to see if the company would find the remaining $290,000 she stole? Or should she 'fess up to it all and plead for mercy? How would she tell her husband and family? She had kept it all from them for years; she and her husband were still on shaky ground, and he was between jobs yet again. Would her friends and coworkers abandon her? What's the maximum jail time for a $300,000 theft? She convinced herself that she would never work in the accounting field again, if she was lucky enough to land another job at all. She was in shock and terrified that someone had finally sniffed out her trail, and completely by chance.

I was on the East Coast and had not been notified of the drama until 8 a.m., Eastern Standard Time, the next morning, when I was pulled into a meeting between Mike and the chief financial officer, Frank Stephens. Frank quietly told us that Betsy had called him first thing that morning to admit that she had taken close to $300,000 over the past few years.

"Betsy is very sorry for her actions," he said. "Even though we only found out about the $9,800 check, she said she actually took around $300,000. She wants to pay us back."

Betsy had stayed up all night waiting for Frank to arrive at the office. After the initial shock of her confession, he said: "We'll need to investigate and discuss the matter further with your attorney. You are not permitted to return to the office nor talk to any Westgrove employees. Betsy, please provide your attorney with the past few years' records of your personal bank, credit card, and mortgage statements in order to assist us in our investigation." In our meeting, Frank requested that we begin immediately to determine Betsy's method(s) and to devise effective internal controls to prevent any reoccurrence.

Mike and I were shocked and angry; Mike, in particular, felt betrayed. He had stuck his neck out for her both times she moved back to California asking to work for Westgrove as a project manager again. Both times management had resisted reinstating her high salary, but Mike convinced them she was crucial to the company's success. To him, she was a long-time, valued employee. She was our "voice" in California; we could rely on her to push our various IT requests through the bureaucratic red tape and assist us when external auditors came knocking. Never believing Betsy would betray his trust for her own criminal interests, he took it personally.

I began the investigation with the only facts we knew. Betsy had successfully used the Great Plains system administrator password to set up a new company ID during the previous year in an unrelated incident. She had no reason to have that password, but Mike had allowed her to keep it as a backup for us, a choice he feared would be another mark against him. She had used the Great Plains system administrator ID to print the check in question, made payable to her credit union. However, the check appeared to be payable to Fielding, our client, when we viewed it on screen in both the general ledger and purchasing module. We knew that she had admitted to stealing around $300,000 in total from at least one of the nine insurance trust funds we maintained.

We hired our regular Great Plains consulting firm, in confidence, to assist with our investigation. I didn't give our senior consultant Betsy's name, but as soon as he knew the barest details of the problem, he pegged her as the culprit. His team quickly wrote a sequel script, a short program used to access specific data elements, to allow us to compare check data in various data tables, including vendor data, vendor history, and general ledger history. We were astonished by what we found. The consultants' report showed that someone, over a four-year period, had written 15 checks, all of which had different payee names in the general-ledger history table than they did in the vendor-data and vendor-history tables in the purchasing module. Ten of these checks had been voided; six had been cashed. In particular, we noted several voided checks made payable to a woman we later determined to be Betsy's sister; all of these had been written and subsequently voided in the span of a few days. We concluded that these were test runs carried out three years before we caught her. She had created false invoices and printed checks to pay them, all as a preliminary experiment. Mike confided to me later that Betsy was astounded that we had found those checks.

In an interesting twist, she wrote three checks to various payees, for her personal benefit, in one week. They totaled exactly $120,000, almost half of the total amount she stole. Seeing those three checks sealed the deal for Mike—together they equaled his base pay. He was livid and wanted to prosecute her.

Reputation vs. Justice

As an insurance agency, Westgrove was highly regulated by all 50 states and the five main insurance agencies for which they wrote insurance policies and paid property damage claims. Many of the largest U.S. mortgage lenders were clients—in addition to some smaller ones. Ultimately, Westgrove was so terrified that the fraud would be leaked to clients that Betsy's attorney was able to negotiate a sweet deal. She was required only to make full restitution and never discuss the details of the fraud with anyone. Westgrove terminated her employment, of course, and mailed her personal belongings to her home.

Betsy's life flipped upside down. She had to cash in her 401(k) and sell her Cayman Islands and Irvine houses. Her husband, an innocent spouse, quickly divorced her and kept their dogs as part of the settlement. Despite Mike's arguments regarding his own professional responsibility to inform the California body that licenses Certified Public Accountants, Westgrove was more concerned about negative publicity. The agency refused to prosecute Betsy or even to notify the California licensing board so that they could begin the process of revoking her CPA license. Human Resources was informed to do nothing but confirm her dates of hire and termination if potential employers called. Betsy had another accounting-manager job with another Irvine company within two weeks of leaving Westgrove.

Mike and Frank had to notify our audit committee, board of directors, and external auditors of the fraud and describe to them in detail our efforts to prevent future occurrences. Mike hadn't eaten or slept much during the first three days after Betsy's phone call; he was nervous about losing his job, particularly since he had gone to bat for her twice with upper management. In the end, there was no fallout for Mike or the company at all. We didn't even receive a negative comment in our management recommendation letter from the external auditors that year.

Lessons Learned

Where there's smoke, there's fire. But if Betsy had not confessed to the full $300,000, I probably would not have looked past the $9,800 check for any wrongdoing. In the future, I will always assume there is more to be found—perpetrators are rarely caught the first time they steal.

Prior to the investigation, Westgrove Insurance Co. had not appreciated the importance of the Great Plains system administrator password and the power it grants. Undoubtedly, we must change the password periodically and restrict access to only those personnel who need it to perform their job duties.

Betsy had charged all of her embezzled funds against the largest premium receivable accounts, knowing that we would be unable to trace the money. After the fraud, Mike declared war on irreconcilable differences and insisted that Escrow, a department that did not report to him, sift through thousands of old checks and cash receipts to determine the discrepancies.

Finally, we realized that the accounting department was partly responsible because we had allowed her to speak for our interests in IT priority meetings. Mike had relied on Betsy to be his "ear to the ground" and "right-hand man" in our Irvine office, where she would participate in IT project planning meetings on our behalf. We now know that she took advantage of this authority to delay our critical reconciliation project with IT so that it would take even longer for us to reconcile the insurance premiums receivable account down to the check level. The IT vice president lamented later that she had been curious as to why the accounting department had told Betsy to give our report fix a low priority, but she had never thought to mention it to us. In the future, we will take a stand and push for our own projects.

Recommendations to Prevent Future Occurrences

Although Mike admitted that "Someone has to have the keys to the kingdom," referring to the system administrator password, we significantly tightened up the internal controls with the following recommendations:

Prioritize

The IT check-detail reconciliation project was a high priority, but we allowed ourselves to become sidetracked and misled, giving Betsy plenty of time to perpetrate her fraud. Know what's important, then outline and implement an effective strategy to achieve those goals to reduce damage.

Representation

We did not have adequate representation in the IT meetings to push the accounting department's objectives forward. It's important to have a voice that will address your department's concerns in company matters.

Limit Access

Betsy, the perpetrator, had 100% access to our systems. Technically, she should not have known the password. The system administrator password should be changed to dual authority, where two users are required to separately initiate and approve system administrator actions. As a further precaution, the accounting manager should also change the system administrator password on a monthly basis and restrict access to only the personnel who need it to complete their regular job duties.

Checks and Balances

The accounting manager should run periodic reports to compare the check data in purchasing and general-ledger data tables. That way, if an error or an instance of fraud has occurred, it will be detected earlier and mitigate the potential for substantial losses.

Internal Audit

I further recommended that the company create an effective internal-audit department. I had already discussed this idea with the CFO several times prior to this fraud investigation, but management had been unwilling to commit the required resources, dismissing the request as unnecessary. Had management agreed to implement an internal audit program, we would have had objective professionals outside of the CFO's influence reviewing operations, looking for ways employees could circumvent internal controls, and suggesting significant improvements in their communications with the CEO and the board of directors.

About the Author

Jennifer Birtz, CFE, CPA, CIA, is a manager with Habif, Arogeti, & Wynne LLP, a fully integrated financial services firm. She is a graduate of the University of Florida and has over 15 years of audit and accounting experience. She is an active member of the Association of Certified Fraud Examiners and the Georgia Society of CPAs.

CHAPTER

32

Keeping It In the Family

ERIC SUMNERS

With two adorable children and a loving wife, Erwin Jacob considered himself a family man. He enjoyed attending his kids' sporting events and participating in family functions sponsored by his employer, Great Members Credit Union. Erwin supported his brood on about $35,000 per year as the manager of the loan department at his credit union, while his wife raised their children as a stay-at-home mom. Despite a moderate income, Erwin had just bought a new home, which caused no apparent financial strain. Most of his coworkers wrote off the financial discrepancy as reflecting significant help from his parents. Overall, Erwin was an outgoing, friendly individual who was quick with an amusing story and a pat on the back.

Despite being the loan manager at Great Members Credit Union, Erwin had no financial institution experience and no post–high school education. This was typical for Great Members' employees. Many of them were referred to the credit union and received their jobs through a friend or family member employed there. Erwin received the job because his father worked for a vendor.

Credit union management maintained a great deal of loyalty to their employees. Many referred to the organization as a family. I was hired as the chief financial officer (CFO). When I arrived, I found the friendly atmosphere much more desirable than that provided by my previous accounting firm employers. Upon initially meeting Erwin, I liked him.

Erwin reported to Carl Blair, Vice President of Lending, Member Services, and Collections. Carl had worked for the credit union for most of his adult life and climbed up the ranks the way many longtime employees had. Like Erwin, Carl did not pursue education after high school. Although Carl was the vice president, everyone agreed that Erwin was the heart and soul of the loan department, and since the loan department was the credit union's major source of revenue, he seemed to be the heart and soul of the entire organization. Also, even though Carl was the senior member in terms of years and rank, many saw him as a lazy dullard. It was Erwin who was the brains of the operation.

As manager of the loan department, Erwin had six employees reporting to him, including hardworking and intelligent Bruce, whose aggressive work style resembled Erwin's more than Carl's. Bruce was another employee who had been referred by a relative who worked for the credit union. He had no financial institution experience but better than average computer skills. As most employees did not have significant computer experience, Bruce was welcomed by managers and staff.

Great Members Credit Union, located in the Midwest, had about 35 employees, three locations, and approximately $85 million in assets. Revenues from loans were consistent but never strong, and it seemed that management was often fighting to maintain a respectable bottom line or net income. New loans were vital to sustaining profitability and, because of this, the loan department and its employees were given a great deal of latitude to develop new products and delivery channels. To keep costs low, employees were typically paid a good, but not great, salary and average benefits. Many staff members noted that the credit union industry was solid work but no one was going to get rich.

Similar to countless small companies, and particularly small financial institutions, Great Members Credit Union had a number of internal control weaknesses. These weaknesses were in both the manual-controls and information-technology areas. They were a combination of business risks taken due to limited budgets and finite resources, and of risks taken simply because they were unknown and thus unanalyzed. The general and application-control weaknesses were in some sense part of the culture, not only the credit union's culture, but that of the industry. Many small credit unions are run like "mom and pop stores" and often ignore these substantial internal control risks until they are forced to react, often due to fraud.

Welcome to the Family

While serving as the CFO for the credit union, I had a fair amount of internal-audit and internal-control responsibilities as well. Although these duties did not seem to be related to my position of hire, my employer was a small financial institution and I was happy to help out in any way possible. My grandfather had founded a credit union, and I had grown up in the industry. So leaving public accounting and "going home" was a welcome change. The CFO portion of my duties accounted for approximately 85% of my time; however, I attempted to institute a sound control environment. Due to finite resources, I tried to take a risk-based approach to controls and, where possible, improve them in the information technology area, including application software, data integrity, and the IT physical environment.

Like many credit unions, Great Members' share and loan–processing database was the lifeblood of the organization. Every employee had access to it and could maneuver within it to some degree. When attempting to tighten user controls, I was often told that the level of access was necessary to conduct business. In public accounting, I argued against this laidback approach.

As my duties were diverse and other employees knew I worked as an auditor in public accounting, I was often given any mail that other departments were not sure how to handle. One cold, northeastern January morning, I was handed a letter from Big Midwestern Mortgage. Upon opening it, I noticed that it was a positive confirmation, which is a letter used by auditors to verify balances, typically used to confirm investments, deposits, and liabilities. This one concerned a loan to one of the credit union's employees. A confirmation was something that I was very familiar with from my public accounting experience and I figured it would be a quick task. I had spent many hours sending out and following up on confirmations as a first-year auditor.

Subsequent to reviewing the confirmation, I noticed that attached to it was a letter from Carl certifying that Erwin had a significant amount, greater than $150,000, on deposit with the credit union and no loans. Also attached was a recognizable printout from the credit union's share and loan database, which agreed to the amounts on the letter from Carl. It did not seem totally out of the ordinary that Carl had completed the paperwork, as he was Erwin's supervisor, but I would have expected that the human resources manager would have completed it for privacy's sake, if for no other reason. However, Carl and Erwin were clearly close and had worked together for a number of years, so the choice seemed to make sense.

Family Secrets

After opening the credit union's electronic share and loan database and pulling up Erwin's account, I was surprised to find that the amount on deposit did not match. There was a $125,000 difference, and although the confirmation paperwork showed no outstanding loans with the credit union, there were two loans totaling about $10,000 displayed on the database. My quick task was looking a little more like a minor project and potentially a rather large venture. At first I was somewhat confused. The loan and deposit amounts did not agree with the reports used by Carl to report Erwin's financial information to Big Midwestern Mortgage. As I reviewed the database report, it did not appear to be altered and the account number was indeed Erwin's, but the amounts on the database were not even close to Carl and Erwin's reports. I thought perhaps there was confusion between the dates reported to and asked for by the mortgage company; this was a common error I'd noticed in public accounting, and it often led to hours of follow-up work to reconcile the differences. A review of six months of activity showed that Erwin never had anywhere near $150,000 on deposit, and he had loans that dated back two and a half years. Also, I noted that the dates requested by Big Midwestern on the confirmation and supplied by Carl were identical. So obviously the documents sent to Big Midwestern had been altered internally.

At this point I realized that the credit union had, at best, a data integrity issue in its share and loan database, and at worst a case of fraud and some serious internal controls weaknesses concerning the primary database. A data integrity issue would imply that the database had been corrupted. On the other hand, an internal control weakness issue would indicate that an individual had temporarily manipulated the screen so that a valid account number would have the corresponding data changed to another account number, making the number and data appear related, although they were not.

I needed to notify my supervisor, the chief executive officer (CEO). This was something of a delicate issue as the CEO, Susan Wren, had known both Erwin and Carl for a long time and looked on them as not just employees but sons. When discussing my findings with Susan, I attempted to focus on its being a potential data integrity issue. Although the circumstances appeared suspicious, I didn't want her to speak to the two men just yet. Telling them might have made the investigation more difficult, and I was still uncertain of the gravity of the situation. Susan didn't seem concerned and noted that she trusted both of them. She considered them part of her and the credit union's family. Fortunately, she did agree that we needed to keep the issue between us until we could clarify the facts.

Getting Down to Business

I tended to prefer my CFO duties, but the gloomy winter weather—snowy and wet—made it seem somewhat appropriate to be investigating a potential fraud.

While there clearly was a discrepancy, the printout that Carl submitted did offer a few pieces of integral investigative information. First, it contained the date that the document was printed. This would be extremely useful in narrowing down the time range of my investigation. Second, it contained the user ID of the employee printing the report. I was surprised once again, because the user ID belonged to neither Erwin nor Carl. It belonged to Bruce, the hardworking and somewhat technologically savvy loan officer.

This truly seemed incongruous. I wouldn't expect an employee to want a subordinate to review his or her personal information. These useful bits of information led me to believe I was not dealing with a data integrity issue, but with the collusion of three employees in a fraud.

Working in a small environment such as a credit union provides certain advantages and risks in terms of database controls. One of the advantages is that, in general, most users do not have a tremendous amount of computer expertise, thus seemingly reducing the possibility of a complex technological fraud. This fact, however, can lull management into a false sense of security. All the employees do have access to the database and are somewhat familiar with a wide array of commands and functions, which can be a fairly risky proposition if not managed correctly. Employees having a range of job duties require broad access rights, which can result in fertile ground for the seeds of fraud to grow.

Based on my experiences as an internal auditor, I was aware of the assortment of reports that were automatically generated daily by the credit union's loan and share database. These reports would be my starting point for the investigation. Unfortunately, they were in computer-output-to-laser disk (COLD) storage, and the only available disk reader was in the computer room. Working at a small organization with few employees, people would notice that I was away from my desk for long periods of time sitting in the computer room—and the last thing I wanted was to create suspicion.

The first step in the investigation was to contact the credit union's service provider for the share and loan database. I needed to obtain an exhaustive list of reports it generated. Although I had a working knowledge of many standard reports, I wanted to make sure that I looked into every crevice and was as efficient as possible. While the potential fraud had occurred about six months prior, it was important to crack the case quickly to avoid suspicion. In addition to the comprehensive list of standard reports, the database vendor was able to use structured query language (SQL) to run some ad hoc reports based on my needs. With the basic tools of information technology investigation on hand, I began my search to determine what had happened.

The computer room was windowless and did not have the normal ventilation systems, so fans ran 24 hours a day to keep the room somewhat cool. The constant hum made it difficult, when concentrating, to determine if someone, namely Erwin or Carl, had entered the room. Erwin did come in a number of times. Though not unusual for him to stop by and converse, it was still unsettling.

The searches based on date and user ID would have yielded a stack of paper. Because of this, I further refined my searches using Erwin's account number, resulting in a more manageable amount of documents that allowed me to conduct a great portion of my review in my office. This provided me with some privacy.

Searches of the documents revealed an interesting situation that I did not realize was possible on the credit union's database system. Bruce, the most technologically shrewd of the three, had gone into another, much more affluent, member/customer's account and changed the account number to Erwin's account number. This had the effect of creating a report with Erwin's name and account number showing no loans and approximately $150,000 on deposit. At the time of the confirmation, Erwin actually had a couple hundred dollars on deposit, and a printout of the account would have shown numerous recent overdrafts in his checking account. In fact, there were numerous periods when Erwin's account was negative for several days. This information would have been useful to Big Midwestern's underwriting process, but also to Great Members, as it showed a loan officer with a money problem. This certainly would not have disqualified him from receiving a mortgage, but it would have changed the way the underwriter viewed him as a credit risk. The reports also showed that, approximately five minutes after making the initial change, Bruce made another alteration to undo his previous modification. This indicated that Bruce was a clever and experienced computer user. The credit union had some issues concerning the assignment of privileges and file access–privilege controls on the share and loan database; all previous risk assessments had failed to foresee this type of fraud. Although I had been reviewing achieved logs as part of my internal audit duties, it was evident that this process would need to be improved with customized triggers, continuous auditing, and e-mail alerts to have a much more inclusive, integrated, and real-time audit and fraud-identification function.

I contacted the credit union's database vendor to go over the reports with a help desk representative to make sure what I was seeing could happen. That was a fairly short phone conversation. The help desk representative was very direct that the change was allowable the way Bruce and all users were set up on the database. At this point I knew I had a very serious situation and, although I would keep copies of all evidence locked in my office closet, it would also be beneficial to keep another set of the documents at home. The credit union maintained fairly laidback controls, and employees came and went from the building at odd hours and on the weekends. I knew that Carl had a fairly extensive set of keys and could get into my office after hours.

Breaking the News

Next, I was faced with the delicate process of informing my boss, Susan, of the situation. Although the facts concerning the fraud were clear, her view of the credit union as a family had me concerned about the possibility of a "shoot the messenger" response. I decided to wait until after lunch the next day. This would allow me to collect my thoughts and conduct a complete review of the documents.

The next day, after lunch, I entered Susan's office and shut the door behind me. She knew from our time working together, and the look on my face, that this was not going to be a short meeting.

"What exactly are we meeting about?" she asked.

"I'd like to discuss the confirmation project we spoke about last week," I replied.

Susan thought that some coffee might help the conversation, so we brewed a fresh pot. Looking over the highlighted detail and listening to my explanation, Susan agreed that there was a serious situation. However, she tended to focus on the use of a member's data to falsify the mortgage application. Since the information had been changed back within five minutes, the member/customer was not harmed and this was not identity theft, so Susan believed a brief suspension for all the players would be sufficient. I agreed it was not technically identity theft and the member had not been harmed; however, I said, there was a serious act of collusion between Carl, Erwin, and Bruce. And an officer of the credit union, Carl, had falsified information to Big Midwestern Mortgage. After explaining to Susan the truly grave nature of this offense, she agreed that, although the credit union family had become a little more dysfunctional, something more serious than a brief suspension was in order.

We determined initially that Big Midwestern Mortgage needed to be contacted. I also insisted that the credit union's bonding company and local authorities needed to be given notice.

A couple of days subsequent to my meeting with Susan, I contacted Big Midwestern Mortgage. They were less than concerned. The mortgage had been sold to another company and the mortgage was currently paid up to date. Although they said they would pass on the information, they seemed indifferent. Due to the cool reception from Big Midwestern, I decided to document the exchange by sending a follow-up memo to Big Midwestern so I could prove that they had been given notice. It was evident that the confirmation process, for Big Midwestern, was nothing more than a "paper control" in place for style and not substance. It seemed to be there to appease their auditors and serve no purpose. Ironically, it had uncovered a fairly extensive fraud at Great Members Credit Union.

Next, we contacted the local prosecutor's office. Although they were interested, they did not believe that the amount and information provided was enough to go forward and press charges against the three employees. I was zero for two with one option left, and the three perpetrators were still employed but on paid leave.

Somewhat defeated, I contacted the credit union's bonding company. The bonding company's opinion as to the seriousness of what had happened was important, as all credit union employees are required to be bonded in order to be hired and remain employed. The representative from the bonding company was very eager to hear the facts and review the documents. After I verbally described the situation and forwarded copies of the documents, the bonding company had me fill out a "Notification of Incident." A few days after the required forms were submitted, I received a phone call from the bonding company's senior investigative analyst. He noted that the situation was well researched and documented. The company would be removing all three employees' bonds. Shortly after this conversation he faxed a notice to Susan and noted that hard copies would be mailed to Carl, Erwin, and Bruce.

When Susan received the notice, she was upset. The three would lose their jobs and not be able to work in a credit union again, which seemed severe to her since "there was no harm done." I reminded her that there was, in fact, harm done and the bonding company agreed. Although she was uncomfortable with the terminations, she realized that the situation was out of her hands due to the bonding company's review and decision.

Knowing the removal of the employees' bonds would cause the termination of Erwin, which would probably result in the mortgage payments becoming delinquent, I wondered if Big Midwestern's attitude concerning the situation would change. I never heard back from Big Midwestern. I did hear, through company gossip, that Erwin refinanced the mortgage about a year later, though I'm not sure how valid the application documents were.

Lessons Learned

One of the most important lessons I learned from this case is that a perpetrator does not have to have a degree in computer science or be an expert hacker to commit a computer crime. In some cases, knowing the computer system well enough to do your job can be enough for a fraudster whose employer has careless user access controls.

I also found it interesting that even though Big Midwestern was defrauded, the company was indifferent about the situation as long as the mortgage was current.

Recommendations to Prevent Future Occurrences

Proper Controls and Annual Reviews

Do not underestimate the creativity of information technology users. Given enough time and the desire to commit a crime, a fraudster can and will find loopholes in a poorly secured or designed system. In this case the design was sufficient, but management failed to secure the system properly. Annual reviews are important to ensure that controls are sufficient and enforced.

Separation of Duties

Separation of duties tends to be overlooked and taken for granted in small institutions. One of the main problems in this case was that I was the CFO but also acting as the internal auditor. Had I been more focused on the internal audit work, it might have been possible to find this situation prior to receiving information from an external source. Years of training and experience in public accounting did not compensate for attention and time spent reviewing and analyzing internal controls and searching for fraud.

Assess Risk

It is important to view fraud in a very broad sense. This case did not result in money being stolen in the typical sense, but in the manipulation of information. An individual received a loan that he, it appeared, did not quality for. If the underwriter had accurate documents, the loan might have been declined. Based on this, it is helpful to constantly ask all employees how and why fraud could be committed, so that tunnel vision is not used when assessing risk. Although potential fraudsters may not be forthcoming about limitations in controls, their peers will often point out the risks and sometimes have recommendations on how to deal with them.

Act on Tips

Internal controls are worthless endeavors unless an institution is willing to act on leads. While Great Members took appropriate action when presented with the facts, Big Midwestern did nothing when confronted with fraud even though it was their positive confirmation that triggered the investigation. All companies face limited budgets and must make difficult decisions in terms of expending resources; however, when controls are implemented, they must be taken seriously, observed, and enforced.

About the Author

Eric Sumners, CFE, CPA, is a graduate of Michigan State University and the University of Michigan, Dearborn, and has approximately 20 years of professional audit experience in an array of industries, including financial services, manufacturing, not-for-profit, and governmental. Mr. Sumners has also had a number of articles published concerning auditing issues.

I Due

REBECCA BUSCH

Jonathan Grant, a successful entrepreneur, was raised with all the benefits of wealth, including a top-notch education—a solid foundation to propel his career. After graduation, he took the reins of a family-run printing business and used e-marketing to successfully lead the company into the electronic era.

Jonathan's home life appeared every bit as successful as his professional one: Jennifer, his high school sweetheart, was a stay-at-home mom who managed the lives of their three children, all active in traveling sports teams. The family enjoyed the traditional trimmings of life in an affluent community. They were living the American dream.

Jonathan supplemented his income from Family Press Publications' successful e-marketing ventures with his personal endeavors. He wrote several books showcasing his savvy in various industry markets. The success of his trainings and lectures prompted a worldwide tour. Jonathan even developed an expertise in trading monetary instruments and applying his e-strategies in the financial markets. Later, he pursued interests in the subprime mortgage market. Needless to say, both he and his company were well-rounded, successful, and growth-motivated enterprises.

Fraud: A Cruel Mistress

Appearances can be deceiving. Jonathan and Jennifer's marriage wasn't as picture-perfect as it seemed. After 25 years of matrimony, Jonathan moved out and the divorce proceedings began. During this process, Jennifer received a call from the well-established Bank Online regarding an irregular signature identified by its fraud unit.

"Did you write an $8,000 check to Business Enterprises on your equity line account?" the investigator inquired.

She was flabbergasted. Eight thousand dollars is no small sum. "What check?" she asked. "Who is Business Enterprises? I don't have an equity line account with your bank!"

That phone call set off a chain of discoveries for Jennifer, whose experience with checking accounts did not extend past the one she shared with her husband. That same week the household bills, which Jonathan had always handled, started piling up. As it turned out, Jonathan had not paid one single utility bill in full over the past 12 months. It wasn't long before her car was repossessed, the gas turned off, and Jennifer had no access to credit cards.

Still reeling from her personal and financial change of circumstances, she went to a local bank to open up a checking account so she could, at the very least, deposit the child support checks she was now receiving from Jonathan.

"An adverse notation in ChexSystems was reported by another bank. That prevents us from opening up an account using your name and Social Security number," the teller explained.

"What are ChexSystems?" Jennifer asked.

"A service that provides deposit-account verification services to its financial institution members to help them identify account applicants who may have a history of account mishandling," replied the teller.

Jennifer shook her head. "What, exactly, does it state I did?"

The response was vague: "Fraudulent irregular signature activity."

The second bank responded similarly. During her attempt with a third bank, she offered to deposit cash on loan from a family member. Jennifer was yet again turned down.

"What good is a child support check if I can't cash it? Will I always have to go to his bank, cash the check, and carry cash? How am I supposed to pay the household bills, pay for the kids' activities, or save money?" she begged.

Jennifer was truly at a loss. She was struggling to provide the basics for her children without the ability to even open a bank account or deposit a check. At her lowest point, she had to ask a neighbor in their affluent community to make peanut butter and jelly sandwiches for her kids' school lunches.

On her seventh visit to a rural bank, she came prepared. Jennifer had obtained copies of the irregular signature first reported by Bank Online's fraud unit. Other evidence included front and back copies of the forged checks, documents proving she did not open the account herself, and letters from the bank acknowledging the error. Upon receipt of the evidence, the bank representative opened up an account without the formality of running her social security number through ChexSystems. This allowed her to open a limited account with significant restrictions including a 10-day hold on all checks deposited.

By the time I talked to Jennifer, she sounded as confused, frustrated, and despairing as anyone I'd heard.

"What the heck is in my credit report?"

Issues clearly existed within Jennifer's credit activity. Banks informed her that, according to ChexSystems, she was listed as being involved in fraud, which disqualified her from opening a checking account. I realized that something significant had occurred to tarnish Jennifer's name.

The financial strain caused Jennifer to forfeit her full-time job as a stay-at-home mom and enter the workforce. But every time she reached the final phase of an interview with a prospective employer, the company would summarily withdraw its offer. Perplexed, she decided to look into the matter. By accessing a section of her online credit report that documented parties who had requested the information, we determined that prospective employers were viewing it and subsequently withdrawing their offers.

After 25 years of marriage with credit cards held in her husband's name, Jennifer tried to obtain her own, but failed repeatedly.

"Have you requested a copy of your credit report?" I asked.

"No," she simply replied.

I requested that Jennifer come to my office immediately. Once there, I told her that she needed to review her credit report. We downloaded it from an online credit source. After patiently waiting for the hourglass to stop spinning, we received a profound shock: Her credit score was 390.

Jennifer's score was in the bottom 2% of the population. This revelation was mystifying for someone who had never requested a credit card, had always used cash provided by her husband, and had never earned her own income. Her only role in the family finances had been signing off on real estate purchases. The print button produced a document containing page after page of credit, mortgage, and finance activity. Jennifer recognized only a handful of these events.

"What does this all mean?" she asked. Unfortunately, these were red flags, glaring indications that a fraud had occurred.

Taking the Necessary Steps

By the time we finished gathering the initial evidence of the mortgage closing statements and documents requested from creditors within her credit report, we had discovered a very extensive history of activity. Jonathan's very complex fraudulent activity featured three prongs:

1. Falsifying up to 17 mortgage loans with 11 different mortgage entities to obtain equity loans of $1.2 million from bank branches in 7 different states for their one single-family home

2. Opening 30 credit cards in over 20 different states (the interoperability of the financial markets allowed him not to get caught)
3. Falsely obtaining a copy of the wife's Social Security card directly from a Web site application

"What do I do now?" Jennifer asked, incredulous.

The first step was to immediately place a fraud alert with all credit agencies. Next, we created a standardized letter to send to every credit company noted in her report. The letter requested the names, locations, and sources of the accounts opened up; a list of all financial transactions, account signatures, and dates connected to the accounts; and, if closed, when the accounts were shut down. Because Jennifer first learned of her husband's activities from Bank Online's investigator, who called into question her supposed signature on a check, we sent a specific letter requesting all bank statements and the front and backs of all checks written. A total of over 50 letters were sent out.

In addition to a fraud alert, credit bureaus allow a 100-word statement by the consumer. I assisted Jennifer in preparing the following:

> My credit report is a reflection of what can happen to a victim of identity theft. I am aware of the perpetrator, and I am taking steps to mitigate the damage. If you are a prospective employer and/or credit agency, please feel free to ask me for specific information. I invite you to make detailed inquiries of me and I will provide information and confirmation that the activity within this report did not occur by my hand.

We forwarded this statement to all of the credit agencies. Within the first week, 20% of the letters were returned, labeled "wrong address; no forwarding information available." This struck us as rather odd since we had used the addresses listed directly in the credit reports. Next, we commenced to contact any creditors who would take phone calls, presenting the available information, account number, and Social Security number in order to locate the branch that issued the credit report statement. We learned that most of the reported companies and banks do not have listed phone numbers. Many banks, in fact, have policies against giving out phone numbers to their fraud units. We simply had to send out letters and hope that someone would respond, at the very least to let us know that we were contacting the right places to begin mitigating the false information.

We faced roadblocks as we moved through the process. For example, one of the bank's support hotlines for reporting fraud told Jennifer, "We assume that the reported fraud is correct. But you can't do anything about this." Next I sent her to the bank's local branch to report the fraud in person to the branch manager, who then put her in contact with the bank chairman's office. A senior executive became involved with reviewing the documents that led one of his branches to report the adverse event into ChexSystems. He reviewed the evidence provided by Jennifer in addition to the documentation in the bank's computer files. The senior executive offered to amend the situation by providing verbal confirmation that Jennifer was not involved with the generation of the irregular check signatures, but his legal department wouldn't allow him to put anything in writing. He stated that he could not make any promises. Reversals in ChexSystems were almost unheard of. But after 45 days Jennifer received a letter from ChexSystems containing a copy of a new report with the adverse false notation removed from her account.

Requesting account information and verification of the debt required proof of identity. I advised Jennifer to obtain copies of her birth certificate and social security card and also to gather up some examples of U.S. mail sent to her address. But she hadn't seen her social security card since college. When she went to the Social Security Administration office to order a new one, she learned that her card was last issued three years ago. I told her to gather as much information as possible regarding how the card was issued and exactly when it was sent out. This date turned out to be significant because, during the same time period in which the card was reissued, the evolution of debt and credit activity reported on Jennifer's credit report where she was listed as the "sole" party to equity lines and credit cards grew exponentially.

By reviewing the ChexSystems report, I discovered that two banks had reported suspected fraud. The first was Bank Online, whose fraud unit investigator's phone call had tipped off Jennifer, helping her to uncover her husband's identity theft activities. This institution had allowed Jonathan to open an equity line in Jennifer's name, but she was supposedly the only party with signature privileges. Establishing this account was an online transaction with a closing that occurred via U.S. mail. In all, 15 checks were found. It was not until the last one, which prompted a call to Jennifer to confirm a particular signature, that Jonathan's fraud had been revealed.

"How could this have happened?" Jennifer asked the bank representative.

"We only check signatures on amounts over $6,000."

"Then why were the checks written for $20,000 and $8,000 approved?" Jennifer asked.

The representative had no explanation for the lack of internal control. Based on the information provided by the bank, it appeared that Jennifer was the only authorized account holder. However, on three of the checks, Jonathan had signed with his own name; Jonathan conceded to Jennifer in an e-mail that he forged her signature on the remaining checks. The account had been opened two years prior to its discovery. In total, Jonathan had signed Jennifer's name 15 different times on this single equity line.

The second bank involved with the ChexSystems reporting report was Family Savings Bank, where Jonathan had a checking account and where he tried to deposit an equity line check of $100,000 from Bank Online into his account. This $100,000 check could not be cleared because of irregular signature activity. Bank Online's fraud unit reported the bounced check to Jennifer. Family Savings Bank then reported Jennifer's irregular signature to ChexSystems.

This trail of wrongdoing prompted a letter-writing campaign to both banks, including the office of the chairman at one. Both admitted that the reporting was in error. But neither bank assured Jennifer of its ability to remove the incorrect report from ChexSystems. The chairman stated that he needed approval from the legal department in order to give acknowledgment in writing that an error occurred. This has yet to happen. In the meantime, Jennifer continued to communicate in writing with ChexSystems; but like most of the banks she and I communicated with, ChexSystems refused to correspond with any party via the telephone.

Jonathan's response to the forgeries and subsequent destruction of Jennifer's credit was nonchalant. "It's no big deal," he said, adding, "This would all go away if she would just write a letter to the bank." But a hundred letters and about 50 phone calls had been made to no avail.

With respect to the credit card debt and the disappearance of equity in the home, he said, "Well, if we both just file bankruptcy, this will go away." Easier said than done. Jennifer had invested three months of her own time—and mine—just to convince the two main banks to acknowledge that an error had been made. The situation was further compounded by the fact that Jonathan generated well over $150,000 in commissions alone, while Jennifer did not produce an income. Furthermore, Jonathan, in some of his business ventures, had generated W-2 income in his wife's name. But he had never disclosed to Jennifer that he was paying her a salary through his business, and, conveniently, had not filed a tax return in three years.

Most victims of identity theft will tell you how devastating it is—particularly when it involves someone you trust. Jennifer's case was particularly burdensome. She was mitigating the effects of her ex-husband's fraud while also hunting for a job, trying to open up her own bank account, paying bills, and feeding, clothing, and caring for three teenagers. In addition to family court proceedings, Jennifer had looming over her bankruptcy court, foreclosure fears, credit collection activity, and a potential criminal division lurking around the corner. How does someone mitigate their own spouse's identity theft, forgery, mail fraud, computer fraud, bank fraud, and a host of other activities? Jennifer's simple letter-writing campaign to all the creditors to correct false information could have, at any time, bitten the hand feeding her and her children.

Each letter built more evidence against Jonathan. To this day, several of the banks continue to request affidavits for documentation that Jonathan had been using Jennifer's identity without her consent and with the intent of not paying off any of the debt. But if he were convicted by any of the parties, such as the mortgage entities or credit card providers, any "time served" by Jonathan would mean unemployment. He would be unable to pay child support.

Picking Up the Pieces

The ability to develop business and banking relationships over the Internet, while convenient, has facilitated personal misrepresentation. Online banking eliminates face time with customers who request credit. Due to the increased technology, Jonathan was able to use the computer to initiate online mortgage applications and to obtain his wife's Social Security card. The only good news is that he monitored all his transgressions from his home computer and kindly left a Word document containing respective passwords to most of the locations where he obtained funds.

Jonathan's fraud totaled $1.2 million in equity line dollars that he obtained on his house, which was reappraised repeatedly at an alarming rate of value. Because the $100,000 transaction was what triggered the ChexSystems notation presenting the greatest hurdle for Jennifer in regards to obtaining a banking relationship, she and I focused first on it, spending 60 hours without a complete resolution.

The $100,000 transaction represented just one item out of 50 from this identity theft. Jennifer is about to enter a lifetime of mitigation. We obtained title companies' closing statements in order to follow the remaining $1.1 million. Subsequent work helped us to understand the credit card activity. One particular problem with the credit cards was that some showed cash advances instead of actual purchases. The damage actually reached closer to $1.8 million. No wonder Jonathan was anxious to rush to bankruptcy court and walk away from the mortgage and equity-line obligations. Jonathan's goal was to eliminate the $1.2 million in loans he obtained from his single-family residence. New bankruptcy laws that now limit activity for those who generate over $150,000 per year and fail to file tax returns, however, may have cramped his plans.

Jennifer is on the right path for mitigation but has at least another 10 years of work ahead of her. Jennifer is considering a civil fraud and identity theft action for damages against her credit and reputation. Repercussions for Jonathan are pending.

Lessons Learned

The first step in investigating a computer identity theft is to recognize the problem. Next, initiate protective provisions such as fraud alerts. The third step is to provide the credit agency with a personal statement that will be documented within your credit report. Exercise your right to obtain information about the source driving the adverse financial reports. For example, it is the consumer's right to report mishandling of account activity and controls within the banking system. It is important to find appropriate legal representation. Issues related to divorce, bankruptcy, real estate foreclosure, fraud, and criminal activity may exceed the expertise of one type of attorney.

In identity theft, it's critical to have a well-organized process for collecting and documenting evidence as it was gathered. It was important in Jennifer's case, not just for creating an audit trial for subsequent presentation, but also for handling the ongoing discovery of new activity. Having a well-organized process can generate unexpected discoveries. Have a systematic decision tree for analysis; otherwise the process may become difficult to manage.

Recommendations to Prevent Future Occurrences

Review Finances and Credit Reports

Individuals should review their finances and credit reports annually, at minimum. If a breach is discovered, act quickly. Notifying appropriate parties of a breach and gathering information will reduce the effects. Furthermore, in the context of marriage, parties should always have their own individual credit in addition to combined finances.

Banking Industry Prevention

Banks' "know the customers" policies should require extra vigilance—not just in marriages but in business enterprises where more than one party has a financial interest. In addition, the banking system needs to check its internal controls for how credit is managed and provided within electronic commerce versus traditional in-person meetings. For example, a follow-up telephone interview with all parties should be made to verify the results of such meetings. If Jennifer had been called to confirm the opening of an account in her name, she would have known of the fraud sooner.

Mortgage Industry Prevention

The act of obtaining a mortgage involves several parties. These may include the borrower, banks and credit institutions, realtors, mortgage brokers, real estate appraisers, attorneys, and title companies. Internal controls for electronic transactions as well as in-person transactions should be part of any annual audit review. The potential for misrepresentation and collusion is a growing problem. Strong internal controls are required to screen for fraudulent activity.

About the Author

Rebecca S. Busch, CFE, RN, MBA, CCM, FHFMA, is CEO of Chicago-based MBA Inc. An expert in the area of health care reimbursement and electronic data analysis, she has participated on expert policy determination panels and has numerous publications and presentations, including *Healthcare Fraud: Auditing and Detection Guide* and *Electronic Health Records: An Audit and Internal Control Guide*, both published by John Wiley & Sons, Inc.

CHAPTER 34

What Lies Inside the Trojan Horse

JOHNATHAN TAL

Raj Mentiri grew up in India. Unlike the vast majority of people in his country who lived below the poverty line, he came from a fortunate household where his family could afford a luxurious lifestyle. Both he and his brother Vignesh were educated in the best schools money could provide. Technology was the "it" subject of study for young Indians, and so Raj and his brother followed suit and mastered it with hopes of moving to America to prosper. When they arrived in the United States in the mid-1990s, they were quite stricken with the realization that, although their new home afforded endless opportunities, the amount of work it would take to attain their goals could take a lifetime. After a couple years in America, the older brother, Vignesh, had started his own software company. "Don't worry, little brother," he told Raj, "Success comes to those who find it—sometimes in disguise. All we have to do is to recognize it when it's in front of us."

Raj was a highly skilled software engineer who was consistently promoted, not only because of his technical prowess, but also because of his powerful personality. His mix of technical knowledge and personal charisma inevitably drew support from his cohorts, and his career blossomed. After a few years, Raj found himself in the position of chief technical officer (CTO) at a new and exciting company located in the heart of where his expertise would be best rewarded—Silicon Valley.

In the late '90s, Silicon Valley was the mecca for tech start-ups. A host of "techies" with bright business ideas were enjoying the height of the dotcom boom. Flying in the face of convention, these budding companies embraced a more casual culture than the large, established, staunch corporations before them. Located in San Francisco's Bay Area, Incurio Inc. was a company in the midst of rapid growth. They employed a host of tech experts, largely brought in from overseas, that provided online and on-site tech support for various computer systems, peripherals, and applications; it was a Geek Squad before its time. Even with the steadily growing trend of telecommuting, the masterminds behind so many of these groups knew that, to be successful, their personnel would be spending a great amount of time at the office. Casual became not only the dress code for most days, but the general attitude of all levels of staff. But in the quest for a more comfortable atmosphere, did some of these organizations like Incurio also relax their control protocols?

Risky Business

The familiar "ding" of a new e-mail arriving in Kumar Singh's inbox reached his ears as he downed his second Red Bull of the morning. Caffeine wasn't exactly what he needed at the moment, as his nerves were already buzzing with the decision he was about to make. Apprehensively, he clicked the mouse so that his e-mail was visible on the screen. The new message was from exactly where he expected. Kumar looked around his cubicle to be sure that no one was behind him, took a deep breath, and opened the message. He tensely fingered the button on the collar of his polo shirt as he read.

> Hi, Kumar,
> The vendor I told you about is on board. We're set to meet next week. I'm really hoping I'll have you along for the ride as well. Someone of your skill level and know-how would benefit my project greatly. Let me know by lunchtime. I can't wait any longer—if you're not in, I've got to find someone else.
> Raj

Kumar was pensive for a moment, and then began to type in a manner quite unlike his usual breakneck pace. "Raj, I've had time to consider the proposition. Call it morbid curiosity, but I'm unable to turn it down. Count me in. –K."

He moved the cursor over to the send button, but hesitated. Kumar nervously rubbed his brow. His finger shook as it hovered over the mouse for an instant, though he was unsure if his shakiness was from the caffeine coursing through his system or the gravity of his decision. Finally, he clicked the mouse and the message was sent out to its anxiously waiting recipient. As of that moment, Kumar Singh's fate at Incurio had been sealed.

A Supposed Software Savior

As with any company armed with a bright idea and the right people to bring it to the public, Incurio enjoyed positive feedback from its growing clientele, largely due to word of mouth. At its peak, the company employed over 500 tech-support experts. But Incurio's success was to be short lived. Within a year of starting the rapid growth mode, the company was already on course for its downfall. Incurio's profitability began to dip in its second year of business. At a loss for answers, its board of directors brought in Chip Dewright, a new and highly respected CEO who had a proven track record of changing the fortunes of companies in trouble. Shortly into his tenure at Incurio, Chip received an e-mail from his CTO, Raj Mentiri:

> Our growth is being delayed because our capability is not meeting our demand. I have ideas—can we meet?
> –Raj

Chip welcomed any input and agreed to a meeting. "So, Raj—lay it on me," Chip said late one evening in his office.

"We need software. The right program that would allow us a greater interfacing ability would boost our response time," Raj began confidently. He went on to describe in detail the exact specifications this software would need in order to be compatible with Incurio's existing infrastructure. "So the bottom line is: Our response time is shortened, our profits go up," Raj finished, setting his notebook down on Chip's desk. Chip unclasped his hands from behind his head and did a few calculations on his computer. He stared at his screen for a moment.

"Where do we get this software? Does it even exist yet?" asked Chip. Raj took a breath before answering with confidence.

"It just so happens I know exactly where we can get it. It's pretty new, but other companies have used it successfully. I believe my team could have it fully implemented within the next month or two."

Chip hesitated and looked at Raj, "All right then—make it happen."

Incurio purchased the software system suggested by Raj from a company called Soclus for $155,000. Soclus, coincidentally, was headed by Vignesh Mentiri, Raj's older brother. As CTO, Raj and his team were tasked with implementing this software into Incurio's daily operations. But his bright promise of having it up and running within a couple months began to dull as the weeks passed by. Gradually, Incurio's distressed CEO noticed that Raj's output had steadily been decreasing; the new software that had been purchased at such a hefty price still had not been implemented as planned, and no solutions were in sight.

Another month passed and Incurio's progress still remained stagnant. Chip was stymied. The only news that he could bring back to the anxious board of directors was that progress had stalled. That was when the focus turned on Raj Mentiri.

Chip pulled Raj aside one afternoon after a staff meeting. He was particularly bothered by the news he had just received that the IT department was still stuck. "Raj, you told me three months ago that you'd have this new software up and running within a couple months at the latest. What's the holdup?"

Raj looked Chip straight in the eye and, without hesitation, answered: "I'm sorry, Chip. We're working hard on it. There have been a couple of setbacks that I didn't foresee, but I assure you, we're almost there." He was exceptionally adept at maintaining his composure, even when put on the spot.

Chip opened his mouth to say something, stopped, then continued. "You have one more week," he said. "If it's not a go by then, I'll have no choice but to move in a different direction. I'm counting on you, Raj."

Deception at the Hands of Their Own

It came to pass that the software purchased at such a hefty price from Soclus was never to be used at Incurio. Those in charge of its implementation alleged that it just wasn't compatible with the company's existing systems. Without the new software system in place, profits were dropping with increasing rapidity. The company was taking a sharp turn for the worst. Raj's deadline of one final week came and went, and still Incurio lacked this new "silver bullet" software that he had so confidently touted. Chip felt he had given Raj more than a fair chance and he could no longer tolerate this lack of output.

At the next board meeting, Chip sadly had no good news to report. The directors shared a collective sigh.

"I thought this great new software was supposed to be the sure cure for Incurio. What happened?" Director Burns inquired of Chip.

"Well, that's what I was told also," Chip answered, frustrated.

Burns exchanged glances with the other board members. "You realize we have no other option but extreme overhaul, don't you?" she said.

Resigned, Chip nodded. By the decision of upper management, the housecleaning would begin in the IT department.

"The board motions that the terminations of Chief Technology Officer Raj Mentiri and members of his team, to include head engineer Kumar Singh, be set for two weeks from today, to allow sufficient time to find qualified replacements. All those in favor?" Every board member's hand rose. "Then it's final," Director Burns concluded.

It was then that our company, TAL Global, was employed by Incurio to provide protective services during the terminations. Leading Silicon Valley in security and investigative consulting services, TAL Global was the natural choice for high-tech companies looking for security solutions.

Just days before the Incurio terminations were to be carried out, a Trojan Horse virus, meant to erase or overwrite data while simultaneously corrupting files, was unleashed onto the company's servers. Fear shot through upper management, and understandably so. They suspected Raj and possibly other members of his team had somehow caught wind of their impending terminations and had, in fact, been the source of the virus. This prompted an immediate call for more extensive action. In addition to our protective services, our expertise in computer forensics work was called upon in order to mitigate the risk posed by the virus of sabotage, theft of proprietary information, and damage or loss of intellectual property. Our scope of work was immediately broadened to include damage control in the form of a comprehensive computer-forensics investigation of Incurio's systems. What we uncovered then proved to be the tip of the iceberg in the culmination of some of the most brazen, unlawful action within a business we had ever seen in our 25 years of investigations.

Incurio's information systems were under attack. The knowledge level of those suspected of waging the assault (Raj and the other personnel) was so technologically advanced, it was necessary to secure Incurio's servers so access would be denied to those unauthorized parties wishing to get a final look (or swipe) at information they would no longer be privy to after their departure. We secured the servers both physically, by locking all the doors to forbid unauthorized access, and by disabling all user accounts except for the administrators'. We also installed all security updates that applied to the operating system and application, removed all nonessential or unknown software, and shut down all programs.

The last thing the already struggling company needed was intellectual property theft in addition to their already anemic profits. Our top-level technical expert, Dr. George Wizen, was summoned the night before the terminations were to take place. In the early 1980s, he had broken ground in researching information protection with the invention of the earliest computer virus defenses. A widely published author and known expert on all things computer security–related, Dr. Wizen had been associated with some of the largest corporations in the world, as well as governmental agencies for the past 30 years. With such rich experience to draw from, this assignment promised to be a routine one for our expert and his team. In addition to securing Incurio's servers, they worked from 10 p.m. into the early morning hours to do "imaging," making copies of the contents of all the company's hard drives. Dr. Wizen and his group began a routine check of the company's external infrastructure. Router settings were being reconfigured to allow the proper network traffic through while disallowing any unlawful use of the company's bandwidth that had been exposed by the virus. They then had to go through the process of documenting legitimate uses of the company's systems so they would be able to distinguish those from any unauthorized activity. It slowly became evident that things were not as they should be. The inventories of each user's system were beginning to show programs that did not belong with the company's infrastructure. In addition to Incurio's regular accounting software and database, a separate accounting system was found, and it was not immediately apparent what or who it belonged to. Evidence of unauthorized virtual private networks (VPNs) that would allow a user to connect to a home network were found. The warning alarms began to really sound as a secondary e-mail system separate from Incurio's was discovered. The only reason a secondary e-mail system would have been created would be to enable correspondence not directly related to Incurio.

"We're gonna need to talk to whoever's left in their IT department." Dr. Wizen made this proclamation, fully knowing it was loaded with the possibility of exposing to Chip the worst nightmare for any company: deception at the hands of its own.

Shadow Company

We arrived on scene that morning in our originally scheduled protective capacity just hours before the ax was to fall. Even as the terminations were taking place, our crack computer-forensics team uncovered evidence showing that Raj Mentiri, along with several of his colleagues, had created an entirely separate company called Dolus. The odd pieces of secondary e-mail systems and accounting databases that were found by Dr. Wizen and his team began to come together: Raj and his cohorts had been running the Dolus infrastructure through Incurio's. Once the existence of Dolus was discovered, concrete documentation showed that its Web site domain, along with one for another separate staffing company, had been registered by Raj Mentiri's wife, and that these new companies were listed as having the same mailing address as the Mentiri household.

The previous misgivings of Chip directed at Raj's lack of output were quickly proven to have merit. Various records of e-mails from Raj and his cohorts' systems showed that the implementation of Soclus's high-priced software had long ceased to be a priority for them. For the past few months, the focus had changed entirely to the operation of this new side company Mentiri and his fellow infiltrators had created. Several other Incurio systems belonging to various employees throughout the company showed evidence of correspondence with Raj that clearly identified them as willing participants in the Dolus venture.

All the evidence uncovered through our computer forensics investigation pointed at earnest efforts towards building this new company, all on Incurio's time and at its expense. E-mails on the secondary system, including the very ones exchanged by Raj and Kumar Singh, confirmed that meetings had been carried out after-hours in which they and other representatives of Dolus had met with unsuspecting vendors and investors at Incurio's facility. As if that were not heinous enough, to give the illusion that Dolus was already a solvent venture, invoices and accounting records showed they presented all of Incurio's assets as belonging to Dolus.

The more layers that we peeled back on this investigation, the more it became apparent just how deep this new operation had gone. Apparently, Incurio was only the latest in a number of companies that had fallen prey to the unlawful intentions of this unabashed group of thieves. More careful investigation of Raj's previous work history showed that he was, essentially, the leader of an infiltration group spread across various organizations whose modus operandi was to make their way into companies based on alleged successes at prior endeavors. Once in, they would siphon funds and resources into their own pet projects. When the company they were bleeding dry went under, they ever so stealthily moved on to the next victim organization.

It had already been discovered that a number of current Incurio employees were associated with Dolus. Those dangling the puppet strings of Dolus even went so far as to begin bringing in new overseas employees, complete with all the necessary documentation needed to work in the United States.

Incurio was being dismantled even as Dr. Wizen and his team were imaging the systems of those who had been terminated. Our investigation of the servers revealed that over half of the information that was being stored on them was, in fact, for Dolus. Raj Mentiri's team efforts were so focused that 2,483 hits on Dolus and 500 hits on Soclus were located, compared with only 4,822 company-wide hits on Incurio.

Mentiri and his associates had grossly taken advantage of Incurio's investors by using the invested money to grow their own side business. They were so absorbed in this vilely illegal and unethical side project that it became totally immaterial that they were doing so using the equipment, resources, and personnel of Incurio. When all was said and done, it was estimated that the operation of Dolus and Raj Mentiri's other staffing company had leeched over a million dollars from Incurio in the course of approximately six months.

Additionally, the tie between Raj Mentiri and Soclus suddenly didn't feel so coincidental. It turns out that, from the beginning of Incurio's association with Soclus, the $155,000 purchase of the allegedly dysfunctional software was simply a front for a means of channeling funds into Dolus, and possibly back into Soclus. Even before all the phases of our investigation were completed, Incurio had been dismantled by its stunned and disgusted board of directors.

Lessons Learned

This case was a classic example of a company doing too little too late. Incurio's investors had poured $16 million into attempts to save the company. The prosecution of the perpetrators would not result in a single cent being recovered. Rather, it would put indelible marks on the reputations of individuals who had proven and branded themselves as having impeccable judgment and business sense. Prosecution was declined and, in the end, the thieves in engineers' clothing got away with everything scot-free.

A company can dedicate large amounts of money into putting together the best-laid business plan and setting up the most avant-garde IT security practices, but all that can never take the place of thorough preemployment background investigations. Stories such as Incurio's emphasize the importance to companies, large or small, of conducting sufficient due diligence on all prospective employees.

Recommendations to Prevent Future Occurrences

Due Diligence

Comprehensive due-diligence background investigations are imperative for companies of all sizes. Criminal and civil court checks can show if a prospective employee has had prior legal trouble in the way of unethical or even violent behavior. Financial asset databases can reveal if prospective employees are facing any financial woes that might prompt them to steal from an employer. Perhaps most importantly, previous employment checks must be conducted. Talking to former employers can either validate or negate what is claimed on an applicant's resume. Pointed questions about an individual's character, including a point-blank question as to whether the reference would rehire that person, could save prospective employers immeasurable heartache.

Project Management

It is important to have a system of persons in place to manage large projects and make sure deadlines are met. Raj was given several months to install the new software, and when he didn't meet the deadline he was able to shrug it off with a few excuses. Micromanagement can lead to lost productivity, but it is also important to have sufficient oversight and management to make sure projects don't veer off course. The tough part is finding the right balance.

Audits and Reviews

By reviewing the system for unusual activity, network administrators and internal auditors can often detect problems early. It is common to come across employees who use the computer systems for personal business, porn site surfing, or even illegal activities such as child pornography and drug dealing. Routine reviews can serve as deterrence to such behavior.

About the Author

Johnathan Tal, CFE, CPI, President and CEO of TAL Global, has extensive experience in emergency preparedness and crisis management, investigative services, physical security management, and risk assessment. A licensed investigator, Johnathan played a crucial role in bringing the first "theft by computer" conviction in California.

CHAPTER 35

Lost in Transition

AMY CRON

Brent glanced at the clock on his office wall and released a loud sigh. It was nearly 7 p.m. *Here comes another fight with Julie,* he thought. He could see his wife now—arms folded, eyes sharp, lips scowling and turned down in irritation.

He'd recite the same script he'd been delivering for months: "Yes, I realize today is Sunday. Yes, I know I promised I would be home earlier. Yes, of course I'd rather be home with you."

Brent wished his wife would understand that he was just under a lot of stress—working unusual hours during the month-end close was just part of his job as plant controller. But he would much rather spend time with his family. He adored Ashley, their bubbly three-year-old daughter with Shirley Temple curls, and missed her laughter and inquisitiveness when he was away. Brent knew his absence was hard on Julie—and the fact that she was seven months' pregnant made it even harder. His wife wanted him home and his job wanted him at the office—on a Sunday night.

Brent had to admit that his work hours had been growing progressively longer in recent months. He felt so overwhelmed. More frequently, he found himself staying late to try and get a handle on the workload.

Brent had worked for Zen Textiles for his entire career. As a 20-year veteran, he was one of the most knowledgeable employees at the Jacksonville plant. Holding various positions in his tenure enabled him to accrue an intimate understanding of operations at all levels. Brent was the go-to guy for all sorts of questions. Even after all these years, he still couldn't believe he was the plant controller. Without a formal accounting degree or a CPA license, the position had initially seemed unattainable. But Brent was persistent. He had applied for a staff accounting position multiple times before finally earning the job 15 years ago. Slowly, he taught himself the necessary vocabulary and skills. Brent's knowledge of the plant operations helped give him an edge in the accounting department. Because of his previous experience, he had a heightened instinct when the numbers looked wrong, and he always knew whom to call in the plant for the right answers. Over time other employees left the company and he remained, acquiring more and more responsibility.

When the plant controller announced he was leaving Zen five years ago, Brent was the next in line to get the job. But he was nervous. He worried that his lack of formal education, especially not being a CPA, would hurt his chances. But his anxiety proved immaterial. Brent was offered the position as plant controller, a hard-earned and deserved promotion.

Four years after the move, Brent was approached by Bill Shah, his boss, who took a deep breath and said, "We've been sold."

After a long conversation, Brent had a grasp on the situation. The Jacksonville plant had been purchased by CheapJeans, a Zen rival that produced essentially the same products. All of Zen's Jacksonville employees had the option of working for CheapJeans, but their specific jobs were not guaranteed.

CheapJeans was a much larger company than Zen, with nearly double the number of plants. They had a fiscal year-end date of December 31, instead of the June 30 fiscal year at Zen. Coincidentally, the external auditor for both companies was the same firm.

With his growing family in mind, Brent immediately decided to accept a position with CheapJeans. He met with the new executive team and was excited when they offered him the plant controller position on a probationary basis. Brent was confident that he would prove himself just as he had in the past.

Over the next few weeks, Brent was surprised to find that many of his long-term colleagues decided to move elsewhere. He was one of the few management employees from Zen to stay.

Although Brent's title stayed the same, the CheapJeans management team quickly implemented significant changes at the Jacksonville plant, many of which directly affected the accounting department. Both companies may have manufactured similar products, but each employed very different approaches when it came to their accounting judgments and decisions.

CheapJeans used a different methodology to account for its costs. Historically, Zen had used standard costing to account for changes in prices in material, direct labor, and manufacturing overhead; rather than assigning the actual costs, they used standards, or expected costs, for each input. Under this method, the inventory and the cost of goods sold were initially recorded at a standard amount for each good. Then they would compare the standards they had developed to the actual costs and record the variances in a separate account. This methodology allowed the Zen management to quickly assess rising costs and implement swift changes to prevent further overages.

Zen had used standard costs since inception, and had the necessary accounting software to process all of the individual variances. The software combined all of Zen's cost data into certain key discrepancies—direct labor, direct materials, and overhead—that management could then analyze. Any significant variances in costs were immediate concerns for local management, and those greater than 10% required a submission of detailed explanations to the corporate office.

In contrast, CheapJeans historically captured its costs on an actual basis. Under their system, inventory and the cost of goods sold were recorded based on what CheapJeans had actually paid. They had an internal software system that they used to capture its costs.

CheapJeans wanted to switch the Jacksonville plant to its preferred cost methodology and cost-accounting software. However, to ease the transition, they decided to wait at least a year before changing the current systems.

The company's decision not to change the cost accounting for the Jacksonville plant put additional pressure on Brent Dobbins as the plant controller. Since the software was unique to Zen, only Brent was familiar with it. Also, closing a period on this cost accounting software was an ordeal; the system was so large that it could only operate on days when the entire computer capability could be focused on this process, which usually meant the weekend. The added strain was hard on Brent, and his decision making suffered.

Off to a Bad Start

I try to make a habit of shutting down my Blackberry on Sunday. As CFO of CheapJeans, I receive around 200 e-mails a day, so my Sunday reprieve is a luxury. It's a day of rest, has been for centuries: a day clearly not meant for the whining vibrations of a Blackberry. But come the workweek, it's back to the grind, starting with a deluge of e-mails. One dreary Monday morning in December, as I scanned through the weekend's messages, one e-mail in particular grabbed my attention. It was sent at 5:15 a.m. from a plant controller in our Jacksonville division with the subject "Audit Reconciliation." I opened it with nervous anticipation:

> Dear Amy,
>
> I have spent the entire weekend trying to reconcile the balance in Accounts Payable Accrued. I am currently unable to explain the balance of approximately $3M (debit) in AP Accrued. I resign from my position as Plant Controller with this email.
>
> Brent Dobbins

I reread the e-mail several times. Debit balance in accounts payable (AP) accrued? That didn't make sense. Why would a liability account have a debit balance at year-end? Brent is resigning? And now, mid-December during our year-end audit and before the year-end financial statements have been filed? It was the worst possible timing. What would the auditors say? Jacksonville was a heavy revenue contributor. Not a good start to the week.

A few hours later, I was on a conference call with the head of our internal audit department, the plant VP at the Jacksonville location, and our general counsel's office, informing them about Brent's strange e-mail and resignation. The plant VP, Bill Shah, had received a similar message. He informed us that, to complicate matters, Brent failed to show up to work that morning. Bill filled us in on the developing situation at the plant.

For the past few weeks, the external auditors had been working in Jacksonville performing their year-end audit procedures in preparation for our December 31 filing. They had requested account reconciliations for all significant balance-sheet accounts, a fairly standard procedure. As the plant controller, it was Brent's responsibility to provide this information to the auditors, which he hadn't done. They were impatient and needed this reconciliation before they could continue. On top of Brent's missed deadline, the balance in the account looked strange. Instead of a credit balance, it read as a $3 million dollar debit.

Because Brent failed to respond in a timely manner, the auditors had contacted Bill. They needed the account reconciliation immediately. Bill calmed the auditors down (they were an excitable bunch) and assured them they would have it by the following Monday. Then he walked down to Brent's office to look into the situation. Brent replied that he was buried in other requests at the moment, but not to worry because this particular account was fine; he just needed a little extra time to complete the reconciliation, he said. Brent promised Bill the auditors would have it first thing Monday morning.

Bill also mentioned during our conversation that Matt Frick had recently come to him with concerns regarding Brent. As a manager in the accounting department, Matt was responsible for the monthly account reconciliations. Despite weeks of work, he had been unable to reconcile the AP accrued account due to activity that seemed irregular. When Matt approached Brent for help, his response was strange: "You just don't understand—I'll take care of it myself!"

Matt was taken aback by Brent's outburst. His boss was normally quiet and reserved; he had never heard him yell before. Furthermore, Matt was simply doing his job. He decided to ask Bill Shah for advice.

According to Bill, Matt was nonchalant when the problems with the AP accrued were brought up; he focused instead on Brent's outburst. Based on his statements and attitude, Bill interpreted the issue to be more about Brent's management style than any problems with an account. Bill had decided to wait until the year-end financial statements were complete before talking with Brent. Closing the books was stressful; he thought Matt had just caught him at a bad time.

At this point, Mary Costello, the general counsel of CheapJeans, spoke up. "Based upon what I've heard, legal steps need to be taken immediately. I'll take care of that. Why don't you try to figure out this account? We'll talk again at the end of the day. We could have a major issue on our hands."

Since the internal auditors and I were located at the corporate headquarters in Texas, we spent a lot of time that day on the phone with Bill in Jacksonville. As a team we tried to understand the various journal entries posted to the accounts-payable accrued account. There were hundreds each month—far too many to analyze effectively in just one day. Neither Bill nor I were familiar enough with the plant's financial statements to easily explain which of these journal entries were appropriate and which were not. However, their frequency and significant dollar value were an immediate matter of concern. Even at first glance, it didn't appear that this account was being used in an appropriate manner.

The general purpose of accrued accounts payable is to properly accrue for goods or services received without an invoice. For example, in the case of a manufacturing company, oftentimes materials are received at the shipping dock during the last few days of the period—sometimes before the invoice sent via regular mail is received. Accrual accounting requires a company to estimate the payment due for these goods because a liability (payment) exists for the company at that time. The entry would be a debit to inventory and a credit to AP accrued. As we analyzed these entries, something didn't make sense.

During our second conference call of the day, Bill and I discussed our initial findings with Mary Costello and the internal audit department. Although we were unable to quantify the possible misstatement, we believed that the activity appeared unusual and potentially inappropriate. Especially given the timing of this discovery, 15 days before our year-end, we decided to initiate an independent investigation of the account. Mary contacted our legal counsel and they suggested hiring forensic accountants for assistance.

Manipulate the Balance

Our external counsel and the forensic accountants began their investigation by conducting interviews with numerous employees. For the next two days, I scheduled interviews with people from the accounting department, human resources, shipping, finance, and IT. Anyone who may have had contact with Brent received a visit. We left no stone unturned.

During the second day of interviews, the lawyers approached me to discuss an issue that had surfaced. An employee in accounts payable had mentioned a potential problem to the investigative team. Mark Johnson, the AP clerk and legacy Zen employee, told the team that a few years back, a new and unfamiliar vendor, Techtronic, had been entered into the accounts payable system. As it was Mark's job to input new vendors, he had searched the entry forms folder for Techtronic but found nothing. He asked his fellow clerks if they knew anything regarding the company, but no one did. Instead of continuing his inquiry, Mark rationalized that Techtronic must be an old vendor they had just started using again.

A few months after Mark's initial discovery, something else unusual occurred. Often, manufacturing companies, CheapJeans included, outsource the printing and mailing of checks to pay vendors. They will give a certain company their vendor master list, contact information, payment details, etc., and then the company will print and distribute the checks. Recently, a few checks were returned to CheapJeans due to missing information on the vendor master list. They were payable to Techtronic.

Mark wasn't quite sure how to handle these returned checks, so he asked his boss, Brent Dobbins, for direction. Brent told him to just leave the checks with him and that he would "take care of it." This became routine. As Techtronic checks were returned each month, Mark would leave them on Brent's desk.

The investigative team also learned from the interviews that Brent had recently been working strange hours. Several employees mentioned that he was at the office unusually late at night and on weekends. The staff had offered to help him on multiple occasions, but he refused any assistance. To some, Brent seemed detached from the day-to-day accounting functions, as if he was working on a special project. Issues that had once concerned him in the past were no longer of importance.

Next the investigative team created forensic images of multiple computers from individuals deemed key custodians, which included Brent Dobbins, those who had regular contact with him, and several executive level employees (including myself as CFO). They needed to review electronic evidence for those whom Brent supervised and those who supervised him.

Around this time, a forensic accountant, John Anderson, who worked exclusively with electronic evidence, joined the investigation. John spent a few days with our IT department to gain a better understanding of the IT infrastructure, focusing specifically on the storage of e-mails and the transition of electronic data for the Jacksonville plant during the acquisition.

After completing the interviews, the investigative team created an extensive list of search terms based on relevant words, account numbers, and other data deemed potentially important. The documents that John had retrieved were filtered and revised based on the search terms, and placed into one of three categories: relevant, potentially relevant, and not relevant. Using this methodology, thousands of documents and e-mails were sifted through until only a small pool of pertinent information, which necessitated further action, remained.

The point of the e-mail review was to uncover any possibility of collusion between the perpetrator and a fellow employee. The investigative team at CheapJeans scoured through thousands of e-mails to identify any individuals who may have or should have known that improper activity was occurring. Oftentimes, e-mail is the best source of information regarding employee relationships, tensions at the company, and the general tone at the top of an organization. The team found no instances of collusion.

The forensic accountants performed an analysis of the accounts-payable accrued balance as of December 31. In order to understand the balance, they requested a detailed listing of all the journal entries that had been posted to the account throughout the year.

The accountants began their analysis by isolating activity for a one-month period. They reviewed the support documentation for each journal entry posted to AP accrued in that month, and they were surprised by what they found. Expecting to see an approved journal voucher and supporting documentation, they instead found a system-generated printout containing the journal entry that had been posted. The majority of entries had no approval or detail attached.

The accountants requested a system list of all journal entries posted to the account. The list should have the following information: transaction date, date posted, time posted, amount, description, and the individual who entered it into the system. After reviewing the requested information, a pattern emerged. Each month, a few standard entries would be posted to the account and then subsequently reversed the following month. They appeared to be standard AP accruals, and when the accountants went back to the journal-entry support file, they had the proper documentation attached.

At the end of each month, another series of journal entries were posted to the account. These were manual and entered by Brent Dobbins. They contained high-dollar amounts, usually round numbers (i.e. 450K). The entries were also unusual in that they were debits to AP accrued and credits to cost of goods sold.

The investigative team, our internal auditors, Bill, and I gathered together in a conference room in order to better understand the impact of all this. We wanted to understand why Brent Dobbins could have been making these monthly manual journal entries. We began our discussion by discussing the journal entries for a typical purchase using a standard cost system. It was clear that accounts payable accrued should have a zero balance at the end of each sale. The amount accrued each month should be reversed as the actual amounts due are either added to accounts payable or paid during the period. However, we had a large debit balance.

Bill suddenly spoke up. "I think I may know what's going on here."

He explained to the group that materials costs had been rising at some of the other plants, but not at Jacksonville. Bill had found Jacksonville's ratio to be unusually steady in the past year. When he asked Brent about it, Brent launched into a complaint about the standard cost-accounting system and how he didn't feel it was reporting the correct variances. In light of these hundreds of manual journal entries, Bill began to wonder, "Was it really possible that Brent had been manipulating the balances in these accounts?"

The impact of the manipulated entries decreased AP and decreased the cost of goods sold. As a result, it appeared that costs were not rising and the revenue was higher than it should have been.

Dinner with a Thief

After a few busy weeks, the investigative team asked me to set up an interview with Brent Dobbins. I arranged the meeting in a neutral setting, a local restaurant's private room.

According to the team, Brent came to the interview alone; he was friendly and smiling. They began by asking him to explain the manual journal entries he had made each month. A few specific entries posted recently were placed on the table in front of Brent to refresh his memory. He shook his head and responded that he couldn't recall any specific details. They showed him more recent items. Again, Brent shrugged his shoulders and held fast to ignorance. The lawyers tried to press him on his responses, but to no avail. He told everyone at the table that he was overworked and just simply couldn't remember.

The team asked Brent about Techtronic. They had been able to trace the payments made by CheapJeans to the rogue company, and coincidentally the deposits were made at the same bank Brent Dobbins used. The team also had determined which employee had entered Techtronic into the vendor system; again, it was Brent Dobbins. In addition, the review of electronic evidence had found a Techtronic invoice in the My Documents folder on his computer. When first questioned about Techtronic, Brent told the team that it was a standard vendor, first at Zen and then at CheapJeans. However, as the evidence was slowly presented to Brent, he began to backpedal and change his story. Eventually, he admitted that Techtronic was his company and that he was using it to steal money from CheapJeans.

After Brent's confession regarding Techtronic, the investigative team searched extensively for any other areas where Brent may have misappropriated funds. They verified every other vendor on the master list over a period of weeks. The team also performed an evaluation of Brent's expense reimbursements; another place where he had access to cash. His office was searched and the documents on his computer reviewed in extensive detail.

The final conclusion reached by the investigative team was that Brent extorted money from CheapJeans through his singular fraudulent disbursement scheme only. The total damage amounted to approximately $100,000.

Take It to the Grave

The team had a hypothesis to explain the errant journal entries in accounts payable. The theory related to Bill's discussion with Brent regarding the increasing materials costs, although Brent had never confirmed his intentions. The team thought that Brent had been concerned when the costs were increasing and that he could have believed the system data was incorrect, given his long-term experience in the industry. Brent might have made these unusual journal entries, debiting AP accrued and crediting a material expense account, in order to hide the increasing costs from management. The effect of the journal entries decreased the material costs and decreased accounts payable. As the costs continued to increase, Brent had to make more and more of these unusual journal entries. Or Brent might have been simply overwhelmed by his new cost accounting responsibilities and wasn't comfortable admitting it to his new employer.

The investigative team found it difficult to determine if the two areas of misconduct were linked. It was possible that Brent had made these journal entries to prevent the corporate officers from inspecting the unexplained variances. Perhaps Brent was concerned that they would discover Techtronic and ask questions. However, it was also possible Brent was simply overwhelmed and didn't want to ask for help or admit defeat. Regardless of Brent's intentions, the investigative team needed to ensure that CheapJean's financial statements were correct.

Due to the quantity of postings by Brent each quarter, the accountants decided that tracing each one was not the best method for determining the appropriate account balances. With so many entries and no clear indication of which ones were appropriate and which were not, it could have taken months to get to the bottom of the matter. CheapJeans wanted to get their financial statements filed on time, and this debacle presented a serious roadblock.

Instead, the accountants decided to rebuild the balance sheet based upon available third-party documentation for each account balance. For example, if an amount remained in the balance of any account at year-end, they required third-party support for that amount. If no support was available, the amount was written off. In this manner all amounts on the balance sheet were eventually 100% supported. In the end, a charge of approximately $4 million hit the income statement that year to properly record the accounts Brent had manipulated.

Lessons Learned

As CFO, I learned a lot about effective internal controls and corporate oversight from this investigation. Under our old system, Brent was able to enter vendors into AP and to approve payments. We were too lax with our passwords for the accounting system. Most employees simply taped their passwords on their desk.

I also learned that we should have more effective oversight for each plant. We need to review the plant controllers more carefully and have a complete understanding of their day-to-day operations. They should have surprise visits from the corporate office and spontaneous audits of their books and records.

Recommendations to Prevent Future Occurrences

At the end of the engagement the investigative team provided us with the following suggestions:

Proper Controls

The controller should not be permitted to write and process journal entries without a second-level sign-off before the entry is processed. Proper controls should be implemented to create a system of checks and balances in order to prevent fraud.

Review

Corporate or internal audit should review a list of nonstandard manual journal entries each quarter. These entries should require sign-off approval.

Maintain the Records

A company should establish and follow a clear policy for the retention of documentation supporting the accounting records. That way, should an error or incident occur, the path to correct the problem will hopefully be straight-forward.

Education

Employees should receive the proper education regarding the appropriate steps to take when confronted with coworkers' actions that seem unusual or suspicious.

About the Author

Amy Cron, CFE, CPA, has spent the past seven years working in fraud and forensic accounting. Ms. Cron specializes in internal investigations and financial statement restatements.

CHAPTER

36

Superhero Syndrome

HATITYE ZHAKATA

Preston "Superman" Dudley had a well-known fetish for electronic gadgets and a penchant for expensive things. At age 33, he was successful. His efforts helped contribute to the expansion of Fast Brands Inc., the company where he worked. In addition to his business savvy, he was an accounting software whiz and knew the system very well. The company rarely called upon the manufacturer's technical support team, as Preston would offer to solve any problem of that sort.

"Superman" Dudley was handsome and confident. His 6-foot-tall frame, glowing brown eyes, and charm made him a hit not just with the ladies but with everybody. His great sense of humor endeared him to everyone he met. Legend has it that this "knight in shining armor" could turn any female into his *chéri amour*.

While he claimed to be a model family man, Preston exhibited a flawed—if not troubled—behavior. In addition to his wife and their nine-year-old son, he also had two mistresses, one with whom he had a three-year-old son. Perhaps then it was not a surprise that he also had a tumultuous relationship with his immediate family.

His eldest son attended one of the most expensive junior schools in the country. Preston and his wife had a house in an up-market part of Nairobi, Kenya, with a state-of-the-art security system, tennis court, and swimming pool. Furthermore, their property was undergoing major renovations. A jacuzzi was being added, as well as two extra bedrooms and a second lounge. He seemed to be living well for someone earning less than $30,000 (equivalent to approximately US$56,000) per year. His wife made an annual salary of less than $10,000 (US$35,000) per annum as an administrator for a manufacturing company. Their lifestyle far exceeded their humble backgrounds, where their parents had to work very hard to make sure the basics were provided.

This fairy tale turned tragedy dates back to when Preston joined Fast Brands as a trainee manager at age 23. He swiftly developed an intricate knowledge of the firm's accounting system, openly boasting that he knew more about it than the manufacturer's technical support team. Arrogance would ultimately cause him to turn to dishonesty. Before long he had risen through the ranks of the firm to become one of its key employees.

Upon completion of his training, Preston was promoted to managing director for one of the firm's operations in Nairobi. Forever smiling and pleasant, he had a good sense of humor and was treated like a hero by his coworkers and superiors. When they had problems with the accounting software, their computers, or any other aspect of their work, "Superman" Dudley would come to their rescue.

He was extremely hardworking and, in later years, became more concerned with his job than anything else. According to his colleagues, he associated with very few people outside of the office. Juggling long hours and a colorful private life kept him busy.

Trusted and very much loved by his employer, Preston was treated as one of their own in this family-run business, which grew from a small operation to one spanning several countries. Fast Brands is a general retailer of major fast-moving consumer goods brands with an interesting and exciting portfolio of products. Its leading brands of food and household detergents have strong reputations and are popular worldwide. New distribution agreements allowed this relatively small company to rapidly expand where previously not popular or available.

Founded in 1985 in South Africa, the company's operations started selling various food products like sea food, condiments, and soft drinks. By 1991 its portfolio had increased to also include nonfood items such as toilet paper, and they continued to add new products over the next decade and a half. Using this business model, Fast Brands managed to successfully develop its operations into four other countries by the end of 2005, but its headquarters remained in South Africa.

The business's income grew from under $50,000 per year to several million. Revenue escalation and a 300-strong workforce were a signal of its increasing market presence and dominance.

While expanding exponentially, the company remained firmly under family control. Given such a close-knit environment, it was difficult to imagine that any sort of deception would occur. It was this trusting outlook, however, that would ultimately lead to the subsequent fraud.

When in Doubt, Ask

One early morning in June, Carmella Brooks, an alert employee in the accounts department, discovered an anomaly during a routine accounting of the preceding week's sales. Damaged frozen vegetables previously written off had been reinstated into the company's inventory system. Carmella thought this discrepancy was strange given that the merchandise had been thrown away about six months prior.

She sent an e-mail to the managing director, "Superman" Dudley, requesting an explanation. Preston did not respond directly to the e-mail. All Carmella received from Preston was a phone call: "Don't worry. Leave it to me. I will sort it out." This was suspicious, given that Preston always told his staff to write business matters down—preferably in e-mails—so that an audit trail was maintained.

This was the last time Carmella heard or said anything about the matter. That is, until the company's external auditors came for the annual audit in July. Because Carmella indicated to the auditors that there had been an anomaly relating to the company's merchandise, they compared the physical count results and the accounting records. It soon became apparent that the quantities in the accounts were inflated. For instance, due to the perishable nature of some of the products, the company had a maximum limit on how much it could hold in its cold rooms at any given time. The auditors assessed the quantities recorded in the accounts and immediately realized that the number listed was more than the maximum permitted. As the audit progressed, they also discovered that the value of the debtors was also inflated. For example, some of the company's customers who always settled their accounts on time were recorded as being in arrears. In some cases, the value of what customers owed was well in excess of their credit limits. Everybody was perplexed. The inconsistencies were too significant to be simple errors and the only person who could provide the answers was "Superman" Dudley.

Call to Duty

Fast Brands' directors were then alerted of the problems by the company's auditors. A meeting was arranged by the board of directors at the Nairobi headquarters, and there Preston was asked to explain to the directors and the two audit-engagement partners the business's present financial position and why the books of accounts were such a mess. He could not provide satisfactory answers and only managed to point out that they could be a result of errors. The directors felt that there was more to the story.

They suspected that Preston had misappropriated company funds and that the false accounting was an attempt to cover his tracks. "There's no way that simple errors could lead to such huge discrepancies," the operations director, Grant Chadway, said to the others after Preston had left the meeting.

The group chief executive officer, Troy O'Donnell, also suspected that the cunning Preston would have gone to great lengths to eliminate evidence. Preston was very intelligent and would certainly cover his tracks if he was indeed involved in any wrongdoing. Therefore, it was agreed by the board of directors that a computer forensic audit would need to be conducted as soon as possible in order to obtain as much evidence as possible.

I was relaxing at home on a sunny late Friday afternoon in September when I received a phone call from Troy asking me to conduct a computer forensic audit as part of a wider investigation. "Is it possible for information that has been deleted from a computer by a user to be recovered?" he asked.

I responded with a cautious "yes," adding that this could not always be guaranteed as there were software programs that could ensure that files were permanently erased from the hard disk drive. Furthermore, the files could be overwritten by new files saved onto the hard disk drive or they could be damaged, in which case the best hope is to try to reconstruct them. I could tell from the tone of Troy's voice and the ensuing response that he was excited.

"Well then, how soon can you come and help us?" he asked. "We have a very big problem at our firm and we urgently need your help."

"I will be able to come in anytime after Wednesday," I responded.

The following Wednesday morning, my assistant, Nelson Trent, and I packed our bags and flew from Harare, Zimbabwe, to Nairobi, where we were to stay for the next five days.

The Computer Made Me Do It

We landed at Jomo Kenyatta International Airport. The city was experiencing a lot of growth after several decades of underdevelopment. The streets were filled with people—some shopping, others on their way to work, and others just lurking about.

Upon arrival at the company's premises we met the company's directors. Grant, the operations director, took us on a sightseeing tour. From the lovely and spacious single-story administration offices we went to the warehouse, where many people worked. Forklifts moved inventory, groups of people conversed, and shouts were being tossed around the shop floor.

"This is our small warehouse," he said of their giant warehouse, which was packed to the hilt with a wide array of products such as fish, pet food, chocolates, soft drinks, and mineral water.

"If this is what you call small, could you please show me large?" I quipped as we both chuckled. I was thoroughly impressed with the firm and its efficiency.

We then convened briefly to discuss where we were to work, what was expected of Nelson and me, and so on. In addition to Grant, the group CEO, Troy O'Donnell, and the finance director, Marshall Courtney, were also present. My assistant and I were expected to perform a data recovery exercise on five computers considered key to the investigation. Depending on the files recovered, the scope of the investigation would then be expanded to include other computers. Nelson and I were also to reconstruct recovered files that were damaged. Once this was done, the findings obtained from the ensuing file analysis would then be compiled into a single report to provide supporting evidence for the fraud charges leveled against Preston Dudley.

During the meeting the directors indicated that, due to the substantial amount of evidence that he had misappropriated company funds, criminal charges had already been filed against Preston and a docket opened by the police's criminal investigation department about three weeks earlier. They hoped that the police would arrest him before he was alerted to the fact that he was under investigation and absconded. As we were sitting in the meeting, the police department phoned to confirm that "Superman" Dudley had just been arrested that morning on fraud charges and had been placed in remand prison. "Well, that's good news!" I exclaimed.

After concluding the cheerful meeting with the directors, we left for the auditors' offices, which are situated on the first floor of a breathtaking skyscraper. After introducing ourselves and breaking the ice with some small talk, we got down to business.

We discussed the auditors' progress. They had completed the inventory count and examined the supporting documentation relating to inventory and debtors. During the investigation, Preston had been on leave.

Their analysis revealed that, while the quantities of inventory were inflated, the prices per unit were accurate. Furthermore, the company's customers did not owe as much as the accounting system reflected. In some cases customers were said to owe amounts that they had in fact paid, and in other cases they were said to owe amounts for inventory they never ordered. As expected, the amounts of cash in hand and those at the bank were far less than they should have been. What immediately came to mind was that Preston had inflated inventory and debtors' balances in order to compensate for the cash he had misappropriated. That way the balance sheet would "balance." Initial indications were that he had been doing this for at least a couple of years and that the losses totaled $600,000.

Depending on the particular circumstances, Preston would "model" his misappropriation in Microsoft Excel either before or after taking the cash from the company. This enabled him to see the effect his fraudulent activities would have on the firm's financial statements *before* capturing the data on the firm's accounting system. That way he would ensure that the data he was entering on the accounting system accurately concealed his fraud.

In order to further cover his tracks, Preston used his computer and the portable document format (PDF) to alter supplier invoices sent to him via e-mail. Essentially, he would inflate the quantities of inventory and thus the total amount to be paid to the suppliers and the tax authorities in sales tax and customs duty for the imported products. In addition, he sometimes used an invoice template to generate false supplier invoices. It is suspected he had obtained this from one of his two mistresses because she worked for one of the company's suppliers.

He would then submit these false invoices with the inflated amounts to the accounting department. By inflating the amount of the "purchases," he could take more cash out of the business while at the same time providing supporting documentary evidence for the inventory "purchases."

The auditors next examined the amount of loss the tax department had suffered with regard to sales tax and import duties on the imported inventory.

The company's external auditors and I agreed to share the information that each side would obtain from its investigation. They would give us regular feedback of their audit findings and I would give them feedback on the information recovered from the computers that Preston used. We were primarily interested in material that would provide further evidence for the auditors' findings and would provide vital clues as to where he could have possibly laundered his ill-gotten gains.

Nelson and I were assigned to recover all the other files from the desktop and laptop that Preston used prior to his departure, including those that had been deleted. Furthermore, we were to examine three other computers, one of which Preston had used in previous years. The other two were used by the accounts department.

First we created images of the hard disk drives of the aforementioned computers in order to preserve their evidence and to enable us to perform the second step of our operation. Once that was completed, we performed the data recovery exercise using AccessData's Forensic Toolkit computer forensic software, endeavoring to recover those files that we suspected Preston had deliberately deleted from his computer's hard drive. In the process, we also tried to obtain those files that might have been damaged or corrupted and reconstruct them.

When we completed the data recovery exercise, Nelson was finished with his duties and the rest of the assignment was left to me. I analyzed all the files that we had recovered, which included Microsoft Word, Microsoft Excel, Microsoft Outlook, and text files. I compiled my findings into a report that highlighted the areas that were of concern to me and provided evidence to address the concerns that had been highlighted by the company directors and auditors.

Fraud Revealed

My findings revealed that, unknown to his superiors, Preston also operated business ventures such as automobile sales and a supermarket. There were Microsoft Excel spreadsheets indicating in great detail each company's purchases, sales, and operating expenses. In addition, I found e-mail communications between Preston and his sister, Sharon, who was also his business partner, discussing matters relating to the ventures. While these may have accounted for some of his wealth, it was my opinion that these operations were too small to adequately account for his lavish lifestyle. In any case, there were questions as to where he had obtained the capital to start these activities.

True, he might have obtained the capital from family, colleagues, and friends. However, when this was considered in the aggregate context of his age, background, and life in general, it became clear that there was no legitimate way—unless he had won the lottery—that he could have amassed so much wealth.

I also came across evidence to support the claim that he had two offshore bank accounts, both of which were in the United Kingdom's Channel Islands. While we did not recover any electronic bank statements, the evidence was enough to ensure that we could obtain the information that we required from the relevant authorities. Preston had typed letters to the offshore banks requesting that money be transferred to the accounts of his wife and sister. When applying for the visas to go on holiday in North America, he referred to these bank accounts to cite evidence of his ability to finance the trips.

While it was known that he had gone on holiday with his family and visited North America, the files that we recovered revealed just how lavish the trip was. He sent e-mails to the various hotels confirming reservations and to travel agents booking plane tickets. His family stayed at five-star hotels throughout their holiday. One particular hotel room cost in excess of $3,000 per night. Taking into account the hotel room bills, the cost of plane tickets, visa application fees, and other expenditure such as shopping, this trip alone could have cost anywhere up to $40,000.

Preston also had file deletion software installed onto the company's computers, which he used. I suspect that after having completed his misdeeds, he would use the file-deleting software to destroy documents that could have proven his fraudulent activities.

From the files that we recovered, it appeared that his rationale for defrauding the company was that he was overworked and underpaid. Of particular interest was a letter addressed to the group CEO, but never sent, that stated Preston's grievances. Preston highlighted how he had been loyal to the company for close to a decade and was disappointed that he did not receive the recognition he deserved. He was unhappy and said he earned half of what his counterparts in the company were being paid. Furthermore, he indicated that he was carrying an unfair burden because his operation was understaffed, forcing him to carry out additional duties to compensate.

Indeed, he even managed to convince his coworkers that he was entitled to the money he was taking when he asked the cashier to give him cash or transfer funds to his accounts whether these were offshore or otherwise.

Due to his authority, nobody questioned Preston's instructions. The accountant, Norton Lake, told me: "Preston would simply ask me to transfer money into his bank accounts. I thought that these amounts were either his salary or bonuses he was entitled to. On occasion he told me it was reimbursement for the company expenses he had paid with his own money, such as air tickets, fuel expenses, hotel bills for overnight out-of-town accommodation, and so on." The cashier, Marian Cook, was similarly convinced: "I thought he was entitled to the funds he was asking for."

During the interviews I conducted with the various members of staff, there were hints made to the effect that Preston might have had a drug problem. Indeed, Carmella pointed out that during his last days at the organization Preston "was not himself." "He had severe mood swings and appeared extremely stressed, exhausted, and depressed," she said. "He was at times lethargic. His memory was failing him and even his decision making became questionable. This was far from the energetic, decisive, confident, and eloquent Preston that everybody knew. When I asked him if everything was OK, he said he was fine." While all of this could have been attributed to Preston simply being overworked, what I believe lent credence to the drug suspicions was that he had been previously able to cope with the pressure of the job. I also suspected that in the final days leading to the unearthing of the fraud, the stress of trying to cover up the fraud and the prospect of being caught had gotten to Preston.

As someone on a salary of less than $30,000 per annum and with many responsibilities, including two kids, two mistresses, and a wife, he certainly could not afford a drug habit.

Interviews with Marian and Carmella revealed another startling fact, which was that Preston knew the other employees' computer passwords and they knew his passwords. This stemmed from the employees' reliance on Preston's assistance when they had problems with their computers or the accounting system and clearly also emanated from the lax internal controls. Since he was the managing director, he had the keys to all the doors. Therefore, there was nothing to stop him from accessing the computers after normal working hours or on weekends. Above all, he was the boss and nobody dared to question or doubt his decisions.

I produced my final report in October of that year, just over a month after starting the investigation in early September. Acting on the advice of the criminal investigation department's detectives, Preston's lawyers indicated that they would like to meet with us in order to negotiate an out-of-court settlement. On a Tuesday morning about two weeks after the release of the report, I received a phone call from Grant, Fast Brands' operations director. We were due to meet Preston's legal team on a Thursday morning in mid-November at the police station where Preston was held. In light of the overwhelming evidence against their client, this was the most sensible action for Preston's lawyers to take.

On Wednesday, a day before the meeting, I returned to Nairobi. Upon arrival, I met the company's management, auditors, lawyers, and the investigating officers, who briefed me on the progress of the investigation. Further evidence in the form of falsified invoices and tax documents had been found by the auditors, indicating the full extent of Preston's misappropriations. Preston indicated, through his lawyers, that he took responsibility for the missing company funds but would not admit to stealing them. We agreed that we would make our way to the venue of our meeting with Preston and his lawyers the following day.

The next morning, after leaving Fast Brands' premises, we proceeded to the police headquarters. As we approached the busy reception area, we immediately met the chief investigating officer, Mason Tennyson, who took us to the third floor of this large complex.

The building is situated in the middle of the city. One could still smell the fresh green paint on the walls. We were led to the detective's office, which he shared with six others. These were fierce-looking guys, all at least within easy reach of the six-feet mark. *Menacing individuals*, I thought to myself.

The other parties finally showed up half an hour late. We went to a spacious boardroom, which was the complete opposite of where we had been waiting for Preston and his legal representatives.

It was my first time meeting Preston Dudley, but I had seen photographs of him on his computer. He was clad in designer-label blue jeans and a matching t-shirt. All were oversized and baggy and must have fit him in better days. Compared to the pictures, he seemed to have lost a lot of weight. I was expecting to see a much bigger figure instead of a skinny, frail young man. I wouldn't have recognized him if we had not been introduced. Clearly, prison life was taking its toll, and he hadn't even been there for three months.

As I greeted him, I noticed that he did not make any eye contact. I thought that in itself was a telltale sign of guilt. Throughout the proceedings he did not say a word and he held his head in his hands. At no point did he lift up his head except when we got up at the end of the meeting.

After about one and a half hours, we could not reach an agreement. Preston's legal representatives wanted us to drop all criminal charges against Preston in return for him paying back some of the money over two to three years. But we were only interested in him returning the full amount he misappropriated—nothing less. Furthermore, the state was not willing to drop the charges of tax evasion leveled against him.

Preston "Superman" Dudley is not so much the superman that people used to call him, given his bleak future. Facing charges of fraud and tax evasion, he will now be sentenced to a minimum of seven years behind bars.

His wife left him after she had had enough of his indiscretions. At the first sign of trouble, so did his mistresses.

Lessons Learned

Audit failures arose because the auditors relied on information that Preston provided, namely the documents that he had doctored in Microsoft Excel. Auditors and fraud examiners alike should examine source documents and the accounting system by themselves and verify the work of the people they are auditing or investigating. For example, they can contact the originating source of the documents, which in this case were the company's product suppliers.

The most valuable lesson I learned from this case was how the red flags and "traditional" hallmarks of a fraud can combine with the new dangers posed by today's proliferation of information and communication technology if its use remains unchecked or if it falls into the wrong hands. As fast as companies are willing to embrace technology, they should embrace the risks that come with it. The failure to do so is a major problem worldwide, but I have found it to be more so in developing countries where the appropriate expertise may not always be readily available.

Great strides have been made in terms of file encryption technology, particularly with the portable document file (PDF) format. However, as demonstrated in this case, such technology may not be tamper-proof against an individual determined to commit fraud. Corporations need to be aware of this threat when adopting any sort of information technology security.

This case also dispels the myth that small companies are not susceptible to fraud, and the loss in excess of $600,000 demonstrates the threat that fraud can pose to a company's survival. Indeed, it's a miracle that Fast Brands is still operating today.

Small and medium-size organizations face staffing challenges. In many cases these companies have to rely on one or a few individuals, which results in a lack of segregation of duties. Preston had unfettered access to the company's premises, computers, and accounting system, which provided him with ample opportunity to commit fraud.

Recommendations to Prevent Future Occurrences

Establish Internal Controls

"Superman" Dudley betrayed the family that had trusted him for 10 years with their company. Businesses need robust internal controls regardless of how well they think they know their employees. A system based on "trust" alone can lead to frauds of major proportions.

Update Controls as the Company Grows

What started as a small family-run business expanded into an operation spanning five countries, yet the company's internal control systems remained the same. It's important for firms to continuously improve and review their internal controls in order to ensure that they remain current with their changing circumstances. One of the best ways of doing this is to conduct the Association of Certified Fraud Examiners' fraud prevention checkup annually.

Hire Experts Who Can Assess Fraud Risks

Furthermore, it is imperative for corporations to engage the appropriate expertise on a continuous basis to advise them of the risks they face and how to mitigate them.

Monitor All Employees

Overreliance on one individual must be avoided at all costs. In the event that reliance must be placed heavily on one person, that individual's work should be monitored closely. Preston succeeded in defrauding the firm for two years because there were no checks and balances. There is no substitute for vigilance.

About the Author

Hatitye Zhakata graduated from Newcastle Business School with a Bachelor of Arts degree in accounting. He worked for Ernst & Young Zimbabwe in a dual role as a forensic financial investigator and risk management consultant. He currently operates his own consulting firm, which has a portfolio of clients in various industry sectors.

Stealing for the Sale

WILLIAM J. PEDERSON AND TIMOTHY M. STRICKLER

People said Max Pruss looked like Gordon Gecko from the movie *Wall Street*—fifty-something, with slicked-back hair and brown eyes. As CEO, his career soared. Max was easygoing and friendly. Employees liked him. He treated them to lunches, took them on excursions, and even offered loans to some. After years of struggling to sell his ideas and build up the business in which he was invested, Pequod LLC, the place was finally running itself. Max relaxed in his office while his controller handled most of the day's details using a system he helped to design and program. Satisfied with the company's financial status, Max felt he had achieved his goals—visibility, control, and financial security.

He decorated his office with the trappings of his personal and professional successes. The wall across from his desk displayed underwater pictures of him and his family on their recent Caribbean vacation, along with a mountaintop group photo from a ski trip out West. Community award plaques and various certificates of merit hung on another wall. From his office, he could look down from his building at his new Porsche Boxster S in the parking lot. Max had a nice income from Pequod, both from salary and his 49% interest. He had only one more bridge to cross before retirement—selling his portion of the company.

This sale would be the critical point he had worked for, the final step in his professional career. His position as CEO and his large ownership interest would guarantee the package of his dreams—a large cash buyout coupled with a nice consulting contract that would run for a few years. With this retirement vision, it was extremely important to maintain the company's profitability and to attract potential buyers. Max wanted nothing more than to have a nice earnings multiple or cap rate applied against last year's or last quarter's results. With these approaches, a single dollar in earnings became a multiple-dollar increase in the sales price, an increase that would ultimately find its way to his pocket.

Pequod LLC was a small company that financed automotive insurance premiums for individuals with below-average credit histories and, often, less-than-perfect driving records. An entire industry is built around drivers of this sort. In many cases, insurance agents are located close to the Department of Motor Vehicles. That way, if someone is in negotiations to secure an automotive registration or to retain (or obtain) the privilege of operating a vehicle, the person can quickly and conveniently purchase his or her insurance, often with financing and interest.

With about 50 employees, Pequod did business in only one state, and it was regulated by that state's banking commission because it was a finance company. It financed thousands of policies each year, with total premiums of $50 million annually. Because interest rates ranged from 19% to 24% before fees, the profitability prospects for Pequod were excellent. Its favorable history allowed the company to effortlessly fund its operations. In fact Pequod was generally borrowing at prime plus 2%. Most of the staff answered the phones to set up accounts, respond to inquiries, or follow up on payments due.

The premium financing process for Pequod was fairly simple. An agent first provided an insurance estimate to a client. Once a quote was accepted, the customer completed a credit application. The premium quoted was used as the basis for the financed amount. The agent then collected 15% of the premium up front, usually in cash, certified check, or money order. Next the agent contacted Pequod and either faxed or e-mailed the application along with a wire transfer of the funds received. Pequod paid 10% to the insurer for the policy (also by wire) and sent a payment book to the insured. The remainder of the premium was billed to Pequod by the insurance carrier. Pequod then paid the balance of the premium only after receiving the first monthly payment from the insured. Virtually all financings were for a period of 12 months. If the insured didn't pay on time, Pequod contacted the insurer to cancel the policy (the application the insured signed allows this). The insurer then refunded any unearned premium to Pequod.

Pequod was profitable on paper. In spite of the high credit risk associated with its clients, the company developed internal procedures that ensured profitability. These procedures kept the company ahead of defaults by always requiring that some portion of the premium payment be submitted in advance of the premium being earned. For example, 15% of the premium was always due up front; the first payment was due a month later. If the first payment was not received within 15 days of the due date, Pequod would cancel the policy. Since the 15% initial payment would cover roughly two months of premium, canceling at 45 days (30 days plus a 15-day grace period) kept Pequod ahead of delinquency. If subsequent premium payments were not received, the policy would be canceled and the unused premium refunded. The key to profitability was to ensure that premium payments were always received ahead of when premiums were earned. When this occurred, the company was always paid.

Crucial to the process of staying ahead of the insured were the procedures and proprietary accounts receivable system developed in large part by Max Pruss. The timing and protocols for Pequod's processing of accounts were paramount to the company's success.

A Check for Christmas

The fall of Enron and subsequent implementation of the Sarbanes-Oxley Act of 2002 induced numerous fallouts in the audit industry. While much fanfare was devoted to new SEC reporting requirements and disclosures for public companies, some trickle-down effects impacted even smaller, privately held companies. Pequod was audited by a regional firm that reacted to some of the changes in Generally Accepted Auditing Standards by modifying its audit procedures to include a review of cash accounts regardless of their relative materiality to the balance sheet. In this case, the auditors chose to examine the Pequod's petty cash account, which revealed a check cut to cover the expense of the company Christmas party. The check was written for $5,000, payable to "cash," and was both signed and endorsed by Max Pruss. Additional analysis of the account exposed several other checks payable to "cash" or "Max Pruss." Because these were not made out to specific vendors, the auditors began making inquiries: first as to why not, and second as to how petty cash was being funded. Max indicated that a number of checks sent to insureds as refunds had not been cashed. He thought it would be appropriate to use these funds for a company party instead of keeping the money in Pequod bank accounts. This was the first indication of a problem. Questioning how accounts were kept in balance, and aware that Pequod would be subject to state escheat laws, the auditors began to look deeper.

Planes, Jewels, and Automobiles

It was determined that Max had been transferring unclaimed refunds back into the company and using these funds for company expenses for a number of years. Upon closer examination, the auditors found that a payee for a check from the petty cash fund was a local auto repair shop. Max admitted that his own car had been serviced and that he had issued a company check to pay for the service. The auditors were now concerned on several levels. Clearly, there were problems at Pequod. The auditors began by approaching the other owner of Pequod to discuss their findings and to suggest removing the CEO until an investigation could be conducted. Due to a conflict of interest with their own firm, the auditors recommended the services of our independent forensic firm, Stellar Services.

We began our investigation by first meeting with the auditors and counsel of the company. A review of the financial statements ensued, followed by interviews with various Pequod employees, and then ultimately, with Max Pruss. As these interviews proceeded, it became apparent that Max's activities extended far beyond issuing checks for company parties or repairs on his own vehicle. The interviews revealed a number of red flags. First, only a few individuals would work with Max each month to balance the accounts, excluding the controller. Furthermore, Max had direct access to the programs running at Pequod and would intervene from time to time if a call representative ran into a software glitch. He relied on a single individual when processing cash and performing bank reconciliations; if this individual was not in the office, the reconciliations were deferred until his return. Max was also known to be on the company system for hours each day, and no one knew why.

During his initial interview, we confronted Max with the checks he issued and with a high-level analysis of the refund account. He sensed the gravity of the investigation and cooperated fully. The way he frankly discussed ways he used customers' refunds for personal gain indicated he didn't realize the illegality of these endeavors. Max willingly divulged how he used his knowledge of the company's accounts receivable system to defraud customers.

Since Max assisted in the development of the company's system, he had the access necessary to alter the databases in which customer account data was stored. There were virtually no controls. The system wasn't password protected. There were no access restrictions for lower-level employees; anyone could manipulate an account. Cash was reconciled daily, but no one reviewed the actual transactions input on this basis. Customer account information was easily altered. This utter lack of controls made the company susceptible to fraud.

The auditors were correct to question why so many customer refunds were unclaimed. Not only did Max admit to not mailing many of these refunds, he also admitted to transferring refunds from one account to another in the company's computer system. Once a number of refunds were transferred to a single account, he would then issue a check from the account for his own personal use. For example, if five customers were each due a refund of $200, Max would transfer the money from each of these accounts into a sixth account, mark it as paid in the account from which it was taken, and then issue a check from the sixth account for $1,000 to his favorite ski lodge as a deposit for his upcoming vacation. Once the check was printed, he would then access the system again and change the payee name from the ski lodge back to the name of the customer, preventing anyone who was reviewing the bank reconciliation from noticing any outstanding checks. During his interviews, Max suggested that this might have happened five or six times in the preceding year.

Based on this information, we knew that we would need to review each refund check from the last several years to determine the extent of the fraudulent transfers. The procedure was simple but time consuming. We input each check the company had issued into a database (payee, date, and amount). This data was then compared to the company's own disbursement records. When the payee name did not agree between the two databases, we pulled the transaction for further investigation. This comparison found no less than 78 instances where the payee name had been changed by Max. Payees included jewelry stores, horse stables, vacation hotels, airlines, a veterinarian, auto repair shops, and even his home insurer.

Max's transfers, however, extended beyond covering some of his personal expenses. He would also transfer balances due as refunds to the company write-off account. Again, his full access to the company's systems enabled him to manipulate accounts without question and cover his tracks. While the theory of the finance company was to always be ahead of the premiums, the employees would not always adhere strictly to these procedures. To cover the write-offs that resulted from the underpaying customers on the books, Max would transfers refunds due to customers to the write-off account, thereby reducing or eliminating write-offs and establishing a false appearance of profitability for Pequod. Max's incentive was obvious: His annual bonus was based on performance (including profitability and write-offs). Not to mention the fact that Max sought to inflate the value of the company for its ultimate sale, which would fund his retirement.

Max undertook other methods to improve the financial statements of Pequod. For example, he reduced bad debt expenses by redepositing refund checks returned from bad addresses into other canceled accounts, ones that should already have been written off as bad debt expenses.

Max also accumulated stale checks (checks over six months old) and carried them over on his reconciliation statement instead of reporting them as unclaimed property subject to escheatment by the state. He then deposited these checks into the company's operating account and wrote checks payable to cash for the company and to himself for personal expenses.

Max wasn't able to commit his fraud schemes alone; he also enlisted the help of a few employees. As mentioned earlier, he treated the employees well, and they followed his orders without questions. When insurance policies were canceled, many times there was a refund check from the insurer. If the check from the insurer was greater than the balance owed by the customer, the customer would be due a refund; if the balance was less, there would be a write-off. Max Pruss directed employees, mainly one specific employee, to intentionally input the checks into the system for an amount greater than the actual check to cover the bad debt expense. Since regular refunds were input at rounded dollar amounts, he used a system to indicate what amount was added to cover the balance. One penny was tacked on when $100 was added, two cents for $200 and so on. He also had them input the transactions dated for the following Sunday, so they could easily be identified by Max later when he would reverse accounts-due refunds to cover the shortfall created and to make sure the daily cash reconciliations balanced.

To identify the bulk of the tampered transactions, we imported Pequod's system data into a database for analysis. While there were millions of records, each one included specific transaction codes listing its purpose. We merely had to establish a pattern to fit the adjustments Max had made and search for those transactions. For example, we determined that Max Pruss was using negative amounts for transactions with normally positive amounts (e.g., deposits of cash, checks, or money orders). All of these negative deposit transactions were identified, reviewed to verify that they were improper, and their totals then accumulated. We did this for several identified patterns including Sunday transactions and transactions that ended in certain decimal amounts. The individual transactions were generally small in amount, but the number of transactions identified for all years was in excess of 20,000.

As part of the investigative process, Pequod, its counsel, and Stellar were in regular contact with the state's regulatory authority. Conference calls were held weekly and reports regarding progress and findings were constantly circulated and updated. Because Pequod was licensed, it was critical to keep the regulators informed and satisfied in order to maintain operation. Pequod was forthright in its disclosures and provided the regulators with the ability to closely monitor operations through Stellar, so its license was not revoked during the investigative process.

Forfeiting the Farm

We determined that almost $3 million was diverted by Max Pruss over a period of three years. Pequod sent out thousands of overdue refund checks to the customers from whom Max Pruss stole. Where these refunds went unclaimed, the state was paid in accordance with applicable escheatment laws.

Time will tell whether or not Max will be formally prosecuted. In the meantime, he has been removed from his position as CEO and required to repay Pequod every penny. Further, he was forced to forfeit his ownership interest for virtually nothing. He resigned as the chapter president of one of the organizations to which he belonged and lost his company-leased Boxster S.

Lessons Learned

We learned that the perpetrator himself can be a valuable resource in fraud examinations. Max's contributions during the interview process were indispensable to our investigation. Although he would not admit to the extent of his activities, he did provide direction. The interview process was not a condemnation of his activities, but an open-ended discussion with a focus on what occurred and how. This nonthreatening angle likely persuaded Max to offer guidance in the investigation.

Recommendations to Prevent Future Occurrences

Implement Controls

Max Pruss did not actually need the money he appropriated from Pequod. He admitted to being driven by the challenge. The almost complete lack of internal controls—Max's full access to Pequod's system, books, records, check stock, and bank reconciliations—granted him ample opportunity to commit a fraud.

We recommended that Pequod implement a new set of internal controls. Checks and balances must be in place to allocate power. The system should be password protected, and the employees should be restricted to accessing only the portion of the system necessary for them to do their jobs. A random sampling of transactions should be tested daily, and any unusual transactions (i.e., negative cash or checks) should be flagged immediately for review. The daily processing functions must be separated properly to ensure that one person doesn't control the entire flow of cash.

Monitor Refunds

Refunds to customers could arise for a variety reasons, but the cause was usually for the cancellation of a policy due to nonpayment. Most of Pequod's customers assumed that if they stopped paying their premiums, they simply lost their insurance. But since Pequod endeavored to stay ahead of the premium, the customers would generally be due a refund. This was especially true for customers who stopped paying toward the end of the policy period. Since most clients were not aware that they would be due a reimbursement, they never complained about not receiving one, so red flags regarding refunds were never raised.

About the Authors

William Pederson, CFE, CPA, is an associate director with Protiviti, where his focus is on accounting and litigation issues.

Tim Strickler has been a financial consultant for nearly five years, working on many different types of cases involving fraud, bankruptcy, and litigation. He specializes in data extraction, compilation, and analysis. Tim became a member of the ACFE in March 2008.

CHAPTER

Do as I Say, Not as I Do

RICHARD WOODFORD

Daniel Lohman appeared at ease as he approached the speaker's platform. At the height of his professional career, Danny was preparing to instruct an audience of government financial managers and systems administrators on how to set up and maintain government-issued credit card accountability programs in their respective federal agencies. His appearance at this national conference was a real feather in his cap, especially since his presentation was based on his expertise in developing internal controls and the success of his policies for dealing with delinquent payments and unauthorized credit card transactions at his agency.

Government-issued credit cards were a recent improvement over the previous travel voucher/expense system. Federal employees could use the cards to pay for expenses incurred during official travel, including hotels, rental cars, and meals; they could even withdraw cash advances while on official business. The cards were issued in each employee's name, but the purchases were backed by the full faith and credit of the U.S. government. Even if the employee should be delinquent in making payments, the bank could ask Uncle Sam to garnish the employee's wages or otherwise make good on the debt.

Before mounting the speaker's platform, Danny reflected on his 15 years as a Certified Public Accountant in the trenches of the civil service. He started off his career as an auditor poring through tax filings and business receipts; then he worked as an internal auditor during the Enron and Worldcom scandals. Danny's perseverance and business sense were recognized with a promotion to project management. By heading more complicated financial systems, he gained a better perspective on the bureaucracy of the federal government and how it might be improved. He served at several different agencies, working on larger and larger financial projects and systems. He soon proved himself capable and tough enough for a position as branch chief over other teams of accountants. He was given the opportunity to develop a policy handbook for handling delinquent accounts in his department, and again his performance was impressive. After several years of success as a team leader, Danny had advanced as the senior accountant and head of payable accounts in the financial operations directorate for the Media Research Group (MRG). He had finally arrived at the top tier of management for a multibillion dollar public agency.

Although his counterparts were making three to five times more in the private sector, as a senior manager at the top of the General Pay Schedule (GS-15), Danny was earning a six-figure salary, equivalent to a one-star general. He had spent most of his adult life in government service as a supporting player, and now it was finally his turn to enjoy the spotlight.

There was just one problem: While Danny was brilliant at managing the government's finances, he was living from paycheck to paycheck at home. A single parent at age 57, Danny was funding the college tuitions of his four children as well as helping to support and raise a few grandchildren. Although his hair remained free of gray, Danny had cause for worry: His personal credit was stretched beyond the limit. Yet he was careful always to keep his personal affairs private.

Danny had boyish looks and an overabundance of nervous energy; he worked hard and was always on the go. Having risen through the ranks, Danny was still proving that he was willing and able to go the extra mile. Unlike many of his peers in senior management, Danny drove himself much harder than he did his staff, often showing up to work an hour earlier and staying an hour later than everyone else. Indeed, it was common for him to work weekends and holidays, especially near the end of a budget cycle or reporting period. Danny's favorite saying was "This job may be over, but the work is never done."

Danny's presentation at the credit card training conference was typical of his driven, no-nonsense attitude toward life; he advocated a fair and firm approach to dealing with employees who abused their government-issued credit cards. He described in detail how to set up transaction-monitoring systems, how to calculate and adjust credit card limits, how to block unauthorized transactions, and monitor and track delinquent accounts. Danny's graphs and charts showed how his garnishment policies and techniques had dramatically reduced the incidence of credit card abuse and delinquent payments by employees at MRG. At the end of his presentation, as the audience applauded, Danny allowed himself a brief, tight smile of satisfaction. His moment in the spotlight was deserved; still, he couldn't help but feel slightly apprehensive. He wasn't just an expert in detecting credit card abuse and debt delinquency, he was also an expert at hiding his own.

Often mistaken as a privately funded venture because of its corporate-sounding name, the Media Research Group is actually an independent federal agency that awards grants to individuals, educational institutions, and research companies for the advancement of public interest causes. As far as federal government funds are distributed, MRG is only a medium-size independent agency but still receives a multibillion-dollar annual appropriation. It employs about 800 technical and administrative staffers to monitor the progress of its grants and cooperative agreements. MRG also invites numerous academic experts and part-time technical reviewers who travel to Washington, D.C., to evaluate grant proposals and make the award decisions for MRG's highly sought after federal grants.

By all measures of effectiveness, MRG was performing well, with several "green lights" in the President's Management Agenda. MRG was one of the first public entities to establish itself as a model for fiscal management and accountability.

As an investigative attorney, I had been part of the MRG investigative group for a little over two years. Most of the work was standard internal investigations fare: padded vouchers, misstatements or falsifications of reports, employees misusing official resources, or grantees taking money and being unable to account for how it was spent. Every now and again, we received some interesting allegations through our confidential hotline. For every solid lead that the MRG hotline produced, there were usually several complaints that were hard to read, much less categorize. Some were half-baked, others were completely bogus. MRG received numerous hotline requests demanding immediate inquiries and investigations into the scandals of the faked moon landings, the water fluoridation conspiracy, and the Area 51/UFO cover up. Some hotline letters offered suggestions (with technical diagrams) on how a nationally funded program to provide aluminum foil helmets could protect the American public from satellite-based "thought probes." In tracking the ebb and flow of these hotline complaints, I noted that there was an apparent pattern of submissions that coincided with the lunar cycle: The high tide of unsigned, mailed complaints seemed to arrive within three or four days of the full moon. They were often handwritten, single-spaced, and richly detailed missives that were copied to multiple law enforcement agencies and congressional offices. Like most federal agencies, MRG maintained Freedom of Information and Privacy Act files, so even the most bizarre complaints and conspiracy theories ended up in a file somewhere.

Not Another Lunar Special

It promised to be another anticlimactic December day on the Monday morning after Christmas. I had just cleared away the last of the holiday tinsel from my cubicle when I received notice of a new preliminary investigative matter under the heading "Anonymous Complaint: Credit Card Misuse."

"Great," I thought. "Here's one that's going nowhere fast."

Like most federal employees, I had quickly learned that in D.C. the week between Christmas and New Year's Day is a time when very little substantive work is accomplished; Congress leaves town, courts are not in session, and many executive branch employees are burning up their "use or lose" annual personal days before the end of the calendar year. For the rest of the feds left in D.C., late December becomes a challenge to schedule any real work. You find yourself navigating a patchwork of holiday parties, religious observances, personal errands, and the two paid holidays.

Inwardly, I was relieved to see that this was an anonymous complaint, partly because there would be one less interview to try to schedule over the holidays on what was likely a dead-end case. I knew that in October, MRG auditors had issued their report on the agency's credit card programs and had found no irregularities, due in part to new policies that dealt with employees who abused their credit cards, policies that were conceived by a respected manager, Dan Lohman. If there were any anonymous complaints about MRG's credit card program, it was likely from a disgruntled employee who recently had his wages garnished. I speculated, "Here's another story of a hapless fed who claimed not to know it was improper to use their government-issued credit card to pay for tattoos." My calendar showed that the complaint had arrived on the full moon—another indicator that this unsigned letter was likely to be a red herring. Looking back, I couldn't have been more wrong.

I picked up the complaint file from our intake desk and noticed that there was a pink Post-It™ on the outer folder that read: "I found this letter under my door when I got back from leave. It looks like an investigative matter. Please see me if you have any questions, Tracy Trost."

Tracy had been the lead auditor on the MRG credit card audit. The envelope bore Tracy's name, yet the enclosed letter was addressed "To whom it may concern." The single white page was computer printed and double-spaced, predictably missing any clues as to the identity of the author. In part, it read, "Someone needs to take another look at MRG's credit card program records. When you do, you will find Daniel Lohman has been using his card for unauthorized personal items and cash advances for some time now; he's been delinquent for several months of payments and Mary

Corrigan in MRG senior management knows about these problems but refuses to take any corrective action.''

Initially, I was even more convinced that this tip was the work of a discontented employee trying to lob a grenade at MRG senior management. Then I started to think about the possible sources of this anonymous complaint. It was obviously not from someone external to MRG because the letter had been hand delivered under Tracy's door. It had to come from someone who knew about her role in the credit card audit, which program records were examined, and the audit results. The tone and language of the note were measured and concise and the details were specific. The fact that the complaint had not been delivered through the e-mail system suggested that the writer did not want to be traced back through his or her MRG computer. Even the envelope appeared to be hand typed and not addressed on a word processor. Suddenly, this complaint didn't feel like a lunar special, but more like the legitimate concerns of someone who was worried about keeping his or her job while exposing wrongdoing in the office.

Give Me the Raw Data

As an investigative attorney, I had seen cases where the whistleblower ended up on the receiving end of an investigation or inquiry and then went on to suffer retaliation, official reprisals, and even personal recriminations. Blowing the whistle is never a sure thing, even when the information being exposed is 100% accurate and the motives behind the revelations are pure. But before this preliminary matter became a full-blown investigation, I needed something besides the anonymous note to go on. The only other lead might be in the audit work papers of Tracy, or perhaps something that she had noticed but didn't add to the report.

Before talking to her, I asked myself what if everything in the anonymous note was true. Could Danny Lohman, the manager who designed MRG's highly touted government-issued credit card program, be abusing his own program for unauthorized purchases and cash advances? How could he be delinquent on his own payments without being detected in the recent audit or exposed by MegaBank, the financial institution that administered the credit card? Even if Danny was abusing his credit card and hiding his unauthorized transactions and delinquent payments, why would his supervisor, Mary Corrigan, allow it? Finally, I thought, how was I going to find support for any of these claims when the audit report on the MRG credit card program was clean?

A week had passed and all I had accomplished was posing what-if questions and confirming that the audit report had indeed positively reviewed MRG's explicit policies and procedures in administering the credit card program. I started to think that maybe the note was just what I had first suspected, an attempt to have two senior MRG managers fired. I needed to interview lead auditor Tracy so I could write up a recommendation for moving ahead or closing the matter.

Tracy was cooperative yet slightly mystified as to why we were spending any time on this tip. The answers to my what-if questions were all a resounding *no*—it wasn't possible that Danny had unauthorized credit card charges because those would have shown up on the monthly account spreadsheets. Dan's name never appeared on MegaBank's records or in the delinquency list during the three-month scope of the audit. Mary Corrigan was not directly interviewed at that time, but she had been present during the audit entrance and exit conferences, and no issues or concerns had been raised by anyone about Lohman or any other MRG staff abusing their credit cards. As the interview was completed, I was starting to think that I needed more red ink for my "case closed" rubber stamp.

While I was writing up Tracy's interview for a close-out recommendation, her words came back to me: "Danny Lohman's name and card charges *never came up* during the scope of the audit."

Like Peter Falk's Columbo, I went back to Tracy's office. "Just to clarify for my report, Lohman's name never appeared in the three months of credit card records?" I asked.

Tracy confirmed it. Then I asked one of the other questions that lingered during the what-if phase: "Who supplied you with the three months of MRG credit card records?"

Tracy blinked several times before answering, "Danny personally ran them for me from the MegaBank database."

"Did Danny ever have any unauthorized cash advances?"

Tracy looked a little crestfallen when admitting that there appeared to be one or two cash advances, but only for $20 each and both outside the three-month window that the audit was testing. She had discounted these minimal advances as immaterial oversights by Danny. Tracy reasoned that because he worked so many late nights and weekends, he must have withdrawn the funds after the bank had closed because they appeared to have been made at the MegaBank ATM inside the lobby of MRG's headquarters after normal working hours.

Suddenly, all my *what-if* questions had some plausible answers: If Danny was the sole supplier of all the credit card data for the audit team, then he was in a prime position to manipulate it prior to any examination. I learned from Tracy that "delinquency" was a term that MegaBank employees used to describe any credit card account that had gone unpaid for *60 days or more*. Given this insight, I saw how Danny could float his credit card payments for up to 59 days before raising any red flags at MegaBank or with MRG. Given the possibility that the first two elements of the anonymous allegations were plausible, I sought out access to the raw data from the MegaBank servers.

It took a while to obtain covert access to the raw data, partly because MegaBank wanted to refer me to the MRG agency contact, Danny. Once I got the information directly from MegaBank, it didn't take long to find that Danny had nearly two years' worth of personal expenses charged to his government-issued credit card. A simple comparison of Danny's authorized MRG travel records and the bank data showed that he had made improper charges or received unauthorized cash advances totaling $3,900. Most of Danny's charges were for basic staples: groceries, gas, or textbooks. The largest single cash advance was less than $300.

Danny had clearly altered MegaBank's credit card data. It was time to interview him to fill in the rest of the story. I was fortunate that another MRG attorney, Isabel Gregory, was available for Danny's interview. Although we felt that the records were a clear indication of his deception, we wondered what Danny would have to say.

The interview was a textbook example of how body language tells the tale before the perpetrator ever speaks. Danny looked like he hadn't slept the night before, his posture was slumped, his body angled toward the exit, and he was carrying a file folder that he placed away from him on the table. Once Isabel and I dispensed with our required preliminary introductions and had Danny acknowledge his statement of rights, we asked him if he knew why we was there. Heaving a sigh of relief, Danny said, "I guess it's about my credit card account and the audit records."

Over the next hour, he admitted that he had been using his card for personal items and cash advances for about two years. According to Danny, when he learned about the audit of MRG's credit card program, he was most concerned that his actions would be blown out of proportion and that the ensuing fuss would derail other financial programs that he was overseeing. Danny asserted that even though he made some late payments on the credit card, he was never delinquent (over 60 days in arrears). Furthermore, he suggested that some of the charges and cash advances might have been made by his children, who had a habit of borrowing his card. When we pointed out that any charges or cash advances made by his children would still be unauthorized purchases *and* a violation of the MRG policies, Danny looked stunned and incredulous that we were quoting his own policies back to him. He also freely admitted that Mary Corrigan was aware of his activities, and said that she didn't particularly care what he did with his personal affairs so long as the MRG financial systems were running smoothly.

Danny provided a typewritten statement that admitted the deletion of his own official credit card records from the data that he provided to the MRG auditors, as well as accounting for the charges and cash advances that we had identified as unauthorized. With Danny's sworn statement and the authenticated and altered records in hand, we were confident that we could find a U.S. attorney who would be interested in prosecuting this fraud case.

In Violation of Public Trust

Assistant U.S. Attorney Kirk Kennan listened intently to our case briefing, and asked three questions for clarification: How much money was involved? What was Danny's current status at MRG? What disciplinary actions, if any, was MRG planning to take against Lohman and/or Corrigan? Although the amount involved was less than $4,000, Danny was in a public trust position, and as he had been cited in trade publications as a model financial manager, the case was really more about upholding public integrity. After his confession, MRG replaced Danny as the agency credit card manager, and he was planning to resign from MRG. Mary Corrigan left MRG for a job in the private sector shortly after Danny provided his sworn statement regarding his abuse of the credit card while under her watch.

As it turned out, Danny's data manipulation fraud was the tip of the iceberg. Through an expanded reexamination of the unaltered credit card records, investigators found seven more cases of employees who made regular unauthorized purchases or cash advances. Danny was not only covering for himself; he was selectively deciding which MRG employees would be disciplined and which would get the carte blanche treatment. Ultimately, the seven other MRG employees were given administrative disciplinary actions ranging from oral reprimands to unpaid suspensions from duty.

Kennan initially thought that Danny's data deception would be too abstract to prove theft, wire fraud, computer intrusion, or obstruction of a federal audit. The dilemma was twofold: Technically there was no direct monetary loss to the government (Danny ultimately paid his credit card debts), and there was always reasonable doubt because possibly he had intended to provide unadulterated data and the computer files had been inadvertently corrupted during the file transfer to the audit team.

In the end, it was Danny's sworn admission and his defense attorney's advice that ended the dilemma: He agreed to plead guilty to one count of willfully destroying a government record, in violation of Title 18 U.S. Code, Section 2071(b), a felony. The case was on the federal district court docket.

At Danny's plea hearing, Judge S.P. Eschell stopped Danny in midsentence during his allocution with this statement: "Mr. Lohman, you took the money because you wanted something for nothing, isn't that true? That was money you weren't entitled to, and that, sir, no matter how you explain it, is stealing, isn't it? The fact that there was no permanent loss to the government doesn't excuse your actions, especially the abuse of the public trust that you were supposed to uphold."

Danny conceded that his deception amounted to stealing and then fell silent. His attorney finished by asking that Judge Eschell take into account Danny's years of honorable service and the many personal commendations that were entered on Danny's behalf.

Judge Eschell accepted Danny's guilty plea to destruction of an official record and sentenced him to 60 days of confinement, a $1,000 fine plus court costs, and two years' probation. As a matter of law, Danny's felony conviction included a permanent bar to any public employment in the future.

Lessons Learned

Danny's case classically illustrated the fraud triangle: He used the opportunity as the single point of failure in the data interface between MegaBank's servers and the MRG financial systems, he was motivated by his personal financial crises and his desire to keep it away from auditor scrutiny, and he rationalized that the deletion of his own credit card records was justified since he was actually helping MRG maintain its sterling reputation for financial management despite his own financial shortcomings.

The computer was paramount in Danny's data manipulation. He downloaded the monthly credit card data into an Excel spreadsheet, highlighted the sections of the spreadsheet that contained his records, and deleted all the entries that contained his monthly credit card charges. Ironically, Danny's deception might have gone undetected longer if he had only deleted his *unauthorized* monthly charges instead of all of his authorized charges. Recall the phrase that auditor Tracy Trost used: "Dan Lohman's name *never came up* in the credit card records." Yet, by being a frequent government traveler, Dan's credit card data should have been coming up on a regular basis. By deleting all the credit card entries associated with his name, he created a hole in the audit spreadsheet between "Lehman" and "Luzinski."

I learned something about making assumptions when it comes to nomenclature and terminology. In this case, "delinquency" had a specific trade meaning that was based on criteria set by MegaBank personnel. I initially assumed that the anonymous tip was bogus because, as I understood it, there were no delinquencies reported in the audit. In fact Danny knew exactly how long he could float his unpaid balances each month in order to stay off the 60-day delinquency list. Even when you think you know what a term or phrase means, it never hurts to ask for clarification. The answers might surprise you.

Another major lesson learned was that one should always ask the question: "What if these allegations are 100% true?" In this case, the anonymous tipster's information was correct: Danny was abusing his credit card, he was floating his card payments to MegaBank (carefully staying under the 59-day grace period), *and* he implicated his supervisor, Mary Corrigan, as being at least acquiescent in the matter.

An audit is only as good as the data being examined. In this case, the perpetrator guessed which records the auditor would be looking for and during what time period. It was an easy task for Danny to retrieve the raw data from MegaBank's servers and download it into formatted spreadsheets. By asking "what if," I eventually saw how it would be plausible for Danny to set up a system for detecting credit card abuse and yet be able to avoid being detected by that same system.

Finally, it helps to remember that audits are snapshots of "what was" and not "what is." Danny's deception was successfully hidden from the auditors, but someone in Danny's department had somehow seen the same raw credit card data that I eventually found. The whistleblower had figured out what Danny was doing with his credit card when he wasn't traveling to make presentations on how to discipline credit card abusers. He or she took the time to write and hand deliver a note, hoping that Danny's own abuse of the system would be exposed. And it was.

Recommendations to Prevent Future Occurrences

In the wake of Danny's resignation and conviction, MRG reviewed its government credit card programs and policies and made several changes to correct the internal control weaknesses that Danny had exploited.

Checks and Balances

Danny insisted that he alone would access the MegaBank database and begin the monthly processing of delinquent accounts. All the raw data was filtered through his computer without a second set of eyes to review it. After his fraud was revealed, I suggested that monthly processing of delinquent and unauthorized accounts be performed by at least two people.

Rotation of Duties

Danny's staff had never rotated work assignments, a factor that made Danny "invaluable" because he could fill in for any absent staffer. This put him in a position to inflict damage on the agency. After his fraud was discovered, work assignments were regularly rotated.

Random Spot Checks

Predictably, once the spot checks were announced, the number and amount of credit card cash advances across the board declined in one month.

Deactivating Credit Card Accounts for Infrequent Travelers

It was relatively easy to temporarily deactivate an account or to request a very low credit limit ($300); it made sense to place such controls on any MRG employees who only traveled once or twice a year. Why place temptation in the hands of employees who don't need a $10,000 credit limit?

About the Author

Richard F. Woodford Jr., J.D., CFE, is a regent and vice chair of the 2008–2009 Association of Certified Fraud Examiners' Board of Regents. Mr. Woodford's federal investigative experience includes public corruption, safety, ethics, and grant fraud cases. He is a veteran of the U.S. Navy and U.S. Naval Reserve. He works in Washington, D.C.

Cinderella: One Glass Slipper
Just Wasn't Enough

ANTONIO IVAN S. AGUIRRE

Hugh Calloway's marriage proposal to Alice Nixon was highly touted as a Cinderella story. A young Prince Charming from a reputable and wealthy family had found his beautiful bride, a teller at a local bank. The forthcoming event was the talk of the town, covered on television by the regional news programs, and written up in the papers. All the local big shots planned to attend.

Alice was from a small rural area, a close-knit community where everyone knew each other. She was well liked and had a reputation as a hard worker who deserved everything she had earned. But before she ever walked down the aisle, a stroll that would remove her from the workforce forever, she sealed her fate by committing fraud that cost Nasdall Bank $7.2 million covering 13 accounts as a result of cash abstractions.

Alice had worked at the bank for over 10 years. The branch head, Neil Wilson, the operating officer, Michael Siefert, and the branch accountant, Jim Denver, had unequivocally trusted her. When interviewed later, they begrudgingly said that they empowered Alice because they considered her a person of undisputed integrity. Nowhere in their wildest dreams did they imagine that they gave the keys of the castle to a criminal.

Lo and behold, the pretty Cinderella had the capacity to comprehend the automated resources of the bank. They underestimated her keen sense of technology, her knack for computers, and her ability to find weak points in the operational processes. These skills enabled her to commit fraud for four years undetected.

Nasdall Bank, in the business for the last 70 years, is a market leader in consumer banking. It has a sizable clientele made up mostly of retirees and traders. Nasdall has been one of the top commercial banks in the region for the last 15 years, and it employs more than 12,000 people at nearly one thousand branches worldwide.

Having been the head of the fraud examination department at Nasdall Bank for several years, I'm accustomed to hearing news of employee fraud, usually minor and poorly planned offenses. However, on a Sunday afternoon I received a call that I considered far more serious than usual. It came from one of our auditors conducting a regular audit on the West Coast area branch. He informed me that he'd been tipped off by a panicked call from Michael, who said a customer's account had been emptied. Furthermore, several unusually large transactions could not be reconciled with his records despite diligent efforts to identify the cause. Together with an assistant, I immediately visited the branch. I noted several accounts that showed discrepancies in their balances when compared with our computer-generated reports; they were directly traced to transactions executed by a teller named Alice Nixon. I discriminately and distinctly identified Alice's thread of fraudulent transactions, which showed manipulated entries on the deposit accounts of several clients.

Trust in Me

Considering the duration of her tenure with the bank, Alice had developed a good rapport with Nasdall's clientele and her superiors. But Alice fooled everyone with a deceitful smile. She was entrusted with too much information—most significantly, Michael, the branch operating officer, had disclosed his user ID and override password to her, enabling her to commit and conceal the fraud.

A cursory glance of the branch records, specifically her transaction journal and its supporting documents, did not indicate any immediate evidence of manipulated deposit accounts. Her records had all the superficial marks of legitimacy—but a closer look showed alterations.

Many customers with deposit accounts carried passbook records, which are small hard-copy booklets used to store records of transactions similar to stubs from ATM machines, in lieu of online and telephone banking. Every transaction is recorded onto a piece of paper inside the passbook by a teller using a small printing machine, then handed back to the customer. In this case, when the passbooks were compared with the bank's records of the transactions Alice oversaw, gross differences existed.

I discovered that she had used Michael's password to access the passbook adjustment/corrections module in order to manipulate the entries printed in clients' passbooks to make them appear as though the transactions were reflected. However, the bank's computer balance displayed the actual amount in the account, which was different in cases where she stole money.

To illustrate, if a client intended to make a cash deposit of $10,000, he would hand Alice both the money and his passbook. She would pocket the cash and type an online entry so the bank records showed a cash deposit of $10,000. Subsequently, Alice would nullify the entry by using Error Correction, an area that was off-limits for other bank tellers and required Michael's password.

In the bank's system, it would appear that no money was deposited to the account of the client. Next Alice printed the reversed transaction documentation into the customer's passbook, then discarded the piece of paper. Thereafter, she would print a record indicating their cash deposit of $10,000 from the passbook adjustments/correction module (which is an offline entry) onto a piece of paper from a batch of passbooks she stole from the vault. Furthermore, each entry required a signature from a manager. Though not authorized to do so, Alice would sign the passbook for the customer. The bank's clients relied solely on the passbook entries to determine their true balance.

Balancing Act

Michael and Neil, the branch heads, failed to closely monitor override requests and perform post reviews of such transactions for the accuracy of entries against the source documents.

The balancing process, which requires comparing physical cash in the teller's custody against the posting media (in this case, the deposit slip), showed no signs of a discrepancy. Because Alice had nullified the previous entry of cash deposit by using Error Correction, her cash and documentation were balanced. Michael failed to require Nasdall's clients to sign deposit slips immediately above any alteration, which was a mandatory bank procedure. Nor did he adhere to the policy requiring him to countersign on the alteration of any information on the transaction or posting media to indicate that it had passed his review. Jim, the branch accountant, did not confirm unsigned corrections, including the physical existence of the slip with the designated officer.

Alice devised another scheme to rob bank customers of their money if they wished to withdraw cash instead of deposit it. If a customer wanted $1,000, for instance, she would have Michael and Neil approve the slips showing the customer's desired withdrawal amount, a bank policy they actually followed. After they signed, Alice would alter the withdrawal amount to $10,000 and record that figure in the computer system, then take the remaining $9,000 for herself. To cover the stolen money, Alice posted cash deposits from other accounts to cover previously manipulated ones. These transactions were not reflected in clients' passbooks. To avoid detection, she created a lapping scheme, posting validated cash deposit entries made by other clients into the accounts from which the $9,000 was abstracted.

Alice allowed the clients to withdraw cash without posting it in the system, and took cash from other accounts to give to the clients as part of her scheme. She gathered the nonvalidated withdrawal slips and used them to abstract bigger sums from clients' accounts by padding the amount and altering the transaction date.

To avoid detection, Alice had a "black book" list of accounts she victimized. She knew approximately when her prey would come to the bank. She regularly intercepted them by personally attending to these customers. From the clients' point of view, she provided excellent service. Alice would go to any length to perpetrate her fraud. She even turned down a promotion. And she never took a leave of absence—taking a single sick day or vacation would prevent her from monitoring her victims. Ironically, her supervisors took this as a sign of hard work.

That is, until Alice's wedding approached, four years after she began her scheme, and she took an emergency leave to prepare for her special day. When one of Alice's 13 victims, Mr. Brantley, came to the branch, he approached a substitute teller and handed her a withdrawal request. The teller was shocked—the computer indicated that Mr. Brantley's account was empty. The teller called over Michael, who compared the data to Mr. Brantley's passbook and found that a vast difference existed. Every transaction displayed a teller's code to specify who processed the request. All of Mr. Brantley's transactions had been processed by Alice.

A year prior to the discovery of Alice's fraud, the human resources (HR) department had issued a memo on her excessive use of Error Correction, which they detected with their monitoring device. Bank policy required HR to send a memo requesting an explanation if a teller used Error Correction more than three times in a week. They intended to suspend her for two days. However, Michael appealed the decision and covered up her violations because he thought he could trust her. He misled Human Resources into believing that it was just a glitch in the system and not Alice's fault. Michael committed gross negligence. Fraternization with staff can result in supervisors forfeiting objectivity in carrying out policies and procedures.

Spend-erella

We traced major portions of the stolen money that were being used to pay for her personal and father's credit cards. She also appeared to be deep in debt from gambling. Alice was living the high life! Unknown to the branch personnel, her after hours were filled with shopping sprees, trips to casinos, and expensive jewelry purchases.

As a result of my investigation, Nasdall Bank filed criminal charges against Alice on multiple counts of theft. To avoid arrest, she went into hiding, jumping from state to state. I coordinated with authorities to conduct a manhunt. Ultimately, Nasdall Bank put up bounty money for her arrest, published nationwide. I was tipped off when she registered in a private hospital for a diabetes checkup and one of the staff members happened to recognize her. In coordination with police authorities, we immediately cordoned that area. She did not offer resistance when arrested, but she showed no remorse either. In fact, she mockingly told me that she loved her job because she could take cash at will! "Where else can you work where everyone is a suspect but you?" she quipped. Indeed, Alice was trusted by all. But everything must come to an end. I acted as an expert witness on the case that led to a conviction. Alice was sentenced to 25 years in prison and ordered to pay restitution for the monetary loss incurred by the bank.

The massive fraud brought shame to the bank officers and left them with the bitter taste of betrayal. Michael and Neil were held liable for exposing the bank to risks and the financial losses arising from policy and security violations, as well as their failure and gross negligence to discharge official functions and responsibilities. Michael was responsible for the concealment and conspiracy in the cancellation of Alice's suspension due to excessive Error Correction violations. Michael, Neil, and Jim were terminated by the bank for gross negligence.

The discovery of her fraud stunned Alice's rich fiancé, other socialites in the community, the bank, and her valued clientele. They never imagined that she had the capacity and the resolve to commit a crime. Her fiancé, Hugh, was mortified that he was about to marry a con! Upon discovery of Alice's transgressions, he broke off the engagement. The story was a fairy tale gone awry: One glass slipper just wasn't enough for this Cinderella.

Lessons Learned

"Trust but verify" was an old adage popularized by the late President Ronald Reagan. Alice exploited the trust and confidence bestowed on her by the unsuspecting branch officers, local community, and even her fiancé. She had a knack for anticipation; she was always several steps ahead to conceal her crime.

Alice was able to master the computer system of the bank and identify opportunities for fraud. She spotted major operational flaws that she used to create havoc and steal from various accounts at will.

During my bankwide lecture to the branch operating officers, I reminded them that we should never underestimate anyone's capability to perpetrate schemes. There is always room for "mastery of the learning curve"—somebody within the organization can identify weak points and exploit the situation for monetary gain.

Alice successfully defrauded the bank and its trusting depositors due to the branch's total breakdown of internal control. In many instances, she had sole and complete control over transactions, including the custody of deposit instruments.

Recommendations to Prevent Future Occurrences

I recommended the following remedial and corrective measures:

- Banks should set up a monitoring list of excessive Error Corrections.
- Passwords must be regularly changed; overridden passwords should be reviewed.
- Branch officers should require a strict compliance policy.
- Approving officers should require clients with withdrawals beyond $5,000 to sign in their presence; authority limits on signature verification should also be defined for control purposes and to restrict employee fraud such as forgery.
- Surprise cash counts and surprise inspections of tellers' work areas should be implemented.
- Employee rotations should be implemented, including transfers to other branches within the locality.
- The organization's official code of employee conduct should include policies and procedures on proper reporting of crimes and irregularities, and management should make sure employees know about the policies and procedures.

About the Author

Antonio Ivan S. Aguirre, CFE, CPA, CSI, MBA, is the chief resident auditor of the United Nations Assistance Mission in Afghanistan, Office of Internal Oversight Services, United Nations. He previously worked with the largest bank in the Philippines as the head of special audit and is an expert witness against numerous white-collar crimes. He is also a martial arts instructor and a strong chess player.

Bloggers: Separating the
Wheat from the Chaff

STEVEN SOLIERI, JOAN HODOWANITZ, AND ANDREW FELO

Richard Fox was, by any measure, Columbus, Georgia's favorite son. He was the founder, CEO, and chairman of the board of Southern Cross Inc., the nation's largest chain of outpatient medical clinics. Despite an inauspicious beginning as a high school dropout, Richard ended the twentieth century as the third highest-paid CEO in the country. He celebrated his good fortune by donating large sums of his company's money (not his own) to local schools and charitable organizations. He hired some of his closest friends as senior executives and nominated others to serve on Southern Cross's board. Richard even visited local job fairs to recruit college seniors for entry-level positions in the company's finance and accounting departments. Grateful for the opportunity to start their careers at a Fortune 500 company, these job fair recruits were extremely loyal to Richard and Southern Cross. They would do nearly anything to please him.

But there was another side to Richard Fox, one that the general public rarely saw. This was the man who ruled Southern Cross with an iron fist and micromanaged every detail of the business. This was the man who hired Audit Enterprises LLP, Southern Cross's independent auditor, to conduct "pristine audits" at the company's 2,000 clinics. Although they were only maintenance and cleanliness inspections ("Are we out of toilet paper?"), Richard spent more on Southern Cross's appearance than he did to ensure accurate financial reports. This was the man who pored over every line in the company's books and then humiliated clinic managers who failed to achieve his profit goals. This was the man who read his employees' e-mails and installed hidden cameras and microphones to catch disloyal workers. And this was the man whom many employees referred to as "Mini-Hitler," but only behind his back.

Like some other CEOs, Richard used a carrot-and-stick approach to keep his employees in line. He rewarded workplace loyalty with accelerated promotions and corporate perks, and he punished disloyalty with public reprimands, demotions, and pink slips. The perks included, but were not limited to, free rides on his fleet of corporate jets, parties with celebrities, and (for executives only) an invitation to play with him in his country band, Hostile Takeover. No other employer in the Columbus area could begin to compete with Southern Cross's cash compensation and generous stock options. Slowly but surely, several of Richard's employees became addicted to life in the fast lane. No one wanted the party to end.

Richard and four of his friends founded Southern Cross Inc. in the mid-1980s, 20 years after Medicare and Medicaid became the law of the land. Medicare is the federal insurance program that subsidizes health care for the elderly. Medicaid is the state-run program that provides health care for the poor. Richard was not the first entrepreneur to exploit these programs for guaranteed revenue, but he was one of the first to focus on outpatient health care as a low-cost alternative to nonprofit hospitals and their exorbitant fees for 24-hour care.

It took Richard just three years to turn Southern Cross into a lucrative company with over $20 million in annual revenues. Confident that he had a winning business model, he hired Audit Enterprises to help him prepare for the company's initial public offering of shares of stock. After Southern Cross went public, its subsequent rise to the top of the health care industry was nothing less than meteoric. During the next 10 years, the company's stock price soared at an average of 30% per year. Richard started acquiring potential rivals, and his company grew at a furious pace. By the mid-1990s, the company was reporting more than $1 billion in annual revenues. Ten years after it went public, Southern Cross was listed as a Fortune 500 company.

Although 1997 was a banner year financially for Richard and his health care empire, it was also the year that President Clinton signed the Balanced Budget Act (BBA) into law. The BBA cut Medicare payments to companies like Southern Cross by $115 billion over a five-year period. As might be expected, every company in the health care industry suffered a significant loss in revenues. Southern Cross's net income dropped a whopping 80% in the following year. Unlike its competitors, however, Southern Cross managed to reverse most of its losses by the millennium. Everyone agreed that Richard had the Midas touch in an industry where most companies struggled just to turn a profit. What could possibly go wrong?

Cyber Gossip: Spreading Rumors on the Internet

Beginning in the late '90s, a number of disgruntled employees, concerned investors, and angry competitors began raising red flags about Richard's aggressive leadership style, the board of directors' lack of independence as corporate overseers, and the absurdity of the company's rosy financial reports. The traditional corporate governance watchdogs (e.g., the audit committee, the internal audit department, the independent auditor, the financial/business media, and the Securities and Exchange Commission [SEC]) either missed the warning signs of impending disaster or simply chose to ignore them. But it was the late '90s and a new technology was turning traditional corporate governance on its head. The age of the Internet had arrived.

Southern Cross, like other major corporations, had its own message board on Yahoo. Their true identities protected by screen names, employees, investors, and other interested parties expressed their opinions of the company and its leadership with no fear of retribution. At first the posts were positive, but they took a decidedly negative turn in the spring of the following year. The bloggers started questioning the numbers in Southern Cross's financial reports, a reaction, in part, to the recent discovery of accounting fraud at Columbus/HCA, a big competitor. Although every major corporation has its share of negative bloggers, some of Southern Cross's Internet critics were obviously knowledgeable insiders with formal training in accounting and finance. Why did these people decide to air their concerns about Southern Cross and Richard on the Internet? Did they have little or no confidence in the traditional whistleblower hotline? Did they prefer the Internet because it allowed them to connect with others who had similar concerns while still protecting their identities? Why weren't the internal and external auditors reading these posts to help them assess the risk of fraud in the company?

Although the Internet has greatly facilitated global communications and instant access to electronic information, it is not without problems of its own. One such problem involves the difficulty of confirming information, especially if the source chooses to remain anonymous. Were the negative comments on Southern Cross's message board credible or were they merely vindictive lies? Consider one of the more outrageous posts written by William Kresge, a former Southern Cross employee. William adopted the name of a fictional porno star as his screen name. He accused Richard of "bilking taxpayers by sapping Medicare reimbursement" and described the company's senior managers as "egotistical yahoos." He also warned readers that "this house of cards is starting to collapse." Unfortunately, William was his own worst enemy. He claimed that he and Richard's wife, Leslie, were lovers. When the posts finally came to Richard's attention, he ordered Southern Cross's legal department to find out who wrote them and sue that person for slander. William was forced to post an admission that he had lied and any credibility his previous statements had were lost. Although he exaggerated his sexual prowess, William clearly knew more about the company's accounting gimmicks than did its corporate watchdogs.

Another Southern Cross employee, Kathy Lewis, also posted negative comments about the company. She called Richard a "crook" and a "megalomaniac" and warned readers that the company's stock was about to fall because Southern Cross had paid too much money to acquire some of its clinics. She even described how Richard helped his parents (and himself) make a fortune:

> I accidentally discovered that [Richard's] parents own the company that all the computers are purchased for all [Southern Cross] facilities. A requisition is sent to Corporate and the computers can only be purchased through this company . . . Fox is a sly SOB. Taking advantage of everyone to make millions of bucks.

In an interview with *The New York Times*, she accused Southern Cross of "keeping the numbers up" by accepting certain Medicare-eligible patients even though it could not care for them. Richard sued Lewis but eventually dropped the suit, citing "an inappropriate use of [Southern Cross's] resources."

Not all of the bloggers worked for Southern Cross. PatientCare, an anonymous employee at one of Richard's competitors, described himself as follows:

> I work in the healthcare field with many companies. I can tell you that the distrust and dislike of Southern Cross and [Richard] is practically universal.

When a blogger who supported Richard criticized PatientCare as a malcontent, he replied:

> I do have a grudge against this company and its senior managers. I think it's the largest mismanaged company in the nation . . . [It] is a house of cards in much the same way Columbia/HCA was . . .

Matthew Pines, a former Southern Cross bookkeeper, was probably one of the more knowledgeable insiders who tried to expose the company's fraud. Although he lacked an accounting degree, Matthew worked in the fixed-asset management department for five years. His department was responsible for processing transactions involving the purchase of major pieces of equipment. After a while, he began to suspect that Southern Cross was deliberately overstating income statement profits by transferring expenses ranging from $500 to $4,999 from the income statement to the balance sheet. As a result, the expenses were never subtracted from the company's net income. Southern Cross's accountants, some of whom once worked as Audit Enterprises auditors, knew that the independent auditor never examined expenses below $5,000. What could be easier?

Uncomfortable with Southern Cross's sleight of hand, Matthew told his supervisor, Karen Foley, that he would not make the necessary accounting entries unless she signed off on them. (She was one of 17 Southern Cross employees who pleaded guilty to fraud.) But Karen needed fictitious balance sheet assets to hide the transferred expenses. She used a computer and a scanner to duplicate the documentation for existing assets and then altered them as needed. Audit Enterprises never realized that $1 billion of the assets recorded on Southern Cross's balance sheet existed only in Karen Foley's fertile imagination.

Matthew started having second thoughts about working for a company that was cooking its books. He quit his job and sent an e-mail to Audit Enterprises urging the audit firm to review the accounting transactions in three accounts: minor equipment, repairs and maintenance, and public information. Matthew never told the auditors to look at transactions below the $5,000 threshold or to verify the existence of the fictitious balance sheet assets. He assumed the auditors would do the right thing. However, one year after leaving the health care giant, Matthew realized that Audit Enterprises had done nothing to stop the fraud. Frustrated, he posted the following message on Yahoo:

> What I know about the accounting at [Southern Cross] will be the blow that will bring [the company] to its knees.

Unfortunately, Audit Enterprises accepted Southern Cross's explanation that Matthew was merely a vindictive former employee who had been fired for fraternizing with women.

Hell Hath No Fury Like . . .

If any person should be credited with exposing the Southern Cross fraud, that person is Richard Fox himself. He knew Congress was working on legislation to prevent a repeat of the Enron debacle. The Sarbanes-Oxley

Act of 2002 would, among other things, hold CEOs and chief financial officers (CFOs) explicitly accountable for the financial information in their corporations' annual reports. Shortly after the law was passed, Richard and his bankers began working on a plan to make Southern Cross a private entity once again. This would enable Richard to avoid the SOX requirement to certify his company's financial statements. But he never executed the plan.

In the spring, Richard sold five million of his shares of company stock for $74 million. Immediately, bloggers threatened to sue and demanded an SEC investigation of insider trading. One blogger named BigMan complained that Richard had talked the stock up on cable television just before he made the sale:

> When you appear on CNBC and look the camera in the eye and say the stock should be valued "north of $20" and two weeks later unload 5 million shares at $14, you are sending a message about the stocks [sic] true value. Not even Richard Fox would leave $25 million on the table. You also provide yourself an opportunity to unload because everyone's eye is off the ball . . .

Richard's stock sale should have raised red flags at the SEC and Audit Enterprises, but neither entity seemed to notice.

Roger Meadows, the CFO at one of Richard's other companies, warned Richard against drawing attention to himself and Southern Cross by selling so many shares. In July, Richard discovered that Roger had embezzled $500,000 from his personal accounts and was having an affair with Faith Brooks, one of Leslie Fox's employees. Despite his outrage, Richard did not notify the authorities. A week later, Roger's body was discovered on a country road. The coroner ruled his death a suicide. Richard finally reported Roger's alleged theft during the subsequent police investigation. He also told Faith's husband about her infidelity, a move that he would later regret.

The day after Roger's suicide, Richard sold another large block of stock for $25 million. Once again there was outrage on the Internet. In mid-August, Richard and his CFO, David Wetzel, certified Southern Cross's financial statements as required by the Sarbanes-Oxley Act. Two weeks later, however, Richard shocked everyone by releasing a statement warning investors that profits would be reduced by $175 million annually due to changes in Medicare billing procedures. Not surprisingly, Southern Cross's stock price fell 44% overnight.

The profit warning was the straw that broke the camel's back. In September, the media reported that the SEC was investigating allegations of insider trading by Richard. A few days later Faith Brooks called the SEC and the Federal Bureau of Investigation (FBI). What she told them is not known, but Richard was soon under investigation by two federal agencies.

Smoking Guns and Poetic Justice

Six months later, the SEC filed a civil suit against Southern Cross and Richard in which it accused him of masterminding a $1.4 billion accounting fraud. Southern Cross immediately fired Richard as CEO and chairman. Eventually, the Justice Department indicted Richard on 85 criminal counts for orchestrating a $2.7 billion fraud. Richard would go down in history as the first CEO to be indicted under the provisions of Sarbanes-Oxley.

Most media analysts assumed that the trial would be a slam dunk. Seventeen of Richard's subordinates, including five former CFOs, confessed to participating in the fraud and testified against him. One of the CFOs had even worn a wire to help obtain evidence for the FBI. Richard's defense team, however, earned its multimillion-dollar fee. Richard waged a two-year public relations war in which he portrayed himself as the victim of an out-of-control legal system. He joined a black church and asked black religious leaders to attend his trial and provide him with moral support. As it turned out, nine of the jurors were black. He paid a local newspaper to print pro-defense stories on page one. His family even hosted a local TV show that aired daily highlights of his trial. The government, on the other hand, almost bored the jury to death with long-winded explanations of arcane accounting rules.

After a five-month trial, Richard was acquitted of every charge. Several jurors explained that the government simply failed to prove its case. It never produced the smoking gun to connect Richard to the fraud. Although prosecutors were greatly disappointed in the verdict, they had the satisfaction of seeing Richard convicted in a separate fraud case one year later. He was sentenced to prison for 6 years and 10 months. It could have been much worse; Richard could have gone to prison for 20 years if he had been convicted of a Sarbanes-Oxley charge.

Lessons Learned

What lessons can we learn from Southern Cross's bloggers? First, a growing number of people prefer the Internet to company hotlines when it comes to reporting suspected fraud and other illegal or unethical behavior. After all, on the Internet they can hide behind screen names and remain anonymous. They can vent their frustrations with management and their concerns about fraudulent activities without fear of retribution. Everyone has heard stories, often apocryphal, of whistleblowers who used the company hotline to report fraud and were later transferred, demoted, or fired. (In reality, of course, the courts can order an Internet service provider to identify the blogger if there is reason to believe a crime has been committed.) Second, the use of screen names makes it difficult, though not impossible, for auditors and other forensic investigators to determine the relative credibility of people writing on the Internet. Third, the Internet is an untapped source of potential clues about a company's culture, the morale of its employees, and the risk of corporate fraud and other illegal activities. While it is true that a single post alleging fraud or corporate misconduct may be meaningless, run across several such posts by different individuals and you have a sign that the company's risk for illicit activity is relatively high. The company's financial audit should be modified accordingly to reflect the increased risk.

Corporate message boards often give bloggers the illusion of standing around the office watercooler exchanging juicy bits of gossip. In fact, the Web site Vault.com trademarked the term "Electronic Watercooler" for its "collection of company-specific message boards for employees." While many bloggers say little or nothing of consequence, some make statements that, if confirmed, could send people to prison. Some hide behind their screen names and make claims they would never make in other venues (e.g., face-to-face conversations). Some take advantage of the added time needed to type a blog entry to calm down and avoid saying something they will later regret. Some seek the catharsis of venting pent-up emotions, while others just want to comment on previously posted messages.

As the Southern Cross fraud demonstrates, it is sometimes very difficult to determine the credibility of individual bloggers. William Kresge's assertion that Southern Cross's "house of cards was starting to collapse" was certainly prophetic, but his claim that he was Leslie Fox's secret lover made him look like a crackpot. Assuming the auditors had even bothered to read his posts, how could they determine William's credibility if they did not know his true identity? In other words, how can they sort the wheat (indicators of corporate fraud) from the chaff (sexual fantasies)?

In a recent paper titled "New Metrics for Blog Mining," Brian Ulicny, Ken Baclawski, and Amy Magnus are grappling with this very dilemma. (The paper can be found at http://vistology.com/papers/Vistology/SPIE07.pdf.) Their research promises to help auditors and other investigators develop a system for measuring and evaluating the credibility of individual bloggers. The system is similar to the ones used by news-tracking agencies such as Fairness and Accuracy in Reporting (FAIR) and online auction and retail sites such as E-Bay and Amazon.com.

Consider the case of a blogger who posts several Internet messages on a single topic over a six-month period. Subsequent events eventually confirm the allegations in the messages and help establish the blogger's credibility as a source of information. That credibility, however, must then be weighted by the relevance, specificity, and timeliness of the individual messages.

Other factors that must be considered include the blogger's motivation and his interest in the subject under discussion. For example, the person writing might be new to a particular issue or organization. He or she chooses a screen name (i.e., establishes an Internet identity) and posts a single message. Assume that the person does not post additional comments; either he or she lost interest in the topic or needed only one message to vent some anger. This writer's credibility would probably be lower than that of one who posts messages on a regular basis, discusses the issue in a rational manner, and makes an effort to understand different opinions. Then there is the blogger whose only goal is to paint enemies (real and imagined) in the worst possible light. This person may post a single, vitriolic message or a series of them. His or her credibility would be lower than that of a blogger who refrains from emotionally charged accusations.

At the end of the day, however, it should make no difference to the auditor if the blogger is motivated by raw emotions or cold logic. Auditors can use entries on message boards (and the postings on real-time chat rooms) to take the pulse of a company and see it through the eyes of its employees, customers, suppliers, competitors, and shareholders. They can, in fact, mine the Internet for signs of fraud and corporate governance failures. After all, the number of potential bloggers far exceeds the number of individuals an auditor can interview in person or survey using a written questionnaire. The trick is to separate the wheat from the chaff.

The blogs about Southern Cross were full of red flags signaling fraud and a lack of corporate oversight. First there was William Kresge's accusation that Richard was "bilking taxpayers by sapping Medicare reimbursement." Then there was Kathy Lewis's warning that Southern Cross's stock price was going to fall because the company paid too much money for some of the clinics it acquired. There was PatientCare's assertion that Southern Cross was "the largest mis-managed company in the nation" and the allusion to Columbia/HCA (a company rife with fraud). And there was BigMan's suggestion that Richard was less than honest because he sold his shares of Southern Cross stock when "everyone's eye [was] off the ball." Even if the auditors could not uncover the true identities of these bloggers, the allegations should have been pursued, given both the health care industry's high risk of fraud and Southern Cross's extraordinary profitability at a time when its competitors were struggling just to break even.

Recommendations to Prevent Future Occurrences

Southern Cross's message board was up and running for more than five years before the public finally learned of the scandal. Hopefully, other corporate frauds can be prevented or detected in a more timely manner if auditors add the Internet to their tool kits for gathering and confirming audit evidence. We strongly recommend that audit firms implement the following changes as soon as possible.

Identify Your Resources

Identify all relevant Internet message boards, chat rooms, and related Web sites for the companies that they audit. It is important to take into account and evaluate any potential resources. The Internet has changed the way we do business, and in turn it should change the way we audit.

Develop Data-Mining Techniques

Research and develop appropriate data-mining techniques for Internet sources. There is a lot of information available and much of it is superfluous or misleading. It is important to develop a system to help sift through and identify the important material.

Train the Appropriate Staff Personnel

Train all professional staff personnel on data-mining techniques. Assign one or more trained members of each engagement team to evaluate the audit evidence obtained from Internet sources. Document completely the procedures used to obtain the audit evidence from Internet sources and the conclusions that are then derived.

About the Authors

Steven A. Solieri, Ph.D., is currently teaching auditing and systems at Long Island University. Dr. Solieri is certified as a CPA, CMA, CIA, CISA, and CITP, and is a practitioner with the CPA firm of Solieri & Solieri, CPA, PLLC, in New Hyde Park, New York. Dr. Solieri's research interests include corporate governance, systems, fraud, and forensic accounting.

   Dr. Andrew J. Felo, CMA, CFM, is associate professor of accounting at the Pennsylvania State University Great Valley School of Graduate Professional Studies. His work has been published in *Accounting and the Public Interest, Journal of Forensic Accounting, Journal of Business Ethics,* and *Strategic Finance.*

Joan Hodowanitz, MBA, retired from the U.S. Army in 1998 after a 23-year career in signals intelligence and electronic warfare. She is a member of the Veterans of Foreign Wars, Disabled American Veterans, the Military Officer Association of America, and the Association for Healthcare Documentation Integrity.

The Campus Con

KEVIN SISEMORE

Rita Wallace would do anything for her family. She had a loving husband and four children, all of whom were frequent visitors to her office at Frankston University, where she worked as an administrator in the Languages Department.

Greg, Rita's husband, worked for another department at Frankston. He was happy in his relatively new position. Not long ago, he had been laid off from another position within the university when a research project was closed. Those were tough times for the Wallaces; eventually, they had no choice but to declare bankruptcy. But Rita was perseverant. She kept the family afloat by managing the money she brought in.

Rita had been working as a department administrator for over 8 years, but had been a university employee for nearly 20. In her current position, Rita's basic responsibility was to manage department operations. Essentially, she made sure everything ran smoothly so that the faculty could teach and conduct research without the distraction of logistics. She made travel arrangements for professors and handled the purchasing of materials and supplies. In order to maintain the stock, Rita had been given a university procurement credit card, known as a "pro card." It worked like an ordinary credit card except the transactions had to be approved first in the computer system by the cardholder's supervisor or someone else designated to make authorizations. This person was called the "approving official," who, in Rita's case, was the department chair. Rita learned the procurement card system so well that she soon took over responsibility for all the cards in the department—issuing them to new employees, setting up the new cardholders' approving officials, and allocating the purchases to the right accounts and expense categories.

When the department chair changed, Rita was responsible for updating that information in the computer system so the transactions would be routed to the proper person. She took this opportunity to reroute the transactions to a professor on sabbatical. In addition to making purchases through the university computer systems, Rita was authorized to make purchases over the Internet using her pro card. Many of the books and supplies needed by the department were more readily attainable from online shopping sites than at local stores. She was given trust and the freedom to make purchases at her own discretion.

The Languages Department didn't have much funding, but it managed to get by with what was available, supplemented by the occasional grant. Over time, Rita earned the trust and admiration of not just her department but nearly everyone she worked with in the university. This was fortunate for the faculty. Department chairs changed with some regularity, but Rita was a constant. She was there to handle all the administrative tasks and keep the funding and expenses properly accounted for in the books, even as chairs came and went. She assured everyone that she had the approval and allocation of every expense under control. When a chair noticed an unusual charge or an unexpected account deficit, Rita was always quick to explain the misunderstanding and show that the accounts were, in reality, just fine. When a faculty member looked at his or her financial statement (which was not often), she would swiftly clarify any misconceptions and show that they were not really in deficit, that there was simply a delay in posting the funds. By the next month, the accounts would look fine. Everyone had great confidence in Rita's abilities and in her integrity. They became comfortable leaving all the computer-related tasks in her capable hands. In fact, a computer was so crucial to her duties that the department bought one for her to have at home. This afforded her flexibility when the weather was bad or when her kids were sick.

The university was well over one hundred years old and set beautifully at the basin base of the Rocky Mountains. Over 200 buildings lined the campus, all with sandstone facades in what was described as a rural Italian style. We always joked that the school attracted as many students and faculty for its access to skiing as it did for its academic reputation. Frankston University was labeled a liberal arts school, but it offered a wide variety of degrees and conducted a phenomenal amount of research. It took great pride in its diversity of people and programs. The campus had a population of 29,000 students, 1,250 faculty, and over 5,000 administrators and staff. Academically, it was made up of nine colleges and schools, each consisting of numerous departments, centers, and institutes.

Each department was chaired by a faculty member and managed by administrators. The larger departments had more resources and could afford a level of segregation of duties, meaning more financial and administrative staff members. The smaller departments, like Languages, usually had only one or two. The university had a long history of letting departments take care of their own finances. So long as there wasn't a deficit, they were left alone.

The Languages Department was part of the College of Arts and Sciences, the largest college within the university. It was small but fortunate enough to have two administrative staff, one being Rita, who had proven experience and familiarity with the university's computer systems. She had it all under control.

However, the dean of the College of Arts and Sciences had been growing concerned by the apparent lack of financial controls and the growing deficits in some of the college's smaller departments. To remedy the situation, he established new financial controls. Specifically, the updated system switched the academic departments to a centralized accounting system that expanded oversight for all fiscal transactions. This meant that all department-level payroll, pro-card, purchase-order, and travel-expense transactions would be reviewed and approved by a centralized center. It was a huge departure from the past. Departments that were accustomed to having complete control over approvals suddenly found themselves scrutinized externally. Departments with deficits, like Languages, were forced to explain themselves.

Rita was among the earliest and most vocal critics of the centralized approach.

"It can't possibly work," she asserted. "The financial-service center personnel will be confused by the unique aspects of this department. They'll never be able to properly handle the transactions."

A Special Mother-Daughter Relationship

Rita was right about one thing. The financial-service center personnel were confused by some of the interesting transactions coming out of the Languages Department. They couldn't understand how this small but adequately funded division continued to run deficits year after year. Even when given infusions of cash from the college, the deficits persisted. Where and how the department spent its money was a mystery. One particular account was even more perplexing than the rest. Every department had to pay a portion of the costs of centralized services, such as facility upkeep and IT support, for which each department contributed an amount based on its size. For some reason, Languages showed expenses charged to the centralized services expense account that exceeded amounts recorded by departments three and four times its size. As the allocation of these costs was based on department size, this raised a red flag with the newly created financial oversight group. Most of the balance was the result of journal entries moving large dollar amounts from other expense categories to the centralized services account. This was also unusual, as expenses normally charged to this account were consistent and routine; rarely was it necessary to move expenses using journal entries. Speculation was that either the department administrator was mistakenly moving other expenses to this account or someone was using it to hide the true nature of certain department expenses.

At the same time as the concerns were being raised about the expenses and the department deficits, a curious payroll transaction made its way to the financial service center. An employee named Linda Wallace was paid for 80 hours as a student worker in the Languages Department. The person processing the payroll had known Rita for more than 10 years and knew that Linda was Rita's daughter. She also knew that Linda was 18 years old and a student at the local high school. The 80 hours worked was for two weeks when school was in session, which cast a shadow of doubt on the legitimacy of the payment. A review of Linda's payroll history showed that Rita had set her up in the computerized payroll system and entered all of her hours.

The college finance officer decided this was enough evidence to take action. As a former internal auditor, she gathered the information related to the deficits, the charges to the centralized account, and the payroll matter, and scheduled a meeting with the university's internal audit group.

At the time, the group comprised nine professionals who worked with the university along with three sister campuses. I was the only auditor dedicated to fraud investigations, but everyone in the group pitched in to help on the larger cases. We met with the college's finance officer and agreed that there was sufficient reason to proceed with an investigation. After reviewing all the documents we were provided, I decided a meeting with Rita was the next logical step.

The Cookie That Crumbled

I asked another audit manager, Cassie Manning, to join me for the interview. I did this for a couple of reasons. First, unless you plan to record the interview, it is a best practice to have a second person present. It's also important for someone to help with notes and offer another opinion on verbal and nonverbal clues. Most importantly, since Rita was female and I'm male, it was legally safer for a female coworker to be present. It would also help Rita to feel more comfortable.

We wanted to catch Rita off guard to reduce the chance of her shredding any documents or coordinating stories with any potential witnesses. To arrange this, we asked the finance folks in the college to set up a meeting between them and Rita, which she had been requesting anyway in order to vocalize her objections and explain the department's deficit.

Deception is not usually a good strategy. However, I have found that some levels of subterfuge can facilitate the process for all parties involved. Telling people that an auditor or an investigator is coming usually hurts productivity, even when the person is innocent. They spend time trying to figure out why we want to talk to them every bit as much as the guilty.

Rita was an average-size woman with long brown hair. She was friendly and receptive when we arrived, even after we told her the meeting was with us and not the college finance folks. Her only concern seemed to be that she really wanted to straighten a few things out in regards to the new system. If she was losing sleep waiting for the knock on the door, she didn't show it.

We started the interview with the standard introductory questions. Then we presented Rita with time sheets that showed her daughter working 40 hours in a week. We asked and she confirmed that her daughter attended high school. Even with that admission, Rita didn't appear nervous. She very casually explained for each and every time sheet we produced that her daughter Linda was very dedicated and frequently worked long hours after school let out. She assured us that Linda was present and worked every hour recorded on the sheets. Rita seemed confident that her explanations were complete and convincing. I wasn't.

We showed Rita two time sheets where we believed she had been negligent. The documents indicated that Linda worked a weekend when Rita wasn't present and on a holiday when the entire university was closed. But she explained that away as well: "Linda came in that weekend without me. And she worked the holiday because there were some urgent tasks to be completed." Though her words echoed earlier statements, something in Rita had changed. Her tone and body language didn't convey the same assurance as before. These two time sheets had shaken Rita. Her confidence was clearly fading. Without producing additional "smoking gun" time sheets, I moved in to challenge the weakened defense.

After only a few probing questions, she crumbled. She hung her head, began to cry, and asked if she and her daughter were in trouble. We let her know that it was not our job to determine whether or not she was in trouble, but rather to develop the facts and provide them to management. We did tell her that being open and honest seemed to go a long way at the university. We also implied that our reports took a couple of days to issue and, if she wanted to help herself, she could write out an admission and give it to her supervisor. That way she could come clean before we issued our conclusions. Rita took our suggestion and wrote out and signed an admission that she had overstated Linda's compensation by $1,350. More than anything, she said, she didn't want her daughter to be held responsible. Rita was placed on paid administrative leave and told to go home. We returned to the office to assess the situation.

When we got back, two College of Arts and Sciences finance officers were meeting with our director. Naturally, they asked how our interview with Rita went. We told them that she had admitted to padding her daughter's pay. "Is that all?" they asked us, disappointment in their voices.

"We don't know yet," I responded. "We still have some big deficits that haven't been explained."

While I wrote up the interview notes, Cassie did some data mining. She had recently been trained on how to access and filter information from the university's procurement card system. In the past, we had to rely on the procurement services group; now, thanks to Cassie, we had instant access.

It only took a few minutes for her to come back to my office. "Languages is a small department, right?"

"Yes," I relied.

"Outside of payroll, they have a pretty low budget, right?"

"Yes."

"Then you need to see this."

The Other Daughter

Rita's pro card history showed $77,855 in purchases over a little more than four years, a much higher volume of transactions than I would have expected from such a small department. But that wasn't all Cassie wanted to show me. In particular, she was concerned about the volume of purchases from certain types of vendors, specifically grocery stores. Rita's card history showed a total of $9,585 in grocery store purchases over the same period. Most food items purchased by university departments were handled by payment voucher with the campus food-services department. Over $9,000 from grocery stores by a single department was suspect. A call to the department chair confirmed that grocery store purchases at this level were never approved and that no one had seen large quantities of food and drink at any social functions.

Further review of Rita's purchases showed $9,431 in expenses charged to faculty member's labs—charges that these employees later confirmed were never authorized. To learn how this happened, we examined the procurement-card system information on Rita's account. We learned that she was set up to allocate her own charges. This allowed her to buy whatever she wanted and then use her system access to place the charges into an unsuspecting faculty member's account. Rita's responsibility of preparing and reviewing the department's financial statements meant that she was aware of which professors had funds in their accounts and which did not. More importantly, this system access let her know which professors were spending money and which ones weren't. During interviews with these faculty members, we learned that some had questioned Rita regarding why the balance in their accounts was so low or in deficit. Each time she had excused the situation as an error and told them the balance would be normal by month's end. Our review showed that the account balances were low due to expenses allocated to them that had been incurred by Rita and were unrelated to any faculty members' work. When someone would question a low account balance, Rita would use her system access to make journal entries moving expenses out of the faculty account and into the account for centralized expenses, where she believed there was little scrutiny.

The activity on Rita's pro card prompted us to examine all the procurement card activity in the Languages Department. So we went back and gathered up all the pro card records. While examining the receipts, I noticed a name that I knew I had seen before—Cory Copek. I called over to the Languages Department and asked to speak with the administrative assistant, Nancy. She was still in shock over Rita being sent home, but cooperated with me.

"Why does the name Cory Copek seem familiar?" I asked her.

"Cory is Rita's other daughter," Nancy replied. Older than Linda, she had worked for five years in the department and had recently left for a job in California. I asked Nancy about Cory's responsibilities.

"Well, I remember that Cory helped with department projects and in the computer lab, but was not involved in department administration," she said.

I immediately realized I had seen Cory's name in Rita's personnel file as a dependent.

Rita set up Cory as a pro card cardholder when she came to work at the university. Shortly thereafter, Rita established herself as the approving official and expense reallocator for transactions made by her daughter. Cory worked for the university for just over three years. During that time, she made a total of $125,697 in purchases. By comparison, Rita, who was responsible for departmental purchases, had only $40,727 in purchases over the same time period.

The charges to Cory's card read like a holiday gift list. One receipt showed $316 worth of items at a bookstore charged to the department's general expense account. Cory had purchased DVDs of newly released blockbusters and books on raising puppies and horses, living and working in Canada, and equestrian instructions.

Most worrisome of all were Cory's grocery store purchases. Over the course of her employment, Cory had spent $39,017 at grocery stores. Many of the receipts showed that her purchases were made within minutes of Rita's at the same store. The department chair reviewed all of the transactions made on Cory's pro card and did not identify a single legitimate incident.

Our review of the procurement card system showed how Rita had managed her scheme without being caught. Since she approved all of Cory's transactions, there was nobody to question them. As long as Rita manipulated the accounts and kept the expenses moving, the chair just thought the department was spending too much money. Rita's own expenses should have been reviewed and approved directly by the chair. However, again she used her system access to avoid detection. She changed her approving official in the system from the current chair to a faculty member who was out of the country on sabbatical. When the pro card statements came in, she forged the absent faculty member's name and filed the statements.

That was enough information to expand our investigation. When we finished with the pro card work, we turned our attention to other areas where Rita spent department money. We focused on purchase orders and travel and expense reimbursement. Again, the computer was Rita's best friend.

Over the course of just a year, Rita spent $2,264 in meals and hotel accommodations that were directly billed to the university for several non-employees. Interviews with these individuals established that Rita had personal relationships with them that did not involve official business. Rita again had used her system access to charge these expenses to faculty accounts. Everyone said that they were unaware of the charges and never approved them.

On three separate occasions, Rita submitted travel reimbursement forms, totaling $3,230, without the approval of the faculty member responsible for the program charged. The faculty member reviewed the charges and indicated that he or she was not aware of them and that they did not relate to the program.

Restitution

After completing our investigation, we turned over our report and work papers to the campus police. I accompanied our detectives to a meeting with the deputy district attorney responsible for prosecuting white-collar crime. The DA took the case and warrants were issued for both Rita and Cory.

They were arrested and each charged with two counts of felony theft, one count of unauthorized use of a financial transaction device (credit card), two counts of embezzlement of public property, and one count of forgery. Initially, Rita's attorney was adamant that his client had done no wrong and that the purchases were legitimate. As part of the discovery process, I provided all our work papers to him for review. Two days after handing them over, I received a call from the deputy district attorney. She had run into the defense attorney earlier that day. He informed her that he had read the file. When she asked him what he thought, he replied, "You got us," and asked what kind of deal could be made.

Rita and Cory both pleaded guilty to felony theft. Rita was ordered to pay restitution in the amount of $90,000, agreed to as part of a plea bargain. As a condition of the plea bargain, Rita cashed out her pension and turned over a check for $60,000 at sentencing. She was sentenced to 90 days of work release, where she was allowed to work during the day but had to report to the county jail every evening. She was also sentenced to 20 years' probation and 100 hours of community service. Since Rita had agreed to repay the entire amount of the loss, Cory was not ordered to make any financial restitution. She was sentenced to 90 days of home detention with electronic monitoring, 20 years' probation, and 200 hours of community service.

Lessons Learned

After wrapping up the investigation of Rita Wallace, we made some substantial changes to our fraud investigation methodology. We changed our practice to include an examination of any area where a subject may have access to resources, not just the one in question. At a minimum, this will now include pro card transactions and expense reimbursements, even in instances where allegations have nothing to do with either one.

We learned that solid internal controls are a great start—but only a start. If there is no oversight to make sure the controls are followed, they won't be effective. The Languages Department lacked proper supervision and Rita took advantage of the neglect.

Recommendations to Prevent Future Occurrences

Analyze Financial Statements

Require department chairs to show evidence that they reviewed monthly, quarterly, and annual financial statements. The Languages Department was aware of their deficits but readily accepted Rita's explanations. Department managers should be educated on how to read and understand their financial statements. If they need help, it should come from someone other than the statement's preparer.

Analyze Journal Entries

As with the financial statements, department managers should review all journal entries on a regular basis. Anything unusual should be investigated with the assistance of someone other than the preparer of the entry. Many of Rita's journal entries were inconsistent or made to dormant accounts, which was obviously inappropriate but never investigated.

Review Dormant Accounts

Require departments to conduct timely reviews of dormant accounts. In addition to reviewing journal entries to dormant accounts, the process to remove dormant accounts should be reevaluated.

Computer Authorization

Rita had easy and unlimited access to the system, enabling her to change who approved her pro card transactions. Any changes to an approving official should be copied to the previous approver to ensure they were aware of the change.

Review Procurement Card Policy

Require department chairs to review and approve the issuance of new procurement cards. In Rita's case, the department managers had given all responsibility for pro cards over to Rita. We recommended the department head review and approve the application before a new card is issued.

Beware of Nepotism

Ensure proper segregation of duties when relatives work together. University policy already prohibited an employee from being allowed to review and approve the credit card transactions of a relative. Since Rita and her daughter did not have the same last name, the procurement card department did not notice that the two were related.

Perception of Detection

We later learned that the extensive newspaper coverage of Rita's case drove a lot of change in our organization. Pro card holders became more concerned about the business purpose of their purchases. Approving officials became more thorough and more skeptical. This might have been due to an increase in the perception of detection. In the end, Rita's case provided a real-life example of the consequences of committing fraud.

About the Author

Kevin Sisemore, CFE, CPA, CIA, is part of the Internal Audit department of the University of Colorado and is an instructor in the university's business school, where he teaches a graduate course in fraud examination. Kevin is also a member of the Boulder County White-Collar Crime Task Force.

CHAPTER

42

One for You, One for Me: A Tale of Crooked Insurance

STEVE MARTIN

Five elderly, distinguished gentlemen by the names of Antonio Ruiz, Alex Garcia, Gus Alonzo, Roberto Gonzales, and George Smith had been successful businessmen in south Florida for decades. They had interests in all phases and types of insurance, from the company financing the policies to the agency that sold them to the company that would underwrite the policies and pay the claims.

The partners began by forming Seralis Management as a holding company for their insurance businesses and the premium finance company. The five businessmen served as the board of directors and the shareholders. There were numerous subsidiaries under Seralis, units that covered every area of the insurance game. It was a vertical monopoly providing services to clients from start to finish. Seralis Insurance, Shine Premium Finance Co., Bailey's Insurance Agency, Lest Claims Service, Lest Insurance, Seralis Mortgage of Miami, Old Line Premium Finance Co., Airport Insurance Agency, Exclusive Underwriters, and Efficacy Underwriters were all under the Seralis holding company. Lest Insurance was especially important because it was the company initially under investigation. Since all of these were interrelated and working together hand in hand when the boat started to sink for Lest Insurance, leaks began to spring in all of the companies under Seralis Management—enough leaks to sink the entire fleet.

Bailey's Insurance Agency was the managing general agent for Lest Insurance, meaning it paid the policy money to Lest, which would then assign a number to the policy, print the policy, and mail it to the customer. As the general agent, Bailey's controlled the flow of money to Lest Insurance because, as policies were written, Bailey's collected the initial premiums, which it held in "trust" while a potential insured's application was being processed by Lest. If the customer was approved and the policy issued, Bailey's would then be required to forward the premium funds to Lest. Since the same individuals controlled the insurance agencies, the managing general agent, the finance companies, and the insurance company, the stage was set for fraud.

Insurance 101

In order to understand this case, one should understand how insurance policies are processed under normal circumstances. The insurance agent writes the policy and collects the premium or, in many cases, a deposit. If only a deposit is received, the balance of the premium is financed by a company that specializes in premium financing. The agent then submits the completed policy to one or more of the insurance agencies that handle that insurance type (e.g., property and casualty, automobile, commercial). This agency is called the managing general agent. The managing general agent submits the policy to the insurance company, which accepts the policy and pays the claims.

The insurance company invests the premium money it receives, while maintaining a specified amount to pay claims. The company makes a profit by keeping claims low and receiving a good return on its invested money. By law, a portion of the premium is paid into the state guarantee fund to guarantee the payment of claims should the insurance company fail. The state requires an annual audit by a firm that practices in the insurance field, to make sure everyone is playing fair. The state also sets the rules for the amount of capital required for the total premium written, specifies what qualifies as capital, and monitors the loss ratios of the insurance companies. Based on the losses, the state may require that additional capital be contributed from the insurance company. It is the job of the audit firm to provide an opinion on the financial statements and ensure that all of the statutory requirements are met.

It's Better to Give Than Receive

For Lest Insurance, the annual audits raised some interesting questions. Wilson Accounting (a large accounting and auditing firm) discovered that Lest was in a precarious financial situation. In its letter to management, Wilson reported "A significant volume of policies written were not processed and recorded on the general ledger as of December 31."

The following year's audit was also conducted by Wilson Accounting. Lest knew it did not have enough funds in surplus (as required by state regulations). To meet the surplus requirement for the year-end financial statement, an accounting journal entry for $625,000 was made for the benefit of the shareholders; however, no cash was deposited until February of the following year. There is no indication that Wilson researched this surplus contribution. A few simple questions would have revealed that the funds were a transfer from Bailey's. The audit report also noted that there was an "Agent Balance due" of $2,121,743, which is 32% of all of the premiums earned for the entire year.

Wilson again issued a management letter in regards to Lest Insurance for its year-end audit and stated that "there was an unreasonable lag time between the receipt of policy applications and the time the policy was entered into the system." This same "lag time" problem was noted in the previous report and nothing had been done in the intervening time.

Under state regulations, the audit firm (Wilson) "must notify the Department of Insurance within ten calendar days when [the firm] has completed the audit or terminated the audit engagement prior to normal termination." This wording was also contained in the engagement letter. But Wilson walked off of the Lest Insurance audit the third year without ever informing the Department of Insurance.

Thankfully, Wilson had submitted the previous audit reports it had completed to the Department of Insurance. Belatedly, based upon the indications of insolvency in the financial statements, the State Department of Insurance put Lest under administrative supervision.

On June 18 of that year, a circuit judge issued a "Consent Order Appointing the State Department of Insurance as Receiver for the Purpose of Liquidation, Injunction, and Notice of Automatic Stay" against Lest Insurance. By this order, a receiver was appointed to salvage what was left of the floundering company; the order deemed the outfit "hazardous to the subscribers, policyholders, creditors, and the public." The receiver in Miami took immediate possession of all records and assets of Lest Insurance and ordered all agents and brokers who sold policies and collected premiums to account for and pay the amounts within 30 days.

The noose began to tighten, not only on Lest Insurance but on all the affiliated companies. Orders were also issued to every other Seralis Management company, requiring them to make their books and records available to the receiver for inspection due to all of the interrelated transactions among the companies.

Unfortunately, the Department of Insurance had many investigations going on, and this one was particularly complicated. Around this time, a devastating hurricane hit the state and a flood of other insurance companies became insolvent overnight. The department had its hands full—the investigation slowed.

Two years after the initial receivership, the department hired my firm to conduct a new fraud investigation. They gave us a two-week contract with instructions to finalize the investigation of Lest Insurance, put a "nice bow" on the report, and submit it. Our two-week assignment turned into six months as the scope of the investigation increased and the discoveries multiplied. What was considered a weak administrative case became a strong criminal case after we discovered such interesting items as casino markers at a Lake Tahoe casino, a beach house in the Florida Keys, and the diversion of $7.8 million.

Follow the Money

We began our investigation by isolating the computer files and learning how policies were processed. First, Lest Insurance would receive the application and premium check from the agent (Bailey's). Lest would then issue a policy number in the 100,000 series for each new policy. A sticker marking the policy number was placed on the check and the application. The policy numbers were sequentially issued. Next, the application was sent to the underwriting department. If underwriting approved the policy, it was placed in the system and the check would be deposited in Bailey's premium trust fund account (as the managing agent, the checks were made payable to Bailey's and deposited into its account; Lest Insurance recorded the premium on its books as a payable due from Bailey's). Bailey's would then transfer the premiums to Lest. Later, if a claim was received on a policy, the claims-processing personnel simply entered the policy number to pull the information up, processed the claim, and sent a check once all the necessary claim information was received.

When I first received the case, I was concerned that I only had two weeks to summarize the investigation, document the evidence, take all of the written summaries, and solve the case. Where should I start with so little time? I knew that the key was always to follow the money.

I conducted a review and summary of all bank accounts and checks for the affiliated companies. As a part of this procedure, the back of each check over $1,000 was examined and a listing made of the accounts where the money was deposited. As this list grew, one account came to light that had five checks deposited into it in the name of Bailey's. I could not find a reference to this bank account on any of the financial statements.

Since the receivership had stepped into the shoes of the insurance company, obtaining bank records was quick and easy—no subpoena needed. When I received the records, much to my surprise, the statements identified an account where $8.8 million had been deposited over an 18-month period and funds withdrawn over a 3-year period—before Lest went into receivership. Obviously, this changed the complexion of the case and further investigation was required of both the deposits and the checks.

The initial inspection of the bank statements provided records of deposits of $8,859,078 and withdrawals of the same amount. I requested and received the details covering the initial two months of deposit. A preliminary examination revealed that some of the larger checks were payments from affiliates. The balance of the deposits was made up of small checks—the initial premiums from new applicants. But in referencing the names on the checks to policies written by Lest Insurance, very few matches showed up.

While it was puzzling enough to have premium checks deposited by an insurance company with no record of the person who wrote the check, the oddities didn't stop there. As you remember, when a check is processed, a sticker with the policy number is placed on the check. The photocopies of the checks all showed policy numbers in the 500,000 range and not the 100,000 range, like the one we had seen previously. Unless Lest Insurance had written 400,000 policies we knew nothing about, the numbers should not have been anywhere near 500,000. It was time to take a trip to the company warehouse to inspect the physical policies. A day of pulling boxes off shelves and inspecting their contents did not reveal a single policy with a 500,000 series number.

What did the 500,000 series indicate? The computer listings of all the policies were back in the receiver's office stored in 18 five-drawer file cabinets. What could be found or proved with such a mess of potential evidence? We were about to find out.

On Saturday morning, the computer listings were pulled from the cabinets and laid out in sequence in the 150-foot-long hallway. The 500,000 series check dates we had were compared with the 100,000 series policy-listings printouts with similar dates. No matches. The names on the 500,000 series checks were matched with the long list of policyholders in the Lest Insurance files. Only a few names showed up. Still no answers regarding what occurred. Next we examined the claims files. Did any of the 500,000 series policyholders have claims? We found only 12 of these policyholders also in the claims file. What could that mean?

With the 12 claims in hand, it was back to the policy listings. When were the policies issued? The records showed that a 100,000 series policy had been issued shortly before each claim filing. All of the original paperwork was in the warehouse, but with the policy date and the claim date so close together the problem took on new intrigue.

Another trip to the warehouse took place the following week, but this time with the copies of the checks and computer listings in hand. I was looking for specific policy files in the 100,000 series to confirm my suspicions. Holding the records, I compared the date of the 100,000 series policy with the original paperwork. They did not match. But when I compared the paperwork to the check with the 500,000 series number, the scheme began to take shape.

While looking at the third set of original policy documents, I made the discovery that every fraud investigator lives for. The original policy did have the 100,000 sticker as it should; however, it had been pasted over another sticker! I held the document up to the light. Clearly visible beneath the 100,000 sticker was another one with a 500,000 series number that matched the number on the check!

The scheme that ultimately developed was a diversion of premiums directly into an off-book bank account. It took collusion between the partners that operated Lest Insurance and the data processing manager who ran the data center handling both the Lest Insurance and the Seralis Insurance files. The software that had been used to process these policies was actually a test module that could generate a policy without creating accounts receivable, billing, or income. These policies were identified with a 500,000 number. If a claim occurred, a check was written from the off-book account, the policy put in the real system, a 100,000 series policy issued, and the claim paid.

Of the $8.8 million deposited into the account, $7.8 million were premium trust funds; the remainder was repayment for loans or checks to cover overdrafts in the off-book account. With all of the money being diverted, it is interesting to note that the five checks that led to the discovery of this account were checks from the on-book account to cover overdrafts in the off-book account. The total amount diverted was almost equal to the real policy amount written; so in essence, for every dollar put on the books, one dollar was diverted to the off-book account. Lest Insurance was created specifically with this fraud scheme in mind. During the first three months of operation, $990,000 was diverted to the off-book account.

The bank withdrawals showed that the money was used to pay any number of personal expenses for the shareholders. Numerous checks were paid to other affiliated companies. Funds were used to pay shareholder loans at various banks. Two checks for $34,260 each were used to pay markers at a Lake Tahoe casino. Some of the money was used to pay for a beach house in the Florida Keys. One of the shareholders purchased the beach property using the name of his elderly aunt. The monthly payments were five times greater than her Social Security income, but money from the off-book account was used to pay the loan and save the precious beach house from foreclosure.

The Outcome of the Investigation

As a result of the investigation, four of the principals were convicted and ordered to pay restitution (one of the original five had been bought out previously by his partners and was not accused of wrongdoing). Wilson Accounting received a judgment against it and was also ordered to pay restitution.

Lessons Learned

This diversion of premiums could not have occurred without the collusion of the shareholders/principals operating Lest Insurance and of the data processing manager.

The auditing firm should have been more diligent in its efforts to analyze the losses and question why the premium trust funds were not being paid as required.

Further investigation should have taken place to verify the surplus contributions, and a higher initial capitalization amount might have prevented the undercapitalized insurance companies from operating at all.

This case also shows the importance of regulatory oversight in the insurance industry. If the Department of Insurance had greater resources, the improprieties might have been detected sooner and the investigation could have been done much more quickly.

Recommendation to Prevent Future Occurrences

Tone at the Top

It is important that upper management set the tone; in this case, the board of directors (who were also the shareholders) was a perfect example of what not to do.

Education

The greatest deterrent against fraud is education, with an emphasis on educating employees. Some of the employees must have known that something strange was occurring, but no one came forward. In the end, however, all of them lost their jobs. Employees should be taught that silence can cause the entire company to fail, as with Enron.

> ### *Hotline*
>
> Every company should have a hotline to report suspected fraud and abuse. In this case, an internal hotline might not have achieved the desired result, since senior management was involved. That is why government regulatory agencies should offer hotline support, allowing the public or insiders to report crimes or abuses. Hotlines can be a safe avenue for blowing the whistle, especially in cases where the perpetrators are in positions of power.

About the Author

Steve Martin, CFE, CPA, CVA, resides in Las Vegas. He has performed investigations for the SEC, shareholders, and receiverships, and for cases involving personal injury, business valuations and damages, and eminent domain. Appointed by the governor as the state controller, he served as an adjunct professor for accounting and is a Marine Corps veteran. Credit goes to Phil Yorston, who provided the opportunity.

Index

Accountant, forensic, 205, 234, 245, 246, 343, 344, 345
Account(s):
  payable, 120, 146, 150, 152, 174, 178, 213, 252, 257, 341–347
  receivable, 365, 366, 418
Advanced fee scheme. *See* schemes
Affidavit, 194, 225, 276, 279, 325
Antivirus, 80
ATM machine, 376, 384
Audit, forensic, 63,85, 93, 95, 202, 354

Background check, 32, 53, 66, 206, 217, 294, 297,
Bank:
  loan, 110–112
  offshore, 357
  policy, 385–386
  reconciliation, 98–100, 103, 148, 150, 200, 203, 205, 366–367, 369
  statement(s), 94, 98, 100, 200, 322, 357, 417
  transaction, 100, 102
Bankrolling, 26
Bankruptcy, 324–326, 370, 401

Cash:
  petty, 214, 289, 365
  receipt, 61,208, 305,
  shortage, 204

CD-ROM, 130, 274
Certified Fraud Examiner (CFE), 259
Certified Public Accountant (CPA), 66,100, 152, 245, 205, 339, 340,
Chat room, 397–398, 45, 47–48, 50, 52–53
Claims, false, 186
Code(s):
  of conduct, 289
  of ethics, 250
  criminal, 35, 295
Company:
  advertising, 14, 126, 242
  bogus/fake, 264
  electronics, 186
  holding, 98, 413
  insurance, 100, 251–252, 414, 416–417
  marketing, 14
  mortgage, 300, 311–312, 315, 327, 413
  policy, 174, 251
  shell, 94
  software, 202, 204, 207, 329
Computer:
  games, 51
  program, 39, 61,177
  programmer, 1, 432
Confidentiality, 32, 118, 133

Conflicts of interest, 87, 366
Control(s):
  application, 310
  automated, 266
  database, 313
  deficiency, 176, 300
  financial, 238, 403
  internal, 30–31, 66,98, 103, 119,
    127, 132, 146, 150, 152, 178,
    188, 242, 249, 258, 268, 303,
    306–307, 310, 312, 317, 323,
    326–327, 348, 359, 361, 369,
    371, 380, 388, 409
  manual, 310
  system, 266
  user access, 316
  violations, 302
  weaknesses, 66, 178, 216, 261, 310,
    312, 380
Corruption, 85, 89, 94, 225, 227, 312,
  333, 357, 378
Counterfeit, 80, 135–138, 140–141,
  151, 155, 224
Credit:
  accounts, delinquent, 372,
    374–375, 380
  agency/bureau, 322, 326
  card debt, 57,144, 324, 378
  government-issued card, 371,
    373–375, 377
  limit, 79, 353, 381
  line of, 206, 262–263
  monitoring service, 82
  report, 82, 321–323, 326
  score, 321
  union, 182, 300, 302, 304, 309–316
Culture, corporate, 103
Cyber:
  crime, 2, 13, 15–17, 19, 129–130,
    133
  security, 67
  space, 67–68, 71

Debt, 23, 57, 143–144, 156, 323–325,
  353, 367–368, 371, 373, 378, 386
Deposit slip, 63–64, 385
Disbursement(s), 72, 146–151, 301,
  347, 367
Document retention, 80, 189, 201,
  204, 296
Drug:
  addiction, 227, 264, 358
  charges, 4–5, 8, 138, 141
  dealer, 4, 222–223
Due diligence, 87, 116, 134

E-:
  account, 72
  bank, 70, 72
  business, 262–263, 265, 267
  marketing, 319
Electronic:
  accounting, 202–208
  bookkeeping, 199
  data, 215, 344
  eavesdropping, 2
  evidence, 54, 139, 141, 195, 206,
    344, 346
  footprints, 78
  information, 233, 282, 391
  media, 284
  monitoring device, 8
  payment, 82
  storage, 142, 313, 344
  time clock, 175, 177–178
  transaction, 327
Embezzlement(s), 29, 62, 106, 115,
  117, 205–207, 305, 394, 409
Employee schedule(s), rotating, 208,
  388
Equity line, 206, 319–320, 323–325
Evidence:
  electronic, 54, 139, 141, 195, 206,
    344, 346
  videotaped, 63, 51, 202,

Expense reimbursement. *See* schemes

Federal Bureau of Investigation (FBI), 2, 16, 42, 76, 79, 129–131, 133
Felony, 64–65, 141, 177, 207, 221, 277, 409
Flash drive, 14–16, 19,
Food and Drug Administration (FDA), 3–4
Fraud:
  awareness, 267
  deterrence, 44, 208, 267, 361
  examination, 205, 289–290, 369, 384
  healthcare, 10, 17, 390, 393, 397
  insurance, 100, 151, 209, 251, 364, 368, 370, 390, 413, 418–420
  mail, 4, 222–223, 324,
  mortgage, 111, 116, 302, 304, 311–316, 321, 325, 323
  organized, 35, 77
  public sector, 144–150, 377–379, 407–409
  risk assessment, 19
  securities, 236, 394–395
  Triangle, 249, 379
  wire, 8, 186, 378
Fraudulent disbursement scheme. *See* schemes

General ledger, 174, 304, 307, 414

Hacking, 5, 13–14, 17–18, 39, 75–83, 128, 170, 282
Hardware, IT, 87, 89, 91, 93
Healthcare. *See* fraud
Hotline(s), whistle-blower, 208, 250, 264, 267, 322, 373, 395, 396, 420

Identification:
  fake, 135, 137, 139–141
  theft, 82, 112, 135–137, 141, 219–221, 224–228, 322–326
Inflation, 25–30, 32, 244, 353, 356, 367
Inspections, surprise, 388, 208
Internal Revenue Service (IRS), 3
Inventory, 26, 157, 159, 340–343, 353, 355–356

Lapping scheme. *See* schemes
Loss Prevention, 155–156

Mail fraud. *See* fraud
Matrix, 68–70
Memory card, 142
Mitigation, 295, 325
Money laundering, 3–4, 869, 151
Mortgage fraud. *See* fraud

Networking site(s), social, personal, 112–113, 269

Obstruction, 378
Organized crime. *See* fraud
Payroll fraud. *See* schemes
Pop-up, 67
Postal Inspection Service, 7, 221
Probation, 64, 66, 151, 177, 207, 219, 228, 273, 277, 379, 409
Pyramid scheme. *See* schemes

Receipts:
  voided, 62, 64–65
  duplicate, 255, 62–63
  check, 201
Restitution, 66, 147, 177, 186, 197, 206–207, 295, 304, 387, 408–409, 419

Safeguards, 31, 132–133, 171, 178, 197
Scheme(s):
  advanced fee, 35
  coupon stacking, 262–263
  credit, 210
  expense reimbursement, 244–248, 408–409
  identity theft, 82, 112, 135–137, 141, 219–221, 224–229, 322–326
  lapping, 386
  misappropriation, 148, 151, 356, 359–360, 150,
  Nigerian 409, 35, 37, 41
  payroll, 110, 175–179, 291, 294, 296–297, 404
  Ponzi, 68, 70–71
  pyramid, 70
Search warrant, 6–9, 93, 129–130, 137, 142, 194, 221–222, 224, 273, 279, 284
Securities and Exchange Commission (SEC), 391, 365, 394–395
Securities fraud. *See* fraud
Segregation/separation of duties, 64,103, 242, 317, 403, 410
Social Security
  Administration, 323
  number, 75, 78, 82–83, 320, 322–323, 325

Software:
  accounting, 30, 64, 109–110, 112, 200, 202, 204, 207, 302, 334, 341, 351–351
  data-mining, 216
  encryption, 8, 10, 19, 76–77, 81, 360
  imaging, 123, 273, 333, 335
SPAM, 1–5, 14, 43, 67
Spyware, 67
Statement, sworn, 378
State Security Laws, 72
Surveillance, 106–107, 139, 222, 284–285, 295

Tax evasion, 94, 120–122, 360
Thumbnail drive, 142
Tone at the Top, 249–250, 258, 267, 345, 419
Travel and expenses, fraudulent, 252–256, 376–378, 405–409

United States Citizenship and Immigration Services, 35
United States Army, 181, 185

Virus(es), 13–16, 39, 67, 332–333

Web page, 71, 169, 226
Whistle–blower:
  hotline. *See* hotlines.
Wire:
  fraud. *See* Fraud
  transfer, 364

Computer fraud casebook.